I0820245

EDWARD L. BLACKSHEAR AT PRAIRIE VIEW

PRAIRIE VIEW A&M UNIVERSITY SERIES

EDWARD L. BLACKSHEAR AT PRAIRIE VIEW

TEXAS EDUCATION CRUSADER

JOHN A. ADAMS JR.

Foreword by John S. Sharp

TEXAS A&M UNIVERSITY PRESS
COLLEGE STATION

First edition

♾ This paper meets the requirements of ANSI/NISO Z39.48–1992 (Permanence of Paper).
Binding materials have been chosen for durability.

Library of Congress Cataloging-in-Publication Data

Names: Adams, John A., Jr., 1951– author | Sharp, John (John Spencer) writer of foreword
Title: Edward L. Blackshear at Prairie View: Texas education crusader / John A. Adams Jr.
Other titles: Prairie View A & M University series
Description: First edition. | College Station: Texas A&M University Press, [2026] | Series: Prairie View A & M University series | Includes bibliographical references and index
Identifiers: LCCN 2025023254 (print) | LCCN 2025023255 (ebook) | ISBN 9781648433368 hardcover | ISBN 9781648433375 ebook
Subjects: LCSH: Blackshear, Edward L. (Edward Levoisier) | Prairie View State Normal and Industrial College (Prairie View, Tex.)—Presidents—Biography | African Americans—Education (Higher)—Texas—History | Historically Black colleges and Universities—Texas—History | LCGFT: Biographies
Classification: LCC LC2802.T4 A63 2026 (print) | LCC LC2802.T4 (ebook) | DDC 378.764/249 [B]–dc23/eng/20250617
LC record available at https://lccn.loc.gov/2025023254
LC ebook record available at https://lccn.loc.gov/2025023255

To a very great friend and raconteur,
William R. "Bill" Page

Contents

Series Editor's Foreword

RONALD GOODWIN

In 1895, organizers of the Cotton States and International Exposition World's Fair extended an offer to the president of the Tuskegee Institute to address their audience. This event showcased the South's recent technological advancements in agricultural research and production since the end of the Civil War. Historians sometimes refer to this period as the dawn of the "New South." Southern officials used this phrase in the last quarter of the nineteenth century to differentiate themselves from their antebellum forefathers. Booker T. Washington addressed the conference attendees and focused his speech on race relations—particularly in the South. His emphasis on education for the region's black populace was well received. However, he also emphatically stated, "In all things that are purely social we can be as separate as the fingers, yet one as the hand in all things essential to mutual progress." This one phrase seemed to overshadow the other salient points Washington made that afternoon. Nonetheless, within a few years, other prominent black leaders chose a path of civil resistance and viewed Washington's approach as outdated and insultingly accommodationist.

This was the political and social environment faced by Edward Blackshear when he assumed the principalship at Prairie View in 1896. Would he follow Washington's lead and merely focus on educating Texas's black children, or would he support the agenda of "agitation" for social equality as espoused by William Trotter and W. E. B. Du Bois? This is the fundamental question that hovered over Blackshear's tenure at Prairie View and is masterfully examined in *Edward L. Blackshear at Prairie View: Texas Education Crusader* by John Adams.

The challenges faced by Blackshear as he attempted to provide leadership to a fledgling school while navigating the political minefields of Jim Crow Texas are almost unimaginable. However, Adams's meticulous attention to detail and exhaustive research provide the reader a greater understanding of Blackshear, those individuals and ideologies that influenced his tenure, and the resurgence of the attitudes of the "Old South" in the supposedly "New South" era.

As a biography, the author begins with Blackshear's early days in Texas, his alignment with what many consider to be Washington's pacifist agenda, and his ultimate dismissal. This is a story about a man many in Texas knew little about. Blackshear often worked "behind the scenes" with Texas's white and black power brokers to ensure that Prairie View received the necessary support to be successful in the state's Jim Crow environment. Adams describes these relationships with a skill seldom seen in this genre. His extensive research into Blackshear's professional and personal life illustrates his desire to bring to light a man whose contribution to furthering black education was overshadowed by his well-known contemporaries. Still, even though he wasn't as recognized as Trotter, Washington, or Du Bois, Adams found that Blackshear was respected and blessed with many talents. There is a reason so many schools and other buildings in Texas carry his name.

As Prairie View A&M University prepares to celebrate its 150th year of fulfilling its primary mission of educating the children of the formerly enslaved, it is time to revisit (and revere) those stonemasons who laid the foundation for this great institution. Edward Blackshear was certainly one of those master builders. While most remember the Progressive era as being influenced by Prohibition and marches for women's rights, for the black community it meant Jim Crow violence and political ostracism. Blackshear lived in this environment and guided Prairie View through this difficult time in the school's history, a time when the black community was asked to "close ranks" while racists continued lynching black servicemen in their uniforms. In many ways, Blackshear stood above the racism of his day and focused on his mission in Waller County. And, as Adams illustrates, he did so with grace and eloquence.

Foreword

The release of a biography on Edward Lavoisier Blackshear (1862–1919) is perfectly timed with the approaching 150th anniversary of Prairie View A&M University. Born in Alabama to enslaved parents, Blackshear's journey is truly inspiring. In 1875, he was sent to Tabor College in Iowa, where he graduated with high honors in 1881. There he met Hightower T. Kealing, a lifelong friend whom he followed to Texas after graduation.

Blackshear's first teaching job was in a small public school in rural Ellis County. The educational challenges faced by rural black communities shocked and motivated him, shaping his future as an educator. After a brief stint in Waco, he moved to Austin in 1883, where he rose from instructor to principal and eventually became the superintendent of African American schools.

In Austin, Blackshear was a tireless advocate for black education. He helped found the Texas Black Teachers Association, chaired the city's annual Juneteenth celebrations, and was active in the local Black Man's Congress. His work caught the attention of Gov. Lawrence Sullivan Ross, who expanded state support for Prairie View.

In 1896, Gov. Charles A. Culberson appointed Blackshear as the third principal of Prairie View State Normal and Industrial College. Blackshear skillfully navigated the complex social and political landscape of Texas, working with multiple governors and securing significant state funding. He also built strong relationships with Texas A&M presidents and its board of directors and maintained a positive presence in white newspapers across Texas through numerous letters, articles, and interviews.

Blackshear's influence extended beyond Texas. He attended regional and national conferences, collaborating with prominent figures like Booker T. Washington. His legacy is a testament to his dedication and impact on education for African Americans.

Under Blackshear's leadership, Prairie View became the largest black land-grant college in the nation. He also made significant strides for rural black Texans through his leadership of the African American extension service at Prairie View. Blackshear founded the Negro State Farmers' Congress of Texas and served as its president for several years. In 1913, he was elected president of the National Negro Farmers' Congress in Birmingham, Alabama.

Despite his numerous successes, Blackshear couldn't escape the political landscape. In the 1914 Democratic gubernatorial primary, he supported prohibitionist Thomas H. Ball against the eventual winner, James E. Ferguson. The following year, Ferguson demanded that the Texas A&M Board of Directors fire Blackshear. Although the board reelected him as principal in the summer of 1915, they ultimately removed him in early August after failing to change Ferguson's mind. That same year, Blackshear was appointed head of federal extension work for black Americans in Texas, Kansas, Louisiana, and Oklahoma. He passed away on December 12, 1919.

Reflecting on Blackshear's life, one is continually impressed by his ability to garner white support in a conservative state. His success was a testament to his humor, intelligence, eloquence, persistence, and exceptional networking skills.

John S. Sharp, Chancellor
Texas A&M University System
2011–2025

Acknowledgments

The path to researching and writing this book has been long and rewarding. Little did I know when I started that we would find such detailed, rich primary documents penned by Edward L. Blackshear. The more we searched the more we found, and I cannot sufficiently thank the score of archives across the nation that helped locate and provide much of the material. Edward Blackshear was all but forgotten, and now—I trust—this will shed a new light on one of the most dynamic, energetic, and dedicated educational leaders in the country at the turn of the twentieth century.

As with any project, those who assisted helped tremendously. After a score of books, I have many to thank and I hearken back to numerous writers, mentors, and friends who humored me and advised on the many projects. First and foremost is Dr. Henry C. Dethloff, who was my mentor par excellence and great friend and collaborator on a number of volumes. He gave me a great insight into Texas history—even given his deep Louisiana roots—and a great appreciation for all things "agriculture," which played greatly into this book. Dr. R. J. Q. Adams (no relation to the author), an old English history professor, unbeknownst to him caught my attention and interest in historical biography back in the early 1970s with his first and last books—the most recent an engaging biography of Arthur James Balfour, a British politician who rose to be prime minister in England during the same era and time frame that Edward Blackshear struggled for equality and educational opportunity for African Americans in Texas and across the South.

I have further had occasion to visit with some of the greatest authors of our generation, each of whom were very engaging and open with their remarks and observations on writing. Of these I recall a delightful dinner with James Michener somewhere at a home in East Texas as he was wrapping up one of his last major books on Texas. He was a bit surprised when I noted his best book, while I awaited the publication of *Texas*, was *The Source* (1965). The opening pages of the book at an archaeological "tel" in

Israel have always caught my imagination. Some years later I had lunch in Austin with David McCullough shortly after the release of the blockbuster chronicle of the life of John Adams (2001). Seated across from me, David looked at my name tag and smiled, "Old boy, you sure have held up well since 1776!"

Having not written a biography, during the rambling noontime discussion I asked David to describe the key elements in setting the tone and tenor of such a book as *John Adams*. He noted he always tried to set his subject and their surrounding situation "in the moment." He went on to comment that he was not into revisionism but instead in history as it is.

The key to being able to compile such a book is having access to the primary material. Some have asked why I selected such a lost-in-time figure to chronicle. The blame rests partly with my good friend Bill Page, who has routinely over the past few decades started a conversation with, "This would be an interesting topic for someone [else] to write a book on"—only to drop it in one's lap and go on to the next topic! And thus the Blackshear research was a transition from my study of the Texas A&M administration of Pres. Lawrence Sullivan Ross during the 1890s (whom, I was soon to learn, was a contemporary and close friend of Blackshear). Yet once into the research, during which Bill was tremendously helpful in locating documents, commenting on drafts, and constantly suggesting new topics, I found myself engrossed like I hope other biographers are—and as Professor Adams would say of a compelling biographical topic, "The central character was indeed a profoundly interesting man."

In short, Blackshear was a compelling figure and his story a pleasure to tell. It became very clear that Blackshear could have embarked on any career he wished to pursue. His educational attainment at Tabor College in Iowa, his keen sense and ability to relate to those around him in difficult circumstances, and the changing post–Federal Reconstruction political and social landscape of Texas and the South are most instructive. Blackshear's crusade into the throes of education from the grassroots of a small, one-room schoolhouse to becoming the chief executive of the largest college of public education for African Americans in the nation served Texas and its citizens well. Thanks, Bill and Dr. Adams, for unknowingly pointing the way.

Without the timely assistance of professional librarians and archivists, research historians are all but helpless. Thus, given the restrictions, delays, evolving archival protocols, access schedules, and the necessary patience to locate and retrieve key documents during the nationwide pandemic of 2020, I am beholden to many. My search began in the birthplace and location of the early education of Edward in Montgomery, Alabama, and I was assisted by Ken Barr of the Alabama Historical Office and Betty Pouncey at the Montgomery County Historical Society. One of the greatest and most pleasant surprises was to locate the records from the 1877–81 period of Tabor College in Tabor, Iowa. The now-defunct college had been closed since 1927, so it was a long shot that any records survived—but they did. Harry and Jeane Wilkins at the Tabor County Historical Society produced Edward's college class records, graduation presentation, and rare photographs that give a critical look into the value of an intense classical education combined with science courses and sheds light on how this education at Tabor served Edward throughout his later years.

Further records were located at the Prairie View A&M University Archives with the help of Phyllis Earles. In Austin at the Austin History Center, I was aided by Molly Hults and Mike Miller, and by many helpful staff at the Texas State Library and Archives Commission and at the Dolph Briscoe and Benson History Centers at the University of Texas. Also helpful were Kaitlyn Price at the Dallas History Center; Kevin Kinney at the Galveston and Texas History Center at the Rosenberg Library; Elizabeth Dunn at the Rubenstein Library at Duke University; Louisa Hoffman at Oberlin College; Benna Vaughan at the Baylor University Archives; and Michael Frost at the Yale Archives.

After over 50 years I am the oldest living researcher at the Cushing Memorial Archives at Texas A&M University. I have outlasted numerous staff changes, yet all have been extremely understanding, patient, and helpful with my forays into research. I would like to thank David Chapman, Beth Kilmarx, Leslie Winter, Robin Hutchinson, Anton Du Plessis, and Vaprrenon "Vappy" Severs.

I extend special thanks to J. Gilberto Quezada and T. G. Webb, who has for the past many years provided great insight into a number of my recent projects, and, along with Alwyn Barr, most recently provided timely comments for this endeavor. Others who have been a tremendous assistance include Jerry Cooper, Carl Walker, John Keck, and Jerry Thompson, as well as Frank Johnson and Ron Goodwin.

Yet none have been more patient and supportive than Sherry—who for way too many years has tolerated my research pursuits, my long nights at the typewriter, and continuing talks about my research of the moment.

EDWARD L. BLACKSHEAR
AT PRAIRIE VIEW

•⁂•

Prologue

A Nobler Future

The years after the Civil War were a tumultuous period across the South. Radical Reconstruction imposed by federal edict changed every aspect of the Southern social, political, and economic fabric. The abrupt transition of the African American population from slavery to freedom was met in the South and in Texas in particular with a mixture of white opposition that would redefine and reshape Southern institutions for decades. As I started this project, I reflected on one book in particular. Some four decades ago I first read C. Vann Woodward's *Origins of the New South, 1877–1913* (1951), and his insights and assessments of the dynamic period still resonate and provide an excellent backdrop to this work. Additional books that provide a tremendous perspective on the response to the era after Reconstruction are Alwyn Barr, *Reconstruction to Reform: Texas Politics, 1876–1906* (1971); Lewis L. Gould, *Progressives and Prohibition: Texas Democrats in the Wilson Era* (1973); and George R. Woolfolk, *Prairie View: A Study in Public Conscience, 1878–1946* (1962). The works, papers, and memoirs of Booker T. Washington and W. E. B. Du Bois, two nationally known African American leaders of the era, have a significant impact on this story. Furthermore, Edward Blackshear knew and worked with both men. In large measure Washington became Blackshear's primary mentor. Thus, the dominant Southern institutions, combined with the trans-Mississippi Western influence on Texas, impacted the economic, political, and social changes in the state. This included the role of education at all levels, which would play a pivotal influence and catalyst in the advancement and quest for inclusive equality of the African American community.

Education in Texas in the immediate post-Reconstruction period was orchestrated by the white Democrat Redeemers as a means to dominate

African Americans. Progressive reformers in the late 1880s and 1890s, however, viewed education as a key aspect of advancing the social and economic well-being of black Americans across the South. While education was promoted by a varied cross section of federal government agencies, northern abolitionist groups, religious organizations, education leaders, and independent philanthropists, as well as, of course, African American leaders, the reality is that the specter of advancing the education of African Americans was met with hardcore political opposition that hijacked and stymied the spirit and intent of universal education for all for decades after emancipation. What type of subjects to be taught, who would fund education, and who would teach and administer education in the South were much debated by those who proclaimed a "separate but equal" mantra.

The political opposition to the advancement of African Americans via education involved a complicated mix of religious, social, and economic dynamics that would be in conflict for decades. The level of advancement of black education was deemed by some to be a challenge to white political-social control in the South. The South in general and Texas in particular well into the early 1900s was overwhelmingly a rural society. What followed was a debate, sometimes violent, mixed with fear and ignorance on the part of those who denied the beneficial impact of education. Political manipulation, such as linking suffrage to a poll tax and literacy requirements, the controversy over Prohibition, and property ownership requirements for voting—the Jim Crow laws—were viewed as a means to keep "the blacks in their place."

If Black voting was suppressed, so too would be their collective efforts to advance the funding and expansion of education that, some whites feared, would interfere with opportunities for whites. Even when votes supporting black educational opportunities were counted and in the majority, progress was slow or nonexistent, such as the vote in Texas to locate the "black university" in Austin that was never accomplished due to postelection legislative manipulation, ballot box irregularities, and questionable court challenges. The ramifications of the political environment and Blackshear's strategies to deal with them, will be an overriding theme explored in detail in the following chapters. From this debate would rise a new generation of black leaders, as well as numerous white advocates, to work to advance the well-being of African Americans in Texas.

While there were scores of Southern black activists and champions of education across the South, this work will focus on the life and times of black educator Edward Lavoisier Blackshear. In the years from 1885 to 1919, he would become a pivotal leader, educator, strategist, essayist, poet, agriculturist, and advocate in the struggle to advance opportunities for black Americans across Texas in spite of a rigid white power structure. His understanding of the agricultural economy of Texas and the challenges facing the small farmer facilitated his leadership in the advancement of the agricultural extension services to assist Black farmers. Politically astute and prudent, he was at ease and conversant with US presidents, Texas governors, national political leaders, and leading agricultural and business concerns in the state. As a crusader for the benefits of black education, he helped advance the social, political, and economic well-being of a generation of Texans. No understanding of the period is possible without a grasp of the influence of transformative figures like Blackshear.

One of the earliest African American newspapers printed in San Antonio, the *Tonguelet*, published the young Blackshear's editorial and his "hope for a nobler future":

> Our growth and power as a people are not to be measured merely or mainly by the number who attend school and acquire some degree of literary attainment, but they are rather to be measured by what those who have received educational advantages actually do accomplish and achieve in the struggle of life. The colored merchant who from a small beginning and with no encouragement builds up a substantial trade, the farmer who adds yearly to his acres, accumulates stock and improves his property; the professional man, whether doctor, lawyer, minister, editor or teacher, who rises by merit, industry and character to a position of influence and financial independence; the thrifty laborer or mechanic who owns a comfortable home, maintains in a respectable manner his family, educates his children and has some cash in the bank—such men as these show forth the capacity of the race and give hope for *a nobler future*.

When the twenty-year-old Blackshear arrived in Texas in the early 1880s, the statewide population was 1.6 million. Over 80 percent of Texans were rural, and the largest city in the state was the Port of Galveston. Education in Texas was at best underfunded, ill-administered, and underserved. Some 73 percent of black Texans were illiterate, along with an estimated 25 percent of the white population. The level of illiteracy among the Mexican

American Texans is unknown. The general consensus in the rural communities was, first, that working the farm and ranch was more important than education. Second, if there was going to be "schooling," farmers didn't want to pay for it, and, third, classes could not last more than a couple of months and could not interfere with planting or the harvest. There were few school facilities in the rural areas, as well as shortages of teachers and funding for textbooks. The larger cities like Galveston, Waco, San Antonio, Dallas, and Austin seemed to be a little better prepared, given broader civic and church support, but they too dealt with poor school facilities, low teacher salaries, and few books.

During the course of Blackshear's career in education, the population of Texas more than tripled (growing from 1.6 to 4.7 million), and farmers struggled to cope with increasingly competitive markets and with concerns over the dominance of the railroads. The issue of Prohibition split political parties and loyalties as well as church congregations. The state was impacted by two debilitating economic recessions. In addition, the combination of the gradual industrialization and urbanization of the state shifted political-social priorities. Each of these dynamics weighed heavily on the role and enhancement of education in Texas.

By the early 1890s, Blackshear was a well-known leader of education reform in Texas. With links to national figures such as Booker T. Washington and W. E. B. Du Bois, he became an active advocate and leader of educational programs across the South. Much has been written about the pioneering programs at Hampton Normal and Agricultural Institute of Virginia, Howard University in Washington, Fisk University in Nashville, and Tuskegee Institute in Alabama, but little attention has been given to African American higher education programs and experiences west of the Mississippi River, especially in Texas. And there has been little scholarship on Prairie View A&M in particular and Edward Blackshear's contribution and impact on his generation. This will be addressed with a wealth of recently uncovered primary research materials that provides new light and perspective.

Blackshear's interests were not limited to his grassroots career in education. While not a full-time farmer, he became one of the most knowledgeable men in the country on the agricultural dynamics of the economy, from the challenges farmers faced in the field to the inequities of the credit-lien system, the dearth of agricultural best practices, and the onerous distance of cotton markets. Furthermore, thanks to his excellent college education, he remained a keen observer of international issues ranging from Africa and Haiti, competitive commercial concerns with the cotton markets in Liverpool and Manchester, to the geopolitical and religious influence of Japan and China.

This pivotal story will be told in the time frame and terminology of the era in which it is set. For example, in the over four dozen newspapers and periodicals I reviewed prior to 1925, the term "African American" or "Afro-American" was seldom used. Quotations will of necessity include terms now considered offensive, or at least outdated. Contemporary accounts known to Blackshear and general news media regularly used "Negro," "black," and "colored," and occasionally "African," with the one lone exception of a Philadelphia newspaper that was called the *Afro-American*. Likewise, the term "white Anglo-Saxon American" was never used during this era, only "white," "whitie," or "cracker," with the meaning of the last ranging from a term of endearment, to "redneck," to a term of slander. Interestingly, during the late 1930s the number one farm team of the St. Louis Cardinals baseball organization was proudly known as "The Atlanta Crackers"—and my father pitched for the team in 1939–40.

The period at the turn of the twentieth century in the South is one of the most turbulent in our nation's history. While the issues and events continue to resound today, by necessity this work will focus on the years of Blackshear's life prior to 1919. No collection of Blackshear's letters or papers survive in the archives at Prairie View A&M University or Texas A&M University, and only a small but important number of his works are found there. However, a broad cross section of research in primary sources in over a dozen archives nationwide, supported by correspondence and editorials in over forty nationwide magazines and newspapers, has uncovered over 370 letters, articles, poems, legislative testimonies, and reports written by Edward L. Blackshear. Unlike others of the period, he did not employ a ghost writer. These sources provide rich insight into his career as well as into the opinions of his colleagues.

Edward Blackshear lived and worked during years of remarkable changes and tremendous challenges for African Americans. When examining documents concerning his life's work, one is struck repeatedly by the fact that he was a man of vision. He knew what was possible at any given moment and had a strategy to work from the possible to the desired outcome. His masterful skills as a communicator are ever present, with the keen ability to motivate audiences—especially whites wielding power—to support each step of his plans. One can only wonder what more he would have accomplished had his death at a relatively young age not occurred.

The author hopes that this work and its companion volume will encourage others to research the writings of additional black leaders. Other than the discussion of Blackshear's tenure at Prairie View in George Woolfolk's 1962 book, *Prairie View*, there has been no other scholarly attention to someone who was in fact an iconic figure in his lifetime. And thus, I have endeavored to present the heretofore lost story of the works, challenges, leadership, and spirit of Edward L. Blackshear and his contemporaries, both friend and foe. Any conclusions gleaned from this presentation are mine alone.

·» 1 «·

The Early Years

> My grandmother, although ignorant, had a profound belief in education. But if she knew absolutely nothing of the world of letters, she had something as good, perhaps better—a warm, honest, loving heart and Christian principles. She had a genuine hatred for dirt and disorder, a regard, amounting to a fearful reverence, for white people of "quality," and a great and ill-disguised contempt for common, shiftless "darkies," and low-bred whites.[1]
>
> EDWARD L. BLACKSHEAR

As Texas was experiencing a dynamic transformation from years of taming its western frontier and the emergence of a growing post-Reconstruction state, Edward L Blackshear arrived in Waco, Texas. Encouraged to make the Lone Star state his home by a college friend, following his education in the upper Midwest he began a four-decade career championing education in Texas. During this period Blackshear would rise as the primary leader and strong advocate of African American educational attainment, first in the state of Texas and then across the South. Beginning as a "common school" teacher in rural Texas, he came face-to-face with the poverty and poor conditions of subsistence farmers struggling to cope with day-to-day hardships. In the process he quickly learned to navigate the political, social, and economic challenges of the Jim Crow South, rising from superintendent of the Austin African American school system to become principal of one of the largest black land-grant colleges in the nation, Prairie View A&M Normal College, in the mid-1890s. The story of Blackshear's focus, drive, and dedication to education, equality, and advancement of the lives and future of African Americans is long overdue.

—⊰⊱—

In the words of Blackshear, his grandmother Harriet Graybill was a most remarkable woman. She idolized his mother, Adaline, the only child whom she was allowed to keep when her plantation owner sold her in the mid-1850s in Georgia to a new home and owner in Montgomery, Alabama. Raised in Georgia and Alabama, Harriet was midwife for her daughter, Adaline Pollard Blackshear, at the birth of Edward Lavoisier on September 8, 1862, in Montgomery. Edward was born into slavery on the Pollard Plantation, home of Capt. Charles Teed Pollard, who appears to be his father. Following his service in the war, Pollard returned home as president of M&M Railroad. Young Edward learned to read and write from his mother, learned math from his father, and added training in the "Big House" from the German tutor who was retained yearly for the white children of the family. After the end of the Civil War in 1865, his mother remained with the Pollard family. The strong personality of his mother, backed by his grandmother, instilled persistence and self-sacrifice in her young son at an early age. Edward attended one of the first public schools for African American children in Montgomery, followed by three years of study at the Swayne School, established by the American Missionary Association (AMA), known in its formative years as the American Home Missionary Society.[2]

By 1870, Edward's stepfather, Abram (Abraham) Blackshear, was trained as a cabinetmaker and employed in the grocery store business, while his mother was employed "keeping house." Abram reported assets of $500 in real estate and $1,000 in personal property. The Blackshears raised four children, Sovellia (b. 1859), Edward L. (b. 1862), William T. (b. 1868), and John (b. 1870). As late as the 1870 US census, Adaline's sixty-three-year-old invalid mother was living with the family. Little other information on the early years of the Blackshear marriage and family background survives except for periodic census information.[3]

The AMA society, founded by the Congregationalist Church, was one of many Northern, Protestant-based abolitionist groups established to promote education and racial equality. Among its first efforts in the South was opening camps during the war to assist former slaves.[4] During the postwar period their aim was to establish churches and encourage educational programs with the creation of schools for freedmen. Reflecting on the dynamics of education facing the newly freed, Edward Blackshear began in the early 1880s to shape his attitudes and approach to education. In 1902, he gave an assessment on the harsh transition from enslavement to freedom in a newspaper article, "Present Needs of the Colored Race": "When the Negroes were set free the first aim of thousands was to learn to read and write. Gray-haired veterans of the plantations sat side by side in the day schools as well as in night schools with the smallest pickaninnies. And all seemed eager to learn the mysterious arts of the school room. The school book in the eyes of the unlettered slave, was a sort of fetich [*sic*] to which he attributed the power of the white man. It was not surprising that the whole race tried to go to school, and it need not surprise us if, in the enthusiasm for book-learning, from which the race had been so strictly debarred, too much stress may have been placed on mere book learning and too much confidence placed in the formal processes of the school room."[5]

Montgomery, the former Confederate capital, was one of the primary communities—along with Charleston, Atlanta, New Orleans, Nashville, and Austin—targeted to deliver the society's services. Edward and scores of black and white Americans greatly benefited from the missionary teachers, who also evangelized their students. Years later, Blackshear, in a 1902 publication, *Twentieth Century Literature, or A Cyclopedia of Thought on the Vital Topics Relating to the American Negro by One Hundred of America's Greatest Negroes*, reflected on the impact of his early education: "A faithful band of Christian missionary white women gave answer by coming in the face of an inevitable social ostracism to light the torch of thought in a region hitherto unblessed by a single ray of education's light."[6]

The AMA sponsored more than five hundred one-room primary schools and a dozen colleges for freedmen across the South. The society's *American Missionary* magazine was one of the first nationwide publications with a broad circulation to advocate the expansion of educational programs for black Americans. The society recruited Northern teachers through the AMA's arm of the Freedman's Aid Society (no direct connection to the Federal Bureau of Refugees, Freedmen, and Abandoned Lands), as well as championed legislative efforts for full voting rights for African Americans across the South. The Freedmen's Bureau, created by an act of Congress on March 3, 1865, had an initial impact beginning in early 1866, providing educational opportunities to black children primarily in rural locations.[7] The bureau, which provided a legal and moral basis for political activity for African Americans in the South, had four divisions: Land, Educational, Legal, and Medical. The land department overshadowed the broader mandate of the postwar agency, given its power to confiscate surplus buildings and transfer them to teachers for dwellings and schools (though in the case of Texas it was not very successful in transferring land directly to the freedmen, despite the myth of the "forty acres and a mule" that persisted for decades). However, private and eleemosynary organizations championed by the AMA provided more funding and teachers across the South, given their long-range horizon, than the bureau. All federally sponsored education efforts during Reconstruction in Texas were abruptly discontinued at the end of 1870, but African American interest in education did not end with the work of the bureau.[8]

While the AMA, a pioneer in black higher education in the South, had assisted the establishment of colleges, there were also some two dozen private, church-funded denominational "academies" and colleges. In the late 1800s, few white or black students had the opportunity for schooling beyond learning basic reading and writing through the equivalent of the fourth or fifth grade. Antagonistic agricultural and labor groups viewed such "institutional" learning as "hampered by ancient conditions and valiant supporters of liberal culture." Thus, "literacy and education was viewed as a means to better their social status and as a benefit of freedom—school attendance symbolized their free status and entry in the body politic." Furthermore, these so-called private colleges were deemed by some as "founded principally to keep students within [the] denominational fences of their parents." Edward was among the students who benefited from these private schools, and his parents and supportive local teachers saw major promise in the future education of the young student.[9]

Tabor College: *Lux in tenebris*

In contrast to most black students, who took local manual labor jobs after a few years of schooling, young Blackshear was sponsored by Prof. James F. McPherson of the AMA school in Montgomery "on account of his love for study and books" for enrollment in Tabor College, in Tabor, Iowa, a predominantly white Christian liberal arts college founded on egalitarian principles. Edward's parents, who could both read and write, were highly supportive of educational opportunities available for their son. Tabor College, affiliated with Congregationalists, was founded in the early 1850s with abolitionists as many of its early benefactors. A committed theist throughout his life, Edward maintained strong ecclesiastical ties as a part of his lifetime moral compass. He entered the Tabor prep school at age fourteen in 1876 and boarded in the home of Professor McPherson's brother, the principal of the Normal Department of Tabor College, Asbury Sullens McPherson and wife Hannah Maria.[10]

Edward worked for his room and board, and after completion at the prep school he was accepted to the 1877–78 freshman class enrolled in introductory classics studies. Thus began his rigorous college experience. While majoring in the "classics," dominated by studies in the ancient languages of Latin, Greek, and German, he additionally received a solid foundation in elocution, rhetoric, and logic. Given his love for learning and self-confidence, Edward thrived under challenging instructors who encouraged him to broaden his intellectual reach and curiosity. Maintaining high grades and with the knowledge of an excellent teaching faculty, he completed courses in algebra, geometry, and trigonometry. Lectures in botany, astronomy, and zoology opened his eyes to the importance of scientific research. He completed a four-year program to earn a bachelor of arts degree in June 1881 at age nineteen. At Tabor Blackshear received a thorough education in the late 1870s curriculum, and this formal education in the classics would be reflected throughout Edward's lifetime in his eloquent writings, breadth of knowledge, and dramatic speeches.[11]

On the occasion of the jubilee anniversary of Tabor College, Blackshear, who was unable to attend the celebration, submitted an original poem, "Memories of Tabor," confirming his "unswerving loyalty" and the educational impact of the institution:

> But here within these leafy groves
> To heart and memory dear
> Abides a peace that soothes the soul
> In the evening sweet and clear.
> As if to see the abundant fruition
> Of the sowing of long ago
> The bread cast on the waters then
> Has returned with the tide's inflow.
>
> Farewell, ye lovely visions
> Of the Tabor that was mine
> Oh, may her radiance never dim
> But e'er more brightly shine![12]

The class of 1881 at Tabor had only two graduates, both black: Edward Blackshear and his close friend Hightower Theodore Kealing of McLennan County, Texas. The two graduates were the featured speakers at the fifteenth annual commencement of Tabor, with an oration by Blackshear entitled "Man and Destiny," followed by Kealing's presentation, "The True and False in Philosophy." Raised in East Texas, Kealing graduated with a degree in science. After working a brief time in Iowa, the new graduates traveled to Montgomery to visit Edward's family, and then went to Waco in February 1882 to seek teaching jobs.[13]

Texas still had a wild, untamed frontier. Only months before Blackshear and Kealing arrived in Waco, Apaches had attacked the Quitman Stagecoach, killing the driver and a passenger. Kealing joined the faculty of Paul Quinn College in Waco, sponsored by the African Methodist Episcopal (AME) Church. This was the first African American college west of the Mississippi River, having been established in 1872. Edward, due to undiagnosed health problems, was delayed in beginning his teaching career and instead opted for outdoor labor to improve his health, taking a job as a lineman on a telegraph gang setting poles between Waco and Gainesville, Texas, for the Texas Midland Railroad. This was an important manual labor experience for Blackshear, to which he afterwards attributed his beliefs on physical health considerations as a key part of a well-rounded and well-educated person.[14]

At an early age and only months into his teaching career in rural Texas, Edward was active in articulating his views on education in general and the critical need to advance educational opportunities for African Americans in particular. When Blackshear and Kealing returned to Texas, the total population of the predominantly rural state was 1.6 million—of which about one-quarter or 400,000 were African Americans—with an illiteracy rate estimated over 80 percent. Blackshear's first teaching jobs in small, unfurnished, one-room black rural country schools were a far cry from the comfortable, bucolic environment of his college days in Tabor. The following March 1883 article, "Evolution of Society," which he penned in Waco for *The Christian Recorder* after months of teaching, marks the philosophical crusade that Blackshear would espouse in the upcoming years:

> The doctrine of evolution is now almost universally accepted in some form or other. It is a fact that in nature nothing is accomplished

suddenly or in a hurry. All is slow, gradual, first lower then the higher. First we have the simple, jelly-like, unorganized nomad, and afterwards by processes of growth, development, natural selection and heredity, we arrive through many varied transitions, to the highest power of animal life. We see the same gradual evolution, not only in the history of species general, tribe and family, but it is equally apparent in the light of the individual, whether man or animal.

How gradual, yet how great the changes from infancy to manhood, not alone in physical power, but also, in mental capacity. The growth and development of civilization is in respects similar to that development which we see elsewhere in the universe. Nations, like poets, are born, not made. You cannot force a child into a man, neither can you force the growth of nations. A child will become a man under proper influences, so a nation will become civilized under proper influences. We apply this thought to the Negro in America. It seems to me that too much has been expected of the negro in so short a time.

We cannot expect that a people, torn from the fetichism [*sic*], and held as slaves for two hundred years, should suddenly and in all respects become equal to that race which stands in the foreground of modern civilization. As a race we have much which we must contend. In the first place, we have the degrading influence of inherited passion and appetite. We must, as a people, learn self-control. It seems as though we were incapable of controlling our passions and emotions. Centuries of indulgence on the part of our ancestors, has made us slaves to our passions. We must rise above and subdue this mighty undercurrent of our animal nature, or it will sweep us into the vortex of natural ruin.

Every generation leaves its impress on all succeeding generations. The work of civilizing a people must extend through several generations. Each must do his part in elevating the race. The more we accomplish in our day, the less will remain for those who follow. If we learn to control ourselves it will be easy for our children to control themselves. If we educate our minds, our children will take to learning more easily and naturally. This influence of heredity we must never forget. We live not for ourselves alone, we live to all succeeding generations. Our race will be just what we who now live, choose to make it.

Of all the influences and forces at work molding society, none are so potent for good or evil as the family. The family should be the

> preparatory school to active life. Here the child should learn self-control, to curb its disposition and rein its desires. The lesson of obedience to authority should here be taught, and in the family the training of the mind, manners and morals of the child should receive most careful and prayerful attention. They should here learn its duties to God and humanity. Our race will never be truly civilized till we have better and purer homes for training of our youth. No school or church can do the work which the father and mother should do at home.
>
> To have good homes, we need purer men and more virtuous women. The development of society among us must be slow and gradual and we must not be discouraged. The full development of the Negro in America we shall not live to see, but that does not lesson our responsibility to do what we may to bring about that full fruition.[15]

Edward's close link with Theodore Kealing would be lifelong, as he briefly joined his friend at Paul Quinn College in February 1882. Eager to be a part of the postwar efforts to articulate the black perspective, Kealing edited the *Colored American Journal* along with Rev. C. W. Porter. The young, twenty-two-year-old Kealing attracted a great deal of attention and was offered a teaching job in 1883 in Austin, where he taught in the Eighth Ward School. And soon, Blackshear, after teaching briefly in Ellis County, followed him to Austin in late 1883, working first as a part-time day laborer in search of a more permanent teaching position. For the balance of the decade, the two men taught at a number of schools. While Kealing remained active in education, becoming president of Paul Quinn College in 1888, increasingly his attention was drawn to the affairs of the AME Church. Thus Blackshear and Kealing entered the leading professions for African Americans during the late nineteenth century, for, as historian Alwyn Barr noted, "teachers and ministers formed the vast majority of the black professional class in Texas."[16]

Kealing's literary interest resulted in the publication of his *History of African Methodism in Texas* in 1885 and later the editorship of the church's literary quarterly, the *AME Church Review*, the primary magazine of the African American community nationwide. The support of black churches played a major role in the moral arguments and organized efforts to ensure educational equality in Texas for black students. One observer, W. E. B. Du Bois, claimed that the church was "the first distinctively" American black social institution and critical to advancing education among African

Americans. Furthermore, after emancipation the church "represented both the institutionalization" of black "community life and defiance to white authority." It became the freedman's sanctuary, as black Americans turned to the church for mutual support and cultural, social, and recreational activities as well as spiritual needs.[17]

—•≫≪•—

On the eve of Edward's Blackshear's death in late 1919, *Dallas Express* writer N. W. Harlee penned an editorial harking back to the educator's formative career and arrival in Austin and telling an old, often repeated, but insightful story: "One day in the city of Austin, while the young Blackshear was carrying a hod on his shoulders, the perspiration running down on his brow, an old gentleman who knew the ability of the boy of destiny, advised him to go over to the legislative hall where an examination for teacher's certificates was being held, and there take the examination. This the young Blackshear did. Now came the turning point in his useful career as well and favorably known by every school man of any note and the young people throughout the state."[18]

—•≫≪•—

While Kealing was devoting more time to church work, Blackshear continued his teaching career, being elected in fall 1883 to the principalship of the Austin Wheatville School, located on what was then the far western edge of the capital city. This was a significant honor for a twenty-three-year-old man with little teaching experience. One of the first freedmen's communities outside of the capital's city limits and predominantly settled by African Americans, Wheatville was founded in 1867 by a former slave from Arkansas. The original plot of land became the home to semiskilled workers, blacksmiths, day laborers, and small farm families and their livestock. In 1877 the Travis County Commissioners Court awarded surplus local funds for the construction of a free public school for African Americans. At its peak Wheatville boasted a population of some three hundred inhabitants, of which an estimated fifty to sixty-five were students. Blackshear quickly learned that local community support with both funding and political influence was critical to placing and maintaining the school on a solid footing. He soon found that one of his key allies was the church.[19]

TABLE 1.1. Enrollment and Attendance for Austin Colored Schools in the Ninth Scholastic Month (Ending May 1883)

		enrollment	attendance	Total students	Rate of attendance
Wheatville	boys	40	37	71	92%
	girls	31	28		
Third Ward	boys	47	27	110	60%
	girls	63	39		
Seventh Ward	boys	36	29	99	76%
	girls	63	46		
Eighth Ward	boys	74	66	126	89%
	girls	52	46		
Tenth Ward	boys	52	30	115	65%
	girls	63	45		
Total colored pupils		521	393		75%

Source: *Austin Daily Statesman*, May 24, 1883.

Veni, vidi, vici

As Blackshear worked as principal to advance the success of the small Wheatville School, he was fully aware of community support, particularly that of the local church. The spread of new AME churches had had mixed success due to competition with already active congregations of both the established AME and Baptists. Notwithstanding, Southern historian C. Vann Woodward notes, "Observers from outside the region were struck by Southern religiosity." Edward was active in promoting the establishment of a local AME church supportive of his school. Efforts during 1882–84 had been sluggish due to a void in church leadership, with what Edward described as "unfavorable circumstances," the "chief among which has been that greatest of hindrances, namely inefficient pastors." The solution was found in the arrival of Elder and Reverend Abraham Grant, about whom Blackshear proclaimed in an article in *The Christian Recorder*, "At last the right man, Reverend Grant, came. *Veni, vidi, vici.*" The new leadership resulted in a successful campaign to raise $4,000 for the construction of the new, three-story AME Church. Concerned with the success of the church and in the planning, Blackshear was vocal in writing the church officials, declaring: "The pastor must be supported . . . [and] thoroughly understand all the intricacies of finance." The great success was noted by the church elders, who wondered if they should send a new bishop. Edward wrote to oppose their sending anyone: our man, Rev. Grant, "is the pastor now in Austin." The involvement in the dynamics of church politics and serving as the private secretary to the bishop proved a great training ground and lesson for Blackshear. Bishop Grant remained a fast friend and influential ally.[20]

In addition to his involvement in church affairs, Blackshear was increasingly active in community activities in Austin. For a majority of African Americans, the church became the focal point of their lives and community events. The church was the only institution in the South over which black Americans had complete control. And no local event was more important than the yearly celebration of the June 19 anniversary of "Juneteenth," the day in 1865 on which Union general Gordon Granger arrived in Galveston with the news of Lincoln's Emancipation Proclamation and the abolition of slavery in Texas. In 1884, the celebration was filled with what the *Austin Daily Statesman* termed a "grand demonstrations [parades] and picnic" at Wheeler's Grove, with "every one invited to attend and bring filled baskets." Edward was a member of the three-man organizing committee that determined the selection of the program, which included a reading of the Emancipation Proclamation by Prof. W. T. Phillips, following orations by Blackshear and prominent black leaders and friends Reverend Grant, J. J. Hamilton, and William H. Holland.[21]

One of Blackshear's earliest mentors in Austin during the 1880s was William Holland. By the time Edward arrived in Texas, Holland was a well-established teacher, civic leader, and legislator. Born in Marshall, Texas, in 1841, he and his brothers, Milton and James, the sons of white planter Capt. Bird Holland, were given their freedom in the late 1850s and moved to Ohio to attend school. In 1864 Holland enlisted in the Union army, was assigned to the 16th US Colored Infantry Regiment, and saw combat in the federal vanguard at Overton Hill and the siege of Nashville. Following the war, he returned to attend Oberlin College for a few years before returning to Texas to be a teacher, where he also received a federal appointment in the Austin post office. As one of the earliest black community leaders in Austin, he was the keynote speaker at the 1873 Colored Men's Convention that convened in Brenham and was chaired by Norris W. Cuney. The annual statewide black conventions championed key issues to promote friendly race relations, enhancement of education, and equal protection under the law, and were held through the late nineteenth century. "The black conventions," Alwyn Barr concluded, "provided one of the strongest voices for black people of Texas."[22]

In advance of the 1891 Colored Men's Convention, the African American paper the *Argus* (Galveston) printed a circular releasing a few suggestions on "things that need consideration" signed by Edward Blackshear and A. L. Maynard:

> Colored young men and women need to be taught how to be skilled in labor. As Hon. N. W. Cuney said in a recent address: "We are top-heavy. We are educating the brain but not the hand and arm. We have too many college graduates and almost no skilled mechanics. As a race we do not read enough. We are not well informed on the public issues of the day. We do not read newspapers. We need some league of which all colored men, regardless of political or religious belief, shall be members. No race can greatly improve unless its homes are the centers of morality, obedience, frugality, economy and true religion. We feel that our homes are not what they ought to be as a rule. It is the women, the mother, that makes the homes and the home determines the character of the offspring. We fear that many of our women, even some of those who have been sent away and kept in school, are not the home-makers that they ought to be. They do not manifest that loyalty to their husbands, families and race that we see in women of other nationalities. As long as so many colored men in our cities and towns allow themselves to be bribed by money and whiskey, so long will other races despise us and declare that we are unworthy of the right to vote. The folly of multitudes of our race in imitating the extravagant habits of white people more wealthy than themselves is still seen on all sides. We know, but we do not make use of the knowledge that economy is the road to wealth. We need more applied religion. *We need to have education show its power, not merely in the schoolrooms but in actual life work and deeds among the people.*"[23]

Following a move to Waller County, Holland was elected to the state legislature in 1876. While in Austin, he was concerned that the implementation of the 1862 Morrill Act in Texas was viewed as only supporting a white land-grant college, and thus he championed and sponsored a bill providing for

Edward L. Blackshear, 1900. From the collection of John A. Adams Jr.

a "black college," which, in time, was instrumental in establishing Prairie View Normal School as well as an equitable distribution of all state and federal education funds. Following his tenure in the legislature, he drafted a detailed proposal for the establishment of a facility for handicapped black children, resulting in the Eighteenth Legislature approving $50,000 for the creation of the Deaf, Dumb, and Blind Institute for Colored Youth, which opened in October 1887. When Holland—a Republican—was appointed by Democrat governor Sul Ross to direct the new institutions, he expressed misgivings as to his ability to perform the duties required. Ross responded to the fellow veteran, "I know you and have known of you for some years and you are the best man in Texas to fill the job." Holland served very successfully as the first superintendent of the institute for over a decade. However, he was best noted for an often-quoted public address at the June 1882 emancipation celebration in Austin.[24]

Uprising Scare of 1883

Shortly after graduating from college and while still in his early twenties, Edward Blackshear began a regular routine of submitting letters and articles to newspapers and periodicals not just in Texas, but also nationwide. Topics he discussed included church doctrine, the role and state of African American society, and the needs of the black community to advance economically. The urge to write was influenced by his broad liberal education at Tabor College and encouraged by his close friend Kealing. Blackshear had grown up in the city of Montgomery, Alabama, but he had spent his formative years in a calm Iowa rural community little impacted by the racial fears and angst experienced by African Americans across the South in the post-Reconstruction period, and he likely lacked firsthand experiences with the struggle of rural black Americans. Clearly aware of prejudice during his early days in Alabama, he was confronted with prejudice, segregation, and "Black Codes" when he arrived in Texas. In the fall of 1883, a number of incidents began in Marshall, Texas, concerning the right of African Americans to bear arms in local militia units (more fraternal gatherings with military trappings) and to organize in public parades and hold private meetings. Complaints from local citizens in East Texas resulted in a reversal by state officials to limit the number of black militia units, which was followed by protest by black leaders. This led the white press to fuel fears of a potential "negro uprising" invoking inflammatory editorials of a "war of races."[25] Rumors spread to other northeast Texas counties, random shots were fired, and the black private Bishop College in Marshall was blamed for the disturbances due to its Northern white teachers who taught malicious ideas such as "social equality." Concerned with the possibility of a volatile confrontation, the governor and attorney general were notified. As the situation cooled down, the new, young common school teacher in Austin was closely monitoring these events. Following a series of inflammatory articles and attacks on black Americans in the local papers penned by reporters whom Blackshear termed "irrepressible reporters, hungry for something sensational," Blackshear began to blame these extravagant journalists for inciting racial tensions between blacks and whites. The *Austin Statesman* did not hesitate to print his highly opinionated letters, which, in one detailed submission, placed the blame on the polarized political system in Texas, which divided and fueled prejudices:

> I long to see the time when in state affairs, at least, the negro shall cease to follow a lot of indigent, office-loving white Republicans (who are even now seeking to drive the negro out of the Republican Party) and vote for the man who ensure us our rights as citizens, not of the United States, but of Texas. Truly, we, the negroes of Texas, are in a dilemma. We are driven out by Republicans, and the Democrats say plainly we are not wanted.
>
> We long to see a party in Texas controlled by men of experience and sagacity, which shall not know men as white or colored, but only as citizens, a party whose leaders shall live and act on that lofty plane of statesmanship where the consciousness and perception of color shall vanish, where men shall be regarded as men regardless of race.[26]

One of the most intriguing aspects of Edward Blackshear was his candid public views on religion, race, politics, social norms of the period, equality, and education.[27] One expected that such observations would be heard with some indignation in Austin—especially from a young, college-educated African American teacher. The state capital and county seat of Travis County in the mid-1880s was a small, undeveloped town, more rural than urban, of some 18,800 inhabitants, of which 8,293 were African American. It was dotted with churches of some ten faiths, a handful of physicians, dozens of small independent merchants, and the expected scores of lawyers banking on doing business with the state and lobbying agencies, as well as numerous, mostly white, politicians. Immigrants from a dozen countries gradually grew in number. For example, rural Travis County (a very far cry from today's Austin metropolitan area) was dominated by farming, with 63,457 acres in cotton producing 18,664 bales (3.5 acres could produce 1 bale on average), followed by 34,638 acres in corn, producing over 800,000 bushels. One event that had a direct impact on how the city was viewed was the loss due to a faulty wood stove of the aging, three-decade-old, two-story wooden structure that housed the state capital and offices in the early 1880s. Up until its loss, little change or growth had occurred in Austin—and none was expected. However, Blackshear arrived in the capital as a small economic growth boom began.[28]

Common Education

Primary or "common" education was a large part of the local economy and social makeup. The first law concerning public education in Texas was passed in 1854 and was further supported by the state Constitution of 1876 under article 7, section 7, which briefly stated, with regard to local education, "Separate schools shall be provided for the white and colored children, and impartial provisions shall be made for both." City and rural school programs varied, and the degree of prosperity or poverty of an area affected the availability of local school tax revenue. For the two decades prior to 1900, the predominantly black county schools, also known as country or common schools, were administered by local county judges who acted as de facto superintendents. The education committee of the Colored Men's Convention, chaired by E. H. Anderson, was the first organization to analyze and document the state of black common school education in Texas. Their study concluded that preparation of an adequate number of teachers was considered the prime priority. For example, in 1887 Travis County had a total school population of 5,309, with half of this number enrolled in the city of Austin. Smaller satellite schools were housed in some fifty one-room schools scattered around the county; they employed an estimated one hundred teachers, with sixty teachers in the city and the balance in segregated rural schools. The average length of the school term in Austin schools was 106 days, and the average attendance in the city was 1,747. With no state standard, average school days ranged from 110 in Galveston to 100 in Dallas, to a high of 120 in Waller County, the home of Prairie View A&M.[29]

Segregation was the norm of the day, and disparities and prejudices were evident in every aspect of daily life. In spite of the mostly ineffective efforts to enhance and expand formal education, most Texas student learning ended in the early grades of the common or primary school. One very glaring inequality was the pay differential of monthly wages between white and black teachers, which ranged from 5 to 25 percent. The quality of any public school system is to a great extent dependent upon its financial base and how revenue is used to support education and employment of teachers. Towns and small communities could levy limited taxes, but most were more willing to give tax exemptions to attract new local investment in railroads and seaport facilities and merchant business. Railroad property was often undervalued below the true assessment worth, and incentive payments (many based on fraudulent land surveys) were made for railroad lines and depots, but little or nothing was spent for local education and much-needed teachers. Thus, local control over school expenditures worked to the disadvantage of African American school programs. The Redeemers, a political group whose goal was to undo and reverse

TABLE 1.2. Average Monthly Wages of Texas Teachers in 1887

	White		Black		
	Male	Female	Male	Female	Population
Austin	$117.31	$60.00	$60.00	$50.00	18,000
Travis Co.	$46.20	$39.18	$43.37	$35.62	37,233
Dallas	$85.71	$67.37	$65.00	$60.00	43,000
Dallas Co.	$53.20	$44.65	$42.00	$28.33	77,323
Galveston	$126.50	$65.00	$75.00	$52.25	25,000
Galveston Co.	$50.00	$31.21	$30.00	$27.00	26,379
Houston	$110.00	$58.44	$56.00	$45.00	30,000
Harris Co.	*data not available*				
Waco	$80.00	$57.50	$60.00	$40.00	18,000
McLennan Co.	$50.00	$40.00	$40.00	$30.00	38,001

Source: Foster, *Forgotten Texas Census*, 312–16.

Republican measures of Reconstruction, to reduce black voting power, and to oust all "foreign" control imposed from the North, neglected their social responsibilities, and public education was the first to suffer. The disparity was reflected across the state, as is noted by the salaries shown in Table 1.2.[30]

It is hard to determine when Blackshear selected a political party affiliation. His experiences and activities in Austin during the late 1880s gradually shaped his political inclinations. To further his awareness and civic community activities, he served as a lay minister at the Austin Metropolitan AME Church and was often referred to as "Reverend" Blackshear, a career in the ministry he was surely tempted to consider. Clearly, his thoughts and actions were focused on improvement in black education, indicated by his appointment by the church bishop to be a "special agent" to solicit funds for Paul Quinn College. In Austin during Blackshear's early days as a teacher, he began to form conclusions on educational and social debates based on a number of the pivotal issues of the day. The issues he contemplated and addressed during the period included the interaction of blacks with whites, enfranchisement of African Americans, compulsory school attendance, the issue of a designated colored university in Texas, and the politically charged proposal bantered around in the press about returning the "Negro" to Africa.[31]

In 1888, Blackshear was promoted to the principal of the Central Grammar School at the youthful age of twenty-six. By 1892, he became supervisor of all colored schools in Austin as well as principal of the high school—succeeding his close friend Kealing, who departed to Philadelphia as editor of the *AME Review*. Convinced by day-by-day classroom experience, Blackshear quickly realized as a school principal and administrator that student attendance was a pivotal aspect of education. On the surface it seemed clear—if you were not in the classroom, you could not learn and improve. Yet even this issue had political overtones. Many in the white political power establishment during the years after Reconstruction were not very interested in education in general, or in education for black Americans in particular. As a predominantly agrarian-rural economy, education was seen by many as a threat, giving children new ideas and possibly driving them away from the farm and ranch to the "sin and corruption" of the blossoming urban areas. Well into the twentieth century, black schools in parts of Texas delayed the start of fall classes so children could help with the harvest. Second, black education was seen by some whites as a means to provide education and job skills that resulted in the loss of white jobs. These whites felt it was best to "keep'em down on the farm" and out of the way. Blackshear and other leaders in the black community were well aware of these opinions, and thus facilitated efforts to enhance education for all. As early as 1885, Blackshear was one of the first Texas educators to strongly advocate compulsory school attendance, three decades before it became state law. Blackshear, in a detailed article in the *Austin Daily Statesman*, noted that increased school attendance would be the catalyst for the future, and he envisioned a statewide, county-by-county improvement: "If, with our already excellent and constantly improving public primary schools, we could have in each county at least one public grammar and high school, with practicable, industrial and commercial departments attached for the Negro needs especially to learn how to work in the various branches of agricultural, mechanical and chemical industry, how to do business, and how to originate and carry on commercial enterprise." The article, one of the very few he did not sign in person, was signed: "Teacher in Colored School."[32]

In responding to an editorial on education in the *Statesman*, Blackshear took direct aim at the white establishment: "We are pleased to know that you hold such liberal, progressive sentiments encouraging the education of our race, and we believe yours to be the sentiment of the majority of the leading white citizens of Austin. . . . We note it with joy; we hail it with delight."[33]

Blackshear followed these comments with an assessment that few, white or black, were prone to speak of so openly, and much less to submit to the local newspaper for publication. Clearly the young teacher was confident and sure of himself and his views:

> Since the white people of the country control the governments, state and federal, since they control every branch of industry, every department of commerce, and own the very soil on which we tread (I had almost said the air we breathe) it is natural that every thoughtful colored man should be deeply interested to know the sentiment of the white people towards himself, since they (the whites) by virtue of their superior power, wealth and intelligence are able to do him (the negro) much good or much harm. Hence the colored people of this and other states receive their school privileges, to some extent gratuitous.
>
> Yet it should be remembered that years the negro labored as a slave and was not allowed to accumulate any of the results of his labor.[34]

Alta Vista

Little did Blackshear know that in October 1885 his editorial comments and public speaking engagements on the prospects for the establishment of a "black university" became his life's work, when he optimistically wrote: "With a colored branch of the state university, soon to be organized, the colored people of Texas could boast of being most highly favored in regard to education." The origins for a black university in Texas began prior to Blackshear completing Tabor College and arriving in Waco and Austin. The new state Constitution of 1876 contained a provision for a designated black, educational "university." The legislative document also contained, upon the recommendation of William Holland, a provision for the establishment of a "colored" branch of the State Agricultural & Mechanical College of Texas. Republican governor Edmund Davis signed the bill to establish Texas A&M as a white-only branch of the nonexistent state university in April 1871, but it would be more than five years before the institution opened its doors. The mandate for a black college was established by an act approved on April 14, 1876, and determined to be a branch of Texas A&M. A commission appointed by the governor, comprised of

Ashbel Smith, J. H. Raymond, and J. D. Giddings, selected a site for "colored youth." The 1500 acres and buildings of the Alta Vista plantation of Col. Jared E. Kirby was purchased from Mrs. Kirby at a cost of $12,000 on October 23, 1877. Thus, the Alta Vista Agricultural College near Hempstead in Waller County for "colored youth" was a reality. Twenty thousand dollars was appropriated as the initial funding on January 22, 1878, for the board of directors of the A&M College to use for the expenses at the new campus.[35]

The new colored branch and its administration by a principal reported to A&M president Thomas S. Gathright, a crusty, old, and opinionated former superintendent of schools in Mississippi. Gathright was hired for the position on the recommendation of Jefferson Davis, who was first offered the presidency of the new college but declined. In addition to being president of A&M College, Gathright received no additional salary for his new management duties at Alta Vista. After hiring former Alcorn professor Lawrence W. Minor, an acquaintance of Gathright's from Mississippi, as the first principal and on-campus chief administrative officer, the college opened for its inaugural enrollment on March 11, 1878.[36] Though they expected a couple dozen new students to study agriculture, only eight enrolled and soon all dropped out. "The primary reason being," according to historian Henry C. Dethloff, "that the Negro youths did not want to go to college to learn to be sharecroppers or dirt farmers," and as such viewed the school as an "effort to hinder their intellectual and social progress." Blackshear confirmed this in his 1901 keynote address to the Colored Teachers Association: "The Negro farmer of that day had not the faintest notion of scientific farming and his boy did not care to go to school and be put at the same old task he was familiar with. And he stayed away." President Gathright reported to the board in late 1878 that all classes were discontinued due to the low enrollment and concluded that "there is no demand for higher education among blacks." Blackshear, a historian of the college's earliest efforts, noted on the delayed opening in 1878, "This conception [of higher education] was entirely alien to the minds of the colored people of that day."[37]

One seldom-noted aspect of the earliest days of the founding of Alta Vista school was that President Gathright and the A&M board attempted to organize the new school with a uniform corps of cadets similar to that formed at the A&M College in October 1876. A&M commandant of cadets Capt. George T. Olmsted was asked to contact the War Department in Washington to request a second regular army officer be assigned to the college. President Gathright then contacted Texas senator Richard Coke to intercede with the secretary of war, who agreed to consider detailing Lt. Henry O. Flipper to have charge as the military instructor at Alta Vista. Flipper was the first African American graduate of West Point, was assigned to the 10th Cavalry Regiment, and became the first non-white officer to command Buffalo Soldiers. Uniforms for the student body were considered a couple of times between 1890 to 1915 yet never adopted. However, due to the low student enrollment, a shortage of active-duty US Army officers, and inaction of the A&M Board, no federal officer was permanently (there were temporary duty officers during World War I) assigned to Prairie View until the opening of an ROTC detachment in May 1942, shortly after the Japanese surprise attack on Pearl Harbor.[38]

However, abruptly closing the only state-supported black institution of higher learning in Texas due to a shortage of students was not a final option. President Gathright immediately informed Gov. Oran M. Roberts, formerly president of the Texas secession convention in 1861 and a regimental Confederate commander during the war, that the situation was in "crisis." Notwithstanding his background, Roberts, a graduate of the University of Alabama, played a pivotal role in establishing the educational system in Texas.[39] Roberts and Gathright, along with Minor, who as a faculty member had experienced a similar disruption during the opening months of Alcorn College in 1871–72, were aware that the Morrill Act of 1862 and the Texas Constitution of 1876 mandated the operation regardless of the resources needed to reopen the college for black students. Aware of the ongoing shortage of teachers for the black rural schools, Gathright and Minor submitted a reorganization plan to the governor that called for the Alta Vista College to be reopened and staffed as the Prairie View Normal Institute for black Texans.[40] Governor Roberts approved the plan, which emphasized the education of teachers, and the legislature provided additional funding on April 19, 1879, along with a generous stipend of $6,000 following a visit to Texas by Dr. B. Sears, general agent from the Peabody Endowment Fund, a private foundation. The conversion of Alta Vista to a normal college was followed by the opening of the Normal College in Huntsville for white students. This was in part a plan to sustain racial segregation in Texas colleges, but also indicated a sincere effort to sustain both higher and common school education for black Texans. By October Ernest H. Anderson, a graduate of Fisk College and former instructor at the Tuskegee Institute with Booker T. Washington, was hired as the new

box 592. aul5 1m

STATE
A. & M. College of Texas
For Colored Youths.
Alta Vista, Hempstead P. O.
THIS SCHOOL will be opened for its first annual session on TUESDAY, the 1st day of October next.
The buildings are in excellent condition, and the opportunities for study are of the best character.
For information, address as above,
LAWRENCE W. MINOR, A. M.,
Local Principal.
jy16 t oc1

One of the first advertisements placed by Principal Lawrence W. Minor to announce the opening of the A&M College of Texas in 1879. From the collection of John A. Adams Jr.

principal (following the death of Minor), at an annual salary of $1,200, along with two teachers. Early registration in the fall of 1879 enrolled sixteen students, which grew to sixty by December. The coursework offered included grammar, reading, arithmetic, and geography. Years later, in spite of Gathright's gloomy misgivings in 1878, Blackshear credited him as the catalyst and father of Prairie View.[41]

Even at this early date questions were raised whether the Alta Vista branch college of Texas A&M was the college for African Americans envisioned in article 7, section 7, of the Texas Constitution of 1876, which mandated a "college or branch university for the instruction of colored youths of the state." The opening of Prairie View had no connection with the intent of the delegates in 1876 to create a "black university." However, the debate raged on for decades, a political football with no resolution, as one scholar of the subject noted: "The underlying issue was whether and to what degree black Texans continued to wield political power in Texas after Reconstruction." In the late 1870s all eyes were on the events and growing pains at both the public colleges in College Station and at Prairie View. Yet still turmoil over this issue of establishing a viable scheme of public higher education in Texas reigned.[42]

At the A&M College in Brazos County the entire faculty, cadets, board members, and a number of local supporters and former students became embroiled in a complicated affair and disruption regarding grievances and counter-charges concerning who should govern the college and the selection of the senor cadet officer in the Corps of Cadets. The heated conflict resulted in the firing, on November 21, 1879, of President Gathright and the entire faculty, except Louis L. McInnis. The statewide media coverage surfaced opposition first from the vocal agriculturists in the Patrons of Husbandry (or, familiarly, the Grange) and second from the Farmers Alliance, who accused the A&M College as being only a haven for "military peacockary [*sic*]" and not providing the mandated agricultural training. Many criticized the award of the Bryan campus to the lowest bidder (and because of its central location on a major rail line) as a poor selection due to inferior soil and inadequate fresh water. The Grange, numbering some forty thousand members in the mid-1870s, demanded that the study of agricultural and mechanical arts be emphasized and that students be required to work on the campus experimental farms: "No systematic and practical instruction had ever been given in what the law commanded should be the 'leading object'—the study of agricultural and the mechanical arts. . . . The college had sedulously cultivated a sentiment antagonistic to the development of these branches of study." Thus, public debate raged for years about the relative importance of agricultural education, with active critics advocating for what they perceived to be the role of Texas A&M and Prairie View. However, agricultural colleges struggled for years across the South, "groping for pedagogic dogma which produced professional agricultural technicians and also produced useful information for farmers." With Gathright's departure, John G. James, director of the Texas Military Institute in Austin, was hired along with an entirely new faculty who took charge in College Station on November 24, 1879.[43]

While there was little or no public response to the location of the Prairie View site, the disruption at the A&M College and termination of the administration and faculty did not help Prairie View, which was struggling to survive and needed timely assistance from the advocacy of Gathright and the board. The fledgling school in Waller County had numerous problems including housing, inadequate water, faculty recruitment, and dwindling admissions. Applications, followed by an entry examination on the "common branches of education" at the college, were encouraged from eighteen-year-old women and twenty-year-old men from across the state.

The cash-strapped college was furthermore caught in the debate in Austin on how to resolve the demands for a black university. A struggling normal college offering primarily remedial courses and no higher education courses to a shrinking student body could hardly meet the requirements of the Morrill Act or be classified as the first-class black university envisioned in the state constitution. Governor Roberts hoped he could clarify the standing of Prairie View and "the university issue" with quick legislative action. However, by late 1881, the struggling Prairie View was soon insolvent, and the governor insisted the A&M board pay the debts until new funding could be appropriated.[44]

In early 1882, Roberts, in a letter to the *Galveston Daily News*, appealed to private citizens to provide "aid to keep up the school." His plea generated $600 from Col. James M. Burroughs of Galveston; merchants Ellis & Carson of Houston agreed to advance $900 worth of provisions; James H. Raymond & Co. offered $300; and an undisclosed amount arrived from Frank Hamilton in Austin.[45] This was followed by a special session of the legislature to pay the college debts from the general revenue fund. Due to a state treasury shortfall, Roberts transferred money from the Permanent University Fund (PUF) to fund Prairie View. In a move to placate the debate on the black university, a statewide election was scheduled to select the site (as required in the Texas Constitution) of the new black university on the November 2, 1882, ballot. Many deemed Roberts's rush to draw attention to the black university as a premature action given the lack of political support in Austin. Nonetheless, African American organizations, communities, members of the Republican Party, and citizens were encouraged to nominate locations for consideration. In Austin, black community organizer and former officer in the Union army William H. Holland was charged by the African American residents to formally recommend to the governor to select Austin as the site for the new institution. Confusion arose when Prairie View principal E. H. Anderson and his brother Laurine C. Anderson, who at the time was serving as a staff assistant to the principal, along with a small group of Waller County citizens, advocated for Prairie View as the site and that the college be designated the new "university." However, when the statewide votes were counted, the citizens chose Austin with 28,329 votes. Houston placed second with 14,000 votes and Prairie View polled 13,160. On December 19, 1882, Secretary of State T. H. Bowman reported that, given the statement of election returns, "I hereby declare that Austin has been selected" as the site for the black university. From that day forward, however, the Texas legislature and white Democratic power structure took no significant action and ignored the outcome of the statewide vote.[46]

Colored Teachers State Association

In the wake of the inaction on the black university location election, L. C. Anderson and black leaders around the state realized that there would be a long road to equality in higher education for African Americans. It must be remembered that this was a racially charged period and the white Democrats took every measure to consolidate their hold and maintain supremacy both in Austin and statewide at the local level, thus eliminating any chance of the Republicans becoming viable competitors. One action that did occur, in the wake of the vote on the location of the black university, was that Governor Roberts rushed the bill through the legislature to open the "white University of Texas"—with no mention of facilities for a black university. In 1884, E. H. Anderson was a part of an organizing group, which included Blackshear and Norris W. Cuney, to form the Colored Teachers State Association of Texas (CTSA), and he was chosen as its first president. In addition to the activities of the Texas Republican Party, the CTSA, at least at its inception—envisioned "as a social movement based upon equalitarianism [*sic*] and compromise"—was one of the first nonpolitical and nondenominational organizations in the state to lead a coordinated effort on the behalf of African American education. However, while it proclaimed to be nonpolitical by its very charge and was opened without restriction to all persons interested in education, CTSA soon became very involved in "education politics," endorsing candidates and lobbying in Austin. Edward Blackshear joined the group, and this was the beginning of his extensive statewide political activities with the legislature, educational groups, church congregations, and leaders, advancing the call for improved conditions for black Texans.[47]

Edward Blackshear's newspaper articles, often reprinted across the state, further enhanced his image and disseminated his views on issues of the day. As one of the leading educators in Austin, he was active in assisting residents with petitions and letters to city officials. During 1885 a serial killer in Austin had attacked and killed six servant girls and family members. Each murder was more violent than the last, and the Austin police were unable to solve the case, despite arresting over one hundred suspects. In early September 1885, another murder occurred: the brutal assault and killing of a young girl and the injuring of her mother. Alarmed at the crimes, Blackshear, backed by a citizens group, drafted a petition to Reverend Grant urging a direct appeal to the mayor and governor, "in view of the fact that similar crimes have become alarmingly frequent and no adequate means" to stop them had yet been found. He advocated for an "offer of a liberal reward" to be established. The crimes continued, however; they were never solved, but abruptly ended in late 1885 with no arrests.[48]

Governor Roberts's efforts to address the concerns with Prairie View were further hindered by aggressive proponents in Austin who wanted a separate University of Texas opened for white students only. During the travails over the reconstitution of Prairie View Normal, the process had already begun to establish the University of Texas (UT) in Austin following a site selection election on September 6, 1881. The first UT Board of Regents meeting was held on November 16, 1881, and Ashbel Smith was chosen as board president. From this date forward, lobbyists, legislative members, and those with commercial interest around the UT campus advocated that a majority of the state's investments earmarked for higher education go entirely into the Austin campus—even to the detriment of all other state public institutions. When the first board of regents discovered that the new University of Texas had access to only $37,025 of the $190,000 approved by the legislature, they appealed to the governor to assign the federal funding from the Morrill Act of 1862—budgeted only for the A&M College—to the university. Roberts, to his credit, refused any such manipulation of funding. Education seemed to be secondary to those who viewed the new campus—and the surrounding real estate—only as a private investment opportunity. State senators and their surrogates, for example, speculated on land adjacent to the new forty-acre Austin campus. Sen. Alexander W. Terrell in particular was strongly chastised publicly for his conflict of interest and duplicity by an *Austin Statesman* editorial, for profiting from speculative land deals around the campus: "Judge Terrell has put his money into town lot speculation [in Austin]. . . . The land boom he helped to start is in full swing, Terrell was in the swim up to his whiskers. . . . He pocketed the big profits . . . it was a 'fat take.'" Nonetheless, the cornerstone for the first university building, only blocks from the state capital, was laid in November 1882 (only weeks after the statewide vote to locate the black university in Austin was ignored), and university classes formally opened in temporary classrooms on September 15, 1883, under the direction of chemistry professor John William

Mallet, a former commander of the Confederate Ordnance Bureau, and with a faculty comprised almost exclusively of former Confederate officers and veterans. Shortly after completion of his gubernatorial term, Governor Roberts, also a former veteran Confederate officer, stepped across the street to be one of the first members of the law school faculty at the new state university.[49]

Incoming governor John Ireland expressed dismay and concern that the legislature, former governor, and board of regents, with such inadequate planning and funding, had moved with haste to open the university. The new staff and administrators, as well as their eager political proponents, received much of the same kind of criticism that on previous occasions had been directed to Texas A&M and Prairie View. The rush to open was largely driven by Austin political officials, land speculators, and business concerns wanting to tap into the maximum amount of the PUF as well as other state appropriations—and thus preempt any other state-sponsored institution from receiving funding. The direction of the new university was questioned by both the media and the Grange—who, while often critical of the A&M College, in fact looked favorably on the College Station institute and did not want its programs diminished in favor of the University of Texas. One observer noted that the "university discomfiture rose precipitously" when the governor appointed Archibald J. Rose of Salado to be Grand Master of the Texas Grange (1880–91) and president of the board of directors (1888–96) at the A&M College for eight years. While university partisans lobbied the legislature to protect their interests, Rose's experience with the A&M College and his political connections proved invaluable during the formative years of the University of Texas. With the excitement over the new white university, no mention was made regarding the establishment of the voter-mandated black university in Austin.[50]

Exodusters

An additional issue that caught Blackshear's attention involved articles and the debate on so-called programs either to return African Americans to Africa or to encourage their migration to northern states. The "back-to-Africa" movement in the United States dates to the eighteenth century, and the idea of "repatriating" black Americans to Africa continued to be discussed through the nineteenth and into the early twentieth century. At early stages of the debate in Texas, the Colored Men's Convention meeting in Houston in July 1879 passed a resolution that concluded, "Negroes [are] urge[d] to emigrate," but recommended that Kansas and Oklahoma, and not Africa, be strongly considered. In 1879–80, as a result of poor working conditions, meager educational opportunities, and discrimination, black Texans, under the leadership of John N. Johnson, secretary to the conference, and John Rayner, an independent entrepreneur and recruitment agent, began to gather in groups for the "exodus" from Texas to Kansas and Oklahoma, seeking free land and a new way of life. This was followed by some black "back-to-Africa" groups, sponsored by the American Colonization Society and the International Migration Society, immigrating to Liberia. This enthusiasm to consider a move to Africa was not new and dated from as early as the 1820s. Yet, due to the high cost to relocate, interest waned, and thus, the "African exodus" included only a small number of black Texans. The majority of those who participated in the trip to Kansas tended not to be established farmers or able to support themselves; knowledge of agriculture would be a critical skill to survive and prosper. Unable to find free land or jobs, many African Americans returned to Texas.[51]

Historian C. Vann Woodward in his classic works reminds readers of the angst faced by the "Great Liberator," Abraham Lincoln, on the future of African Americans regarding "racial segregation and negro subordination."[52] President Lincoln remarked to a delegation of black leaders at the White House in 1862, "There is an unwillingness on the part of our people, harsh as it may be, for you free colored people to remain with us." Lincoln expressed sympathy for their wrongs as slaves, "but even when you cease to be slaves," he said, "you are yet far removed from being placed on an equality with the white race. . . . The aspiration of men is to enjoy equality with the best when free, but on this broad continent not a single man of your race is made the equal of a single man of ours. . . . I cannot alter it if I would. It is a fact. . . . It is better for us both, therefore, to be separated." C. Vann Woodward concluded, five decades after Blackshear and others had fully questioned any such exodus, "This idea of separating the races led Lincoln to support *the most impractical and illusory plan of his career*, the plan for colonizing the freedmen abroad or settling them in segregated colonies at home."[53]

These activities and rumored departures triggered a number of published responses by Blackshear, two decades after emancipation and Lincoln's remarks, regarding an article (further indicating that Blackshear

TABLE 1.3. Texas Population, 1870–1930

Year	Total	White population	Black population	% Rural blacks
1870	818, 579	564,700	253,475	88.0*
1880	1,591,749	1,197,237	393,384	86.0*
1890	2,235,521	1,745,935	488,171	83.7
1900	3,048,710	2,426,669	620,722	80.8
1910	3,896,542	3,204,848	690,042	74.1
1920	4,663,228	3,918,165	741,694	69.9
1930	5,824,715	4,283,419	854,964	61.4

Source: U.S. Department of Commerce, Bureau of the Census, *Negro Population in the United States, 1790–1915*, 43–44; Bureau of the Census, *Negroes in the United States, 1920–1932*, 813. * indicates estimates.

was well read) by a Prof. Edward Winslow Gilliam, MD (1834–1925), in the February 1883 *Popular Science Monthly*, "The African in the United States." The doctor boldly stated the "future of the African [American] in the United States is the gravest question of the day." The article, following a detailed assessment and conclusions drawn from the 1880 census, outlined his proposed remedy to establish "colonization, forcible if necessary, of Negroes in Africa." He noted other options that had been proposed, including to have Congress acquire suitable territory in Central America or, as ex-president Ulysses Grant suggested, to buy San Domingo to "afford a home for our black population." Notwithstanding, Debra Reid observed, "Black agrarians criticized those who favored migration because the tactic undermined their goal to strengthen rural black communities in Texas." The vast majority of articulate African Americans opposed emigration or colonization schemes as a solution to the so-called race problem. Blackshear's response to the inflated hype and promises was an emphatic NO: "The scheme is impracticable. Educate the Negro. Make him an American citizen, no need for removal."[54]

Evidence of backlash to the migration northward was found in a February 1885 notice in the *Texan-Telephone* (Canton, TX) newspaper: "One by one the negroes who went from Texas to Kansas, to better their condition, are drifting back. They have learned by personal experience that the Republicans are not half so much their friends as are the Democrats of the South."[55]

—·⊱⊰·—

A decade later in the spring of 1894, while Blackshear was director of all black schools in Austin and his articles were read by an even larger audience, he once again responded to an editorial noting a new "scheme to emigrate [*sic*] all the negroes of America to Africa." He submitted a letter to the *Austin Daily Statesman* that was published under the heading of "Advice from His Colored Brethren." The ensuing years had only strengthened and confirmed Blackshear's strong belief that the best course and opportunities for African Americans were in the United States. Any such schemes were "wild, impracticable and positively injurious" and those that promoted migration did so at the threat of undermining rural black communities in Texas. This time the argument centered around the discussion that the rush to judgment was reported as a means to escape competition with white people. He was very blunt, "The black man must harmonize himself with civilized conditions or disappear as the Indian is doing." Blackshear's views were echoed by Booker T. Washington.

In a clear and eloquent assessment:

> You cannot force the real growth of a race or nation. It must come spontaneously, in accordance with fixed laws of social development. It is by no means certain that the Negro in America or Africa has reached his highest development. As a negro I hope, and sincere men of all race will hope with me, that there may be in the future a development of negro character and social life creditable to itself [and] helpful to the progress of the world. Emerson, the great New England poet and essayist, has said: "America is but another name for opportunity." I believe America will yet mean opportunity for all men, regardless of race, for the black as well as the white.
>
> Personal improvement in character and industry are needed now far more than a chance to be an "African King." There is no better country on the globe for the American negro than the United States, and no better state than Texas.[56]

Interestingly, William Edward Burghardt Du Bois, known to his friends as Willie, from his home in Philadelphia became engaged behind the scenes in correspondence with representatives of the Belgium government about the intriguing possibilities of connecting African Americans with Africans. The Congo Free State, under the personal rule of King Leopold II, was in chaos with the spread of epidemic diseases (smallpox and sleeping sickness), famine, and violent atrocities. At this point, as far as is known, Blackshear had not met Du Bois in person, but was well aware of his reputation and work. Du Bois's prime contact was the Belgium consul-general Paul Hagemans, who recommended that an arrangement be established between the American Negro Academy (an organization established by Du Bois) and the Belgium government, which, as a possessor of vast holdings in the Congo Free State of Africa, "welcomed Black American emigrants [*sic*]." The reason for such arrangements was to foster Du Bois's own "Pan-Africa dream" in order to "see the Negroes of the World unite for uplifting of Africa." In a detailed memorandum, he concluded that the "cause" for African Americans "is after all the cause of the vast historic Negro race; and that Africa is in truth his greater fatherland," concluding, "Hitherto this has been little more than a pious ideal." He called for a five-to-ten-year plan (which never materialized) to determine a carefully selected class of immigrants who could go back to Africa. Apparently, Du Bois's grand Belgium scheme was never discussed with black leaders in the South, who first learned of its planning in newspaper coverage. Following increased reports of despair and rising death toll in Congo, a growing number of black leaders and clergy, including Blackshear, began to question the harsh treatment of the Congolese people and indicated these oppressed Africans needed aid and protection and not new immigrants from America! Outspoken Harvard paleontologist Nathaniel S. Shaler countered Du Bois's grand relocation plans, saying it would "trespass on the right of blacks" and further would be "all too impracticable to deserve a moment's attention. . . . The exodus would mean the commercial ruin of a half dozen great [Southern] states." The debate continued for decades, with Du Bois immigrating permanently to Ghana in 1961.[57]

The debate on black immigration or "exodus" lingered on for a decade into the 1890s, with Booker T. Washington, himself opposed, taking a keen interest in advising African leaders on his "industrial education" ideas and programs. In addressing the growth of the black population in Texas, candidate for reelection Sul Ross in 1888 appealed to black voters and wondered about the intent of those who wanted to export their people out of the state, noting, "Speculative colored and white Republican politicians have hatched schemes to carry off the colored population of Texas to Kansas, Missouri,

AFRICA: A NEGRO PATRIOTIC HYMN.

Adaption of "America" by Edward L. Blackshear,
Superintendent of Schools of Austin, Texas, June 13, 1893.

I

Our Country 'tis of thee,
Dear land of Africa,
Of thee we sing;
Land where our fathers died,
Land of the negroes' pride,
From every mountain side.
God's truth shall ring

II

My native country, thee,
Land of the black and free,
Thy name I love;
To see thy rocks and rills,
Thy woods and matchless hills!
My heart with rapture thrills;
Like that above.

III

Let music swell the breeze,
And ring through all thy trees,
In sacred song;
Let Africa's tongues awake,
Let Ham's black sons partake,
Their shouts the silence break,
In countless throng.

IV

Jehovah, God, to Thee,
God of land and sea,
To Thee we sing;
Yet may our land be bright,
With Thy Son's holy light,
He'll raise us by His might,
And be our King.

V

Then when our glorious land,
Is snatched from Error's hand,
Saved from above;
We will ascribe to Thee,
Throughout eternity,
Honor and majesty,
Our God of Love.

Mexico, and South America. If Cuney, Dick Allen, Radcliff, Platt and other bloody shirt shriekers in Texas are correct, many of their race have been murdered by the white Democrats. But the race has more than doubled in Texas in ten years! The ability to destroy [immigrate] lags behind the will [to leave]." Shortly after the political disruption in Fort Bend County in 1889, a plan was drafted to "colonize" three hundred families near Veracruz, Mexico, yet the scheme came to naught. While it is estimated that some 2,500 to 3,000 black Texans departed the state, given the growth of the black population in Texas from 393,384 in 1880 to 488,171 in 1890, the "exodus" had very little impact on the state. And, interestingly, while Blackshear opposed any schemes to exit, he staunchly maintained an ethic identification with Africa and penned a hymn in honor of his African heritage.[58]

Links to Africa

Years later Professor Blackshear and his staff were active in recruiting students nationwide, for example with advertisements like "Colored Youth, Come South!" in the Indianapolis paper *The Freedman*. They were pleased to announce that the grandson of a "real" African Nigerian king was enrolling as a student. A seventeen-year-old of the Yoruba tribe, whose homeland was in present-day southwestern Nigeria, Lattevi Ajayi became aware of Prairie View when professor of agriculture John Wesley Hoffman was visiting the tribal king. By the invitation of the secretary of colonies for Great Britain, Joseph Chamberlain, Hoffman was invited to assist farmers in British West Africa. His main assignment was to establish a program to overcome primitive farming methods and increase the production of cotton to support the cottage loom industry. With the approval of the king, Hoffman arranged for Ajayi to travel to New Orleans, where he spent a year learning English and then enrolled in Prairie View College. Following Professor Hoffman's return, Ajayi arrived on campus in the fall of 1908 to complete a three-year course in agriculture. Famed Texas folklorist John A. Lomax, on one of his several visits to Prairie View, met Lattevi and interviewed the young prince and chronicled his knowledge of Yoruba tribe traditions and folk-tales. These stories were delivered by Lomax as the central theme of the December 1912 keynote address at the American Folk-Lore Society annual meeting in Cleveland, Ohio. Thus, agricultural expert Hoffman from Prairie View delivered the first American agricultural extension course outside of Texas and the United States, as well as recruited international students to advance efficient farming. After graduation from Prairie View and a brief period studying with Booker T. Washington at Tuskegee, Ajayi returned to West Central Africa in 1913 to lead his tribe and raise cotton.[59]

Transition: The Business of Schools

Upon the death of Ernest Anderson on October 29, 1885, after six years as Prairie View principal, his brother Laurine was appointed the new principal. The *Texas School Journal* noted the institute "is in excellent condition and it certainly is doing a great work for the colored people." Thus, his combined roles as president of the CTSA, a position he held until 1889, and principal at Prairie View Normal made L. C. Anderson the most prominent African American educational advocate in the state. By the mid-1880s the annual appropriation for Prairie View was raised to $7,500 and four additional teachers were hired for a student body of over one hundred students.[60]

The hands-on knowledge gained by Edward Blackshear at the Wheatfield School teaching job and his administrative responsibilities in the Austin school system was a major formative experience for him, leading to his first job as principal, beginning at the age of twenty-three. In addition to organizing the curriculum, hiring teachers, furnishing the school, budgeting, and arranging class schedules, he was tasked with raising funding to support a school without books and supplies—a common dilemma of one-room black schools across the South.

During the next few years, he continued to make improvements at the Austin school while spending time during the summer months in Goliad, Texas, teaching black high school teachers the best teaching methods and class supervision. In April 1886, Blackshear married Amanda Cravens, but within three years she died of heart disease, with the funeral sermon preached by Bishop Grant. Blackshear's teaching success resulted in first a promotion in 1888 to be the principal of Central Grammar School, followed by appointment as the supervisor of all African American education in Austin in 1892. Two decades after his earliest teaching experience in the primary school, Blackshear wrote a book, really a brief pamphlet, *The Education of Childhood*, reflecting on his early years, the importance of primary education for children, and the challenges of teaching: "Intellectually, the *business of the schools* for childhood is the development of strong vital precepts or ideas by means of the fundamental human arts and sciences preparatory to the acquisition of concepts or general notions in scientific form and their use and organization as instrumentalists to useful and efficient thinking and living. And the fundamental human arts and sciences must have their roots in the primary school."[61]

His success in enhancing education for African Americans was recognized, yet not in his salary. Like his teachers, he was paid hourly. After receiving a "Permanent College State Certificate" from the state superintendent of public instruction in 1895, he requested the Austin City School Board to provide an annual salary of $750.00 to address his expenses and to support "a wife, and two children and a father who is not self-supporting. I am getting on in life, being thirty-three and want to go forward not backward."[62]

One observer noted that "A life of sacrificial effort of painstaking care and of judicious service to the people of his race has been peculiarly [Blackshear's legacy]." Active in education, politics, and his church, Blackshear found himself in a very high-profile position with the new city-wide school appointment, which soon intertwined his educational experience with the ongoing public oversight and statewide political maneuvering for a better way of life for his fellow citizens.[63]

·›› 2 ‹‹·

Education and Politics

> Emerson, the great New England poet and essayist, has said: "America is but a name for opportunity." I believe that America will yet mean opportunity for all men, regardless of race, for black as well as the white.
>
> EDWARD L. BLACKSHEAR

> The manly and statesmanlike attitude taken by Governor Sul Ross and the unanimity of the Afro-Texas press in thanking him for his impartiality and humanity, ought to be a positive that all the negro asks for—all he requires—is equity, justice and civil rights.
>
> AFRICAN AMERICAN: *THE TEXAS BLADE,* MAY 3, 1888

Education has long been intertwined with politics and efforts to educate the citizens, and Texans in the late nineteenth century was no exception. The political dynamics of universal public education would be a challenge that continues to this day. Edward Blackshear, like all advocates for equality and accountability in education, would be straddled with decades of discourse and opposition long before he arrived in Texas fresh from college to teach in 1882. The transition in Texas at the end of Presidential Reconstruction resulted in bitter animosities between the Radical Republican government of Gov. Edmund J. Davis and the old Texas Democratic machine, which had regained political control of the state. After rolling back all vestiges of the Radical Republicans, the restoration of home rule by Texas Democrats swung abruptly in another direction. The centralized state school system in Texas had been poorly supported by a 1 percent ad valorem tax for construction and upkeep of schools statewide. Federal authorities reported over two thousand public schools in 1871 with a total of 125,000 grade-level students and an acute shortage of teachers. There were attempts to establish "subscription schools" for those willing to pay. However, most wanted "free schools." Yet as Edward King noted in his classic *Texas: 1874*, "There has been much objection to the compulsory feature of the free [education] system, parents furiously defending their right to leave their children in ignorance." Thus, first and foremost the Texas Democrats wanted to squash the centralized control from Austin under Davis and shift the responsibility for education to the re-empowered local political level.[1]

Federal action at the time of the state's readmission into the Union prohibited state officials from discrimination against African American educational programs and required equal access to schooling. Implied requirements for segregation were driven by white Democrat supremacists with the extension of the notorious Black Codes (a form of extralegal discrimination), which were implemented after the war to limit the lawful rights of black Texans. Although the rising demand for a poll tax for voting and inequities in rural areas proved detrimental to black Americans and black educational attainment, it did not silence black political discourse. Sen. Alexander W. Terrell introduced the first Texas poll tax bill in 1879 (which failed), followed by plans for literacy tests and property qualifications for voting, purportedly as a means to raise revenue—when in fact it was a measure to reduce black influence in elections.[2] Black Texans were entitled to the same pro rata portion of state school funding as white students, yet local officials failed to comply with the mandate and used local funding as they deemed necessary. However, incoming Democrats made the Republican school system a chief object of their crusade to regain control, and in its place they created a new school system that was little more than a vast political machine from the top to the bottom, focused on education at the grassroots in rural Texas. African American education was not a high priority in these actions.[3]

In the formative post-Reconstruction years, the most influential champion of public schools in Texas was O. N. Hollingsworth, who entered the office of superintendent of public instruction on the Redeemer Democratic ticket with Governor Coke in 1874. The founder of the *Texas Journal of Education* in 1880, Hollingsworth was concerned that public schools should be sustained by active public sentiment and adequately funded. He defined the mandate of public schools in Texas as

1. A school organized in a manner prescribed by the general school law, and one that recognizes the legal authority of public school officials.
2. A school taught by a teacher holding a lawful certificate of competency.
3. A school from which none who desire to participate in benefits are excluded from the organization.
4. A school with no extra charge for tuition from parents for branches prescribed by law and in which public funds are not credited on private tuition rates.
5. A school taught in the English language.
6. A school that is nonsectarian in religious matters.[4]

—•⊱⊰•—

Jim Crow laws, by the early 1890s, crippled the civil rights of the African American population in Texas and their ability to impact key issues at the ballot box. At the local level, the Democratic political machine made the black and Mexican Texan voters (as well as poor illiterate whites) very vulnerable to fraud and intimidation. The white Democratic political machine used a number of methods to steal elections and systematically disenfranchise black voters. Sen. Alexander Terrell continued his ongoing goal to do all he could do to limit access to the political process in Texas, spearheading efforts to disenfranchise black Texans by endless attempts to impose a poll tax.[5] Practices such as rigging the primaries, under-counting votes, and, when needed, stuffing the ballot box were common. "Not only among the Negroes," as noted by Woodward, "but among objectionable whites as well." Many times, the number of ballots were limited and election judges refused to make corrections. And one final trick, which became a common practice by the mid-1890s, was to close the polls early and refuse any additional voters. When state officials refused to take any action, a federal investigation followed, but with little results other than to document the abuse. Elections were controlled at the local level, and county officials were the critical actors with the authority to administer and interpret federal and state election laws the way they saw fit. For example, one witness testified, "In the town of Terrell [no relation to the senator], the partisans and friends of the contestee destroyed the tickets [ballots] upon which the name of [the] contestant was, and [by] that they prevented many persons from voting for [the] contestant thereby."[6]

The decentralized delegation of education at the state level—shifting the requirement for private funding to local jurisdictions—at first benefited more white students in black-majority communities, but over time all students suffered from a lack of quality facilities and overcrowding, compounded by irregular attendance, shortage of teachers, and a dearth of supplies and educational materials. State budget cuts to reduce the debt in 1879, forced by Gov. O. M. Roberts, significantly harmed public education in general and black schools in particular. Concerned about having enough field hands at harvest time, Texans abolished compulsory school attendance. To address the shortfall of school facilities, an estimated two-thirds of black children met in churches, barns, and private homes. Furthermore, rural schools suffered more than urban educational programs, due in large part to the fact that municipalities were better organized to support education, primarily because lawmakers grandfathered incorporated municipalities to organize into school districts and levy supplemental citywide taxes. However, the particularly conspicuous, statewide need for improved education at all levels, especially in rural areas (which at the time comprised over 70 percent of all Texas students), was hobbled by the Democrats efforts in the initial post-Reconstruction period. The fledgling State Board of Education initiated the publication of the *Texas Journal of Education* to address the need for educational reforms and give teaching professionals in Texas their first medium of expression. Concerned with the poor status of education statewide, a group of eager reformers successfully lobbied for the passage of the School Law of 1884 with little or no funding or oversight, and thus by the mid-1880s the system of local control and financing of education collapsed.[7]

Anderson

Laurine Cecil Anderson, born in Memphis in 1853, was among the first black students to attend city schools organized by the AMA. He studied for the Methodist ministry at Fisk University in Nashville, followed by a teaching assignment at Tuskegee Institute. In early 1878 he accompanied his brother to Texas, landing a prestigious job teaching in Brenham, Texas—where the first municipal African American high school in the state opened in 1875. He joined the Prairie View staff as an assistant to the principal, teaching and gradually becoming politically active in black education issues. His primary challenge as the incoming president of Prairie View in the late 1880s, following the death of his brother, was to best determine the status of the black university movement, either with the creation of a new university or the enhancement of the programs at Prairie View. While Blackshear continued his teaching in Austin, Hightower Kealing, following his experience at Paul Quinn College, joined the Prairie View staff as assistant principal in 1886–87. To assist with day-to-day operations, the A&M College board assigned former general William P. Hardemann, chief business officer of the A&M College, to work closely with Anderson to address the needs of the Hempstead campus and its sixty-five students. A visitor to the campus in the fall of 1885 was impressed with the small but growing school, noting, "It is one of the best managed and conducted schools I have visited in the state. The method of teaching can't be excelled and if the students don't learn it will not be [the] state's nor the teachers' fault." Additionally, Anderson's presidency of the Colored Teachers State Association of Texas placed him in the center of the debate in Austin, as recalcitrant white Democrats were loath to allow any significant gains by African Americans for fear such advancements disrupted the political, social, and economic balance in Texas.[8]

Interestingly, the debate regarding what was to be the role of public higher education first began with strong objections to the classical courses and programs being offered at the A&M College near Bryan. The rocky start of the college and the dismissal of the entire first administration and faculty in 1879 did not fully redirect the school to reduce its classical education curriculum in favor of what the Grange and Alliance demanded should be an agriculturally oriented institution. One significant reason for the delay and the impossibility of extensive introduction of agricultural education in the college was that there were few teachers prepared to teach agriculture subjects, a significant lack of materials and textbooks, no established experimental farms, and no farm equipment to conduct courses. Notwithstanding, as a branch of the A&M College, Prairie View was generally expected to have a similar course offering and to adhere to the "agricultural and mechanical" curricula and mission outlined in the Morrill Act of 1862. The political elite and traditionalists of the two leading agricultural groups, who feared losing the expertise and supply of farm and ranch labor, were in full bloom in the 1880s and into the 1890s.[9]

Even more intriguing in what was to be a decade-long debate, people on either side of the issues were concerned with solutions or compromises on how best to implement the agricultural mandate. Additionally, the chairman of the A&M College Board of Directors who oversaw both A&M and Prairie View, Archibald Johnson Rose of Salado, also helped organize the first Texas Patrons of Husbandry, the Grange, and was elected to be its Worthy Grand Master from 1880–91. The African American counterpart to the white Grange was the Colored Farmers' Association of America, with chapters of the "Colored Grangers" sprinkled across Texas. A lifelong vocal advocate and foremost Texas crusader of education and better schools at all levels, Rose was appointed to the A&M board by Gov. Sul Ross in 1887, and in 1895 Governor Hogg selected him as the Texas commissioner of agriculture. Thus, Rose exerted a very strong influence in shaping the agrarian education reform and priorities during the late nineteenth century. As the members of the two leading farm organizations fought in the trenches over the small details, Rose developed a more strategic view of structural changes to address the covenants of the Morrill Act. At the same time, he gave the agricultural sector what it *thought* it needed, in the form of ag-oriented programs and accountability from the state A&M College.[10]

A treasure trove of primary documents can be found on the Texas farm movement in the Rose Collection in the Dolph Briscoe Center for American History in Austin, Texas, including remarks drafted in bold pencil on a light tan Big Chief Tablet, notably a presentation by Rose simply titled, "Agriculture":

> Farming is the noblest calling of man.
>
> From the products of the soil all classes are fed and made to thrive. Without the farmer they could not exist. The farmers produce [the] wealth of the nation. But they are like the fountain heads of the crystal stream that continuously pours out their sparkling fluid—sending them forth to increase the Plan adopted by the Grange will do this and nothing short of this will ever do.
>
> Every encouragement should be given the farmer to encourage agriculture in all its branches and every legitimate means should be used to enable them to retain from the farm the profits made there. There are other reforms necessary that must be made by the farmers.

> There must be closer economy by them until they can afford ready money and it is an unjust thing not to give full value in exchange for these things.
>
> It is a great and good work enough by farmers in producing for the world all the necessaries to sustain life, and the material from which they are to be clothed. To pay for luxuries—again there must be more system [of education] and industry to many who consume too much time around their grumbling.[11]

Thus, Texas was in the throes of a fight over the type of curriculum that prevailed in the state institutions of higher education: a traditional classical-liberal education (viewed as the path to social mobility and racial equality), tech-oriented manual and skills-based training programs, or aggressive agricultural courses. Blackshear was fully aware that the industrial education approach provided a more rapid path to gainful employment in what many Texans felt was a shift from an agriculture-based economy to one that was more industrially oriented. Black leaders quickly concluded, however, that the purely manual training approach limited the opportunities for young African Americans. As one contemporary observer noted, "The freedman imagined that whatever superiority white people have over the blacks is owing to education . . . so the ordinary African [American] thought if his child could only read, write, and cipher, he would be in every way the equal." The classical approach to education, which Blackshear and most of the early teachers in the colleges received during this period, was adequate for a few professionals, such as teachers, lawyers, and preachers, yet this did not satisfy the demands of the agricultural sector, who strongly believed colleges were emphasizing career choices that did not correspond to their perceived agricultural needs. And as one observer of this battle noted, throughout this period the fight was "felt at every level of schooling and politics in both white and black communities."[12]

A system for new, incoming student appointments to enter Prairie View was approved by elected Texas representatives and the A&M Board of Directors. The program was established to attract students from across the state. Such students agreed to the following requirements to encourage more teachers for rural African American schools, as outlined by Sen. Charles Stewart of Harris County:

First, to be a resident of this state.
Second, ladies must not be less than eighteen and gentlemen not less than twenty years of age.
Third, each student must make a written pledge to teach in [a] public free school of their respective district as many years as they have attended the institute; and said service is to render in the year or years immediately succeeding graduation.
Fourth, candidates must be examined in orthography, reading, penmanship, arithmetic, grammar, English grammar, English composition, and history of the United States in all of which a reasonably [*sic*] degree of proficiency must be demonstrated in order to warrant an appointment.[13]

The fight between the classical versus industrial-vocational training approach would be at the center of the Washington–Du Bois education priorities debate for years. In Texas, this argument found a fertile ground for debate and advocacy in the Democratic-Republican struggle for power and control, accented by the rise in the 1890s of both the Progressive and Prohibition political factions. It is important to note that to some degree the debate reflected conflicting needs of rural and urban populations and engaged extensive support by the black Texas Baptist Educational Society for the first time. Furthermore, the debate was fueled by the concerns of Blackshear, Cuney, and Grant about the growing resentment toward African Americans by some whites who did not like the social and economic ramifications of improving black educational levels.[14]

A vocal advocate of third-party farm issues, candidates, and education, the *Southern Mercury* was published in Dallas and was hailed on its masthead as the "Official Journal of the Texas State Alliance and of the National Farmers' Alliance and Co-operative Union." Representatives of the Alliance were clear in their concept of education: "No man has a right to deny that it is education to be able to use the hands in any kind of honest labor. Our public schools are kept up at the expense of the taxpayers. In the present course of study are many high branches, which take up time and serve no good purpose. These could be dropped out and some books on industrial training put in their places. Thus joined to substantial common-sense school education would be of great benefit to the vast majority of young people who will in the future be obliged to work for wages."[15]

"Bugologist"

One important event during the Ross governorship that helped calm concerns of farmers and ranchers, as well as the vocal leadership of the Grange and agricultural populists, was the establishment of the Agricultural Experiment Station at Texas A&M in 1887 following a $15,000 per annum appropriation by the Hatch Act of the US Congress. While, as historian Irvin May noted, "the public was still skeptical of book-learned agriculture," the act was welcome news by agriculturalists. Placed under the direction of the A&M Board of Directors, an "Agricultural Experiment Council" was convened to encourage direct feedback from agricultural producers and members of the Grange and Alliance, noting, "Suggestions will be gladly received at all times from any one who is interested in advancing the agricultural interests of the State."[16] Prairie View was one of the only black public colleges to receive Hatch Act funds. The Experiment Station and the agricultural outreach (primarily through the Farmers' Congress) to work with producers statewide proved critical to countering misinformation and rumors about the role of the college. Texas farmers and ranchers faced many of the same problems regardless of their race. Cattle and cotton were the first two products given extensive study. Procedures to disinfect, "dip," and inoculate cattle against Texas Tick Fever soon proved a success, thus strongly reducing the potential destruction of the Texas beef industry. This event and the public's perception on how such a cure was obtained from "scientific research" proved vital to the credibility of Texas A&M and the Experiment Station mandate. Failure was not an option, as *Farm and Ranch* magazine reported. The search for a cure was assigned to famous A&M veterinarian Dr. Mark Francis, who, after trying numerous remedies, needed more testing stock:

> Perhaps no single conflict ever waged in this country for the solution of a vexatious problem in behalf of the economic life of the nation can be compared, either in extent or in beneficial results, with the century of warfare by the federal and state government and by scientists against the Southern Cattle Tick and its ravages.
>
> The development of this immunization process encountered conditions and prejudices and sundry impediments which might have entirely discouraged a man of less persistence than Dr. Francis. Funds were never too plentiful nor even plentiful enough. The legislatures

> could not be brought to enthuse over spending time and money in what they considered a futile effort to change the natural environment of the Southland. The legislators were not alone in their ridicule of the scientists, for the editors and cattlemen themselves, in any case, pooh-poohed the idea of a lot of work done with ticks by the "Bugologist" and it was frankly and freely stated that the people's money could be better spent. It was hard to get cattle on which to conduct experiments. Thus, the ranchers-researcher connection was paramount.
>
> Once when Dr. Francis went to Governor Sul Ross for funds to buy some cattle, he found the Governor as usual sympathetic, but with no way in which to give the required aid. The Governor, however, did suggest to the Doctor that he go to Col. John T. Lytle of San Antonio and Col. George W. Fulton, of Rockport, saying that they were progressive, big hearted cattlemen and might lend him some aid. This proved to be a valuable tip, as the cattlemen agreed to back the project and gave Dr. Francis several cars of cattle for experimental purposes.
>
> Finally in 1898, during Ross' last year at Texas A&M, and after ten years of the most intensive devotion of his time and thought to the problem, Dr. Francis found a cure and inoculation solved the tick infestation and saved the Texas [and national] cattle business. Concluding, the economic effect of this discovery cannot be estimated.[17]

The angst over the cotton blight fully had Texas in a "boll weevil" panic by 1903—the blight was equally as destructive as the tick fever. The continued

TABLE 2.1. Average Price Per Pound of Cotton, 1875–1900

1875	$0.111	**1884**	$0.092	**1893**	$0.070
1876	$0.099	**1885**	$0.085	**1894**	$0.046
1877	$0.105	**1886**	$0.081	**1895**	$0.076
1878	$0.082	**1887**	$0.085	**1896**	$0.066
1879	$0.102	**1888**	$0.085	**1897**	$0.066
1880	$0.098	**1889**	$0.083	**1898**	$0.057
1881	$0.100	**1890**	$0.086	**1899**	$0.070
1882	$0.099	**1891**	$0.073	**1900**	$0.086
1883	$0.090	**1892**	$0.084		

Source: *USDA Yearbook of Agriculture, 1901*, 754.

fall of cotton prices, the leading crop produced in the state, further created disruption in Texas. With pricing and speculation of cotton market demands determined in New York and Liverpool, English farmers had little or no control over the value of their products. The *Galveston Daily News* (owned and published by Alfred Horatio Belo), the primary source of agricultural news and pricing data in the state on produce-commodity markets, confirmed, "As about two-thirds of the [Southern] cotton crop finds a market in Europe, the demand there in a great measure fixes the price of cotton." While the white-dominated Texas legislature wanted the Hatch Act funds to go directly to the state treasury—thus limiting support for Prairie View—Ross and Rose interceded, and in 1889 Prairie View opened a limited experiment and extension office to assist local black farmers.[18]

Early in the L. C. Anderson administration at Prairie View, Anderson, while a vocal proponent of increases of all levels of support for African Americans, realized that there should and could be a balance with offering a classical course of study while at the same time providing agricultural and industrial education, noting: "This question of labor is the distributing one of present and is destined to still further complicate politics, unless it is met and solved in the schoolroom. . . . This can be accomplished without materially changing the literary instruction given." While the ardent agricultural proponents lobbied the governor and legislature to limit classical instruction, Anderson and the A&M College found a balance of course offerings and programs and endorsed components of the agricultural and mechanical mandate to address both the spirit and letter of the 1862 Morrill Act so often quoted by the Grange. Both A&M and Prairie View dropped liberal arts courses in Latin and Greek, while at the same time implementing compulsory hands-on student work schedules on the college farms. All the while, A&M Board of Directors member Archibald Rose, while in full support of the direction taken to address the needs of students, made sure that misguided damage from outside groups and zealous agricultural populists was not done to the base operations and growing pains at both colleges. Given the mission of the Prairie View "normal" school, mixed with the agricultural backing, Anderson made sure that Prairie View was first producing much-needed African American teachers and second, providing agricultural and industrial skills for those not so motivated. And as George Woolfolk concluded, L. C. provided the leadership for a "quiet atmosphere of disciplined pastorial [*sic*] education."[19]

Political Transition

A decade after the Democratic Party regained dominant political control, the passage of the Texas Constitution of '76 realigned the state political power structure. Following the death of former governor Davis in 1883, black politicians expanded their influence and dominance within the Republican Party, representing over 90 percent of the party membership. The leadership of the party shifted to Norris Wright Cuney, the son of an enslaved woman, Adeline Stuart, and a wealthy white planter, Philip Minor Cuney, the owner of the 1,800-acre Sunnyside Plantation ten miles southwest of present-day Hempstead, Texas. Norris was given his freedom in 1859 at age thirteen, and his father sent him and his brothers to Pittsburgh, Pennsylvania, for their education. Cuney's rise to power began in Galveston as a stevedore contractor on the Galveston wharves, where he soon became a savvy leader of the African American unions and an organizer of longshoremen and screwmen. The Port of Galveston (the third major US seaport by 1892, behind New York City and New Orleans) was a major commercial metropolis on the Gulf Coast and a springboard for Cuney's political aspirations. Galveston was the largest city in Texas with a prosperous natural seaport. It was the terminus of four major railroads bringing products for export, and home of the largest circulation newspaper in the state—the *Galveston Daily News*. In 1883, he was elected as an alderman-at-large on the city council. Cuney's activities in city government as well as business, social, political, and educational organizations gave him the ability to work for the advancement of African Americans in Galveston, as well as across Texas. He first met Blackshear at the organizational meeting of the Teacher Association in 1883. A shrewd customs manager, Cuney was named the first African American sergeant-of-arms of the Texas Legislature and won election as the national committeeman of the Republican Party in 1886, making him the most powerful black politician in the state. In 1889, following a strong recommendation by Methodist bishop Grant at a White House meeting with the president, Cuney was appointed by Pres. Benjamin Harrison as "collector of customs" in Galveston, considered at the time as "the most important post ever given to a colored man in the South." His rise in the leadership of the Republican Party resulted in internal party conflict and the bolting of the white majority Republican members to form a separate, "lily white" branch of the party, backed by member "clubs" primarily in urban areas of the state.[20]

These actions coincided with the gradual rise of third-party politics. "There had grown up an unusual interest in politics among the farmers and other laboring classes in the state"—best represented by the Grange and Farmers Alliance—to challenge the Democratic Party, which consistently commanded a three-to-one winning margin at the ballot box. Furthermore, Cuney could not unite the anti-Democratic voters and miscalculated black dissatisfaction forces; nor could he resolve the black-white racial disputes within the Republican ranks. In an effort to gain more political recognition, black farmers organized the Colored Farmers' Alliance and Co-operative Union in December 1886.[21] Supported by their paper, *The National Alliance*, Texas membership exceeded sixty thousand by 1890. As farmers increased their vocal, "powerfully aroused" campaign to represent their sentiments, Cuney maintained political power, with a large—though shrinking—number of Texas Republicans, and remained the most important black politician in Texas until his death in 1897.[22]

Newspapers were the primary means of day-to-day news and information of the era, and poems were a popular means of communication and a much-read feature of newspapers across Texas. For example, to applaud the role of Texas farmers, Blackshear appealed to black Americans in verse to consider the rising grassroots rumbles of the "populist throng."[23]

Politics in Texas, regardless of the number of third-party movements, changed little in the last quarter of the century and into the early 1900s. Long before the rise of the large metropolitan areas in Texas, the political power center of the state, dominated by the white Democrats, was in an area that stretched northward from Brazos County to just south of Dallas and was bounded on the west and east sides by Waco (today IH-35) and the Texas-Louisiana border, respectively. The area comprised about 25–28 Texas counties, out of a total of 254. The list of Democratic politicians Blackshear worked with from the region is long and distinguished: Gov. Sul Ross (Waco), Sen. Richard Coke (Waco), political operative George Clark (Waco), C. B. Kilgore (Wills Point), Sen. John Reagan (Palestine), future governor Thomas M. Campbell (Palestine), attorney general and future governor James Stephen Hogg (Rusk), future governor Charles A. Culberson (Gilmer and Jefferson), Gov. Oran M. Roberts (San Augustine), John S. Ford (San Augustine), William P. Hobby (Moscow), George W. Chilton (Tyler), Morris Sheppard (Morris County), and Joe Henry Eagle (Vernon). However, Col. Edward House—whom Gould called "an adept manipulator"—became the overriding political

SONG OF THE TEXAS FARMER
by E. L. Blackshear

Oh, times they are hard, and money is scarce,
We're viewing the future askance;
And thousands of farmers are idle and poor,
Wear a patch on the seats of their pants, pants, pants,
Wear a patch on the seat of their pants.

Vote for Culberson, and hard times will stay,
Our troubles will only enhance;
And more Texas people will wear the new badge.
A patch on the seat of their pants, pants, pants.
A patch on the seat of their pants.

There's many a Texan who aches for a change,
You can spot him the very first glance.
There's a look that implies when you gaze in his eyes;
"Kick the patch on the seat of my pants, pants, pants,
"Kick the patch on the seat of my pants."

Kick it hard, for it means that I've been voting wrong;
For Democrats I'll no longer dance,
"At the polls I will join the Populist throng,
"And then buy a new pair of pants, pants, pants,
"With no patch on the seat of my pants."

Source: *Southern Mercury*, October 29, 1896.

kingmaker in Texas political circles during this period. A confidant of Blackshear, his influence and counsel spread over the next two decades from key Texas political races to the chief presidential adviser in the Woodrow Wilson White House. Thus, a majority of the US congressional delegation from the state was from East Texas. Grange Grand Master Archibald Rose and future governor James Ferguson were both from Salado, Bell County. Jim Crow control of voting, primaries, education,

Lawrence Sullivan Ross played a key role, both as a state senator and governor, in ensuring support and funding for Prairie View. Ross and Blackshear were friends from the mid-1880s in Austin until Ross's death in 1898. Blackshear penned the eulogy for Ross's funeral. From the collection of John A. Adams Jr.

and commerce by white Democratic politicians remained centered in East Texas up until World War II.[24]

In spite of rising random agricultural organizations and third political parties—Grangers, Lily-White Republicans, Populists, prohibitionists, Gold Democrats, and Greenbackers—the strong Democratic Party power structure controlled the majority of the state's politics and laws for decades. By the 1890s, however, the hold on state politics by the white Democrats faced a formative challenge by third party movements hoping to capitalize on voter discontent and apathy. In this vein, the Populist movement for one brief moment took center stage. "The wonder is not that the Populists eventually failed," Woodward concluded, "but that they made as much headway as they did against the overwhelming odds they faced."[25]

Sul Ross

One of the greatest champions of free enterprise, fiscally conservative government, and education in Texas was Lawrence Sullivan Ross, known to all as Sul Ross. As the fourteenth governor of Texas, he arrived in Austin fully aware the state was in transition from the days of the wild, uncharted frontier to the slowly emerging "modern age," and thus, he assumed a pivotal leadership position to strike a balance in the rapidly growing state. The times were marked by farmers and ranchers irritated with the monopolistic railroads, the disposition of open public land, fencing, and grazing and water rights, as well as years of overlooked citizen services in education and special needs for all Texans. Raised on the open frontier and hardened by experience, Sul Ross effectively dealt with numerous races and political groups. He was the right man at the right time for Texas.[26]

Sul's parents insisted on his education. He and his older brother Pete attended the common school for Indians at the Brazos Reserve near Graham, followed by classes in Austin. During these early years he gained the next phase of his training on the frontier working with his father at the Reserve at the headwaters of the Brazos River, leading friendly Native Americans in the defense of the indigenous population and settlers against renegade raiders. This was followed by a brief stint at Baylor University, and he finished college at Wesleyan University in Florence, Alabama. Returning home, Ross joined the Texas Rangers, going on to have a notable military career during the Civil War. After the conflict he returned home to Waco. In spite of efforts to open the frontier west of Austin, Central and East Texas were dominated by King Cotton. In the years after returning home from the war, Ross worked on the family farm along the Brazos River in an effort to recover his failing health.[27]

With the end of Reconstruction, Ross was elected sheriff of McLennan County, a member of the state constitutional convention (in 1875), and a key member on the special educational committee. After ratification he was elected to the Texas Senate. By 1885, Sul Ross was drafted to run for governor. A slender, sensitive state senator with a camp-meeting drawl, Sul easily received the Democratic nomination. One of the most popular Texans with the highest name recognition in the last half of the nineteenth century, rivaled only by his mentor and commander Gen. Sam Houston, he won the governorship in a landslide with nearly 80 percent of the popular vote. A Jeffersonian Democrat, Ross arrived as a fiscal conservative to the statehouse and, as historian Randolph Campbell notes, "leaned more toward moderation than old fashioned 'Redeemer' conservatism." The state was entering an economic boom period. The years between 1880 and when Ross entered office in 1887 was one of the fastest-growing periods in the state's history. The state census of December 31, 1887, indicated a statewide population of 2,015,032—a gain of 423,283 or 27 percent since 1880—in spite of an exodus of hundreds of African Americans to Kansas on the rumor and promise of free land and jobs. Lafayette Lumpkin Foster, commissioner of the Texas Department of Agriculture, Insurance, Statistics, and History, reported cotton production was up fourfold from 350,628 bales in 1870 to an estimated 1,380,000 in 1887, even after a severe drought that lasted from 1884–87. Railroads across the state nearly doubled track mileage from 4,216 in 1881 to 8,161 in 1888, with the total value of the roads and rolling stock valued at over $56 million. During the Ross administration statewide tax assessments fell, yet revenue rose due to the expanding economic base.[28]

Governor Ross became the leading advocate of improved education for all Texans. Ross bridged frontier Texas and the changing political structure during the state's transition into the dawn of the twentieth century. During the 1880s Ross had regular contact with Blackshear, Holland, Grant, and Anderson, who pressed upon the then state senator, and later governor, the views and concerns of the black community. Shortly after his inaugural address on January 18, 1887, he outlined a number of priorities, even though the Texas Constitution of 1876 limited gubernatorial powers and crafted a relatively weak executive. Thus, the governor's powers rested in his ability to serve as commander in chief, to make appointments, and to exercise the veto, as well as to recommend and champion new legislation. His recommendations were taken very seriously. Within weeks of Ross taking office, the legislature followed his lead, addressing relief for the 1886–87 drought sufferers in West Texas, enacting fence cutting laws, and providing for the destruction of predator wolves. However, Ross's most meaningful actions in his first term were programs for the youth of Texas, with the establishment of an "orphans home" in Corsicana, a reformatory facility for teenage convicts in Gatesville, and a Deaf, Dumb, and Blind Asylum for Colored Youth (for which the legislature appropriated $50,000) located in Austin.[29]

Interestingly, the one action by the legislature that Sul Ross opposed received the most political and statewide public attention—a resolution drafted on March 4, 1887, for a vote of the people on August 4 to prohibit the "manufacture, sale, and exchange of intoxicating liquors (except for medical and sacramental purposes)." Heretofore, Texas had dealt with the issue of alcohol sales and Prohibition by means of the "local option," where individual counties and cities decided whether to allow the sale of "spirits." Ross, attacked by prohibitionists as "a saloon stump speaker," supported the local option and condemned the amendment with a statement that such an action was "impolitic, unwise and against the genius of our free institutions." Ross was joined by Senator Coke, who noted that this was not a political issue and could only harm commerce and "stimulate illegal liquor sales." Prohibition produced what one observer described as "the most exciting political contest that had occurred in Texas for a number of years," which "enlisted in the canvass not only the habitual politicians, but also citizens of every class, including preachers and women, both white and black."[30]

The Texas governor's campaign during the fall of 1886 and the excitement over the Prohibition vote in August 1887 were the first major elections Edward Blackshear was actively involved in. It is unsure how he voted for governor, but given the pro-education and anti-Prohibition stance of Sul Ross, and as a result of his acquaintance with Ross in Austin, Blackshear likely supported him. Newspapers during the campaign reminded readers that during the Texas Constitutional Convention in 1875, Ross served on the Select Committee on Education and the Special Committee on Public Schools. The Wheatfield School and Blackshear's role in managing the education programs for the African American students of the city, as well as his active role in the AME Church during the balance of the 1880s, gave him a front seat to state government and access to the key Austin and state leaders of the day. In Waco, Governor Ross was a strong advocate of predominantly black Paul Quinn College, encouraging private investment in the "pride of the AME Church in Texas." Furthermore, Ross, along with Blackshear and other African American leaders, advocated for the legislature to give attention to the realization of the colored university envisioned in the state Constitution of 1876. Ross's recommendation and the approval of the colored asylum, as well as his vocal campaign against mob violence and "lynch law," dating from his days as a McLennan County sheriff, addressed critical issues for the black community. Beginning with Ross and continuing through the next three decades, Blackshear would routinely have acquaintance with and access to five Texas governors' offices.[31]

Prohibition remained the controversial overriding political issue and captured the attention of Texans statewide. The German Texans agreed with the African Americans and wanted no interference with their access to "spirits." Black church congregations were mobilized in the anti-saloon fight. Blacks Texans were suspicious of Prohibition and the implied interference with personal freedom. Political leaders crossed political lines as Prohibition became an intensely personal matter. Private brewers and distributors were very free with anti-Prohibition campaign funding. The bitter fight, drawing more voters than the 1886 governor race, ended with an overwhelming victory for the "wets"—220,627 to 129,270. The issue of Prohibition lingered on for a quarter of a century before it again became a statewide political and social debate—and in time dramatically impacted Blackshear's career. The *Galveston Daily News* prophetically noted in the fall of 1886, "Some day there may be a radical Prohibition party in Texas." After Ross's overwhelming reelection to a second term, he dealt with a number of key events and issues: unrest and lawlessness in Fort Bend County, a new state capital, debate over the control of the railroads, and enhanced funding for local education and higher education.[32]

The Politics of Education in Texas

The ongoing political struggles to fund higher education in Texas, both the public debate and the political maneuvering behind the scenes, are legend. It became quickly apparent after the opening of the University of Texas in 1883 that advocates of the new institution exercised all means to provide as much funding as possible to the Austin campus. A group of Austin legislators led by Sen. Alexander Terrell and a group of private investors and land speculators demanded that the state comptroller of public accounts, William J. Swain, conduct a full investigation and audit of misappropriation of funds and disbursements held in the Permanent University Fund (PUF). Any "improperly dispersed" PUF funds, regardless of the impact on the organizations involved, were to be recovered and redirected to the immediate expansion and land acquisition of the University of Texas. In April 1888, at a time when Governor Ross had balanced the state budget and accumulated a small reserve, Terrell, supported by the administration of the university and a number of key politicians, submitted the university's claim of $431,687.53—a combination of principal withdrawn from the PUF and accumulated interest (8 percent) dating from January 1861.[33]

The amount Terrell demanded to be restored to the PUF was a combination of state debt incurred during the Civil War (paid for with [worthless] Confederate paper notes) and interest, totaling a reduced amount of $408,478.86. As it was questionable if this wartime sum could be recovered, it remained unresolved, and thus a majority of the recovery was directed at attacking funds Governor Roberts had advanced to Prairie View Normal by acts of the legislature between 1879 and 1881 in his effort to save the fledgling college. Of the $27,600 appropriation, only $14,495.73 was disbursed to the college from the PUF and not from the general revenue fund (due to a shortfall in the state treasury). Governor Roberts wanted to ensure the college received funding at this critical period. Upon demands from Terrell for an audit, the comptroller concluded that the "claim is founded on the fact that the Prairie View Normal School is in no sense of the word a part or branch of the University [of Texas] and the school is not entitled to this appropriation" and "has not the shadow of a claim on the University."[34] In fact, Prairie View was a branch of Texas A&M, which under the state constitution *was* a branch of the University of Texas—a point that no one appears to have mentioned. Further demand was made for $8,214.25, with interest at 8 percent, dating from April 1881 to May 1888—a total of $22,712.99. The governor was urged by a high-powered group of university supporters to repay the PUF even to the detriment of Prairie View, if necessary deducting funds from the college's 1888 legislative request of $35,000. Sen. Samuel Maxey advised the governor, "It is needless to remind a gentleman of your intelligence and broad views of the inestimable advantages to the state of a well conducted [white] University." Texas regent and university president William L. Prather along with Thomas D. Wooten urged Ross to use his "personal influence and deserved popularity" to secure the funds. In addition, a letter from Benajah H. Carroll, president of the Southwestern Baptist Seminary in Waco, noted, "The people desire to see this institution [in Austin] put upon a first class basis as to material resources and facilities." There was no concern expressed in Austin for the well-being of Prairie View.[35]

As the political wrangling subsided, the governor allowed an adjustment in the PUF and also provided adequate funding to continue the expansion of facilities at Prairie View. Concerned with the lack of attention to assist the expansion of Prairie View, two black citizens groups met in early 1887 to advocate for an expanded state appropriation for the college to establish an "agricultural and mechanical college for the benefit of the colored youths." The first group met in Galveston, chaired by city alderman Norris Cuney, and the second "colored citizens" meeting was in Austin, led by the committee of J. J. Hamilton, Rev. A. Grant, T. H. Smith, W. H. Holland, and E. L. Blackshear. These individuals, tasked to call on Governor Ross and the legislature with a formal petition, worked for the next decade for the recognition and expansion of higher education for African American in Texas. One important link among all these men was that they, including Ross, were active members of the Masons.[36]

The political focus by late summer was on the election of 1888. The campaign centered around a detailed debate concerning Democratic commitment to and funding of education, which impacted both white and black students. Governor Ross highlighted the issues:

> In ten years the colored scholastic population increased 134 percent, and the white 113 percent. Owing to overestimates of the available school fund in 1885 and 1886 there were deficiencies which had to be met out of school revenues of the years 1888 and 1889, reducing pro-rata, by which reduction the white and colored children suffered equally.
>
> During this period up to this date the Democrats of Texas have established 2,981 colored schools, employing as many colored teachers, paying teachers $590,000 per annum. These teachers are officers of the state and 99 out of every 100 of them Republicans. Their politics are not inquired into. Then for the same ten years the state has been educating colored teachers at the state normal (Prairie View) near Hempstead. Not less than 400 teachers have been rendered proficient as pedagogues by that institute. Large and commodious additions to it are now under construction paid in the main by Democratic taxpayers.[37]

Ross's second term victory was nationwide news. The New York *Evening World* published a front-page special story by Professor Blackshear, termed as "one of the foremost colored men in the State," with his endorsement: "I believe the incoming administration will do all it can to improve the condition of the Negro—Governor Ross and Attorney General Hogg in their official acts have convinced the intelligent negroes of Texas that they intend to administer the law without regard to race, color or previous condition of servitude."[38]

In spite of the higher aims to improve education for Texas youth, a culture of discrimination and violence simmered in communities across the state.

Violence: Jaybirds and Woodpeckers

During his career, Sul Ross had fought against lawlessness and mob violence—much of which concerned the safety and concerns of the black community. Just below the surface there were a number of racial tensions in localized pockets across the state. During the last two years of his governorship, mobs lynched thirty-two people, of which twenty-six were black and six were white, across the state. The lawlessness was totally unacceptable. Ross was fully aware of the impact of mob violence, dating back to the time he was sheriff in Waco, and this was the reason he called all Texas law enforcement to enforce the rule of law. History has failed to record the near dozen times the governor dispatched law enforcement or voluntary militia units to calm racial unrest. The most volatile community incidents occurred in Laredo, Texas, in 1886 and in Richmond, Fort Bend County, in the late 1880s. In Laredo the local political power struggle was between immigrant Mexicans and local whites who did not want to share power, while tensions in Richmond had been growing for months, rooted in a heated battle for white versus black local political control. A small group of disgruntled white Democrats in Fort Bend County organized the Young Men's Democratic Club, known as the Jaybirds, in 1888 to oppose the elected black county officials. Black and white county officers who held local political power, long after white supremacy had taken over the state in the post-Reconstruction period, formed a counter group known as the Woodpeckers. The Jaybirds hoped to intimidate, assault, and, if necessary, kill anyone who opposed them. The classic study on Texas feuds by C. L. Sonnichsen, *I'll Die Before I'll Run*, captures the context of the conflict:[39]

> The colored folks [in Ft. Bend County] outnumbered the whites approximately four to one in those days. Furthermore they could and did vote and were the deciding force in local elections. That was why there was

> a feud. The Woodpeckers controlled the Negroes and ran the county. The Jaybirds (who included the majority of the white people) waited and hoped and damned the Woodpeckers until they could stand it no longer, after which the shooting started.
>
> Add to this the fact that everybody carried a pistol, and that everybody in town was related to everybody else, and you have the groundwork for the feud. By 1888 Fort Bend was one of the few counties in Texas where the Negro vote, controlled by a few white men, swung the big stick.[40]

In hopes of controlling the next local election, the Jaybirds ordered at gunpoint a number of black election officials to leave the county, but retained the black tax assessor in charge in an effort to engineer the upcoming election. In spite of all the intimidation the incumbent Woodpecker slate won election, causing the Jaybirds to surround the courthouse and open fire, killing three men. Unable to control the situation, the county sheriff, Jim Garvey, called the governor's office for assistance. Governor Ross, viscerally opposed to any form of "mob law," without regard to "race, color or previous condition," ordered the Texas Rangers to Fort Bend, along with the Houston Light Guard, a quasi-military militia unit (forerunner of the Texas State Guard). Ross traveled to Richmond to take personal command of the situation, setting up headquarters in the National Hotel. After two days he departed, and the incident was in the hands of the Texas Rangers to restore calm. When no local compromise could be arrived at to maintain calm, authority to administer the county and enforce the law was left in the hands of Ranger Sergeant Ira Aten, who replaced the sheriff. Ross's strategy had been reasonably successful in earlier incidents of violence, but fell short of a truly peaceful resolution in this case. The racial tension remained, but the shooting had stopped. Other white men's associations were active in nearly a dozen counties to protect their claim of white supremacy. Hundreds of African American voters statewide were blocked from voting, and the last handful of black state legislators were defeated in the elections of the 1890s.[41]

Second Morrill Act

The Republican Party in Texas and their majority African American membership had had little success regaining the political control they once had in the Reconstruction period. They secured, through the mid-1890s, only a very few seats in the Texas legislature. They had better luck in elections for local offices such as county commissioner, justice of the peace, and constable. Until its defeat, they hoped to use the Prohibition issue to regain some form of impact in the state. Republican Party chairman Cuney decided the next struggle for political power should be over education, particularly Prairie View Normal College and the allocation of federal funding for higher education to Texas A&M. Cuney's daughter Maud noted in her father's biography that in 1889–90 he became vocal on education. "The colored institutions of learning were rapidly growing in Texas, and father, alive to their needs, was constantly in demand—giving advice and working for their cause." Yet in the end he viewed his role as measured through the degree of political gains by the black community, come what may.[42]

The passage of the Second Morrill Act of 1890 by Congress on August 30, 1890, with an annual appropriation of $15,000 to Texas, presented a new opportunity to reassert Republican political influence. Prairie View was one of only four black public institutions in the South (Alcorn in Mississippi, Hampton in Virginia, and Claflin in South Carolina) to annually share in funds from the Morrill Act of 1862. The Second Morrill Act of 1890 specifically set aside funding for black higher education. Thus, Cuney initiated a drive to have all Morrill funding from the federal government rescinded on the grounds that the current funding for the A&M College and the pass-through of funding to Prairie View was affected by "systematic discrimination" and decided only along political lines. His overall argument was that the ongoing Democratic-administered school system statewide had provided unequal funding and treatment of white and black schools. Cuney was very critical of the use of public-school lands to fund Texas A&M and the University of Texas but not black higher education. Furthermore, there was an ongoing call by African American leaders, championed primarily by the Colored State Teachers' Association, for the constitutionally mandated black university approved by Texas voters in 1882 and ignored by politicians in Austin. At the local level there was indeed disparity, but overall, Governor Ross (in response to the politically motivated charges) noted that funding equally benefited white and black children. Cuney filed his complaint with the federal government, and absent any federal agency to handle education issues, the matter was deferred to the secretary of the Department of the Interior (who staffed a federal office of education affairs), under whose authority, from the US Congress, federal educational funding to states in the South was monitored and dispersed.[43]

The detailed response by Governor Ross—"Education of the Colored Race"—is seldom noted, but stands as one of the unique documents in Texas history. At a time when he could have ignored the protest by Cuney, and against the wishes of many in the Democratic power structure, Ross addressed the charges head on. Stating that Cuney's allegations were politically motivated, he drew attention to the local and state educational pay for teachers, regardless of party affiliation, despite the charge they only employed and paid so-called Democratic teachers. Ross noted, "The Democrat loves his money as well as other people. How is it he pays so liberally to evaluate and care for the negroes always found voting against him? Certainly there is only one explanation, and it is that the Democrats of Texas have agreed that the negro shall enjoy equal rights before the law . . . cost what it may." Secretary of the Interior John Noble agreed with Ross's response, tabled the protest, and advanced the prescribed Morrill Act funds to Texas without any objections or restrictions (see the appendix for the full text of the document).[44]

Ross knew more than most that the Morrill funding was a major windfall for higher education in Texas. If Cuney's complaint, driven purely for political purposes, prevailed, it would have set back public higher education funding in the state for years to come and actually cut significant funding for Prairie View. Furthermore, Ross avoided a major crisis at the fledgling college and prevented the funding for Prairie View from being cut back or its programs limited. The new appropriation of $15,000 for the benefit of higher education was to be increased for ten years by an additional sum of $1,000 each succeeding year, and thereafter at $25,000 annually. The Grange also made an effort to control federal Hatch Act funding for the experiment stations, but the governor and the schools quickly stopped this attempted power grab. Ross made the preliminary division of the funds, one-third (33 1/3 percent) to Prairie View and two-thirds to A&M. Combined with the first Morrill Act, the Experiment Station endowment, the Second Morrill Act, and matching funds from the state, Prairie View annual funding increased by over $10,000 (a smaller share than what Ross proposed), despite the fact that the Texas legislature passed a measure to allow funding on the basis of only one-fourth: 25 percent to Prairie View and the balance to A&M (the state-national average of the seventeen black land-grant institutions that received Morrill funds was 29.4 percent).

Additionally, the Second Morrill Act recognized and, in essence, "institutionalized" Southern black land-grant education in the 1890s under the rubric of separate but equal education.[45]

The challenges facing African American education in Texas remained critical as black illiteracy remained high, teachers for rural schools were in short supply, and farm organizations continued to push for farm and ranch "hands" (not scholars) to work the fields and voiced their concern with the role and benefit of a "classical" education in an agrarian economy. Further concern continued regarding the land-grant schools providing the type of education they were mandated to teach. Efforts to provide much-needed annual federal appropriations for educational programs to reduce illiteracy stalled in Congress with the defeat of the Blair Bill in March 1890. Texas senator Richard Coke was suspicious that the measure, crafted by northern Republicans, was little more than a new "element to the various others growing out of the race question to be agitated in the political arena and foment discord and trouble."[46] One of Edward Blackshear's most insightful articles on African American education was featured in the Fort Worth *Star Gazette* and published in papers across the state. His candid assessment quickly placed him among the leading advocates of equal access to education: "This question [of education] was once seriously discussed, and many held and firmly believed the negro incapable of education. But, fortunately, the experience of the last twenty years has settled this question by demonstrating the fact that the negro is susceptible in a high degree to those influences which, in their entirety, constitute education. His mind is certainly capable of development. His capacity to comprehend those sciences and master those arts which constitute the college or university curriculum is undoubted by any who have taken time to investigate."[47]

The quality of education in all land-grant institutions across the South—regardless of the debate and disagreements about the merits of either Hampton or Tuskegee and the Washington–Du Bois debate—remained inferior in both the white and black land-grant colleges and most public schools of higher education. In the case of the black land-grant colleges, this was routinely blamed on white "control" of black schools. A "normal" college could hardly be called a full-fledged university. It soon became evident that while the black land-grant schools had a mandate under the Morrill Acts, their best path toward success was to adhere to these guidelines while also producing teachers. In the mid-1890s, long before the Nelson Amendment of 1907 to the Morrill Act of 1890, which allowed land-grant institutions to use new additional annual appropriations increased to $5,000 for teacher instruction and certification, Principal Anderson and Prairie View, with the full support and endorsement of Sul Ross and the A&M Board of Directors, made the curriculum adjustments to train more teachers.[48]

Sul Ross was a transformative governor who for decades did not get the full acclaim for steering the state on a fiscally strong path in the midst of great changes, population growth, and industrial advances in the emerging lumber, cattle, and railroad industries (the Texas oil and gas boom had yet to be fully realized). His approach to all areas and issues was more objective (pragmatic) and results-oriented. For example, in the case of railroad regulation, he clearly knew it was necessary but not to the extent of doing harm to the investment and economic benefit derived from connecting Texas producers with markets for their products. Incoming governor Stephen Hogg, who claimed credit for creating the Texas Railroad Commission while pleasing a certain group of rabid farm advocates, lawyers, and Populists, sent mixed signals to those who wanted to invest in the future of Texas. One contemporary observer, Maud Cuney Hare, noted that the result was "the stagnation in business, no new enterprises, every industry paralyzed, money driven from the state, with the rate of interest gone up to 10 and 12 percent, so that Texas is doing business at pawn shop rates." Blackshear was a keen observer of these issues and gauged their impact on educational advancements in Texas.[49]

Ross's governorship bridged the closing of frontier Texas with the emergence of the state as an agriculture and industrial launching site for the next century. His actions as governor expanded significant health care services to black Texans and to individuals with special needs. He reduced taxes and expanded services to veterans and widows as well as encouraging the legislature to address education at all levels. He pardoned more African Americans for questionable sentences and on technical grounds than the combined number of actions by all previous governors. Near the end of his administration, he was offered the presidency of Texas A&M in late 1890. While he could have stood for political office for the US Senate or departed for a corporate job, he felt well suited to accept the A&M College offer. Texas A&M was once again in a state of turmoil and welcomed his leadership and gravitas at this pivotal juncture. Ross's accepting the A&M presidency and his friendship with Blackshear proved to be a major plus in the coming years, for the benefit of Prairie View and the advancement of black higher education in Texas.[50]

The Early 1890s

With the victory of James Stephen Hogg in the 1890 governor race, Ross moved as president to the A&M College campus south of Bryan. The college was a long cry from the political dynamics and drama of Austin, but early on in a letter to his former chief of staff, Ross confessed, "I think I am going to like it." His first attention was a close review of the operations at the A&M College and then, in his dual role as "president" of Prairie View, attention to that campus. Ross's close ally on the A&M Board of Directors and chairman of the three-man oversight committee of Prairie View, William R. Cavitt of Bryan, was extremely helpful in representing and addressing the needs of the Hempstead campus. Prior to leaving Austin, the former governor had double-checked that all the currently allocated funding for both colleges was secure and untouched. Blackshear, in a guest editorial in the *Austin Statesman*, "The Condition of Negro Education in Texas," made crystal clear the significant role played by Sul Ross: "It is certainly fact, as testified to by the noble governor, a man whom all classes and races in Texas love and delight to honor, it is, I say a certain fact that the negro is advancing in all that constitutes a Christian civilization." Notwithstanding, a report by the state superintendent of public schools highlighted the fact that educational attainment for black Texans in 1891 was dismal.[51]

The new federal appropriation under the Second Morrill Act of 1890 was a timely funding windfall and used to improve both the facilities and staffing of the two public college campuses. As Ross began the process for the state to accept the terms of the new federal legislation, he increased efforts to add improvements at Prairie View and supported the clamor once again to provide the Texas constitutionally mandated black university.[52] It is assumed that many had hoped that the call for the new black university would subside with the growth and improvements at Prairie View. The sole day-to-day flow of information and the status of the new university came through the scores of Texas newspapers. The full scale of distribution is unknown and few of these papers survive today, yet we are able to track many of the key editorials and stories that were subsequently reprinted in larger newspapers in Galveston, Austin, Dallas, and Houston. Texas by 1890 had some twenty papers edited by African Americans. However, any

TABLE 2.2. Texas Schools and Attendance, 1890–1891

	White	Black	Total
Total number of districts in the county	131	8	139
Number of graded schools	296	23	319
Number of ungraded schools	4,011	852	4,863
Number of high schools	83	3	86
Number of sittings for children (number of seats)	141,767	18,143	159,910
Average school term in months (20 school days/mo)	5.25	4.52	4.89

Source: *Report of the State Superintendent of Public Schools* (Austin, 1893), 22. Note: Only 130 counties reported.

gains at Hempstead and the growing popularity of the college were viewed by advocates of the potential new black university as secondary to their efforts to address both the letter and spirit of the state Constitution of 1876 and the results of the 1882 election regarding the new university site.[53]

Nearly a decade of teaching and administrative duties in Austin as well as work with educational programs across the state ranked Blackshear among the most well-known and respected educators in Texas. Having personally taught kindergarten through high school, Blackshear actively participated in the Colored Teachers State Association (CTSA). A prime example of his role in education was displayed at the 1891 CTSA annual conference, where he was the only member who was a discussant on all the academic papers presented. The presentations included discussions on the finer points of education: "The Relation of Kindergarten to the School"; "Mental Arithmetic: How to Teach It; Its Relation to Written Arithmetic"; and "School Management" (which advocated a "mild form" of corporal punishment). The final topic of the meeting was a discussion led by Blackshear: "Resolved That There Is a Necessity for Establishing a State University for the Colored Youths of Texas." It was concluded that the need was supported by the hundreds of "colored youth that leave the state" to acquire university knowledge elsewhere. L. C. Anderson, principal of Prairie View, favored the university but noted "resolutions wouldn't get it, but hard work by the people of the state would." Lastly, M. N. Brown thought "it well to ask for it now, whether you need it or not, as he thought you will need it before you get it." The final action of the conference was a unanimously adopted resolution offered by Blackshear: "Resolved, that it is the sense of this association that the time is ripe for the establishment of a state university for the colored youths, as provided for by the constitution of Texas and located by popular vote at Austin, and that a committee be appointed to wait on the governor at Austin and memorialize the next legislature relative to this matter."[54]

The driving force behind the black university was a coalition of the predominantly black Republican Party, the Colored Teachers State Association, and the editors of the *Texas School Journal*. During the 1891 annual meeting of the CTSA, a committee of teachers and administrators were appointed, including H. B. Fry and E. L. Blackshear of Austin; M. M. Rogers of LaGrange; G. W. Jackson of Corsicana; S. J. Jenkins of Brenham; L. H. Tindall of Mount Pleasant; I. B. Scott of Houston; and J. P. Starks of Dallas, "to call on"—lobby—political leaders in Austin. Additionally, the front page of the *Galveston Daily News* reported Professor Blackshear would be in Lockhart for a gathering of citizens to represent the association and speak "on the political issues of the day." They drafted a detailed resolution in 1892, addressed to Gov. James Hogg, "respectfully making a strong claim of the colored citizens to establish the 'black university.'" They gave the governor and the state detailed credit for the success of the teachers' colleges (Prairie View and Sam Houston Normal), yet indicated the state was ready for a new university. One key point of their presentation was that other states, many "less able than Texas," including Louisiana, Alabama, Mississippi, Tennessee, and Georgia, maintained separate, state-funded black universities and that "over 100" Texas students were leaving the state to attend these colleges. In their petition they quoted the senior politician in the state, former governor Sul Ross, encouraging a cooperative effort with the "white" university (in Austin) to share a portion of the PUF: "The question of higher education as well as ordinary education of the colored race is one which demands attention of the university regents [of the University of Texas], as well as of the legislature, under the requirements of the law for a colored branch university."[55]

These actions started a decade-long quest in January 1892 to establish a new university predicated on the following justification published in the *Galveston Daily News*: "The time is ripe for a university. The colored population do not presume to make a demand for a university, but they ask it because they believe it to be in justice to their numerical and material increase; because they believe it to be due them as citizens of the commonwealth; they ask it because the state presumes to educate her colored population; they ask it because they believe it will take university training to prepare the young men and women of our race to act well their part of life and to make them worthy citizens, and they ask it, finally, because they believe Texas to be as liberal as any other state; as generous to her colored citizens, and because they believe the public school resources of Texas will warrant the state in providing a university for the colored people equaled by no other state."[56]

A broad base of support would be marshaled in an effort to gain legislative approval in Austin. African-Texan church groups in Austin were well aware of the impact a black university in Austin would have on the local economy and prestige of the black community. Church groups led by Rev. Mark Henson and Rev. L. L. Campbell enlisted Blackshear in early February 1893 to draft a standardized petition to acquire as many signatures from congregations and communities across the state as possible, to send to their legislative representatives in Austin. Blackshear, following his first visit to Washington, DC, was chosen as the spokesman to appear before the Texas House Education Committee. Following what the *Galveston Daily News* reported was "quite a moving appeal," the representatives tabled Blackshear's request for a motion to move forward without further action. While shrouded as a church representative, Blackshear, an employee of the City of Austin, was increasingly becoming more politically active, allowing his name to be attached to newspaper reports urging the completion of the following form letter (drafted by Blackshear as an example) or a letter-petition of their own design, with date, county, and signatures:[57]

> _______ Texas, _______ 1893
> To the State Legislature:
> We the undersigned colored citizens of
> _________, _________ County do
> hereby petition you to establish and put in
> immediate operation of a State University
> for the Colored Youth of Texas, as provided
> by the State Constitution.
> Signed By—[58]
>
> _________

Political activist John Rayner sarcastically called the ambitious Governor Hogg the "piney woods' parvenu"—with Rayner attacking the governor and his party on the stump and in print: "After the proud, greedy and wicked shall have been driven from our legislative, judicial and executive chambers, then God will turn the big end of his cornucopia toward us, and then will commence the human development, which will continue to evolve until humanity is made perfect." Hogg expressed interest in the black university but, after playing both black and white farmers against the railroads to ink the Texas Railroad Commission legislation, was not very active in promoting education in general or a new institution. Furthermore, Hogg chose to ignore the farmers' demand, much to their consternation, for an appointment of an Alliance-man to the new railroad commission. Where Hogg was equivocal others were more vocal.[59]

Proponents for the black university took their message directly to the state legislature. A visitation committee from the Texas legislature attempted to find fault with the results at the public colleges, yet Texas A&M and Prairie View received a laudatory report. The Texas House Committee on Education held an extensive hearing in February 1893, calling on the crusty "Old Alcalde" (former governor and UT law professor Roberts) to comment to the legislators on the views of the Texas public domain and the question of funding higher education in Texas. In a detailed presentation, Roberts gave his strong advice on how to fund the black university while protecting public lands dedicated to the University of Texas: "When it comes every session to asking for taxes to support the main university and the college and the medical branch, and as you know it is agreed to establish the nigger college—I beg pardon, the colored college, as named in the constitution—I say, when it comes to taxing the people for those institutions or supporting them by endowment, the people will say they should be maintained by endowment. I am opposed to taxation when we can help it. How can we help it? By a liberal donation of land." Roberts was followed by Blackshear and W. R. Cavitt of Bryan, longtime A&M College board member. Cavitt witnessed the presentation by Blackshear, with the *Statesman* noting the "committee was very favorably impressed" by the Austin school professor's detailed and reasoned testimony. One critical item was a discussion of a suitable site in Austin, with the recommendation that the state purchase the existing property of Tillotson Institute east of the state capital to organize a new university. The excitement and lobbying soon died down, however, and no action was taken.[60]

The Iron Is Hot

As he prepared to play a major role in the ongoing crusade to establish a black university, Blackshear remained exceedingly active in civic activities in Austin, always mindful of the political history and social dynamics of the growing state. During his life he would be chairman of over two dozen civic and church activities clearly outside of his avocation for education—but amply related to the support of his goal to expand the inclusion of black Texans in all aspects of American life. This work doubtless expanded his statewide contacts and recognition. These activities included the endorsement of political candidates, such as Joseph Sayers's race for Congress, as reported in "a colored man's paper at Austin," the *Illuminator*: "I believe in supporting the best man regardless of party. I heartily indorse [*sic*] Mr. Sayers. He is unquestionably an honest, efficient, patriotic and conscientious statesman, *a rara avis* in these piping times of political degeneracy and apostacy [*sic*]." While Blackshear was deeply involved in Austin, one curious event that could have catapulted him to Washington, DC, was an announcement in the Philadelphia *Freeman* that the Texas educator, unbeknownst to himself, was under consideration for the position of recorder of deeds for the District of Columbia. The possibility of a higher salary influenced him to consider this move. While little resulted from the announcement, Blackshear, a strong supporter of the Grover Cleveland (D) presidential campaign, said he "believe[d] that the war is over and that the Negro has a right to support any party he chooses without being dubbed by the unthinking and prejudice[d] as a traitor." This also clearly indicates Blackshear's increasingly close connection with political affairs in Texas and beyond.[61]

In early 1895 Blackshear promoted the idea of a grand exposition to celebrate and highlight the semi-centennial of his adopted state. His excitement and prose hailed the grandeur of Texas and the opportunities for a prosperous future for the state—and he argued Austin should host such an event, writing in a feature article in the *Austin Weekly Statesman*: "Imperial in extent, strategic in position, protean in resources, glorious in history, resolute and progressive in spirit, Southern in ardor, Western in breadth of view, Eastern in sagacity, national in patriotism, Texas is the Goliath of the federal brood, with no David to endanger its supremacy. Texas is a commercial commonwealth of unusual importance and needs more capital, more people and the exposition would bring both."[62]

Blackshear, after years of writing articles and editorials for papers across the state, was selected as the "conductor" or contributing editor of the "colored department" in the *Texas School Journal* for educational activities around the state, to "represent impartially and correctly the educational movements of our race—in Texas particularly—and to champion the interests of the colored school children of Texas." An extensive plan was drafted to take the fight for expanded educational support (and funding) to Austin and to heavily lobby both sitting representatives as well as candidates for the state senate and state house of representatives. Lobbying continued at the state Republican Conventions in 1892 and 1894, each drafting platform resolutions that "favored equal school accommodations for all races, and thus putting into effect the expressed will of the people." The Democratic-controlled legislature ignored the demands. Hogg—who during the election had promised black Texans a university at Prairie View "similar to the state university in Austin"—and the governor's office were fully preoccupied with his agenda surrounding the railroads, insurance industry, and big business regulation, and they took no action on the university. It was not until the spring 1895 Texas legislative session that the black university issue received yet another hearing in the House Committee on Education.[63]

As the fight to secure a black university heated up, Blackshear, as chairman of the university committee of the Colored State Teachers Association, released the following editorial, "To the Good People of Texas," which received statewide coverage in the media:

> Probably one-fourth of the population of Texas is of African descent. Numerically and industrially this is an important factor. The condition and destiny of this element can not be matters of indifference to the patriotic and far-seeing people of this empire state. History teaches us that the elements of any social body, of any commonwealth, are interdependent, regardless of social class or distinction. The commonwealth of Texas can not be what it should be if the true interests of any class be neglected. Does any one believe that the white people of the South can make the South, which is the most favored and fertile region of our country, what it can be and ought to be if we be left in ignorance, darkness and superstition? The destinies of white and black are bound together by inevitable laws of social action, reaction and progression. Justice is the best policy, as all good men agree. The most dangerous man in any commonwealth, community or party is the demagogue

> who, under pretense of statesmanship and by appeals to prejudice and passion, seeks to deprive any class what is justly due it. The true statesman is he who seeks to do justice to all men, to give every man the opportunity to develop the best in his nature and to make the best use of such talent as nature may have bestowed upon him.[64]

There is little doubt that by 1895 Blackshear knew the only resolution to the quest for improved education for African American Texans rested on the statesmen in Austin and a political solution. Unless there was a political will of the white Democratic power structure both in Austin and at the local level around the state, there would be no measurable attention and funding of black educational programs. Blackshear's connections with political strategist Col. Edward House—the kingmaker of Texas governors from Sul Ross to O. B. Colquitt—were critical to any success or measurable change. The pragmatic House supported Blackshear and Prairie View and the efforts to either open a black university in Austin or, if that was not feasible, to enhance Prairie View Normal.[65] While the emerging Populist Party was advocating African Americans take an activist roll with Prohibition to gain leverage to improve their plight, House advised Blackshear to be wary of the upstart Populism sweeping the West and "work within the system." House was the master of the Texas political system that organized the Democratic platform and the primary strategist for winning gubernatorial and senatorial seats for over a decade, with one contemporary noting, "Colonel House gives to political conceptions a deftness, a sureness in execution, which is really beautiful to the trained observer of the political field—he kept his trusty ear close to earth, sensed the movement and pace of the groundswell, and handled his forces accordingly." An introverted, behind-the-scenes operator and skilled negotiator, House was sometimes categorized as a frail man, due to his poor health. There was no one in this era in Texas whose political clout could equal the influence (both real and imagined) that he has been credited with. One example of his working in the system was exercising influence, against vast opposition, over the planks of the Democratic platform and showing expertise in grassroots organization to ensure victory during the primary.[66]

Knowing that any Republican witness or advocate would not be heard or welcomed, the CTSA selected thirty-three-year-old educator Prof. E. L. Blackshear, chief principal of the Austin African American school district, to deliver the message and appeal before the legislators. The Teachers'

Association informed its membership, "Now is the time to strike for a colored university. The iron is hot—the political iron—it will soon be red hot. We must prepare to strike." Well known in education as well as Democratic political circles in Austin and statewide, the strategy presented by Blackshear was fourfold: (1) remind the legislators of the education mandate in the state constitution and the resulting 1882 site election; (2) highlight the need and obligation to provide equal educational opportunity; (3) distinguish the difference between the current Prairie View "normal" college and the proposed university; and (4) outline for the elected representatives how the new university could be funded by the university land set aside in the public domain for education.[67] Blackshear's testimony and appearance before the committee was carried in the media statewide, including in the *Galveston Daily News*, an excerpt of which follows:

> We appear before you today to ask that provision be made for the immediate establishment of a branch university for colored youth. We are entitled to an equitable share of the proceeds from the sale or investment of the 1,000,000 acres of the university lands, and if a university tax of 1 percent is levied, as has been suggested, provision should be made to give the colored branch a just quota thereof.
>
> There is at present no provision made by the state for the higher education of its colored youth, except what is being done to educate teachers at Prairie View. Prairie View is a normal school, with agricultural and mechanical adjuncts. It is a necessity. We are grateful for its establishment and maintenance, but it is not the college or branch university contemplated in the constitution, and which the people [all] over the state are expecting this legislature to establish.
>
> At first it must necessarily be small, but if wisely planned and planted it must have an ever widening sphere of influence. It will be a mighty incentive to the colored youth in our city high schools and higher grades of town and country schools. Standing upon the summit it will ever beckon them upward; would be a ceaseless inspiration to higher intellectual life. Figures show that there is real need, actual demand for this university, and that there is a constituency from which it will constantly draw. The establishment of the university will be a stimulus to all the high schools and collegiate institutes of the state, which are doing much but are unable to give us what the state will in this school.[68]

What followed was another statewide petition campaign and solicitation of local and state elected officials to support the black university efforts. In addition to Blackshear, key African American leaders such as Paul Quinn College president H. T. Kealing, Rev. I. B. Scott of Houston, W. H. Holland, J. J. Hamilton, C. H. Anderson, and Norris Cuney were enlisted to gather support. As the university campaign continued, changes were underway at Prairie View. There was reasoned concern in some quarters that the campaign to establish the black university could impede the growth of Prairie View. Most likely surprising to Blackshear and his committee, the 1896 president of the Prairie View Alumni Association, Nat Henderson (class of '85) from Columbus, Texas, issued a statement to the *Austin American Statesman*: "The colored teachers of the state are turning every stone to have the state erect a university for colored youths. The university talk is all bosh. It could only benefit the favored few—and very few at that. It is the masses that should be reached and aided to sustain themselves in the race of life."[69]

The petition and lobbying effort were conducted on the basis that the black university had been provided for by the constitution and also given a location by a vote of the people. Blackshear and the CTSA worked to gain a political solution. The two primary political parties in their 1896 platforms put forward the following: the Republicans added a plank, noting colored youths of Texas should have the opportunity for a university education; and the Democrats (with a recommendation by Colonel House), in control of the legislature and most elected offices in the state, held that the Prairie View Normal school should be enlarged, maintaining the provisions of the industrial features of the institution and "gradually [being] convert[ed] into a university for colored people." The A&M Board of Directors and Principal Blackshear were clearly advocates of a separate university. Much to the surprise of the CTSA and supporters of the black university, the legislature passed a law setting aside one hundred thousand acres of the "remaining unappropriated public domain." The public acres, so-called choice lands, were in Presidio County, according to the *Southern Mercury*, which downplayed the first tangible legislative victory, noting the land "today would not net 25 cents per acre" and that it was an "insult to Texas negroes who spurned the proffered gift with contempt."[70]

Shortly thereafter, in 1899, the Texas Supreme Court, in a very questionable decision, blocked the legislation to provide the acres, declaring unequivocally that no unappropriated public land was available. However, the court further noted that any lands returned from the railroad allocations should be considered. In hindsight, then-governor Roberts had basically committed all Texas public lands, and thus tied up all remaining land grants for the University of Texas. In fact, the Texas Land Office had no clear idea how much free land was available and only after an extensive audit of millions of acres in land grants to the railroads did it become known with documented evidence that, first, the state had granted too many acres to the railroads, and, second, over one million, over time, would be returned to the state. The magnitude of the situation is noted by the fact that Texas granted a total of 32,400,000 acres to twelve railroad companies.[71]

The squabble over higher education in Texas was contentious among many Texans. Of special concern by the farmers and ranchers were the efforts in Austin to increase funding for the University of Texas and the medical branch in Galveston over the needs of the agriculture community. The *Texas Farmer* was very direct upon learning of the desire to add "a chair of dentistry" to the medical school: "There is an effort to add a chair of dentistry to the medical branch of the State University. To complete the folly illustrated by educating lawyers, doctors and dudes at State expense, why not add a department to grind out preachers, race-horse trainers, merchants, aurists, opticians, chicken doctors, snake charmers, etc.? If we're going to be fool all, why not be all fool?"[72]

The last elected voice for black educational issues in the Texas legislature for the next seven decades, Rep. Robert Smith introduced numerous bills with mixed results. His support of the black university ended in defeat in the twentieth-fifth session (1897). Notwithstanding, Smith voted for the biannual funding of the University of Texas. Openly chided by a fellow white representative about his vote for the white university that refused any admission to black students, Smith responded: "I know that I cannot enter The University of Texas as a student, but I would rather place the fate of my race in the hands of the educated, rather than to put it in the hands of the ignorant." By 1900 the Lily-White Republican movement, the powerful Democratic white man's grip, the loss of political clout by black Texans, and the growing economic pressure in concert brought a halt to black educational advances in Texas. While black Texans never considered Prairie View as the branch university promised in the Constitution of 1876, the movement to demand a separate university waned and gradually became absorbed in a larger effort to expand the academic programs at Prairie View.[73]

—•❧❧•—

As the black university crusade unfolded over the late 1890s, Principal Blackshear's primary duties following his appointment as principal of Prairie View in 1896 were the management and expansion of the college. The Texas A&M Board of Directors approved an expansion of academic programs as the school was organized into separate academic departments and classical subjects, such as Latin, were added back to the curriculum. And with the death of Norris Cuney in March 1897, following years suffering from pulmonary tuberculosis, Blackshear, while not directly active in the leadership of any political party, gradually assumed the leading role and active voice in the advancement of African Americans in Texas. Signaling the legislature's intent to ignore the black university movement and instead enhance Prairie View, in 1899 the state authorized more funding for the school and renamed it Prairie View State Normal and Industrial College.[74]

3

Called to the College

> The negroes are learning that a little goes a long way sometimes, and they are not being rushed into complications by hot-headed, brainless leaders as formerly. They are finding out that political activity is to be gauged by the sentiment of the community and by the inherent strength, social, political, commercial and civil, of those who engage in it.
>
> EDWARD L. BLACKSHEAR,
> *EVENING STAR* (WASHINGTON, DC), MAY 14, 1905

> The colored teacher has been a herald of civilization to the youth of his people. The colored school teacher is leading his race "up from slavery," that is from the slavery of ignorance and superstition, of intellectual and moral inertia, of aimlessness and shiftlessness, into the freedom of intelligence, of energy, ambition, and industry.
>
> EDWARD L. BLACKSHEAR, 1902

By the early 1890s the Hogg administration was bogged down in the status quo ante, with Texas in the middle of a devastating, nationwide economic depression and the rise of a number of upstart third-party movements to challenge the Democrats. The Panic of 1893 ushered in a serious financial crisis that resulted in the failure of 573 banks nationwide, including a couple of dozen in Texas. The Great Railroad Strike of 1894 was followed by the failure of the corn crop and a decline in demand from Europe for both cotton and wheat. At the local level, Texas was in the midst of increased population growth in the urban areas and a struggling rural economy. Farmers across the state were increasingly pressured by rising production costs and dropping commodity prices due to surplus production that lowered the unit value of crops, especially cotton, corn, and wheat. Small-farm bankruptcy increased due to the perpetual cycle of debt and poverty that turned owners into tenants and sharecroppers—all resulting in lower incomes for the average farmer as well as the basis for social control of poor blacks and whites.[1] In an analysis by E. D. Ball, director of scientific work at the USDA, the land-grant colleges in the emerging industrial age of America were faced with mounting challenges to fulfill their mandate: "By the 1890s the concentration of production and increased transportation facilities had combined to produce the inevitable complication of the agricultural problem. New weeds, pests, and diseases had been introduced and widely disseminated; continuous cropping had brought on soil problems, and troublesome marketing factors were beginning to develop. Overproduction was reducing prices, and the problems of decreasing the overhead and lowering the cost of production were attracting attention. The land-grant colleges must become State leaders in fact as well as in name."[2]

As new immigrants arrived and once-dry Western land became irrigated, competition increased and tension rose among the cattle barons, who demanded an open, free range as well as control over water rights. As ranchers faced drought in far west Texas, farmers in Central and East Texas struggled to hold onto their land. The one dynamic that Ball failed to mention was the impact of the credit-lien system on the struggling farmers. While there were a great number of black tenant farmers, the economic upheaval resulted in a far larger number of foreclosed white farmers being classified as tenants.[3]

Both black and white farmers found themselves in a state of perpetual indebtedness when the price of cotton declined, coupled with the onerous credit-lien system that put many farmers further in debt. In 1895 over six million acres in Texas, some two-thirds of total productive acreage, were planted in cotton—and the more farmers planted and produced, the lower the market price. While there were major efforts to encourage more planting of corn and wheat, farmers were stubbornly resistant to change and thus much less self-sufficient. Constantly cursing the evils of the middleman, Texas farmers knew nothing about supply and demand and failed to recognize or understand the dynamics of market pricing associated with overproduction, with one Texas farmer claiming he could "make more money out of cotton at five cents [per pound] than out of corn at fifty cents." Rising land prices, the crops lien system, discriminatory freight charges, and volatile, unregulated international cotton markets left the small farmers little room for sustained profits.[4]

For all their bluster, neither the always-opinionated Grange leadership nor the Farmers' Alliance provided any sustainable economic relief or guidance for the constantly embattled farmer and rancher. The prime publication of the farm movement in the 1890s, the *Southern Mercury*, began to lose circulation and readers. The incremental reforms obtained by the Hogg-Democrats, such as the Texas Railroad Commission (upheld by the US Supreme Court in 1894), antitrust and monopoly laws, and insurance reforms, did little for the small farmer to combat the rising cost of supplies, inflated land values, taxes, and dropping market prices. White Southern leaders like Henry Grady, owner of the *Atlanta Constitution*—which had the largest circulation of any weekly newspaper in the United States—spoke eloquently of "The New South" but were hard pressed to match their rhetoric with solid results (Booker T. Washington biographer Louis R. Harlan called Grady the "leading myth maker"). Like the earlier prohibitionists, the Populist Party, Texas Republicans, and "Gold" Democrats hoped to take advantage of the deteriorating economic and farm conditions to gain a foothold in state politics by promising reform and change, but they offered no solid means to assist the farmers other than more promises of underfunded government assistance and higher taxes. A keen observer of trends across the South, Edward Blackshear concluded his keynote speech at the National Educational Association convention in Charleston with a call for a future of progress, stating, "In the spirit of Christian forbearance let the black man lay aside every vestige of race . . . [and] make ourselves useful factors in the state and nation's citizenship in the developing, not of a New South, but of a New Nation."[5]

While Hogg has been touted as a harbinger of change in the Progressive movement, his record is mixed when it comes to African Americans and education. While he supported a home for disabled veterans and extended the public-school term from four to six months, he did little to direct additional funding to either rural black or white schools to help pay for the extended school term, teachers, and facilities. While he supported penal reform and increased the number of black Texans who received pardons, he curiously, in spite of being supported by the black community in his last election, signed a Jim Crow law forcing the railroads to supply separate facilities for blacks and whites. Railroads generally did not like the "separate but equal" laws because they added extra cost to operations and placed railroad employees in the position of being expected to enforce laws over which they had no jurisdiction or authority. Undeterred by local segregation policies, Blackshear surprised many with the announcement in March 1896 that he was chairing a committee to open a black YMCA in downtown Austin. The interest in the Y began in 1892 when Blackshear and some friends organized an athletic club known as the Peter Jackson Club in honor of Peter Jackson (known as the Black Prince), a heavyweight boxing champion in both Australia and Britain. Austin Y committee members T. H. Love, L. J. Jordan, Tom White, and L. M. Mitchell were in contact with the national headquarters to make arrangements and had to counter slanderous local rumors and opposition that the Y group only wanted a private social club and "wine room." Notwithstanding, Blackshear had very good working relationships with Austin politicians and the governor's office, as he and the state prepared for the next governor, and he continued to champion the cause for higher education and the black university in the legislature.[6]

Changing of the Guard

Texans and educators statewide were surprised in 1896 with the announcement that L. C. Anderson, the Prairie View principal for over a decade, had been fired by the A&M board. His termination was preceded by reports of a verbal confrontation at the July A&M board meeting, held on the Prairie View campus, between Anderson and board member David A. Paulus of Hallettsville, Texas, who apparently made a derogatory remark about justice and equal rights for African Americans. Heated words were exchanged between the two men, and Anderson was fired on the spot. Anderson had a solid performance record at Prairie View and was a rising leader in the Texas education ranks, which caused the *Galveston Daily News*, the leading newspaper in the state, to conclude, "It is demoralizing to our free [public] institution and discouraging to true merit and manly courage when they are pushed aside for political preference."[7]

The dismissal of L. C. Anderson ran deeper than the heated dust-up at the A&M board meeting. The firing to many looked overtly political—and it was. Anderson had worked closely for years with vocal Republican leader Norris Cuney to throw his political support to the CTSA in an effort to defeat the white-dominated Democrats. Anderson's firing reflected the reality that educators employed by the state had to exercise caution with political affiliations. His fate was part of a pattern across the South. While Cuney might have been a voice in Republican circles at the national party level, after 1895 his political power in Texas waned due to three key factors: the exodus of a large portion of the Lily-White portion of the Republican Party, Cuney's deteriorating health and inability to be active, and the rise of third parties to dilute the opposition votes as well as bleed off Republican support. The result was that James Newcomb, publisher of *The White Republican* newspaper, emerged as the titular leader of the Lily-White opposition, who expressed a desire to protect black civil rights yet with no tangible action.

The Texas Republican Party during the "last quarter of the Nineteenth Century," writes Alwyn Barr, "resembled an iceberg in a Democratic ocean, continuously in existence, [but] often in turmoil beneath the surface."[8] The friction between black and white Republicans was further impacted by bitter infighting over the role of African Americans in the party and bickering over who controlled nominations for federal patronage. Thus Republican strategists surmised that the education issues could bolster their slumping influence. Cuney agreed and launched an extensive propaganda campaign statewide, in the press and with pamphlets and speeches. Highlighting what they deemed their right to economic, social, and political opportunities, the black Republicans concentrated on a message focused on the "inequalities of Negros [*sic*] in Texas." One primary plank of their agenda was the demand for the realization of the separate but equal black university set forth in the state constitution. These vocal political activities resulted in raising concern among Democrats in Austin.[9]

The challenge to the separate but equal laws appearing in states across the South in the late 1880s began in New Orleans in 1892 with a case to challenge the Louisiana Separate Car Act (1890). While *Plessy v. Ferguson* dealt with railroad car seating issues, a seldom-stated nuance is that the majority opinion (7–2) by the US Supreme Court in March 1896 placed education standards and laws front and center. Written by Justice Henry B. Brown, the conclusion relied on precedents in numerous state court decisions that affirmed the constitutionality of laws establishing the separate but equal doctrine and facilities in public schools for white and black children. Education—and those who had the support of the majority to determine how it was provided to all citizens—remained a perpetual political issue. The argument went that since the commingling of children did not (or should not) exist in public schools, it also could not exist in public transportation conveyances. Thus, *Plessy* was initially used to deny African Americans the public education opportunities available to white Americans. The most vocal dissenting vote was by Justice Louis Harlan, who argued that "our Constitution is color-blind and neither knows nor tolerates classes among citizens." Notwithstanding, the decision served as the controlling judicial precedent until it was overturned in *Brown v. Board of Education of Topeka* (1954).[10]

In the meantime, undeterred by events in Washington, DC, former governor Ross was in good standing with the black community for supporting equal access to education. Ross countered the "Cuney Gang" with good news on the improvements in the black school systems across the state as well as key social services to serve the indigent. Improvements in education had been difficult and not at the speed most wanted, but the lag in results impacted both black and white students. Emboldened, the CTSA explored options to move the organization's headquarters from the Prairie View campus to Palestine, Texas—a somewhat strange location to consider, deep in the heart of staunch white Democratic control. The Palestine relocation never materialized and the organization moved most of its meetings to Galveston, the home of Norris Cuney. Anderson's extensive role with the CTSA and his ongoing close relationship with the Cuney Republicans during the 1895–96 election season was the primary reason for his termination.[11]

W. R. Woodruff was elected principal pro tem at Prairie View by the Texas A&M board in June 1896, until a new principal could be named at the next board meeting, scheduled for July 1.

The Hounds and the Hares

The mild-mannered and astute Anderson had made tremendous strides at Prairie View given the resources and challenges he and the fledgling college faced. While active in the Colored Teachers State Association, he was ever mindful of the aggressive campaign to establish a black university—without doing harm to his college. In early July 1896 Anderson was selected principal of the Austin city schools, the position Blackshear previously held. The firing of the overtly Republican Anderson was further questioned by many when he was replaced by his good friend, educator, and Democrat, Edward L. Blackshear, effective September 1, 1896. Still irritated by the firing of L. C. Anderson, a *Galveston Daily News* editorial questioned whether Blackshear had the “broadmindedness, the executive ability and the disciplinary power” needed to succeed at Prairie View. Following a joint meeting of the A&M College board and the Board of Regents of the University of Texas at College Station to review a unified approach to higher education funding, Blackshear, with the approval of Governor Hogg, was confirmed the fourth principal and chief administrator by the A&M board.[12]

Given the crosscurrents of Texas politics and the high expectations of Principal Blackshear, Woolfolk, who considered the new principal “a strong man with a silver tongue,” wrote, “Caught within the swirling currents of disagreements about the aims and ends of education for Negroes in the South and Texas and doubted by a vocal segment of his Negro public, this principal of Prairie View perhaps faced a greater challenge than that confronting any of his predecessors.”[13]

President Ross had maintained a good working relationship with principals Anderson and Blackshear since arriving at the A&M College in early 1891, as well as encouraging the A&M Board of Directors to take a more active role in the Waller County college. Ross was in routine contact with John D. McCall, Texas comptroller of public accounts in Austin, to release funding (not connected with the PUF) for improvements and operations of both campuses. A request of $25,000 was made by Prairie View for “maintenance and support” as well as funding for a new mess hall. Water quality, a perpetual problem, was resolved with the sinking of an artesian well and raised standpipe (water tank), and they improved electrical service. Concerned with the progress and facilities at the Prairie View campus, President Ross and A&M board member W. R. Cavitt made numerous trips to campus.[14]

The new principal had a high profile in education and political circles both in Texas and across the South. Proof of this is the planning he made for his “inauguration” at Prairie View on June 4, 1897. For the event Blackshear shrewdly invited Booker T. Washington of Tuskegee College, one of the leading education advocates for blacks and whites in the nation. With the death of African American leader Frederick Douglass in February 1895, Washington became the new national leader and spokesmen of the race (with Du Bois, at twenty-seven years of age, yet a rising voice). Washington’s appearance at Prairie View attracted the hearty endorsement by the A&M Board of Directors and Texas House Speaker L. Travis Dashiell, as well as local and state elected officials and key business leaders from across the state. The stage party for the commencement was a who's who from across the state: A. J. Rose, House Speaker Dashiell, W. R. Cavitt, J. B. Long, R. L. Smith, Sam J. Jenkins, N. W. Cuney, L. C. Anderson, and G. W. Bowman. Washington's national acclaim was high following his keynote speech at Atlanta's Cotton States and International Exposition in the fall of 1895, called the "Atlanta Compromise" by the *Atlanta Constitution.*[15] Blackshear, while still in Austin; L. C. Anderson of Prairie View; and political operative N. W. Cuney were appointed as delegates from Texas by Governor Culberson to attend the exposition. Washington's presentation gained instantaneous recognition and influence with his gospel of mutual progress and industrial education. Black economic and educational progress was further enhanced by the distribution of the patronage of Northern philanthropists across the South. Washington was clear in his view of the future of black education:

> Our greatest danger is that in the great leap from slavery to freedom we may overlook the fact that the masses of us are to live by the production of our hands, and fail to keep in mind that we shall prosper in proportion as we learn to dignify and glorify common occupations of life. No race can prosper till it learns that there is as much dignity in tilling a field as in writing a poem.
>
> People tell me that the young colored man is cramped, and after he gets his education there are few chances for him to use it. I have little patience with such argument[s]. Heretofore we have had too much of the idea that an educated colored man must either teach, preach, be a clerk or follow a profession. Our educated men more and more, must go to the farms and into the trades. They must apply their education to conquer the forces of nature. Education within itself is nothing except as it is used in a way to produce something.
>
> We must bring our education down to the plain, practical, hard every day facts. As a race we are very emotional. We are inclined to spend more of our time preparing to live in heaven than on earth. We like to talk about living in the white mansions in the upper world, and at the same time live in one-room log cabins here. We like to preach about wearing golden slippers and long white robes in the other world, and go barefooted and nearly naked in this world. We like to sing about living on milk and honey in the next world, and eat cornbread and peas

> here. I believe that living right in this world is the best preparation for a happy life in heaven.
>
> At the Tuskegee Institution we are not saying that the education in the classics, of ministers, lawyers and doctors is not necessary and important, but we are saying with every atom of our being that since 90 per cent of the black race depends at present on the common occupations, and that since 85 per cent depend on agriculture for a living, it is of the utmost importance that we supply them as fast as possible with educated leaders with the highest training in agriculture and the mechanical arts. With us, as a race, this is a question of growth or decay, life or death.[16]

Washington's appearance at Prairie View was a public relations coup for Blackshear that resulted in tremendous publicity for the college. When asked what the effect of Professor Washington's visit was, Blackshear was candid with the reporter: "It was to deepen the interest of all who heard this remarkable man in the matter of industrial education. All who heard him felt that the negroes must learn to be intelligent, skillful and reliable laborers or [be] doomed to extinction or serfdom. There is no room in America for an idle, ignorant class." Thus began a tradition of bringing leading civic, education, professional, and political leaders to the Prairie View campus to address students on the key issues of the day. By the fall of 1897, both Prof. H. T. Kealing of the *AME Review* and Bishop Abram Grant had made presentations to the students and staff. Woolfolk was a bit more shrewd about the new principal's debut: "Blackshear knew that both political parties in the state were searching heaven and earth to find a solution to the persistent demand of the Negroes for the University promised them, and Blackshear would not have been a typical principal of Prairie View had he not attempted the maneuver of running with the hounds and the hares on this issue with the hope of turning the situation into progress for his little pastoral hybrid Normal College."[17]

As the chairman of the university committee of the Colored Teachers State Association, Blackshear continued the campaign for the university by actively producing press releases—called "circulars" in that era—as well as encouraging political and public participation from across the state. While principal of Prairie View and with the full knowledge and support of both A&M College president Ross and A&M board liaison William

Cavitt, Blackshear urged all interested parties to contact their elected officials and come forward to endorse the call for the new institution. Cavitt's experience supporting Prairie View dated from his term as a Texas state representative from Bryan in 1884–85, and he proved valuable in advising Blackshear, who pledged: "We want to be brought into fruitful contact with the best thought of the age that we may develop the best possible type of individual and social life and become a really helpful element in American society." Such political actions and public appearances by a state employee, especially a black employee, were unusual.[18]

Blackshear and Ross had known each other while Sul Ross was a state senator and governor during the 1880s, and the two may have first met earlier in Waco. Blackshear was a member of an African American group of leaders who routinely met with the governor on issues of concern to black Texans—education, prison reform, judicial concerns, indigent care, and curbing violence. Some of these men were appointed to key state positions when the governor added new special service agencies for indigent blacks, poor whites, and veterans. A&M board member David A. Paulus of Hallettsville apparently took an active role in encouraging the appointment of Robert L. Smith, founder of the Farmers' Improvement Society (FIS), who was reportedly opposed by several directors on the "ground that he is a politician."[19] And while there is some indication that Texas commissioner of agriculture (and former A&M board chairman) A. J. Rose weighed in on the final selection, there is little doubt that Sul Ross was directly involved with nominating Edward Blackshear as the new principal (with the endorsement of Col. Edward House). These men had discussed educational issues for nearly a decade. Both as governor of Texas and as A&M president, Ross encouraged the fight to secure funding for a black university. Major Rose and William Cavitt supported the efforts of the normal college. Sul Ross hosted Blackshear and educators as well as African American church leaders, very crucial advocates for all levels of education, numerous times at his home on the A&M campus to discuss means to advance opportunities for black education. Ross further recommended that Prairie View strongly consider the active formation of an alumni and former students association.[20] Principal Blackshear was clear in his appreciation for the leadership of Sul Ross: "Prairie View is a branch of the A&M College of Texas, he [Ross] is also [president and] treasurer of both institutions. It affords me pleasure here in the home of General Ross [Waco] to testify to the nobility of his character and to his genuine interest

SUL ROSS

A hero's a gone' We are wrapped in gloom,
sadness fills the soul,
O'er all our lovely commonwealth,
bells of sorrow toll.

They mourn the loss of a soldier true,
Who never knew to fear.
Who loved his State with devotion rare,
Holding life not dear.

By Academus' shady groves,
He shapes the future State,
Leading the Youth to nobler things,
Teaching to be great.

Source: E. L. Blackshear, *Houston Post*, January 9, 1898

in the education not only of the white youth but of the colored youth as well. Governor Ross recently paid a visit to Prairie View, and in a short talk to the young men, fraught [with] wisdom, urged them to cultivate true manhood and to prepare themselves for the high duties of citizenship. The negroes of Texas have never forgotten him as the founder of the colored deaf, dumb and blind institute at Austin, nor have forgotten that he first in a message urged the establishment for negroes of a branch university or college as provided for in the state constitution."[21]

Within months of Blackshear's comments, President Ross died suddenly in early January 1898 of congestive heart failure after a cold and wet hunting trip on the Navasota River bottoms south of the campus, due to complications from pneumonia, at the age of fifty-nine. Thousands gathered at his funeral in Waco, including African American leaders from across the state. The passing of Ross was the loss of one of the leading pioneers of the Texas frontier. Blackshear was moved to pen a poem and eulogy to his close friend and colleague, "SUL ROSS," as was traditional in those days,

TABLE 3.1. Texas A&M Presidents, 1891–1925

Lawrence Sullivan Ross*	President	January 1891–January 1898
Roger H. Whitlock, ME*	Acting President	January 1898–July 1898
Lafayette Lumpkin Foster*	President	July 1898–December 1901
Roger H. Whitlock, ME*	Acting President	December 1901–July 1902
David Franklin Houston, LLD*	President	July 1902–September 1905
Henry Hill Harrington*	President	September 1905–August 1908
Robert Teague Milner*	President	September 1908–October 1913
Charles Puryear, LLD*	Acting President	September 1913–August 1914
William Bennett Bizzell, PhD*	President	August 1914–September 1925

*President of Texas A&M during the term of Edward Blackshear (1896–1914)

to herald the strong personality and astute leadership of the man known by all Texans as simply "Sul."[22]

The remarkable length of Edward Blackshear's tenure at Prairie View, beginning in 1896, can be gauged by the fact that no Texas A&M president, with the exception of Thomas Walton (1925–43), came even near his years of service to higher education as a head administrator of Prairie View. While A&M presidents came and went, Blackshear established substantial, longer-term relationships with the staff of the college and key A&M board members. Engineering professor D. W. Spence, as well as board members William Cavitt, J. Allen Kyle, and L. L. McInnis, were regular visitors to the Prairie View campus, providing several continuous years of oversight and assistance with administrative needs and legislative interface, as well as repairs and construction of new facilities, additional water wells, and electrical service on campus.

Colored Teachers State Association

The crusade during the late 1890s for improved educational opportunities for black Texans in general and the quest for the black university in particular remained a pivotal challenge for Edward Blackshear as he expanded his role and leadership in the growing Colored Teachers State Association. His advocacy continued to be voiced in his numerous articles, presentations to the CTSA, and in official reports submitted from his institution and the A&M College. Blackshear's primary objective remained "the improvement of the teaching profession and the offering of an opportunity for higher education for those desiring it until the State deemed it necessary and practicable to establish a branch of the University for negroes ordained by the State Constitution." To further encourage his efforts to enhance the programs at the college, Blackshear extended an invitation to Pres. George T. Winston of the University of Texas in March 1898 to make a day-long series of presentations on campus. This was a bold move for both campus leaders given the Jim Crow sentiments of most of the Democratic leaders. The *Southwestern Christian Advocate* noted with caution that the "pleasure of anticipation was not wholly unmixed" given tension with Austin, but that the Texas president, stressing that the destiny of the race was to make the most of present opportunities, was very well received and welcomed by all.[23]

Blackshear realized that, in spite of his efforts to remain professional and above the political fray, political implications dominated the public debate in Austin, as he had long known. The CTSA gave him and other supporters of black education a broader representation, yet Blackshear remained the primary messenger for change and improvement. Leadership in the African American community extended to Prof. H. T. Kealing, editor of the *AME Review*. Kealing was a direct link to black churches across Texas, and he made two keynote addresses at Prairie View in 1898 and 1899 on the high calling of education as "The Way Out." By 1899–1900, following the death of Norris Cuney in 1897, black educators in Texas were divided on the desired location and structure of the black university. Brenham educator and active CTSA committee member H. M. Tarver made remarks concluding that the focus of a first-class university be placed on an expanded Prairie View. At this point Blackshear shifted his quest, and with additional endorsements from the black community and from this point forward, he focused on Prairie View only.[24] Following the private counsel of Colonel House, this course of action was clearly more politically expedient. Correspondingly, the leaders of the CTSA shifted the organization's mission to reduce its militant approach to higher education and the Texas legislature and instead focused on producing high-quality, certified teachers. From this day forward candidates for elective office were prohibited from making presentations at CTSA gatherings. Notwithstanding, the debate over curriculum—classical or industrial—continued among educators. In the middle of the debate, W. E. B. Du Bois published an article in the *Texas School Journal*, "The Two Sorts of Schooling," that further fueled the quarrel:

> With two different and yet closely allied aims—classical vs. industrial—the attitude of the college and industrial schools toward each other should be that of cordial cooperation. Let us then bend actively and courageously to the burden, helping in every needed enterprise with broad charity and quick cooperation; remember that in this problem the aim of all men, black and white, is one—uplifting of the negro people to their highest capabilities, and if these capabilities are what most of us so firmly believe, we can work the more joyously,

TABLE 3.2. State of Texas Budget and Appropriations, 1898–1899

	1898	1899
Executive office and mansion	22,806	19,707
Department of State	10,410	10,210
Comptroller's office	67,280	65,780
Treasury Department	24,010	24,010
General Land Office	65,070	65,070
Attorney General's Office	15,110	5,110
Court of Criminal Appeals	21,260	21,260
Supreme Court	21,290	21,290
Department of Education	20,010	19,510
Railroad Commission	27,290	27,290
Department of Agriculture	19,710	19,710
University of Texas and medical branch	**426,049.96**	**97,984.96**
Court of Civil Appeals – First District	14,000	14,000
Court of Civil Appeals – Second District	13,710	13,710
Court of Civil Appeals – Third District	14,270	13,790
Court of Civil Appeals – Fourth District	13,480	13,480
Court of Civil Appeals – Fifth District	13,500	13,310
Judiciary Department	686,000	686,000
Pensions	58,950	58,950
Public debt	224,420.20	224,420.20

"Knowing this, that never yet
Share of Truth was vainly set
In the world's wide fallow."[25]

This was followed with the timely recognition of Washington and Du Bois as two of "American's greatest Negroes" in Blackshear's article entitled "What Is the Negro Teacher Doing in the Matter of Uplifting his Race?" The *Houston Daily Post* extolled the progress of education, influenced by Washington, "to settle the negro question in their respective localities until the negro question there exists on paper only." Finally, in this brief, insightful, and thoughtful memoir, Blackshear reflected on the importance of his grandmother and mother on his early education. He heralded the teaching profession as "a labor of love."[26]

TABLE 3.2. (*continued*)

	1898	1899
Relief of liquor dealers	10,000	10,000
State orphan asylum	48,270	29,270
State lunatic asylum	233,485	121,285
Southwestern insane asylum	234,000	110,040
North Texas insane asylum	172,160	63,160
Blind asylum	44,197	40,447
Deaf and dumb asylum	69,790	57,200
House of corrections and reformatory	33,340	33,340
Confederate House	56,393	48,230
Quarantine Department	33,000	33,000
Deaf, dumb, and blind asylum (colored)	52,910	17,910
Sam Houston Normal Institute	29,500	29,500
State penitentiaries	71,000	71,000
Agricultural and Mechanical College	138,000	30,500
Prairie View Normal School	**39,550**	**39,550**
Adjutant General's Department	55,470	55,370
Public printing	42,950	33,950
Public buildings and grounds	29,660	22,400
Totals	$3,129,394.11	$2,280,744.16

Source: Texas State Library and Archives Commission.

The inequality of "equal" higher education in Texas is clearly demonstrated in the level of appropriations from the state legislature in the late 1890s. It was very apparent to Blackshear and the dedicated advocates that the black university would not be reality once they saw the 1898–99 state budget. The majority of funding for higher education in Texas was directed to the University of Texas. The dominant white Democrat control over the legislature had absolutely no intention of funding a new university. The total allocation in 1898–99 for the University of Texas, $524,034.92, was nearly double the combined amount appropriated for Texas A&M, Prairie View, and Sam Houston—with Prairie View at $79,100 (see table 3.2).

Milestone

The year 1900 was viewed by Professor Blackshear as not just a turning point for the new century but also a major period of transition for Prairie View. He looked forward to championing the college's emergence from a simple pastoral normal school in the closing days of the 1890s to higher diversification and a growing status as a model of "Texas and Southern Negro higher education." While not formally lobbying in Austin, Blackshear continued to communicate with a wide cross section of friends and elected officials to encourage the support of the fledgling college. One key event that attracted attention was the annual graduation ceremony, and every effort was made to have the highest officials in the state as well as A&M College board members in attendance. Leading the Austin delegation to the June 1900 commencement was Gov. Joseph Sayers, twice severely wounded during the Civil War and one-term lieutenant governor under Oran Roberts. Sayers had been a school teacher in Bastrop, Texas, before becoming a lawyer. He served in Congress starting in 1884 until he stood for governor and was endorsed by Blackshear. The governor's remarks centered around the devastating 1899 Brazos River flood, which gained national media coverage and killed and displaced thousands of African Americans in the river bottom lands, and the recovery events that followed.[27] The depth of the disaster and the request for immediate assistance was made known in Washington, DC, by Blackshear's friend and ally John. N. Johnson.[28] Given the focus on the flood, little was said by Sayers about the growing movement to create a black university other than his strong view that the public land reserves of Texas should be saved for homesteaders and the support of schools. The most interesting remarks, which surely received the attention of the diverse audience, filled with politicians and leaders from across the state, were those fearless and prophetic words by Principal Blackshear recorded in the *Williamson County Sun* under the heading, "A Remarkable Speech":

> The audience may not agree with me, but I predict that there shall yet be erected in the rotunda of the National Capitol three statues. All three will be majestic and of historic proportions. In the center, towering over the others, being the fullest embodiment of American citizenship, will stand the statue of Lincoln, the great emancipator and apostle of liberty, humanity and national unity. To the right will stand the statue of Jefferson Davis, purest of statesmen and the incarnation of principles in social and political life which did not perish when Lee surrendered, but whose truth and potency become more evident year by year. To the left will stand the statue of Frederick Douglass for his freedom and eloquence. These statues shall be erected and shall stand as typical of the union of the three great elements of American citizenship—the North, the South, and the Negro. With these elements, distinct, yet indissolubly joined together, America will move forward in her leadership toward the higher civilization.[29]

In June 2013, the statue of Frederick Douglass was added to the rotunda of the national Capitol, next to those of Abraham Lincoln and Jefferson Davis.

—⁂—

The fall of 1900 marked a major milestone as the school (renamed Prairie View State Normal and Industrial College) prepared for its twentieth academic session to open on September 5 and for administrative leadership changes. The state legislature authorized the A&M College board to approve a four-year college program at Prairie View. Optimism for continued growth was high following a visit to Prairie View by Texas A&M board chairman Frank A. Reichardt, newly inaugurated A&M president L. L. Foster, and Gov. Joseph D. Sayers. The selection of Foster had been strongly recommended by Colonel House, based on his prior position as Texas agriculture commissioner and his work with the A&M board. While House strongly felt the practice of making key appointments for political reasons at universities was ill-advised and even "reprehensible," he overlooked the fact that Foster had been the nominal manager of Sayers's campaign for governor.[30]

Governor Sayers declared that the enrollment at Prairie View (which stood at about two hundred) should be brought up to one thousand students (more than twice the number enrolled at Texas A&M), and thus "made fully worthy of its mission as a part of the grand public educational scheme of Texas." Tuition and expenses for nine months, not including clothing, was one hundred dollars, payable in three installments. Growth of the student body brought expansion of the mess hall, dormitories, and class facilities as well as a campus ice plant. An acetylene gas plant was completed to provide additional lighting for the dorms and academic hall. A&M College campus architect Frederick E. Giesecke and superintendent of construction Henry Rollins, working with a facilities budget of $11,000, supervised the design and construction of all new campus buildings. Blackshear noted, "This is the finest dormitory for colored boys ever built in the South and an additional evidence of the impartiality of the state administration and its interest in negro education. The dorm was furnished by President Foster of the A. and M. College, and is incidentally the same quality of furniture selected with equal care at A&M."[31]

The faculty and staff by 1900 reflected the leading purpose of the college—to train teachers—but as Bishop A. Grant, a visiting lecturer, observed, "Year by year industrial features have been added to meet the growing sentiments of the times." While Principal Blackshear was firmly focused on training teachers and the Tuskegee model developed by Booker T. Washington, W. E. B. Du Bois submitted his conciliatory ideas on the merits of a "hybrid" education to the *Texas School Journal*. The way forward was very challenging, as noted by Nathan M. Sorber in his book *Land-Grant Colleges and Popular Revolt*: "Land-grant colleges needed to maintain curricula, campus life, and academic standards that appealed to the ambitions of burgeoning numbers of high school graduates without alienating farmers and rural communities who wielded considerable influence on state appropriations."

However, the surprise of the fall session in 1900 was the high storm winds that hit the campus following the landfall of a massive hurricane on the Gulf of Mexico on September 8, which devastated Galveston and killed over six thousand residents in the city, in addition to hundreds more further inland. Some ninety miles north from the coast, a number of roofs at the college were badly damaged. President Foster took personal charge to ensure that the repairs to the Prairie View campus, totaling over $3,500, were completed. Later that fall, in a short talk in the chapel on the

TABLE 3.3. Prairie View Faculty and Staff, 1900

E. L. Blackshear	Principal
W. B. Woodruff	Assistant Principal and Professor of Agriculture
C. W. Luckie	Professor of Latin and English
M. H. Bryier	Professor of Mathematics
E. H. Holmes	Professor of Mechanical Industry
J. E. Gunn	Professor of Science
H. M. Tarver	Professor of History
Harriet F. Kimler	Preceptress
Hattie E. Lee	Librarian
R. L. Isaacs	Monitor and Assistant Teacher
W. C. Rollins	Secretary
H. C. Aldridge	Steward
Callie Willis	Sewing Teacher
A. D. Ewell	Foreman of Laundry
A. E. Fiewellyn	Teacher of Blacksmithing
J. J. Burnett	Assistant in Mechanical Department
R. H. Hines	Foreman of Farm
R. F. Johnson	Tutor in Shoe Shop
Luella Craig	Music Department

Source: "The Prairie View Normal," *Houston Post*, September 1, 1900; "Midnight's Musings," *Afro-American Ledger* (Baltimore), October 15, 1904. The 1900 US census for Waller County listed Edward Blackshear (37) as principal, along with wife Rachel (33), son William (8), and daughters Eddie (6) and Rose (1), along with one boarder, Rosa Wyatt (16).

opportunities awaiting the students, Foster declared, "The colored race is at a critical period. It is on trial, and its future depends very much on the way the individuals which make up the race improve present opportunities. You are fortunate in being born in the United States. How much better your opportunities than if your lot was cast with less favored people." The *Austin Daily Statesman* noted, "The remarks were very impressive and the students seemed to appreciate fully the earnest import of them."[32]

The Galveston hurricane created a tremendous amount of news coverage across the state and the nation, and even around the world. Coverage included articles on both the damage at Prairie View and the highlights of the progress the college was making. Given the additional programs and need for larger facilities to expand the enrollment, black Texans launched a petition drive prior to the twenty-seventh legislative session in February 1901 to earmark increased funding for Blackshear's new proposed programs. It is not clear who organized the statewide appropriations request campaign (or whether it was approved by President Foster and the A&M Board of Directors), but there were three specific requests: $12,500 for a new Mechanical and Agricultural Industry building; $2,500 for a building for "female industries"; and $2,500 for the next two years to "formally" establish a college department and inaugurate a "college course of classical and scientific studies." Always looking toward the future, the following proviso was added: "Said appropriation to receive such additional appropriation by successive legislatures as the growth of such college department shall warrant." These efforts were endorsed and promoted by the Prairie View Alumni Association.[33]

Surely at the request of Blackshear, his Tabor College classmate H. T. Kealing was a key voice in focusing attention on the significance of Prairie View to the citizens of Texas. In part, Kealing wrote a feature article in the *Houston Daily Post*: "No one can contemplate the far cry from the Prairie View of twenty years ago, when the very question of continued existence was debated, and the magnificent institution of today, broad in curriculum, thorough in instruction, and expanding into an ever-widening usefulness, without seeing in this growth the fostering care of a broad statesmanship in the State government from without, and faithful, firm and efficient administration on the part of the principal and faculty within."[34]

Whistle Stop: Presidential Visit

The first visit by a sitting US president to any college or university in the state of Texas occurred at Prairie View Normal with the arrival of Pres. William McKinley on May 3, 1901. When Blackshear learned of the recently reelected president's Southern victory tour in early 1901, he wrote Texas representative Sheppard requesting he extend an invitation to visit the institution, as well as sending a letter to the president's private secretary on March 7, 1901, encouraging the White House to consider a stop at Prairie View. Blackshear quickly made his intentions public with an appeal in the *Houston Post*: "I wish to suggest that in case the President McKinley visits

Prairie View students in May 1901 greeting President William McKinley at the first presidential visit and stop at a Texas college or university. Courtesy of Cushing Archives, Texas A&M University.

Texas, it would be well to have him make a stop at Prairie View College to the end that he might see what Texas, the foremost Southern State, is doing for negro education." A third letter, from the female students at Prairie View, was sent to the president's wife, Ida, appealing to her to encourage the visit to the campus, noting, "Striving as we do and as [we] must against difficulties of which the young women of your race are aware, you will be better able to sympathize with us as part of American womanhood." The letter, signed by Blackshear's wife, Rachel, was endorsed by five pages of student signatures. To follow up on these invitations, Blackshear's younger brother, Dr. William Blackshear, professor of anatomy at Howard University in Washington, DC, called on friends in the president's scheduling staff at the Old Executive Office Building next to the White House to strongly endorse a visit to Prairie View. To confirm the presidential visit, Blackshear had his friend Congressman Albert Sidney Burleson, a former cadet at the A&M College, to double-check and confirm that the stop at Prairie View had been "adopted" and officially scheduled by the White House.[35]

On a grand railroad tour across the South and Southwest to California and back to Chicago and Buffalo, the president made campaign-style "whistle stops," first in Memphis, followed by New Orleans and Houston, coupled with visits at three black institutions: Tuskegee Institute, Southern University in New Orleans, and Prairie View. Principal Blackshear and the staff at Prairie View had about a week's notice and an advance visit by the US Secret Service. To allow more Texans to see and hear the president, the Houston and Texas Central Railroad advertised a special round-trip "Presidential Excursion" rate of two dollars for the passenger train from Galveston, with a stop for events in Houston and arriving in Prairie View before the president. After extensive ceremonies in Houston, the presidential train—accompanied by Governor Sayers, a former colleague of McKinley's in the US House of Representatives in the mid-1880s, along with a number of cabinet members—arrived to a waiting crowd of over two thousand students and local citizens at the Prairie View train station at 11:10 a.m.[36]

The special platform and pavilion built for the occasion near the college railhead was surrounded by hundreds of Texans, "75 percent of them being colored," as the *Houston Daily Post* noted. The *Galveston Daily News* reporter somewhat dramatically wrote, "The exercise took place at a cross road on the open prairie. The school buildings were discernible on the horizon. Thousands of Western range horses and every kind of nondescript vehicle which had been used to bring the people formed a novel picture." The fraternal lodge members of the Knights of Pythias served as an honor guard for the president, who was a member of the association. Following the student band playing the Star-Spangled Banner, the governor introduced the president. After the warm welcome, McKinley applauded the students and staff for their tremendous accomplishments and critical role in the economy and future of the state and the nation. As the crowds pressed closer, the president welcomed the students and staff and "held a little informal reception from the rear platform of the train . . . shaking several hundred black hands." President McKinley's remarks on the contributions of African Americans at Prairie View were reprinted in newspapers nationwide, especially those papers published for the black community.[37]

President McKinley was assassinated six months into his second term of office in Buffalo, New York, at the end of his grand Western tour. Many black-owned newspapers then reprinted his last public speech to African

Americans, given at Prairie View, in his honor. In addition to his patriotic reference to black military service and contributions in bearing federal arms for the first time since 1865 in Cuba and the Philippines during the Spanish-American War,[38] President McKinley noted:

> It has given me great satisfaction to observe your advancement since the immortal proclamation of liberty was made. The opportunity for learning is a great privilege. The possession of learning is an inestimable prize, and I have been glad to note your endeavoring, to enlighten your minds and prepare yourselves for the responsibilities of citizenship under this free government of yours.
>
> What we want more than anything else, whether we be white or black, what we want is to know how to do some one thing well. If you will just learn how to do one thing that is useful better than anybody else can do that one thing, you will never be out of a job and all employment is honorable employment.
>
> Be true to right, to home, to family, true to yourself, to your country, and true to your God.[39]

President McKinley's accolades for African American service during the 1898 Spanish-American War proved bittersweet for the returning soldiers. Col. Charles Crane, commander of the 9th US Voluntary Infantry of four companies of African American troops, spoke highly of the service of the "stalwart colored men" under his command to no avail. Although black Americans hoped their military service in wartime demonstrated their patriotism and good citizenship, the white power structure in Jim Crow Texas was unimpressed with their active-duty contributions. The rigid color line they had lived daily before departing to military service had not changed, and in an environment of racial animosity there was no mood to afford any new level of equality.[40] Black newspapers across the country attacked McKinley for not publicly challenging and lambasting the Jim Crow policies of the Southern white power structure. Despite a general disdain for the president's tour in the media, his mere presence at three of the primary African American institutions of higher education received a great deal of positive publicity. Additionally, returning soldiers did have the ability to apply for government pensions and disability benefits. Looking for a show of unity in the postwar South, President McKinley ended many of his brief talks in 1901 with the following verse:

North and South, together brought,
Now own the same electric thought,
In peace a common flag salute,
And with free and unresentful rivalry,
Harvest the fields whereon they fought.[41]

The "Salad Years"

The first decade of Edward Blackshear's term as principal at Prairie View Normal was marked by a striking string of accomplishments and enhancements of the college. A growing student body and faculty, the expansion of the curriculum, and a name change, as well as the positive nationwide publicity from the visit of Pres. William McKinley, all supported Governor Sayers's compliment that the college was "in excellent condition." While active in the late 1890s in promoting the cause of a black university, Blackshear managed to avoid political entanglements that negatively impacted either him or the college. He did, however, work within the political system to promote the college and African American education in general. For example, he encouraged petitions to members of the legislature by the "undersigned colored [constituent] citizens" to draw attention to the needs of the college. The key to the governor's accolades rested largely with Blackshear's successful working relationship with the A&M Board of Directors and most especially with the A&M presidents—Sul Ross, L. L. Foster, and David F. Houston.[42]

President Ross's untimely death in early 1898 was followed by the administration of L. L. Foster, the former agriculture commissioner, who established himself as a competent and progressive president, demonstrating a true interest in the advancement of Prairie View. Foster, like Ross, worked with board member W. R. Cavitt to inquire about the possibility of expanding the College Station campus for the enrollment of women.[43] Foster's energetic approach was cut short: Following a case of pneumonia, the A&M College was stunned with Foster's sudden death, at age fifty, on December 2, 1901. Foster was the first A&M president to be buried on campus. As a sign of the positive success and strong condition of the A&M College, some two dozen prominent candidates were considered by the board to be the next A&M president. Looking to avoid a political figure, Col. Edward House recommended Sidney E. Mezes, a professor in Austin, who declined, before the A&M board hired accomplished academician

State Council of the Association of Colored Teachers in late 1880s. Top row (L–R): Professors Lewis, Jackson, Frige, and Atherton. Bottom row (L–R): unknown, L. C. Anderson, M. W. Dogan, and Edward Blackshear. Courtesy of Prairie View A&M University Archives.

David Houston, the dean of faculty of the University of Texas, at a salary of $4,000 per year. Born in North Carolina and educated at South Carolina College and Harvard, Houston came to Austin as a professor of political science in 1894. In the capital he became acquainted with the state's political leaders and was close friends with Colonel House. House recommended that Houston, a dedicated Progressive Democrat, take the A&M presidency and stay quietly involved and informed—but not publicly politically active—on national trends and the party's affairs.[44]

Houston's tenure as president was built on the success of his two predecessors and was marked by a period of growth and an enhancement of the academic programs at the College Station campus, but with less building construction. Degree programs were modified, the minimum age for admission to the college was raised to sixteen, and entrance requirements were stiffened. In addition to new engineering faculty, Houston added extensive new programs, textile machinery, and staff in agriculture. Houston also sponsored the white Farmers' Congress in 1904, the format of which was adopted a few months later by Blackshear at Prairie View. Houston worked closely with Blackshear to ensure needed funding as well as behind-the-scenes support in Austin and Washington, DC, all with the quiet and stealthy assistance of his close friend Colonel House. Especially noteworthy was the fight to eradicate the boll weevils attacking cotton crops through a coordinated program by both College Station and Prairie View agriculturalists to conduct a statewide train-tour conference. Sponsored in part by the US Department of Agriculture, the traveling exhibits and programs presented by the Texas A&M and Prairie View staff highlighted the "A&M way" of farm-extension "specialists" and farm-demonstration programs for the farmers and ranchers of Texas.[45]

Houston and his staff, as well as A&M board members, made numerous visits to the Prairie View campus to consult on new programs, facilities, and staffing. Campus operations were significantly enhanced with the installation of a telephone line from the college to Hempstead in the fall of 1901. Funding from the Hatch Act, while small, provided subsidies to the Prairie View staff that were critical in helping black farmers after the disastrous cotton crop failure in 1902–3. Historian Lawrence Rice noted, "By 1902 Prairie View occupied a rather peculiar status in the educational life of the state. It was the agricultural college, the state normal school, and the college of industrial arts, and the university for negroes." Blackshear was encouraged to expand the academic programs at Prairie View, while the college was setting the stage for robust black extension programs and cooperative demonstration work. David Houston's work with Blackshear and his familiarity with the Prairie View programs, as well as his knowledge of the Farm Improvement Society along with the Women's Barnyard Auxiliary and Colored Farmers' National Alliance, proved pivotal in future years when he became US secretary of agriculture during the Wilson administration. Interestingly, Houston, who headed the nation's agricultural policy and programs from 1913–20, while at A&M in the early 1900s often resented the "northerner's intrusion into Texas' [agricultural] affairs," fearing the USDA and cookie-cutter agency policies from Washington would undermine and compete with the A&M's extension efforts to educate Texans.[46]

Thus, the period from the inauguration of Sul Ross through the administration of Foster and ending with the resignation of Houston at A&M

on August 24, 1905 (to assume the position of president at the University of Texas), was known, in historian Henry Dethloff's words, as Texas A&M's "salad years," as "Houston's presidency marked a high point in the affairs of the college thus far." Blackshear's tenure as principal at Prairie View coincided with these years, and the gains he accomplished helped set the institution on a solid footing. The principal maintained a large part of the classical curriculum while roundly promoting the industrial-vocational program and agricultural courses. Blackshear, ever mindful of potential critiques, finessed the mixture of programs by requiring students to work on the improved four-hundred-acre campus farm or in the industrial shops a couple of hours every day. One measure of success was the high employment rate of graduates and former students, with Professor Blackshear boasting that in Houston alone Prairie View had recently placed "eight teachers in the colored schools, four railway postal clerks, one in business, one carpenter, and one blacksmith." His statewide visits to communities and citizen groups along with teachers was a pivotal means to advocate for local support of public high school programs for black students—resulting in the establishment and staffing by Prairie View graduates of over three dozen black high schools. These efforts to enhance education in Texas were confirmed by the US Bureau of Education in the first extensive report on African American education in the South, *Negro Education: A Study of the Private and Higher Schools for Colored People in the United States*, published in 1917, which concluded, "The most urgent need of the colored schools in Texas is for trained teachers . . . but the supply of new teachers now depends almost entirely upon the [graduates] from secondary [high] schools." While it takes many individuals to ensure success and growth, the achievements of this fifteen-year period were critical to the foundation years of both Texas A&M and Prairie View.[47]

Reflecting on the changes and image of Prairie View during the turn of the century, Professor Woolfolk noted, "The religious tone undergirded and typified the life of the Negro" and "say what one will, education was viewed still as another dimension of a total enterprise that would not only save a life, but a soul as well." And changes were not limited to Prairie View: Blackshear proposed and organized a statewide committee of leading educators—including L. C. Anderson, superintendent of Austin colored schools, as well as college presidents R. S. Lovinggood of Samuel Huston College (not to be confused with Sam Houston Normal Institute) and M. W. Dogan of Wiley College—to recommend to the Texas legislature that "an industrial school for negro girls in Texas" be established. While no direct action was taken in Austin, this initiative was part and parcel of Blackshear's strategy to maintain a high level of awareness for educational needs in the African American community.[48]

Freedmen's Marching Song

In addition to articles in popular magazines and newspapers and his public speeches, Blackshear remained a regular contributor to the *Texas School Journal*. The fight to secure funding for the black university had elevated him to the key voice in the African American community in Texas. Other civic activities included work with educational associations like the Colored Teachers State Association, active membership in the Second Baptist Church of Austin, and close ties with his brother Dr. J. J. Blackshear, pastor of Bethel Baptist Church in Houston. In September 1904, Principal Blackshear hosted and introduced Texas governor Samuel Lanham (1903–7) for remarks to over two thousand delegates at the Negro Baptists of America convention in Austin. Blackshear was a member of Masonic Silver Trowel Lodge No. 47, A. F. and A. M., in Houston and the Hempstead Lodge of the Grand United Order of the Odd Fellows, as well as a charter member of the Pride of Austin Lodge, Knights of Pythias. Blackshear was also routinely involved in black communal events in Houston (forty-five miles south of Prairie View but quickly accessible and connected by the H&TC railroad), especially when he could promote the programs of the college. One such major event was the annual fall festival known as DE-RO-LOC NO-TSU-OH ("Colored Houston" spelled backwards). The event was formed in response to segregation laws that prohibited African Americans from attending the established white NO-TSU-OH carnival. One day of the DE-RO-LOC event was designated "Education and Industry Day," which allowed Blackshear and other black educational leaders to promote their colleges. The festival, which added football games in West End Park, continued into the early 1920s, when it was determined the event had "outlived its days of usefulness." In addition to urban activities, Blackshear was always mindful of the role and importance of the farmer. During Blackshear's career he strode forward confidently, with one foot supported by farmers and the other braced by the growing urban populace.

He was also a very active member and leader of the "Colored Farmers' Congress," held annually either in Houston or at the Prairie View campus.[49] And he drafted the following song for the Washington, DC, edition of *The Colored American*:

THE FREEDMEN'S MARCHING SONG
by E. L. Blackshear,
to the Tune of "Battle Hymn of the Republic"

Mine eyes have seen the glory of the
freedom of the slave,
Seen him rise from shackled bondage
as one risen from the grave,
On his face the light of Liberty the
light that never fades,
Up ye Freedmen, march ye on.

As they catch the step of liberty, they
raise its chorus grand,
While their shouts of Hallelujah wake
their echoes through the land,
As they move a wonderous multitude
obedient to command,
Up ye Freedmen, march ye on.

But their march is one of danger from
the sloughs of deep despond.
Up the Hill of Difficulty to the Heights
as far beyond,
And in the Vales of Tribulation still I
hear their hopeful song
By God's help, we'll march along.

Though sorely tried and erring from
their path they sometimes stray,
As did once the Sons of Israel in
Moses' Ancient Day,
In great humiliation see them kneel
and weep and pray,
God help us as we march along.

God gives them faithful leaders,
Douglass, Langston, Washington,
Whose counsel and example guide the
struggling host along,
By and by ye'll reach Canaan fair
of Justice, Peace, Sing
Up ye Freedmen, march ye on.

Our warfare is unto Ignorance and
Poverty and Sin,
Our battle-axe is Industry, our war-cry
"Right shall win!"
On yonder glorious summits, Hymns of
victory we will sing,
Up ye Freedmen, march ye on.

Source: *Colored American* (Washington, DC), February 20, 1904

By 1904, Blackshear was the leading education advocate in the state of Texas. Growth at Prairie View continued, with an enrollment of 320 students and two dozen permanent faculty. The principal astutely stayed in contact with Austin political leaders and the A&M Board of Directors. He welcomed official visits to promote the college as well as to draw attention to the needs of the institution. In January the A&M board sent a special inspection committee chaired by W. J. Clay, ex-officio board member and Texas commissioner of agriculture, insurance, and statistics in Austin. Clay was accompanied by board members Judge K. K. Leggett, A. J. Brown, and Louis Amsler of Hempstead. Brown and Leggett were on their first visit to the college and expressed surprise at the extent of the development of the campus, comprising five substantial brick buildings and twenty-three frame buildings. During the first evening after dinner, the status and needs of the college were reviewed by Blackshear and the professors. The committee rose before sunrise and visited the dairy barn to witness the milking of Jersey and Holstein cows, followed by a presentation on methods of processing raw milk through the De Laval separator, testing the milk, and making and handling butter. This was followed by visits to the farm, mechanical shops, dormitories, classrooms, business office, and mess hall. That evening, the guests were hosted and treated to a dinner prepared by the students, as well as by songs and a special piano recital by the college music director, Mrs. Maud Cuney-McKinley. The tour and briefings were well received, with Clay presenting his findings to the A&M board. Ever mindful of media coverage, Blackshear submitted what was known as a "special," an anonymous article he penned on the success of the inspection, to the *Houston Daily Post*.[50]

Blackshear's advocacy for improved higher education for African Americans was not just for public sector institutions; he also championed the growth and advancement of private colleges. In June 1902, Tabor College conferred upon him the honorary degree of master of arts, and in 1903 Wilberforce University voted him the degree of doctor of laws in recognition of his services as a teacher. The growth of the colleges was directly impacted by the number of high school graduates qualified to enroll in college courses. The predominantly black private colleges were not viewed as competing with Prairie View but instead as a true complement in advancing higher education in Texas. To further this goal, Blackshear convened the leaders of the five private black colleges in Texas to form, along with

Prairie View, the Texas Association of Negro Colleges (TANC). Gathered in Austin on March 19, 1904, were Pres. M. W. Logan of Wiley College in Marshall; Pres. I. M. Burgan of Paul Quinn College in Waco; President Lovinggood of Samuel Huston College in Austin; Pres. Marshall R. Gaines of Tillotson College in Austin; and Professor Fuller of Bishop College, also in Marshall. By this union, Blackshear continued to build and strengthen a network of Progressive black leaders in Texas. Principal Blackshear was elected the first president of the association, along with executive members Lovinggood and Gaines.[51]

The TANC association was formed in part to formalize a statewide gathering to have an "oratorical contest on the history of negroes of Texas" and to provide training for teachers across the state. Blackshear and the staff at Prairie View took the lead role and were further charged with providing summer training for black teachers who wanted to improve their skills and obtain teaching certificates—establishing "The State School of Methods for Colored Teachers." The object of the summer school training program was to provide a "careful review of studies: to impact a scientific knowledge of methods, to awaken an interest in the history of education and in child study; to create a deeper enthusiasm for the proper education of the colored children of Texas and to produce a deeper devotion to the work of the elevation of the colored race in all the elements of American citizenship." Blackshear simultaneously served as president of the Texas Colored Teachers State Association, which had become more of a political lobbying organization, while TANC concentrated on continuing education programs and certifications. Attendance at the summer school gathering at Samuel Huston College in Austin was by invitation only and for only those teachers "who are honestly—by honorable means and merit—seeking for improvements in knowledge and methods [of teaching]." Speakers for the training sessions included H. T. Kealing, editor of the *AME Review*; L. C. Anderson, former president of Prairie View and principal of Austin High School; and college presidents Lovinggood, Logan, and Burgan. These activities would be key to Blackshear's statewide strategic efforts to foster attention on the need and financial support for more black schools and teachers, as well as enhancing his role as the lead proponent of black education in Texas.[52]

The visit of Pres. William McKinley to Prairie View in May 1901 received laudatory mention in articles for a number of years afterward. Such mentions generally accompanied an update on black education in Texas in general and Prairie View in particular. The most widely read African American publication in the country, the *Colored American*, was very complimentary, noting the college was "the Pride of the State." Continuing a legislative budget trend started by Gov. Sul Ross, Texas spent "more money for negro education than any other state," amounting to over $50,000 from annual state appropriations and the supplement received from the Morrill Act. Furthermore, the media praised the citizen services, such as the institution for the Deaf, Dumb, and Blind, which provided significant support for disabled African Americans. Prairie View was reported in 1904 to have an enrollment of 320 students and twenty-three faculty, further noting that 318 diplomas had been granted since 1885. The debate on what courses to offer continued. Booker T. Washington published what many considered a controversial article in 1903, "Industrial Education for the Negro," which contended that—while he did not object to a formal liberal arts education—the best form of education for the greatest number of black Americans in the shortest time was the type of "industrial education" offered at the Tuskegee Institute. The *Houston Post*, which was generally very supportive of Prairie View and Blackshear, published an editorial that supported Washington: "A great deal of money and energy have been wasted in the vain attempt to give the Southern negro an academic education (in many negro institutions Latin, Greek and philosophy are in the prescribed courses) instead of teaching him farming and trades that helped him."[53]

Notwithstanding, Blackshear strongly advocated college-level courses supporting industrial training specialties, including mathematics, science, language and literature, history, and mechanical drawing, as well as programs for blacksmithing, plumbing, carpentry, shoemaking, millinery, agriculture, and music. Blackshear's own agricultural expertise was reflected, for example, in his specialty articles on boll weevil eradication. Funding for Prairie View programs increased yearly, but in the Jim Crow environment funding was allocated unevenly between predominantly white and African American land-grant institutions across the South. Blackshear's increasingly vocal stand for improvements in black education resulted in attacks and rumors he had been fired or had resigned as principal at Prairie View—all unfounded. By 1905, the total 1890 Morrill Act allocation for Texas had increased to $25,000. Prairie View, with an enrollment in agriculture of 379, was allocated 25 percent of the total or $6,250,

Table 3.4. Second Morrill Act (1890) Land-Grant Funding, 1905

	White Land-Grant Institutions			Black Land-Grant Institutions		
	Allocation	Students	Per	Allocation	Students	Per
Georgia	$16,667	184	$90.58	$8,333	418	$19.94
Louisiana	$13,159	578	$22.77	$11,841	409	$28.95
Oklahoma	$22,500	555	$40.54	$2,500	363	$6.89
South Carolina	$12,500	673	$18.57	$12,500	815	$15.34
Texas	$18,750	414	$45.29	$6,250	379	$16.49
Virginia	$16,667	731	$22.80	$8,333	1,281	$6.51

Source: *Report of the Commissioner of Education*, 1905 (Government Printing Office, 1907).

which came to $16.49 per student (the average funding per student at black colleges in the South was $15.58), compared to the allocation of $45.28 per white student (slightly more than the average of $40.09 for white students in the South) at the A&M College. See table 3.4.[54]

Blackshear's increased activities with educational associations and projects in Texas resulted in more published interviews on issues facing African Americans in the South. He was routinely asked questions about the national debate on the "role of the black citizen." Questions of most interest concerned the impact of the disenfranchisement and education of "colored people," as well as specific inquiries on what schools should teach and the role of women in education and society. Blackshear did not receive as much press as Booker T. Washington and Du Bois, yet he was a major barometer on education issues and the black community in Texas. The pending Terrell poll tax issue in the state, yet another Jim Crow law, was of major concern. In a front-page feature article in the Washington, DC, *Evening Star*, Blackshear reconfirmed many of the views he had harbored for years: "A restricted suffrage with educational character and property qualifications would if—impartially, honestly and fairly enforced—inspire the rising generation of negroes to educate themselves, acquire property and become good citizens. Instead of a sober political conviction, based upon civic experience, there was only political agitation and a fanatical partisanship that destroyed the individual and social perspective, relegating intellectual, moral and economical strivings and aspirations to the background, when they should have been in the fore."[55]

Without a doubt, the "political agitation" by Sen. Alexander Terrell in Texas and other white leaders disadvantaged black Americans because of the latter group's low property ownership, the poll tax, and the white control of the Democratic primary, all of which slowly diminished the legal status of African Americans in the South. Politics increasingly promised many risks and few rewards for black Texans. Many were motivated to participate in the third-party movement for individual gains—backed by hollow promises of "equal rights to all and special privileges to none." The *AME Church Review* further weighed in, noting on occasion that the only way to make the vote of the Southern Negro valuable "was to divide it." However, a divided vote did not ensure success at the ballot box. In a 1945 interview with Populist activist William "Gooseneck Bill" McDonald, the corrupt failure of this tactic was detailed: "The leadership of the Black Populism fell to [the] disgruntled or adventures from the Republican Party and to jealous and unsuccessful men who possessed a grudge against the existing order. Most of the politicians had been unsuccessful, even in the management of their private affairs. Indeed, most of them had no business, except that of politics. The most fruitful method the populist had for securing Negro votes was to bribe them with whiskey."[56]

Populist Party champion John Rayner from Calvert, Texas, felt that the backlash from the disillusioned upstart political movement in the late 1890s "had been a tragic mistake for blacks"—a failure. The so-called Peoples Party had been mute on many critical issues facing African Americans and made little or no mention of lynching, the right to vote, blatant discrimination, the right of black Americans to be jurors, segregated public facilities, or concern with the underfunding of black schools. The widely held assumption that Populism inaugurated a new era of black-white relations is without foundation. Thus, Populism's promises of black equal rights, meaningful representation, and suffrage were not realized.[57] Senator Terrell's continued obsessive campaign to disenfranchise African Americans across the state, as well as poor whites and Mexican immigrants, had dramatic results. Texas, with the smallest percentage of black Americans compared to other Southern states, suffered a decline in the participation of qualified black voters, dropping from about one hundred thousand in the 1890s to some five thousand in 1906, primarily as a result of Democratic intimidation and the onerous Terrell poll tax. For example, in the 1900 primary in Bryan, Texas, friends of the two local mayoral candidates "made a display of force and permitted no

Negroes to vote." Thus, the white Reformers, like the white conservatives in the Democratic Party, remained loyal to white supremacy and the inequality of racial separation.[58]

The frustration and disappointed efforts of Blackshear and other black leaders to craft a united front among African Americans in Texas are reflected in a critical article by J. B. Rayner in the *Houston Daily Post*, "A Negro on the Negro": "Again some ambitious Southern Republicans are responsible for all political hallucinations and utopian dreams of worthless negroes, that this hallucinated and utopian dream has greatly hindered the negro's moral, intellectual and industrial growth. But the negro is gradually coming to his senses."[59]

As African American political power was drastically reduced at the ballot box, black leaders led by Principal Blackshear and the extension service agents stationed at Prairie View continued their efforts to organize and educate as many as possible in the "worthy occupation of farming," with the inauguration in July 1906 of the first Colored Farmers' Congress. One impetus for the organization of the congress was Blackshear's concern that a wave of Italian immigrants, whom he termed "white foreigners," arriving in the Brazos Valley "threaten[ed] to supplant the negroes in the mills and factories and in the fields." Other leaders from across the state included R. M. Jones of Minneola, E. C. Branch of Houston, W. E. King of Dallas, R. C. Chatham of Hempstead, and Jesse Washington of Marlin. Ever mindful of the agricultural underpinning of the state economy, the Colored Farmers' Congress more so than any other black organization worked to make farmers successful and competitive with practical education and the support of the community. The aim of the organization was to take action to strengthen farmers' economic foothold in their farms, with some 30.7 percent of black farmers in Texas owning their own land. The primary objective was to encourage the purchase of land to break the bonds of tenant farming and also to combat an "influx of foreigners into Texas"—Mexicans and Italians—who competed with the black farmers and drove up the price of land. The turn of the century proved to be a dynamic period, with census data indicating that between 1900 and 1910 the number of black farmers in the South increased by more than 20 percent. During the same period, the value of land operated by black Americans more than doubled.[60]

Blackshear provided the leadership and inspiration for the Farmers' Congress and outlined the importance of working with the agricultural information provided by the extension service to spread the best methods of farming, as well as organizing local farmers' informational clubs or "institutes" in each county. Frederick Hoffman, in his detailed assessment of African Americans for the American Economic Association in 1896, noted in *Race Traits and Tendencies of the American Negro* that "with less than one-half as large a colored population as Mississippi, the state of Texas produced in 1894 almost three times the cotton crop as Mississippi." The abundant production of the cotton "black belt" through central Texas was a welcome change to those who had departed depleted lands in the old South to make their future in Texas. This success also involved the critical component of understanding "better methods of doing business and marketing their products." Thus, Blackshear (along with Robert Smith) stressed the nonpolitical content of the Farmers' Congress meetings; the goal was to give the farmers a sense of purpose, confidence, and a forum for self-governance to plan programs and convey best practices back in their communities. Success in these areas would, it was hoped, discourage the migration or "influx of colored people from the country [farms] to the cities." The Colored Farmers' Congress, later rebranded as the Annual Agricultural Short Course, was held annually at Prairie View through the 1920s.[61]

Washington vs. Du Bois

The struggle over the course and makeup of African American education and social equality during the early 1900s was dominated by the debate between Booker T. Washington and W. E. B. Du Bois. The voluminous record compiled by these two men and the debate over their approach to education, politics, and equal rights both contemporarily and in subsequent scholarly works over the past century have overshadowed the topic. As an educator and one dedicated to advancing black education, Edward Blackshear and a small group of black leaders across the South studied the teachings of these two men and were faced with the challenge of how to selectively implement the best aspects and most realistic approach with what was possible, given the resources, concerns, and what best addressed the needs of the primarily rural population. Conflict with the white power structure, who were suspicious of any actions that they deemed an infringement on their social, economic, and political rights (as they saw them), was omnipresent. Washington, born a slave in rural Virginia and educated at Hampton Normal and Agricultural Institute, believed that a classical (liberal arts) education was impractical for former slaves and their descendants, and that all should be trained in an industrial "trade" or pursue an agricultural vocation. Du Bois, Harvard-educated and raised by free parents in a cloistered, urban, middle-class Massachusetts community, articulated that the most reasonable path to lift African Americans was higher education in the humanities and science. Furthermore, he preached that an elite few should be highly educated to lead the balance of the black population. Their lifelong debate on the best way forward established the tone of the so called "Negro question" during the 1890s and into the turn of the twentieth century.[62]

What is sometimes missing in discussions concerning the merits of Washington's approach versus that of Du Bois is any consideration of the assumptions underlying their respective proposals. Washington's well-crafted argument that you had to build a public school system before you could fully develop higher education made sense in many Southern states, where black schools were inadequate by any measure. Du Bois's argument that colleges offering classical education were necessary to advance African Americans made sense in states where sufficiently well-funded public schools existed to prepare students for those colleges. In addition, a fundamental and well-debated question is whether life on a farm is better or worse than life in a city. As expected, Blackshear expressed a clear opinion in numerous presentations across the state, like these comments at the Lavaca County Colored Fair in Sweet Home, Texas: "It will be a glad day for the colored people of the South when they turn their back on the uncertainties of urban life and return to the virgin soil—the farm." This was the ongoing debate from the post–Civil War period to World War II. How one answers that question bears directly on whether Du Bois's or Washington's approach is more effective. People in the twenty-first century may well answer the question differently than people would have in the early 1900s.[63]

Following the accolades Washington received with the famous "Atlanta Compromise" presentation, Du Bois in his first book, *The Souls of Black Folk* (1903), seemed perplexed by the continual focus on industrial training: "Mr. Washington's insight cannot see that no such educational system ever has rested or can rest on any other basis than that of the well-equipped college and university, and they insist that there is a demand for a few such institutions throughout the South to train the best Negro youth as teachers, professional men, and leaders." Polar opposites, historian H. W. Brands noted, "Du Bois was as different from Booker Washington as a black man in America could be, and his comparatively privileged background informed his rejection of Washington's accommodationist philosophy."[64]

In the case of black higher education in Texas, it proved difficult to have comprehensive higher education without the funding, facilities, faculty, and qualified students to advance what Du Bois articulated was the best course of achievement for African Americans: fast-forwarding their opportunities by providing a formal, classical college education. A Northern freeman by birth and Harvard-educated, Du Bois felt that the privileged education model he was exposed to could be quickly implemented in the post-Reconstruction South. These lofty ideals were commendable and critical to "rising" the African American community, yet not doable overnight. This led to his refinement of his views on education to call for the advancement of the "talented-tenth" comprised of college-educated black Americans to be prepared as soon as possible to advance and help uplift the balance of the race. Conversely, Washington advocated working for the *gradual* advancement of their race, demonstrating proven results and avoiding an open challenge to the prevailing order. One key to shaping Washington's public image, prestige, and influence was his active financial subsidization of newspapers and journals favorable to telling the self-help, economic-advancement, and industrial-educational aspects of the "Tuskegee story"—including, for example, the *New York Age*, the *Colored American* (Washington, DC), *Alexander's Magazine*, the *Colored Citizen* (Boston), and the *Washington Bee* (Washington, DC). He was not opposed to all higher education for black youth, but given the political environment and scarce resources, he felt the focus should be on industrial training. Interestingly, A&M president Thomas Gathright's 1878 plan submitted to Governor Roberts, well before Washington's activities, proposed converting the Alta Vista College into what would be Prairie View College and a normal school to prepare teachers. Prairie View principals L. W. Minor and the Anderson brothers added industrial education courses to help address the educational attainment of entering students as well as the real-world demand for skills development.[65]

Blackshear, as a result of his dozen years as a common school teacher and administrator in the black school system in Austin, realized the limitations and challenges of preparing students to enter colleges, especially given the lack of teachers to provide such education. Private, mostly denominational, colleges or "academies" in Texas were faced with the same challenges and approached the situation more as a remedial educational bridge to address the interests of their sponsors and the abilities and educational attainment of their students. In contrast, Blackshear, as well as administrators at Texas A&M, was confronted with the demands by farm groups for the public college to provide a narrow agricultural and mechanical curriculum. Blackshear's savvy ability to navigate between what was demanded and what was possible and practical is a hallmark of his success in dealing with the white power structure for the advancement of black education in Texas. While mindful of the high ideals of Du Bois to advance classical education, Blackshear crafted the programs at Prairie View Normal along the lines of Washington's objectives and the industrial education programs at Tuskegee Institute, with the eventual goal of expanding the college's mission as the number of black high schools and prepared graduates increased and resources and circumstances progressed.[66]

The Tuskegee approach was apparent from Blackshear's first days at Prairie View and highlighted by the fact that he was able to secure Washington as the keynote speaker at his investiture at the college in 1897. Advancing programs for teachers was always an objective, but providing industrial (sometimes termed "vocational") training to prepare black students for the jobs that were in demand was also necessary and seemed prudent. Furthermore, such training was becoming a prerequisite for entering a skilled occupation. Blackshear's like-minded approach to education resulted in routine contact with Washington, both by written correspondence, during his January 1903 visit to Texas, and in visits at professional meetings across the South and in Washington, DC. As an active organizer of the annual "Juneteenth" celebrations in Texas, Blackshear suggested to Washington in 1909 in an open letter in the *New York Age* that the National Negro Business League (which Washington had founded in 1900), the most influential nationwide African American organization promoting racial solidarity (predating the NAACP), lead an effort to begin preparation for national observance of a Fiftieth Anniversary Emancipation Celebration on June 19, 1913. In response to his proposal, Blackshear was appointed to the national executive committee of the league—which by 1910 had grown to over four hundred chapters in twenty-four states—at their national gathering in Louisville in October 1909.[67]

During a number of visits of Booker Washington to Texas, Blackshear was an active member of the host committee, escorting Washington from city to city. In San Antonio, greeted by a crowd of over three thousand in Beethoven Hall, the Tuskegee educator was presented with a picture of the Alamo by the Second Baptist Church, inscribed, "In the spirit of the heroes of the Alamo who thought so little of life as to die for a principle." One of the biggest receptions was held during Washington's return visit to Prairie View Normal and Industrial College. The greeting party, in addition to the students, faculty, and staff, included Bishop I. B. Scott, the only black bishop in the Methodist Episcopal Church, and R. L. Smith, president of the FIS. Over eight hundred students lined the walkways to give him a "royal welcome." With what was hailed as a remarkable demonstration of support, the students sang a college "yell" or cheer:

> What's the matter with Washington,
> He is our leader loved and true,
> He, large of heart and broad of view.
> Then Rah, Rah, Rah, Booker T,
> He is the man for me.[68]

A grand luncheon in the campus mess hall was followed by a tour and inspection of the industrial divisions of the college, culminating with a presentation by Washington to a crowd of over five thousand citizens from across Waller County, before he departed for Temple and Austin. In a follow-up letter to Washington, Blackshear wrote: "I cannot refrain from expressing a feeling of satisfaction with which all thoughtful colored people in Texas and thoughtful white people as well regard your recent visit. Its influence is unquestionably for great good among both races and all reports and comments are distinctively and positively favorable. I can see that your influence is steadily growing, gathering in momentum and in wisdom."[69]

Blackshear remained in close contact with Washington through the league and correspondence until the Tuskegee educator's death in 1915—which also proved to be a major transition period for Blackshear.[70]

·» 4 «·

Benevolent Principal

> Blackshear came to Prairie View when the dynamism loosed [*sic*] by the Southern search for a solution to bi-racial power had already begun to feel its way toward answers.
>
> GEORGE RUBLE WOOLFOLK

> Our growth and power as a people are not to be measured merely or mainly by the number who attend school and acquire some degree of literacy attainment, but they are rather to be measured by what those who have received educational advantages actually do accomplish and achieve in the struggle of life.
>
> EDWARD L. BLACKSHEAR, *GALVESTON DAILY NEWS*, FEBRUARY 9, 1903

The growth of Prairie View Normal after the turn of the century surprised and pleased supporters and confounded detractors of black education in Texas. The college was emerging from the simple concerns of a pastoral normal school to a growing college offering diverse coursework. The sheer force and diligence of Edward Blackshear transformed the small, struggling African American college into what would become by 1910 the largest black public institution of higher education in the nation. He assumed the helm of Prairie View at a time when "the South [and Texas] stood in the twilight zone between two eras." In addition to Blackshear's persistence and skill, a number of factors and individuals impacted his ability to enhance the image and growth of the college.[1]

Blackshear in 1896 inherited the foundation of a promising yet challenging job to instill confidence in and raise support for the college. One often-overlooked dynamic was the positive and continuous support he received from A&M president Sul Ross and the A&M Board of Directors. The close relationship between Ross and Blackshear dated from the early 1880s, and in the 1890s Ross was once again in a position to have a major influence on Prairie View. Ross, under the legislatively mandated organization of Prairie View as a branch of A&M, was in fact designated both president and treasurer of Prairie View. Blackshear, with the title of "principal," was the chief administrative officer in Hempstead, reporting to Ross. During the early years of the Blackshear administration, he met often with Ross and a select committee from the board to advance the interests of the school. In addition to Ross's numerous visits to Hempstead, Blackshear, along with his faculty and students, were often guests of the president both on the A&M campus and at events in Waco.[2]

Prairie Harmony

Ross was tremendously helpful; if for no other reason, he had encountered many of the same problems and challenges at A&M that Blackshear faced at Prairie View—constant need for more funding, shortage of housing for students and staff, poor water supply, no ice, demand for additional classrooms, no electrical lighting, issues of student discipline, shortage of textbooks, lack of equipment for the farm programs, and constant political pressure from Austin legislators and lobbyists as well as vocal farm groups who felt they knew more about education and what "Texas needed" than Blackshear, Ross, and the A&M board. Col. Edward House also gave behind-the-scenes strategic political advice and support, and the supportive A&M board chairmen (also known as the presidents of the board) Archibald Rose (1888–96) of Salado and Frank Reichardt (1896–99) of Houston helped influence and shape the future of the school. In addition to the hands-on approach of Ross and the board chairmen, the A&M board designated a three-man "Prairie View Committee" to have direct oversight and to ensure the needs and requests of the institution were fully considered, evaluated, and acted upon. After Ross, longtime A&M board member William R. Cavitt (1883–96) of Bryan had the most direct contact with, knowledge of the operations of, and influence at Prairie View.[3]

Within days of Blackshear's arrival at Prairie View, the newspaper "stringers" or reporters began to routinely visit the campus. Prior to 1896 Blackshear was periodically in the news in Austin, yet most of his local press were articles he himself submitted to the *Austin Statesman*. This immediately changed as he and Prairie View became regular news items. Reporters from the *Houston Post* and *Galveston Daily News* regularly rode the Houston & Texas Central Railroad between Galveston and Dallas, stopping along the way to file stories. Other papers that were active in covering Prairie View included the *Austin Statesman*, *Brenham Banner*, *Houston Post*, *Bryan Eagle*, and the *Dallas Morning News*. Stories published in those papers were picked up by other publications, not just in Texas but also in out-of-state papers. At each stop of the H&TC train, reporters could spend some time collecting stories and then catch the next train to the next town. Short news stories could be filed immediately by telegraph from the train station back to the newspaper, and if longer documents were involved—for example, city council agendas, A&M Biennial Reports, or commencement schedules—they could be hand-carried back to the newsroom for next-day publication. Blackshear, both well spoken and written, was acutely aware of the importance of the print media, as the only means of public information in the era, and became adept at keeping the college in the news. Newspapers were the only source of information and editorials in most regions of Texas and thus played a powerful role in shaping public opinion. Blackshear was very concerned with the image of Prairie View to outsiders who had not visited the campus, and he made every effort to publicize the school. During the first years it was a challenge, given the poor conditions of the campus and the small size of the student body (ninety-five) and staff (nine), to constantly direct reporters to the positive aspects of the educational programs and how they impacted the state. As time passed Blackshear became an expert in public relations and in promoting the accomplishments of the college. In spite of the rough campus conditions, Blackshear was heartened when one of the first feature *Houston Post* article headlines read: "Prairie View: The Colored Training School in Excellent Working Condition" and "Great Work for Negroes," noting, "The campus is almost devoid of shade but the constant gulf breezes, which often become strong wind, ensure a cool and pure atmosphere and the healthfulness of the place can not be excelled. The broad view from the college buildings and the wide arch of heaven bending over the dusky reaches of prairie sod and field seem in harmony with the purposes of the school and the motives of the State." A generous article for sure, given the facilities shortage, staffing challenges, poor access to water, and student turnover at the college.[4]

Transition

The efforts to establish the constitutionally mandated black university in Austin initially distracted attention from efforts of Prairie View supporters and their attempts to increase funding for Prairie View. When the vote was taken in 1882 to locate the new university in Austin, Woolfolk noted, "The A. & M. Board considered the establishment of a University for Negroes as sheer folly and waste, and recommended that all of the educational facilities for higher education of the Negroes of the State be centered at Prairie View." Yet the issue lingered on for two decades. From 1896–1900, Edward Blackshear, seemingly with the approval of presidents Ross and Foster as well as the A&M board, was, as principal of daily operations and academic affairs at Prairie View—and thus a rival of any new public institution for African Americans in Texas—the chief spokesman and advocate both in Austin and statewide of the new proposed university.[5]

By 1900, the political reality became clear that the white-controlled Democratic Party operatives, while holding hearings and giving lip-service to a possible black university, never had any intention of appropriating state funding or designating university lands for a new institution. Confronted further by the rising expectations and frustrations of his own people, Blackshear faced the responsibility of charting a course for a diverse audience. Some in the Texas State Department of Education voiced strong support in pulling control of Prairie View from the Texas A&M board and having it come under the same oversight management as the white normal school in Huntsville. Political adviser Colonel House, knowing full well that the outcome of the new university demands would not produce the expected results, advised Blackshear and supporters of Prairie View to stay positive and display to the legislature that while disappointed with its failure to create the new university, Prairie View should be funded and improved to provide a substantial institution for higher education and the training of teachers.[6]

The minutes of the A&M Board of Directors are somewhat void of information or resolutions on the impact of the new attention given Prairie

View, most likely due to the fact that any new appropriations would have to flow though A&M first. State budgets for the two campuses were developed and reported separately, and A&M was careful not to let the University of Texas or any other state agency tap into either the 1862 or 1890 Morrill Acts funding, nor the funding flowing to College Station from the Smith-Lever and Hatch Acts that supported experiment-station and extension-service programs (as well as other subsequent federal appropriations earmarked only for land-grant institutions). Henry Dethloff notes, "Perhaps because of the political uncertainties, and because of Lawrence Sullivan Ross' presence at A&M, Prairie View shared in larger legislative appropriations during the nineties, despite the [economic] depression." Texas A&M was careful not to commingle federal funds with Texas state appropriations to prevent funding from the state. The primary underlying tension for funding higher education in Texas that impacted funding for Texas A&M and Prairie View was the often-heated maneuvering by the University of Texas on the control and disbursements of the Permanent University Fund.[7]

One of the first major outward indicators that Prairie View was expecting more attention and support was the formal change of the institution's name to Prairie View State Normal and Industrial College in 1900.[8] While still referred to by most Texans as the "Normal School" or the "State Normal School for Colored Youth," the new name brought with it a new spirit and direction for Blackshear and advocates of expanded educational opportunities for African Americans. Prairie View was at a crossroads. Like Principal L. C. Anderson before him, Blackshear embraced Booker T. Washington's concepts and philosophy of industrial education. With a finely tuned ear, gained in the halls of the Texas legislature during his advocacy for the black university, Blackshear "played" political concerns and social tensions waged by the white Democratic Party power structure over the education of black Texans to the advantage of Prairie View. The industrial education programs were critical to expanding the vocational aspects of the school, yet he was concerned with the level of academic preparation of entering students to engage in college courses. Blackshear never lost sight that the paramount focus of the college was to train teachers, who in turn could go out across Texas to educate and improve the life of black Texans. Fully aware that Prairie View was a separate but unequal institution, Blackshear's goal was to upgrade the college to advance the needs and quality of life of his race, while avoiding a confrontation with the white power structure.[9]

The changes and improvements needed came through in 1901, when Blackshear received legislative approval to offer a four-year course in "classical and scientific" studies. To support the new coursework, the legislature provided $4,300 for the first two years and further enlarged the program of student scholarships from across Texas to 159 students.[10] This was a mixed blessing given the fact that the college did not have the facilities to handle an increase in enrollment. The new course of study was open to all normal students in the teachers' program without examination and to new students upon completion of entrance exams. The course of study was challenging, and few students qualified for the program. A&M board chairman Archibald Rose included a detailed assessment of Prairie View in the A&M College 1896 Biennial Report to the governor and expressed concern—for the first time publicly and on the record—that black high schools across Texas were not producing enough students who were prepared for college courses in a new university. Rose proposed that a black university could be co-located on the Prairie View campus, thus noting:

> It is hoped that the university for higher classical education of the colored youth of Texas will eventually be located at this school [Prairie View]. This can be done at comparatively little expense to the state by addition of a few buildings and teachers, and by this means the colored race could obtain both industrial and classical education. The former, all will admit, would be of untold advantage in connection with the higher education, especially to the negro race. We are informed that the negroes throughout the state are practically unanimous in favor of this university plan. We particularly invite your excellency's careful attention to this matter. We believe it would be a great saving to the state, and expedite the establishment of the colored university which has so long been asked for by the negro race, and at a point [Prairie View] that can not be excelled in all things anywhere in the state. While *there are not now and not likely to be soon a sufficient number of the negro youth in the state who are far enough advanced in their studies and who are pecuniarily able to attend to justify the early establishment of a separate university* for their benefit, yet the immediate organization of a university branch, as above suggested, *would supply the demand for a classical education for the limited number of colored students* who are now compelled to go out of state to find it.[11]

The few black students that did excel academically opted for private colleges in Texas or left the state to attend other institutions. This provided a great deal of angst for Blackshear and black educators and advocates, who canvassed the state speaking to African American teacher groups, farmers, and church congregations on the need to better prepare black high school students. The Texas State Department of Education confirmed Blackshear's concerns, reporting for the school year 1901–2 black students comprised only 6 percent of the state's high school population, and those who did attend were present fewer class days than their white counterparts. Between 1901 and 1906 there was little or no increase in black enrollment. The result was that when Prairie View held its first four-year commencement in 1904 there were only three graduates—J. E. Davis, Ruth King, and G. A. Randolph. Professor Woolfolk, in his 1962 assessment of Blackshear, was very candid: "It was almost a foregone conclusion that the Blackshear drive for [a] State-supported 'college' in any real sense of the word for his people was doomed by the hardening social philosophy of the white South and the incapacity of his own people." Concerned with the prevailing attitudes toward education in the early 1900s, Blackshear set as a major goal to support and lobby for an increase in the number and quality of black high schools—staffed by his Prairie View teachers—across Texas.[12]

Undeterred by the disappointing initiation of a formal classical program, Blackshear used the experience to strengthen the teachers' certification program. After a weeklong visit to Alabama to confer with Booker T. Washington, Blackshear proceeded with a full embrace of Washington's Tuskegee industrial-style education programs, with one exception:[13] Blackshear expanded the agricultural curriculum and farming operations given the arrival of the experiment and extension programs. Blackshear had little patience with those who wished to teach purely abstract academic subjects. Instruction was to be conducted with an "applied" approach to ensure a better understanding of efficient and profitable agricultural methods. He concluded that the pursuit of agriculture—fully complemented by teacher certification—should be looked upon as the premier program and catalyst to advance the well-being of black citizens across the state. Fully aware that his graduates were succeeding in teaching jobs and professions statewide and were increasingly acceptable to both white and black Texans as the best measure of Prairie View success—regardless of the political-social undercurrents—Blackshear framed the role of Prairie

View: "As there is probably no single agency in the state doing more than this institution to bring about that proper understanding and relationship between the races, which harmonized with Southern sentiment and tradition and which in turn is so essential to peace, happiness, prosperity, and progress of both races in the South, there seems to be wisdom and propriety in an enlargement of the school to meet the growing needs educationally and industrially of the Negro race in Texas."[14]

To accomplish these aims required a greater understanding and buy-in among black communities to support local educational programs and teachers, as well as the addition of "industrial" or vocational training to high school programs. These goals and planning were well timed to address the growing outcry of African Americans statewide for access to skills training that resulted in jobs. The A&M board endorsed Blackshear's emphasis on practical education and his expanded brand of "Washingtonism"; while higher education was always important in the near term, they believed that "it is practical education that the Negro race needs for its development." The directors approved the enhanced approach: "The state of Texas is committed to the wisdom of industrial training for the colored youth and the industrial work here needs to be put on a firm and adequate footing."[15]

Addressing these challenges required a number of items to be accomplished, including a continued commitment to providing as many teachers as possible for black communities, the expansion of campus farming operations and facilities, increased ties with farming communities statewide, and the general expansion of campus facilities to address an influx of students, faculty, and staff. To address the growth, telephone connections were expanded, a campus-wide sewer system was added, and an improved direct road to the new H&TC Railroad depot was completed, as well as a new dormitory. The education and certification of teachers at Prairie View was the core function of the normal school as well as the most outward indication of the success and product the college was producing. Thus, Blackshear broadened admissions for those enrolling in the "normal" curricula and challenged his students and faculty that those who were certified should pledge to teach in the public schools for at minimum as many years as they attended Prairie View. To support this action, he increased the summer school programs for teachers to achieve and maintain certification.[16]

A lifelong advocate of agricultural education, Blackshear was no stranger to the agricultural movement in Texas and across the South. He had a close working relationship with Robert L. Smith, founder of the Farmers'

Improvement Society (FIS), who had accomplished a tremendous impact in a short period of time in black rural communities. As a legislator in the late 1890s, Smith aggressively advocated for financial funding of Prairie View. The two leaders helped establish the Farmers' Congress short courses each summer at Prairie View, as well as working with the expanding extension service programs to assist farmers to increase production and gain greater profits for their efforts. Blackshear traveled across Texas speaking to farm and ranch groups, educators, church congregations, and the business community on the role and importance of the black farmer as best suited for success, when given the know-how and resources to prosper. Blackshear endorsed a key tenant of Smith's "preachings" to farmers that land ownership was critical to success and a better way of life. Thus, in Smith's estimation, "The Negro problem [was] to teach him to live and how to take hold of things about him." Furthermore, Blackshear urged broad community participation in the installations of a "co-operative" cotton gin, shared baling equipment, and the need for crop rotation away from the sole dependence on "king cotton." And rural schools, while teaching "the three Rs" and the basics of industrial education, should also include agricultural instruction.[17]

Student Life

Blackshear's prime challenge was the management and enhancement of the Prairie View campus and its growing, rambunctious student body. With a small staff and increasing number of students—given the pivotal priority to increase enrollment—he exercised what was termed the "full power of a benevolent despot" to instill discipline and habits of self-control, self-respect, and a strong work ethic. Students came from across Texas, many encouraged by a growing number of black high school teachers. The requisites for campus conduct were found in his fundamentalist Protestantism and social gospel beliefs of personal conduct, dating back to his formative years at Tabor College. Furthermore, these ideas and a sense of honor and moral responsibility and integrity appeared often in his speeches and writings for the balance of his life—hallmarked in his key publication *The Education of Childhood* (1911), which concluded that education required supervision of the life of a student.[18]

Nowhere is Blackshear's approach to the changing dynamics of the Prairie View campus more evident than the formation in early 1905 of the Faculty Committee. That body was created as an advisory and academic review assistance group that would also assist with the routine operations of the campus. The weekly meetings were held in Blackshear's office and were comprised of the principal, assistant principal, and five faculty and staff members. During the first twenty years, the college was managed by the principal and assistant principal with occasional assistance from a committee of A&M board members. By 1905, the student body had increased from two hundred in 1900 to over four hundred, and thus, new measures were needed to address the changing demands of the college. Entering students had to be at least sixteen years of age and pass an entrance exam. In addition, the faculty committee consolidated the day-to-day management of the college at the local level, with increased input from the teaching faculty. The detailed minutes of the meetings, located in the Prairie View archives, are a tremendous window into the operations and challenges at the college over nearly a decade. One key aspect of these documents is the leadership of Blackshear and the degree to which he and his staff had local control of nearly all aspects of the college—except possibly the direct state appropriations of annual funding. For example, the committee set the requirements for graduation and promotion to the next class, approving a minimum of 65 percent average for passing for each subject and a "general overall average of at least" 75 percent to graduate. In addition to determining academic standards for graduation, they approved each annual college calendar, which included holidays for Washington's Birthday, Texas Independence Day, and San Jacinto Day. Furthermore, the faculty committee approved travel requests, selected and approved by majority vote the selection of commencement speakers, approved all athletic activities and clubs, determined facilities usage and allocations, and oversaw discipline.[19]

Prior to Blackshear's arrival, there were basically no student organizations or extracurricular activities for the students. Discipline was hard to enforce and students often came and went as they pleased. Housing was always a problem, along with good water and a well-stocked dining hall. Blackshear and his staff tied all non-class activities to organized clubs and events that enhanced the students' education and work toward completion. In October 1905, the campus Philomathean Society, a combination literary and debate forum, was formed to promote learning. Its motto, most likely inspired by the classically trained principal, was *sic itur ad astra*, Latin for "thus we proceed to the stars." Other key organizations included the Young

Men's Society, the Literary Society, Men's Glee Club, and the "Rhetoricals" (to promote more debate). These organizations were pivotal to the college's admission to the Epsilon Pi Tau Honorary Fraternity, making Prairie View the first black institution to be so honored. Formal athletic activities were slow in forming; W. P. Terrell was hired in 1904 to head varsity athletics and the faculty approved an "Athletic Association" in January 1905. The first team sports, baseball and football, were primarily an intramural activity prior to scheduling a few games with teams in the local communities of Hempstead and Navasota. A college band was created in 1905. By 1908, the Committee on Male and Female Athletic Policy established guidelines for student travel and stipulated football games would only be played with "bona fide college students at the different colleges." Intercollegiate games were scheduled in Texas between the so-called Big Five African American colleges—Prairie View, Wiley, Samuel Huston, Tillotson, and Paul Quinn.[20]

Discipline issues generally occupied some 30–40 percent of each faculty meeting. The strict campus rules were adequate grounds for numerous infractions that were immediately noted and addressed. A system of demerits was maintained and punishment assigned to varying degrees of violations. The committee was swift to suspend a student for a few days or weeks. Yet they were also very receptive to review appeals for readmission of violators. "Irregular conduct" was broadly interpreted, for example, as disruption during chapel service, smoking on campus, skipping class, "continued nagging," hunting in a posted pasture, cooking in a student dorm room, or leaving campus without authorization. Mentoring teenagers in the remote campus location, isolated from the influences of a major town and with few local amenities and required attendance at such weekly events as 'chapel,' resulted in the following communication to the Discipline Committee: "The majority of girls who go to the Christian meeting on Sunday evening after tea, go for no good and get no good out of it. I advise that the young ladies be not allowed to attend for it is for their good." Disruption in chapel was not limited to the girls, as boys were reprimanded weekly—including high-profile African student Lattevi Ajaji, who told folklorist John Lomax, "I was more interested in the girls than I was with the boys on campus." For these reoccurring violations, boys were punished by being assigned the duty of "cutting a cord of wood," while girls were assigned extra laundry or kitchen duty. Blackshear and the faculty promoted the advantages of education, but were clear in their expectations: "All students are required to improve their advantages to a reasonable degree and according to their ability, and when it becomes apparent that a pupil's time is not profitably employed he will be requested to withdraw."[21]

The most significant campus discipline situation was a threatened riot in late September 1904. The events were triggered by unrest against the reinstatement of a teacher, and the "student insurrection" resulted from student demands for a "sociable" (a dance and campus social mixer). Blackshear banned the playing of any "loud and boisterous" music such as "the kind of music popularly called 'rag time,'" labeling its effect "degrading." The student "revolt," a rarity in the college's history, for more campus social privileges and popular music resulted in the dismissal of six students and closer monitoring of student activities by the staff. Restless students were not unique to Prairie View, though much of this campus unrest was due to overcrowding and the shortage of facilities to accommodate the surge in growth, coupled with a dearth of student activities. Student disruptions also occurred on the Texas A&M campus; however, when Pres. Henry Harrington issued a special order in the fall of 1907 to the effect that the cadets could not travel to out-of-town football games, backlash and protracted turmoil created a unanimous feeling of dismay resulting in the demand for the resignation of the president.[22]

One source of frustration at Prairie View was that students holding "scholarships" or appointments by their local state senators and representatives, numbering over 150 annually, were more apt to offend the rules of the college, believing that the influence of their hometown legislator who had made the appointment tended to intervene and soften the punishment. The state of Texas established the student assistance program of ninety dollars per nine-month session for Prairie View in the mid-1890s, with one student being appointed by each of the thirty-one state senators, in addition to three students at large and three by each of the six directors of the Texas A&M board.[23] The faculty, interestingly, noted the fact that the staff at the college referenced the "same trouble to deal with that is met [by political appointments] by the authorities at West Point and Annapolis." In 1909 all sponsored appointments were eliminated, so that every student was "on his or her own resources and [stood] upon a discipline record that [was] enforced on all alike."[24] The end of the statewide scholarship program did not affect attendance, with over eight hundred students enrolled by the fall of 1910. However, this did not reduce the irritation among the boys or girls, who were stickily kept separate except for formal occasions, chapel, and the dining hall. The Committee on Discipline drafted the following provisions to set the limits of contact between the women and the men:

> The place for the young ladies upon the campus is defined by a line that runs from the west front door of the chapel to the steps of the frame dormitory, then a line from through this building to fence beyond, also a line from front fence up the middle walk which passes the flag pole to the first line described heretofore. The young men are not to pass beyond these lines at any time without permission, and further that they are not to pass the middle walk by the west side of chapel. The daily routine at the college was spartan with the day beginning at 5:40 a. m. followed by study hour, breakfast and 8:00 a. m. chapel assembly for devotions. Six periods of 'recitation,' averaging forty-five minutes, lunch and practice sessions followed in mid-afternoon with a period of manual labor, and supper at 5:40 p. m, concluding with study-hall, and the 'retiring bell' at 10 p. m.[25]

A special ad hoc Committee on Uniforms was established in the hopes of reducing social dress competition on campus and set the following proposed dress guidelines: "That the uniform for young ladies shall be of navy blue percale [cotton cloth], made in shirt waist suits, with hats to correspond. The uniform of the young men shall be dark navy blue suits made on cadet order and cap to match."[26] In spite of the faculty adopting a student dress code on a number of occasions, however, none was ever successfully implemented.

The most significant annual college event was commencement. Blackshear and the staff held yearly planning sessions for commencement, well aware that this event attracted a great deal of attention from not just the families but also political representatives, the A&M Board of Directors, and the general public. To this end, Blackshear invited some of the most prominent leaders in the South to be commencement speakers. In advance of diplomas being conferred by the chairman of the A&M board, keynote presenters included Dr. J. W. E. Bowen of Atlanta, Georgia; Texas state Methodist bishop Seth Ward; Prof. Hightower T. Kealing of Paul Quinn College; Rev. J. J. Blackshear of Houston Bethel Baptist Church (Edward's brother); and Pres. L. J. Rowan of Alcorn College in Mississippi. By 1908 Prairie View commencement became a two-day event that began midmorning with the annual rhetorical program, featuring student and guest presentations along with music provided by the Glee Club, followed by commencement at midday, and concluding in the evening with dinner and the Annual Program of the Prairie View Alumni Association (formed in 1901).[27]

One of the greatest challenges was the poor condition of the older buildings and the yearly demand for more facilities to address the growth. Blackshear inherited a campus in disrepair and decay in the late 1890s. Capital investment in campus buildings during the first twenty years did little more than repair and maintain old structures. The A&M College board, which had struggled with the same problems at the College Station campus, was well aware of Prairie View's problems and worked continuously to solve the demands and enhance campus facilities. Prior to 1910, the campus had no safe, dependable source of water—in spite of the fact they were only a few miles from the Brazos River, as well as seemingly abundant supplies of artesian wells in nearby Hempstead. There was no electricity, lighting, refrigeration, dependable sewer system, or phone service. Expensive ice and water had to be hauled in from Hempstead. In the early 1900s, the campus comprised the main building (Kirby Hall), a half-dozen poorly ventilated frame dormitories (heated by coal oil and firewood box stoves), four old brick structures that had been damaged in the winds during the historic hurricane of 1900, and a few cottages for married faculty (single faculty and staff lived in the dormitories). The long-term damage of the windstorm was noted in this brief item from Blackshear to Governor Sayers, which appeared in the *Bastrop Advertiser* weekly: "Tin roof torn off academic hall and tin roof torn off mess hall. Slate and tin roof on girl's dormitory blown away, and building greatly damaged. Big chimney fell through the roof. Chapel blown off pillars and windows crushed in. Galleries to teacher's cottages destroyed along with four thousand dollars damage done to stable."[28]

One of the anomalies was that the two-story mess hall, in an effort to maximize all usable space, housed both the kitchen and dining facilities, the mechanical engineering department, and the blacksmithing and carpenter classrooms. Planning and the identification of funding for building began in the late 1890s under the direction of President Foster and college architect F. E. Giesecke. A robust, long-term building program did not begin until 1903–4, with the completion of Foster Hall dorm in 1906 and Luckie Hall in 1909. Excitement spread over the growth of the student body and new dorms after a meeting of the Texas A&M Board of Directors at the Prairie View campus. The growth was greeted with a *Houston Post* headline: "TAKE CARE OF ALL: None Will Be Turned Away from Prairie View." An auditorium–dining hall was completed in 1911, and in 1912 they added Crawford Hall, expanded cow barns, a new residence for the principal, a hospital, and an agricultural building. After years of service by board member William Cavitt, the A&M board appointed a special building committee comprised of Major L. L. McInnis, Col. R. T. Milner of Austin, and Walton Peteet of Dallas to work with plans drawn by Prairie View mechanical department chairman Prof. W. P. Terrell to implement the construction. To defray costs and maximize the available funding to build new structures at both Prairie View and the A&M campus, Terrell installed a kiln at Prairie View to fire over one million bricks—the first profit-making auxiliary enterprise on campus.[29]

For the first several decades, legislative appropriations were determined by separate biennial budgets for Texas A&M and Prairie View, with much of the funding earmarked for specific building projects or infrastructure at each campus. There was always a concern that funding was inequitably divided for Prairie View, yet it should be noted that funding for Texas A&M was rarely adequate either. In 1908, for example, A&M began housing large numbers of cadets in tents (with no water or electricity, and only limited heating) because funds were not available for additional dormitories. In 1913, during a cut in state funding for political reasons, the chairman of the board, Edward B. Cushing, wrote personal checks to keep the A&M College afloat. At Prairie View, hyper-growth of the student body and large capital expenditures for dormitories and infrastructure placed a strain on adequate funding, budgeting, and oversight of projects. A host of other challenges threatened the schools, yet they persisted. In hindsight, it seems somewhat surprising that Prairie View received as much money as it did. Without the annual federal funding that supplemented state appropriations, neither college could have survived.[30]

Blackshear was very proud of the progress and growth of Prairie View, as he demonstrated not only by his continued advocacy of the college statewide but also by his eagerness to place the institution on the national stage with other African American colleges. One means of doing this was advertisements in leading national publications such as *The Crisis*, sponsored by the NAACP and published in Philadelphia:

> Send your boy South—the land of Opportunity
> The Prairie View State Normal and Industrial
> College of Texas. E. L. Blackshear, Principal.
> W. C. Rollins Treasurer. Largest State institution for
> colored youth in the United States. Excellent
> literary, scientific and industrial advantages.
> Expenses low—ideal climate—new buildings.
> For particulars address: H. J. Mason, Secretary
> Prairie View Waller County, Texas[31]

—•⟫⟪•—

Public education received a significant boost at all levels during the governorship of Tom Campbell. The former I&GN railroad executive and manager, who campaigned as one of the "ordinary folk," pledged to support the Texas Railroad Commission championed by his boyhood friend and mentor Stephen Hogg. The bold, progressive agenda of the Campbell administration introduced a number of social and legal reforms, including penal and tax system reform, additional railroad regulations and safety measures, judicial and criminal court reform to ensure speedy trials, and educational changes. "The 'battle cry' of his administration," according to historian and Campbell biographer Janet Schmelzer, "he declared fervently, was reform, and the guiding force embraced the 'principles of Jefferson, Jackson, Coke, Ross, Reagan, and Hogg.'"[32]

Campbell advocated that education was the means to a better life and foundation of a democratic society and nation. To ensure public support, the governor established an advisory group of powerful educational leaders from across the state, the Conference for Education in Texas. The panel on public education included David Houston, Clarence Ousley, H. C. Pritchett (principal of Sam Houston Normal College), Oscar H. Cooper, Theodore Harris, J. L. Long, and Dr. W. S. Sutton (of the University of Texas). There were no African Americans appointed.

Many of the grassroots suggestions to enhance education were forwarded to the governor and legislature and resulted in changes. One key change was to improve funding of public education by raising the local ad valorem tax rate. Bills were signed to improve textbooks, to require agricultural and industrial instruction, and to create the first statewide kindergarten classes. Local school superintendents were given more authority, and the annual school term was expanded from five to seven months. The practice of separate school boards for African Americans in public school administration ended, considered a positive change for Texas education. Blackshear and other black education leaders generally supported these actions in spite of the fact that Campbell viewed black Texans, in Schmelzer's words, "through the eyes of paternalism, segregation and Jim Crow. . . . [For Campbell,] black men were not equipped to make political decisions. From Campbell's view, Texas did not have a 'negro problem' because black men knew their place and accepted social [in]equality."[33]

"The Vexed Negro Problem"

Given the broad number of subjects addressed by Edward Blackshear in both print and from the podium, it is not surprising that he expressed strong views on race relations and what he called the "vexed negro problem." As one observer noted, "It has kept alive sectional feeling, has inflamed partisanship, distorted party politics, barred complete reconciliation, cost hundreds of millions of dollars, and hundreds if not thousands of lives, and stands ever ready, like Banquo's ghost, to burst forth even at the feast."[34] Blackshear's earliest known thoughts appeared in an article in a December 1888 issue of the *Fort Worth Daily Gazette*. During his adult life, hundreds of articles and books by authors from both the North and South were published on the "Negro problem" in publications across the country. Detailed and strong views were routinely expressed by African American leaders including Frederick Douglass ("The Negro Problem," 1886), Booker T. Washington (*The Negro Problem*, 1899), and W. E. B. Du Bois (*The Souls of Black Folk*, 1903). Blackshear's college classmate at Tabor College, Hightower T. Kealing, also authored a number of opinion articles, including "The Character of the Negro People" (1899). One of the most detailed studies, sponsored by the Carnegie Corporation, was Gunnar Myrdal's *An American Dilemma: The Negro Problem and Modern Democracy* (1944). The subject of the "Negro problem" was part and parcel of the racial discourse across the South that impacted all aspects and complexities of social, political, and economic understandings—and especially education.[35]

Blackshear's mentor and confidant as well a leading civic and religious leader, AME Church bishop Abram Grant, expressed his concerns at the annual church conference in Texas: "I have taken the ground that there is no race problem any more than there is a German, or Irish, or Italian, problem in this country. There is only an imaginary race problem. There is a prejudice against us in Texas, in Kansas, in Pennsylvania, and in some form it is all over this country. Furthermore, the Negro race has as many enemies among themselves as there are on the outside." While Grant strongly advised Blackshear to be careful of political entanglements, he observed they should support men who would do the most for the race and not engage with the so-called Lily-White contingent that expelled African Americans from the Republican Party.[36]

Thus, an assessment of Blackshear's views on race, in the context of the post-Reconstruction challenges and adjustments that were taking place in race relations across the South and in Texas, is warranted. Reflecting on his early twenties, fresh from college and teaching in a small, one-room, rural school, he observed, "It seems to me that too much has been expected of the negro in so short a time." Notably, Blackshear had to address these issues in a way that motivated cooperation from Southern whites without alienating potential allies. In an article he summarized his early views: "He [the Negro] is a source of concern to those who love their country and to those who are interested in the progress of humanity. Many questions are asked concerning this rather unpleasant 'brother in black.' Is he improving or is he retrograding? Is he destined to dominate those Southern states whose population he forms so great a part? Is not a race war a thing to be expected in the South? Ought not this race be transported to Africa? These and many other questions are asked. . . . [But I am] not so absurd as to imagine myself about to settle this controversy, which many think shed[s] some light on a problem in which many thinking people, north and south, are interested."[37]

In one case during the Texas legislative session of 1907, Blackshear was confronted head-on with what he routinely addressed as the "race question." In a series of presentations to black teacher groups around the state in which his theme was "the duty to humanity," he advised them "to be loyal to their race" given the rising tide of prejudice and the need to bring the issue of the race problem "to the minds of the world." He cited a series of tragic racial riots and confrontations—for example, the August 1906 Brownsville, Texas, incident involving Negro troops; turmoil in Haiti; and King Leopold of Belgium, whom, he reminded audiences, was responsible for "causing 15,000,000 of the race, 'helpless' and 'harmless' Congolese people, to be killed"—concluding that the Negroes had been "oppressed as no other race had ever been."[38] Blackshear's remarks were not always well received, especially by white Democratic politicians who reeled at any remarks that seemed to lay blame or appeared to be taking a stance to address due process and social equality (in the case of the soldiers tried and executed in Brownsville). Blackshear's remarks were thus politically charged and resulted in an attack on him in the thirtieth session of the Texas Legislature. To attack and chastise Blackshear, Sen. Robert M. Brown of Wharton accosted Prairie View, making a motion to "strike out" the entire biannual appropriation for the college. The senator spoke on the floor that "he was unalterably opposed to the education of the Negro, although he was not an enemy to the Negro per se. He held that the educated negro was a greater menace to the country than was the uneducated one. And that it was the former class that incited the [recent] race riots." Concluding to the surprised senators on the floor as well as the media and guests in the second-floor gallery that he was sounding the alarm on the race question, Brown declared that, while he may be standing alone, "I am opposed to putting tools into the hands of the Negro that would dig their graves and thus would like to see the torch applied to the walls of the Prairie View Normal." Thankfully, there was no organized support for the hostile senator's proposal and the motion was tabled.[39]

Blackshear addressed the general questions that concerned the status and advancement of African Americans as they became freedmen and citizens. Not surprisingly, his first focus was the need for and benefit of a broad availability for black Texans to be educated. Education, he felt, was the primary avenue to advance both social position and prosperity without a dependence on or hindrance from the white power structure. The improvements and advancement of his black students in the Austin schools in the 1880s were a prime example, given the results of education: "His [the student's] mind is certainly capable of development and his capacity to comprehend . . . is undoubted by any who have taken time to investigate. . . . The negro's comparable progress is remarkable." While education was viewed as critical to economic success, the influence of the church caused him to conclude that education would also help foster higher morals, self-help, and personal responsibility. Blackshear noted, that the morals of the Negro are "improving is indisputably true," and he did not shrink or minimize the dynamics of the problem, directly pointing to the actions of the "white race" as complicit in limiting the advancement of his race, especially as it involved African American women: "The negro women [*sic*] is subject to the double trail of temptation from her race and from the immoral men of the white race. The poverty and menial condition of the negro women [*sic*] renders her liable to temptation and insults at the hands of the base and depraved of the white race. The scoundrel, who, to gratify his beastly lust seeks to spoil the virtue of the race, inferior to his own, is a wicked coward, who ought to be tabooed among respectable white people, and subjected to punishment at the hands of the law."[40]

In spite of numerous social and economic impediments facing black Americans across Texas, Blackshear felt that there was clear evidence of improvement: school enrollment grew, property ownership gradually increased, and African Americans were increasingly entering professions not just as teachers but also in medicine, law, ministry, and business. However, he noted, "We can understand a prejudice which excludes negroes from white society . . . but we cry out against prejudice which prevents a fair and free competition of labor. The enlightened, liberal Christian sentiment, North and South, ought to put down such a prejudice." In a letter to the *Austin American Statesman* in April 1890 to thank the "noble" Governor Ross for his steadfast support of black educational attainment across the state and the continued funding of the Deaf, Dumb, and Blind Asylum in Austin, Blackshear wrote, "Ross, a thoroughly representative Democrat and Southerner, states the further fact that the negro has advanced marvelously in personal independence and in education." Blackshear concluded, "The colored and white people of Texas are solving the race problem. The vexing Negro problem of the United States is not 'Shall the Negro gain political or industrial supremacy in the country?' This is out of the question. The real [Negro] problem is, can the Negro acquire property, wealth and education and discharge the duties and enjoy the rights and privileges of [a] citizen in this country? Thus, remove as many as possible of the restrictions with which prejudice of race so heavily handicap him and the Negro will finally become what? Why, simply, an American citizen."[41]

Edward Blackshear included these priorities and messages of encouragement in his writings and presentations to teachers, farmers, and church groups for the balance of his life. One challenge that concerned Blackshear was the idea by some that foreign immigration could solve the "Negro problem." Addressing the statewide annual meeting of the Colored Teachers State Association in 1894, he was direct in his assessment of race relations in Texas: "The destinies of white and black are bound together by inevitable laws of social action, reaction and progression. Justice is the best policy, as all good men agree. The most dangerous man in any commonwealth, community or party is the demagogue who, under pretense of statesmanship and by appeals to prejudice and passion, seeks to deprive any class of what is justly due it. The true statesman is he who seeks to do justice to all men, to give every man the opportunity to develop the best in his nature and to make the best use of such talent as nature may have bestowed upon him." Blackshear was very proud of his country and often expressed this publicly, reminding audiences that first and foremost the "negro is an American citizen." And as a citizen and under the covenants of the Texas Constitution, they were entitled to equal common school education as well as higher education—thus, Blackshear, who was never far from his strong fundamentalist church roots, admonished all to "give him [the Negro] the opportunity to develop the powers of mind and soul with which God has endowed Him."[42]

By the late 1890s, Blackshear, along with other African American leaders in Texas, was quick to point out the impact of elections and political maneuvering on the Negro problem. The rise of third parties and efforts to defeat the Democratic machine's hold on Texas politics and elected officials was, as John Rayner conceded, a near total failure. With the 1896 US Supreme Court decision on *Plessy v. Ferguson*, which justified states' rights agendas to pass segregation laws, and after the demise of the Populist movement, both Texas Democrats and Republicans abandoned rural African Americans. The result was to drive a wedge further between the two races, with the white majority controlling all statewide offices and the legislature for decades to come. Black Texans held only a few local elected offices, such as constables, county commissioners, and justices of the peace. Blackshear noted: "The material prosperity of the South, dependent as much upon this co-work and co-operation of what may be termed its two native races, has been disturbed by politics. And it has taken time for the negroes to get over the political prejudice under which they have [been] controlled by the Republican Party." The disastrous result was an increase in the enforcement of Jim Crow laws across the South.[43]

Booker T. Washington, in private conversations with Blackshear, broached an additional dynamic to the "race problem"—incoming foreigners, primarily from Italy. Immigrants were eager for jobs as well as interested in establishing merchant businesses open to doing business with both whites and blacks. Washington's interest in this topic must have given Blackshear pause given the increasing number of Italians arriving in Galveston and settling in the Brazos Valley. The generally non-judgmental openness of Italians to African Americans "violated the white man's code" in the eyes of some Texans and possibly posed a threat to Negroes as these immigrants were competitors. Washington reflected the sentiments of white Southern nativists by warning that "southern European immigrants might create a racial problem in the South more difficult and more dangerous than which is caused by the presence of the Negro." Progressive activist John Rayner of Calvert, Texas, also expressed concerns about the disruptive influence of new immigrants to Texas. The racial nativism was further fueled by a wave of anti-Catholicism.[44]

While Blackshear had a life-long opposition to the migration of black Americans out of the United States to Africa or locations in Latin America—which misguided schemes he concluded were marked by "failures and sad disappointments"—he did consider other options that seemed less traumatic. Booker Washington agreed with Blackshear, telling the National Council of Colored Women at their annual convention in Chicago, "The plan of transporting the American Negros [*sic*] to Africa I consider impracticable."[45] Shortly after the American occupation of Cuba following the war with Spain in 1898, Blackshear penned an article in *The Washington Post* modifying his stance by wondering if "the serious aspect of the negro problem in the South suggests that Cuba should be an open door for the American Negro." His justification in this case was that "this Cuban safety valve" had less racial prejudice and could offer a new start. The African American in Cuba would not be expatriated, and he would still be an American. The future of his race was the key component of the article: "Will the negro question be always an unsettled one in the United States—I think these race problems are given an exaggerated importance." Blackshear concluded, "I believe the worst fate that could befall my race just now would be to leave them entirely to themselves. What the race needs is a wise curbing of its aspiration and far-seeing. Self-subordination of its own present will and temper, and this with no aim or intent of finally when stronger seeking to dominate any other race, but with the aim and for the purpose of securing the black man in his personal and private rights. If the negro can enjoy property rights, can be protected in life, liberty, and the lawful pursuit of human happiness, can have his family respected and protected, and can be secure in his rights and opportunity to do ordinary or skilled labor, to engage in agriculture and its kindred pursuits and in commerce, he will certainly be on the high road to progress."[46]

As the debate heated up on the best solution to the "high road to progress," Blackshear, following an extended visit with his brother (a professor at Howard University in Washington, DC) and ever mindful of the ongoing geopolitical debate on European colonial activities in the Congo and the actions of the Boers in South Africa at the turn of the century, as well as America's rising global position following the acquisition of Cuba and the Philippines, penned a grand plan and solution to address the "race problem":

RACE PROBLEM SOLUTION

Proposed South African Colony Might Lead to Negro Republicans
Washington Post—June 5, 1905

Editor Post: Through your columns, permit a suggestion bearing on the much mooted "negro problem." It is simply the exchange between the governments of Great Britain and the United States of the political control of South Africa and the Philippines Islands. Great Britain would find the Philippines contiguous to her East Indian possessions, a valuable naval and commercial base, while her experience with the oriental peoples would afford her a superior fitness and facility over the United States in controlling and developing the islands. At the same time the United States could view the transfer of the islands to Great Britain, a natural though not formal ally, with equanimity, retaining possibly a suitable naval base in the transferred islands to meet the requirements of the American interests in the Far East.

On the other hand, with equal equanimity the British government and people might witness the passing of South Africa to the control of the United States, retaining reciprocal advantages. As for the Boers, these could be encouraged to settle in the Southern States of our country to replace the negroes, who would be induced and encouraged to settle in the Americanized South Africa by either private or governmental agency.

The advantages of such a proposition to the United States are evident. The negroes would have an outlet, a place where under the powerful but friendly guidance and control of the United States they could find an opportunity for a freer expansion and development than is possible here. At the same time, the American negroes would be the agents in the civilization of their African kinsmen. Valuable trade

> and commerce, ever increasing, would spring up between the South African republic and the American republic, its guardian. A great negro republic in South Africa, under American guardianship, is an alluring picture to the minds of the ambitious and progressive negroes of the United States, many of whom are deeply imbued with the American spirit of enterprise and liberty. The South experienced a deep sense of its burden by ridding itself of its excessive negro population, and white immigrants would begin to go South as the disadvantages of competition with the negroes began to be removed. The difficulties of the race problem would be materially lessened, while the people of the United States, by affording American negroes an opportunity for a freer development without the fatal limitations of American sentiment on racial relations, would unfetter the hampered genius of a race. The American race prejudice, as effective on Beacon Street, Boston, as on Canal Street, New Orleans, must remain indefinitely a bar sinister to the development of personality and society to all Americans of negro origin. But the proposed South African colony, which would some day become a republic under American protection, would be a measure of recompense on the part of the white people of the United States for what the negro has suffered and done since his forcible deportation from his native land and his enforced and uncompensated labor during more than two centuries.

No action was forthcoming, yet his engagement with the future of his people continued.

Blackshear was well aware that unequal justice under the law, the limitations of social equality, and economic determinants had a tremendous impact on the "Negro problem." John M. Langston of Virginia, a contemporary of Frederick Douglass, had a major influence in the debate, noting the Negro problem "would be solved by the Negro himself through the cultivation and intelligence, virtue, and wealth—with good understanding in a wise community of interest with those who today are the masters of knowledge, power, and wealth." As Blackshear traveled across the South to visit colleges, to see family members in Washington, DC, and to attend professional events—especially after attending the National Educational Association meeting in Charleston, South Carolina, followed by a week-long visit with Booker T. Washington at Tuskegee—he further understood the "wise communities of interest," noting, "It is one of the anomalies of the Negro problem that in the old South, as typified in Richmond, Raleigh and Charleston, the Negro is at his best at the highest title of social, intellectual, moral and economic improvement; also there is a false prejudice against him as a laborer, a man in business and as an industrial factor than in other sections." These visits to the Deep South further confirmed there were fundamental differences between deeply rooted Southern traditions and norms and the approach to race relations in Texas. Far too often, the trans-Mississippi Southwest has been painted with a broad brush, obfuscating its more Western leanings. These observations helped confirm Blackshear's commitment to industrial education, concluding, "Industrial training will help to better relations by making the Negro labor more useful to the white employer," and thus more in demand as a worker, resulting in higher-paying jobs and self-sufficiency to acquire property, achieve home ownership, and build an improved lifestyle for the family. The US Department of Agriculture, which seldom made any comments on race relationships, in an official thirty-page report that supported the message of Washington, Smith, and Blackshear, entitled *A Decade of Negro Extension Work, 1914–1924*, opened with this sentence: "Home ownership is the largest factor in the solution of the so-called negro problem." These ideas became a pivotal part during the last years of Blackshear's career working to expand the agricultural extension services across Texas and the Southwest. Notwithstanding, a boxing match threatened to derail whatever goodwill and progress was being made to reduce racial tensions.[47]

Pugilism

One of the most explosive racially inspired events in Blackshear's life was his stance against the July 1910 heavy-weight world championship fight between Jack Johnson—born in Galveston, Texas, in 1878 and the son of former slaves—and John Jeffries. Billed as the sensational "Fight of the Century," Jeffries was undefeated and in retirement when boxing promoters lured him from retirement as "the Great White Hope" to fight the recently crowned Johnson, the first African American champion after taking the title belt from Canadian Tommy Burns in 1908. Blackshear, a lifelong sports enthusiast and amateur boxer himself, had been active in sports clubs and helped establish the black YMCA in Austin. However, in a feature column in *The New York Times*, Blackshear expressed serious reservations, as he noted the prize fight was being "rapidly regarded as a racial test . . . increasing a tension already stretched to the snapping point." He concluded the fight ought to be called off: "If Johnson wins the anti-negro sentiment will quickly and dangerously collect itself ready to strike back at any undue exhibition of rejoicing on the part of the negroes. Race prejudice is already sufficiently acute in the United States." The fight was held on July 4 in Reno, Nevada, before a massive crowd, with a championship purse of over $100,000 championship purse at stake. Johnson dominated the fight and defeated Jeffries with a technical knockout in the fifteenth round. The violent reaction that Blackshear had feared exploded across the country as African Americans celebrated the victory in a series of the worst riots prior to the 1960s. Within three days after the fight, over two dozen black Americans were killed in racially charged confrontations in eighteen separate states. In the aftermath many called for the ban of boxing, and films of the fight were banned in theaters, though leaders in Texas took only limited action in banning only images of "prize fights" and other "glove contests."[48]

Soon after the fight in Reno, Johnson was charged and convicted for violations of the Mann Act, a Jim Crow–era law that made it a felony to transport any women across state lines for illegal or immoral purposes. Purely a racially motivated injustice, the conviction resulted in Johnson being sentenced to a year in jail. Once released, he promoted US war bonds

Edward Blackshear (center) with the 1907 Prairie View football team. Courtesy of Prairie View A&M University Archives.

during World War I and continued exhibition boxing bouts until his death in 1946. Numerous failed pleas were filed to review the case since the late 1990s, with both the US Congress and White House taking no action, until Pres. Donald Trump posthumously pardoned Johnson in May 2018.[49]

Thus, Blackshear and other key black leaders in Texas were well aware that the prime approach to the "vexed negro problem" was not accommodation but instead reasoned cooperation with the white-dominated political and social structure in order to reach their objectives and goals. It was hoped that the "boxing riots" of 1910 would soon pass. The observation by Prof. George Woolfolk that "a solution to bi-racial power had begun to feel its way toward answers" is reflected in Blackshear's guarded optimism: "Ethnologically speaking, a few centuries is but a short time and the negro a patient race, and somehow in spite of temporary discouragements, he has a deep-seated conviction that his great republic will be too strong to feel the need and too magnanimous to cherish the disposition to do real and permanent injustice to the humblest black citizen. And if patriotic Americans of affluence will aid in the coming centuries [we] will witness a solution of the negro problem which shall involve no detriment to the white man and no injustice or inhumanity to the black."[50]

—•»«•—

The growth of Prairie View and expanding public acceptance of the role the college was playing in teacher education, industrial education, and agricultural programs for farmers across the state was on full display at the 1908 commencement. Professor Blackshear presented what the *Houston Post*—which referred to the professor as "one of the leading Negro educators of the South"—called attention to as a "testimony" of the institution's progress:

> The school stands as a living monument of the good will of the State of Texas toward its colored citizens and of their desire that our youth receive such training as will fit them to make an honest livelihood and to live good, honest lives. Its students are found in every part of Texas and they stand recognized as good citizens and as conservators of good order and promoters of peace and good will between races. They are found on the side of temperance, industry, education, patriotism and religion. They are property owners and home builders, and hence good neighbors and good citizens.

> Under the present State administration this institution has received the greatest appropriation in its history. The sum of $72,000, one of the largest appropriations ever made by any state, North or South, for negro education. Indeed, it is a fact that Texas has spent more money for negro education than any other state in the Union. This is seen in the much higher salaries paid to negro teachers and in the longer school terms. Texas has provided a splendid eleemosynary institution for her negro population. The school law of Texas calls for an equitable and impartial division of the school funds of the state. These facts combined constitute the ground for a strong bond of gratitude and affection on our part for the State of Texas.[51]

By the end of the decade the benevolent principal had charted a solid path for Prairie View. The enrollment growth (exceeding 850 students),

Prairie View was a leader in pioneering agricultural extension service for black farmers in East Texas. Blackshear worked closely with Booker T. Washington at the Tuskegee Institute to development outreach by extension agents, using what were called "Jesup Wagons" filled with farm implements to provide hands-on training. Courtesy of Prairie View A&M University Archives.

successful job placements of graduating teachers, enhanced agricultural programs in cooperation with the extension service programs, and the continued offering of industrial education courses gained wide approval. Demand for more housing and funding was a constant challenge, yet the college was largely successful, with the active A&M board providing as much support as possible. In the process Blackshear had become the most high-profile African American leader in Texas—and, some argued, had a growing positive reputation across the South. Woolfolk was candid in his assessment of Blackshear's impact, noting, "His position as head of the only [public] institution of higher learning for Negroes [in Texas] . . . entitled him—if it did not impose on him—a measure of leadership among his people." Blackshear's efforts to enhance and fund a broad base of education in Texas required direct involvement and a larger role in the political dynamics of the state to succeed. His ability to navigate the swirling, often turbulent waters of political discourse proved critical. And thus by 1910 his skillful avoidance of any political blunders that had no connection to his passion and advocacy for education became even more evident.[52]

5

Demon Rum

"Wets" vs. "Drys"

> The best protection, the only salvation for our boys and girls, is to be found in keeping them busy at useful employment and getting them to cultivate a love for honest toil and decent, moral and economical living.
>
> EDWARD L. BLACKSHEAR, AUGUST 1912

> I don't have to give any reasons. I am Governor of the State of Texas.
>
> GOV. JAMES FERGUSON, MAY 1915

> Educational politics has always loomed large in Negro thinking because it was accepted as the main channel, and in the case of the Negro in the South the only channel, through which the fruits of the American dream of unrestricted opportunity that could be realized.
>
> GEORGE R. WOOLFOLK

The experience and reputation Edward Blackshear had developed would be tested by 1910. His ability to deal with a cross section of educational, religious, civic, agricultural, and political groups and their leaders was a major strength, yet many of his opponents challenged the demands of his allegiance and objectives to advance his interests in education. During the early years of the twentieth century, Texans were once again faced with the issue of Prohibition, which disproportionately overshadowed all other political and social issues confronting the voters of the state of Texas. The lines were drawn along the stance citizens would take on the manufacture, sale, and consumption of alcohol. Blackshear maintained his affiliation with the Democratic party. The restless Progressive movement endeavored to co-opt the Prohibition question to advance their social agenda, and by 1910 they concentrated their political energies on this effort to develop social and cultural reform. The identification of the rise of Progressivism with Prohibition was far from perfect. The "dry" versus "wets" fight disrupted all aspects of the Texan approach to individual rights and common culture, as well as challenging moral convictions and obligations. The dominance and institutionalization of the Democratic, one-party system in Texas created conflicts on its own; as Lewis Gould noted, "Questions of personality and friendship in many instances transcended ideological barriers and produced strange, if temporary, alliances."[1]

In October 1909, Hempstead hosted a second presidential visit with the brief stop of William H. Taft. This visit did not receive as much attention as the 1901 McKinley visit, but Republican Taft, who had lost Texas in the 1908 presidential race to William J. Bryan, was warmly received. Blackshear and Prairie View students and staff were in the welcoming party, joined by county officials, to present him a caged possum, knowing the tremendous appetite of the 325-pound president, in case his cook wanted to prepare a "possum-and-tater" lunch! The *Washington Herald* noted that Taft asked the large crowd from the rear platform of the rail car, "Where is Hempstead in Texas, in the south or east or center of the state, or where?" "Why," sang out one man, "it's in Waller County, of course—known among Texans as Six Shooter Junction" (nicknamed such because it was the site of a major gunfight at the courthouse a few years earlier). With possum on board, the president "seemed perfectly satisfied" with the visit.[2]

However, the prize Hempstead possum was again to make national news before the president departed Texas. The report of the events filled papers:

> The president's train developed a full fledged mystery today. Railroad detectives, special police and secret service men to the contrary notwithstanding, someone stole the president's possum. It happened in Dallas where it seemed as though there were at least a million policemen and special officers on guard.
>
> A fat, sleek, shiny looking possum was put aboard the train yesterday at Hempstead. He occupied one-half of an orange crate, while on the other side was a "mess" of sweet potatoes intended to be served as a

> concomitant of the feast. The possum and potatoes were safely stowed in the presidential baggage car. With memories of the possum dinner in Atlanta last winter still fresh in mind, the president suggested this morning that the Hempstead gift should have the place of honor among the viands for dinner on the Mayflower that evening.
>
> Then came the astonishing news that the possum had disappeared. The man in charge of the baggage car had set the crate on the platform last night at Dallas and despite the fact the train was surrounded by blue-coats throughout the period of darkness, the morning light revealed the fact that the "bird had flown" taking the sweet potatoes with him. The woeful loss in Dallas traveled ahead of the train and when it arrived in Longview [Texas] another possum was put aboard.[3]

—•⊱⊰•—

The always politically aware and savvy Blackshear, who had gained a reputation of representing his key issue of education, was caught in mixed loyalties and the struggle to address the way forward with the Prohibition issue, like other leaders and citizens of the era. He was a leader in a number of major black civic, educational, and religious associations that would be among the prominent groups drawn into the fight. As we have seen from the earliest days of his relationship with the AME Church in Austin in the mid-1880s and early 1890s, and later the Baptist Church, Edward knew better than most that local churches of all denominations were a focal point of African American community life—and a platform to shape political opinion. Prohibition organizers soon realized a major source of support could result in a two-fold win if they could enlist black church members across the state. The black community statewide, while numbering nearly seventy thousand citizens, represented some 18 percent of the Texas population in 1910. Blackshear, in a detailed assessment of the Texas population trends from the 1910 US census, noted that the data posed no numerical threat to the white majority. However, when combined with German, Italian, and other European immigrants, as well as Mexican Americans in South Texas who comprised a relatively small but solid minority swing vote, these totals could help determine the outcome of local elections—especially votes on the local option and the statewide Prohibition issue. The *Temple Daily Telegram* noted: "What the good Democrats should worry about is the Mexican vote—the horde of Mexicans vote the Republican ticket almost solidly."[4]

Prohibition

The jockeying for the fall governor's election was in full steam. The outgoing O. B. Colquitt administration completed its final months without controversy and generally remained above the fray. The overwhelming issue looming over the Texas governor race for years had been Prohibition. Nearly three decades previously, the fight at the ballot box against "demon rum" was first addressed and defeated in 1887 during the Sul Ross administration (1887–91). At that time a coalition of German, Czech, black, and Mexican voters in South Texas favored local option, agreeing with Ross that Prohibition was "presumptuous and paternalistic." They opposed any efforts deemed to interfere with an individual's right to have unfettered access to "spirits," and thus, the wets won the day—220,627 to 129,270. Then in 1908 and 1910, as a result of statewide whites-only Democratic primaries, prohibitionists gained enough ground to pass a Prohibition amendment in the legislature, against the objections of the anti-prohibitionist governor. A statewide referendum was set for July 22, 1911.[5]

Additional factors impacted the Texas political scene. The growing population of Texas was far from homogeneous. Research by Terry Jordan provided significant revision to the notion and make-up of immigration into Texas between 1890–1910. Many assumed that the major influx of Mexicans coincided with the onset of the Revolution in Mexico that began in 1910. However, the major influx from south of the border began in the early 1890s. Approximately 150,000 immigrants from Mexico arrived by 1910, representing a 300 percent increase in the Mexican population in Texas. During the same period, by contrast, the total number of existing Texas inhabitants only increased by 75 percent. While the impact during elections among newly arrived Mexicans was minimal statewide, they did influence elections in communities along the border since Texas law allowed immigrants to vote by filing a citizenship intention petition—known as "first papers." Fraud was de rigueur, due in large part to high illiteracy, low voter turnout due to the poll tax, and the domination of the white Anglo–machine politics in the cities and counties across South Texas. However, while the Mexican population of the state in 1887 (only 4 percent of the Texas population) was outnumbered five-to-one by black Texans, the rapidly growing Hispanic population by 1910, as noted by historian Larry Hill, was accompanied by a proportional (although not numerical) decrease in the black population.[6]

—•⟫⟪•—

From the time of the Sul Ross administration in the late 1880s, Blackshear had maintained close working contact with each Texas governor and his staff. The capital of Austin in those days was small and regular contact with state elected and appointed officials was not uncommon. Blackshear's interaction was primarily intended to be "informational," yet clearly it was in his best interest as principal at Prairie View after 1896 to keep close watch on legislative activities and most importantly appropriations for the college. While directly reporting to the president and board of Texas A&M, he was given wide latitude in his dealings in Austin—if for no other reason than he was recognized as one of the top black leaders in the state. During the Thomas Campbell (1907–11) administration, Blackshear supported the governor's moderate, local-option approach over the radical Progressives who demanded more regulation. For this reason, the prohibitionist leaders wanted Blackshear and his followers in their camp. Prohibition was a politically charged social and moral issue that was more than a "bizarre aberration." The anti-saloon movement tested the emerging social structure of Texas and resulting gradual shift in power from rural to urban and a resulting reorientation of political loyalties. While a Democrat, Blackshear had largely succeeded in remaining apolitical. This changed in 1910.[7]

In an effort to maintain good relations with the governor's office, Blackshear met privately with gubernatorial candidate Oscar B. Colquitt prior to the 1910 democratic primary. During this heated election, Prohibition, which "wringing-wet conservative" Colquitt opposed, once again became a prime issue. Following the election, Blackshear almost ran afoul of Colquitt when he was accused by a disgruntled former employee at the college, T. M. Tarver, of "raising a campaign fund" for another Democratic candidate during the primary. To calm the waters, James H. Quarles, former *Houston Post* reporter and communications manager for Texas A&M (as well as a close personal friend of Blackshear's), was asked to check into this. Quarles assured the governor that Blackshear, whom he had worked with closely, had not "engaged in political controversies between Democrats." Governor Colquitt followed this up with a letter to A&M board chairman Walton Peteet, with further instructions: "Now that the fight [election] is over, I am going to ask you to weed out the men who are not in sympathy with efforts to build up the A. & M. College.

I do not think that a man who cannot give his approval to an administration ought to continue to receive his bread from it." The Anti-Statewide Prohibition Organization and the German American Alliance of Texas quickly pledged their support to Colquitt. The Anti-Saloon League (dry) had been successful in adding a few elected representatives to the legislature and won a number of local-option elections but as of yet had not made inroads into the churches. Under what some considered to be pressure from the governor and disillusioned with the racism of white prohibitionists, Blackshear backed Colquitt and the wets, and continued his support into Colquitt's second term.[8]

The dynamics of Prohibition politics and allegiances are captured by historian Brendan J. Payne:

> Black Texans did not all agree on this issue, but both sides operated under similar motivations. The chief issues were protecting black suffrage and upholding racial dignity, causes that the drys and wets alike claimed to act in support of but did so by aligning themselves with different people. Dry African Americans sought to align themselves with the "best people": middle-class white progressives who usually shared their religious tradition—Methodist or Baptist—and offered the most obvious route to racial uplift through social respectability. Wets, however, turned to the alcohol lobby, one of the most powerful interest groups in the nation. The desire for political success as vote-getters also motivated African Americans on both sides. Deep-seated convictions for or against prohibition likewise mobilized thousands of black voters; wets sought to protect individual liberties such as the right to drink, which became particularly pressing as African Americans watched their rights contract further with the rise of Jim Crow, while drys sought to advance the Kingdom of God by dethroning King Alcohol. A few activists were driven by the desire for financial advancement through connections with wealthy patrons, particularly brewers. Several or all of these motives could be present in a single person at a single moment, and competing motives sometimes prompted actors to shift their positions over time.[9]

The resulting fight to secure voter approval involved most of the coalition from the 1887 heated election, yet this time the pro-liquor forces gained added assistance with financial backing from the Retail Liquor Dealers

Association and the Texas Brewers Association. To combat this, the prohibitionists appealed to all who supported their cause—especially across party lines. The black community's strong opposition to Prohibition was soon countered by the organization of black educational and religious groups to help abolish saloons and their suppliers. Black political leaders believed the rising Prohibition movement would help them regain political power, and thus the Negro Statewide Prohibition Association was formed in Galveston in late 1910. This movement fostered political evangelism and soon attracted support from a growing number of the members of the Texas Negro Baptist Convention, as well as the AME and CME Church Conferences. The church often defined the community. Not all members of each church were in total agreement; for example, there was conflict in the Negro Baptist Convention between "separatists" and "co-operationists." The Colored Teachers Association responded by passing a resolution endorsing "temperance" (akin to local option), rather than an organizational position on Prohibition. As historian Lewis Gould noted, "Prohibition represented more than a bizarre aberration. The place of a rural resident in an urbanizing state and nation, the position of racial minorities in a white culture, the relations of special interests, and the proper role of religion in life all found expression in the debate over prohibition."[10]

As the debate over Prohibition spread across Texas, Tom Ball, leader of the Negro Statewide Prohibition Association, increasingly worked to gain the support of black churches and leaders. Blackshear endeavored to work behind the scenes, but was soon drawn into Ball's interaction with Governor Colquitt. Blackshear had taken careful steps not to be the subject of statewide political news, knowing full well that factions on both sides of key issues stopped at nothing to advance their candidate or cause, but an energetic Ball drew attention to what he deemed were "anti-pro activities of the principal," interjecting in an article in the *Galveston Daily News*: "Yes, I wrote Governor Colquitt a letter calling his attention to offensive allusions to prohibitionists in a catechism sent out by E. L. Blackshear, principal of the colored normal at Prairie View. As to Blackshear's being an anti-prohibitionist, it is a matter of no concern to me, nor do I question the right of any teacher to take a stand in any matter pertaining to the interests of the state. I consider Blackshear's reference to prohibitionists, however, as calculated to do his race and the institution over which he presides a great injustice and not one calculated to promote good feeling between white people and his own color. It is a matter of indifference to me whether the [Texas A&M] board keeps him or not. Governor Colquitt, in his reply to me says that he had no control over the matter, as Blackshear's retention is entirely with the [A&M] board." While there is no indication that Blackshear's job was in jeopardy, neither Dr. J. Allen Kyle of Houston, a close acquaintance of Blackshear's and head of the Prairie View oversight committee for the A&M board, nor W. A. Trenckmann, president of the board, had any public comments or expressed concerns.[11]

African American churches were the first gatherings of postwar freedmen in Texas and across the South. Black congregations, while very mindful of their spiritual callings, were the epicenter of generally closed-door religious and political discourse. From the pulpit they heard both preachers and lay civic leaders discuss, debate, and recommend guidance—with little or no pretense of nonpartisanship. Religion and ethnicity shaped politics. Pivotal to the community's moral and social fabric, black women increasingly played a key role in patronage and the leadership and discourse. These black female congregants in the early twentieth century often accounted for over 60 percent of the black church's active membership. Ties between the Republican Party and African Americans were both historic and strong, and penetrating these long-held views and allegiances was a major challenge for third-party activists. Increasingly, by the mid-1890s, black church congregations hoped to avoid any divisive politics in order to help steer the shifting political winds in Texas.[12]

The "old time" religion, as presented by Methodist and Baptist preachers from the pulpit, did not soften or ease the black-white tension, as white Protestants were apprehensive and fearful of African Americans seeking social equality—with a major white Methodist church publication noting: "Mobocracy, martial law, or almost anything beats Negro rule." Notwithstanding, African Americans, though divided, voted mostly against Prohibition. One overriding irony was that at the moment the dry campaign needed the largest black voter turnout for such a key issue, state laws advanced for over a decade by politicians like Sen. Alexander W. Terrell (one of the leading anti-black exponents of white supremacy in Texas) to impose a poll tax of $1.50–$1.75 had limited the numbers of blacks as well as poor whites and Mexicans who could vote! And thus Blackshear's pragmatic approach to maneuvering within the white power structure allowed him to maintain the struggle for equality for black Texans.[13]

Any doubts that Edward Blackshear was not known statewide as an influential black leader were put to rest by a headline personal attack on the front page of the Marion County *Jefferson Jimplecute*. While the paper's masthead slogan—"Independent in All Things—Neutral in Nothing"—suggested an attempt at a nonpartisan approach to news, the editors regularly published politically charged attacks such as the following: "Prof. Blackshear of the Prairie View Normal permitted himself to be dragged into the anti-campaign, and he used his influence to deliver the ignorant Negro vote to the saloons and succeeded; but he made the supreme mistake of his foolish life. He has turned the great majority of the best white people of the State against him, and now it devolves upon the saloon influence to save him from his predicament. He has ruined himself and done untold damage to the Negroes of the State. Poor old Blackshear!"[14]

Increasingly, African Americans in Texas realized the right to vote—even at the cost of a poll tax (just or unjust)—was pivotal to their advancement. Black leaders including R. L. Smith, W. M. McDonald, J. B Rayner, and J. N. Johnson, along with Blackshear, constantly encouraged black landownership, improved local public schools, and gradually pushed back on the white establishment in order to gain more access to the political process.[15] In the fall of 1911, Booker Washington, skirting any direct political comments, returned to Prairie View, noting the need for cooperation and lauding the state of Texas for "handsomely and generously maintaining" the college.[16] While the white Democratic primary and the Lily-White Republicans limited access to federal and state elected positions, local elections, especially in counties that had a black majority in the early 1900s—such as Robertson, Burleson, Fort Bend, Wharton, and Brazos Counties—could be "swung" by the local black vote. Gains during Jim Crow were indeed very slow and irritating. While many criticized the poll tax, Blackshear in 1911 endorsed the poll tax as an "honorable" rite of passage: "Many states have absolutely or practically disenfranchised the negro people. In Texas we can exercise this right if we pay a poll tax. Our friends everywhere, in and out of Texas, North and South, regardless of party, are advising the colored man to qualify for the privilege of voting. To qualify in Texas for voting requires but the simple payment of the tax before February 3. The payment of taxes is a patriotic duty. It is an honorable thing for the colored man to be a tax payer and contribute to the support of government, of law and order, whose benefits in a general way, we all enjoy. The poll tax goes to support of the public schools. This is an additional reason why the colored man should cheerfully pay his poll tax, as it comes back to him in the way of school advantages for his children."[17] This opinionated stance confounded Senator Terrell and the

Democrats, who presumed their passage of the poll tax was nearly foolproof to limit Black voting. While there were hundreds of poor whites, blacks, and Mexicans who could not pay the poll tax, many of the blacks who could pay did not do so as a means of protest.

Campaign Outfit

In mid-April 1912, Blackshear and Prairie View treasurer W. C. Rollins, accompanied by J. H. Stewart, superintendent of the Colored Deaf, Dumb, and Blind Institute in Austin, visited Governor Colquitt in Austin to encourage his support of the college and present him with a "new campaign hat." Along with a custom-made Prairie View hat, the principal jovially delivered a new pair of custom-made six-dollar shoes, a silver whisk broom engraved with the governor's name, and two sweeping brooms—all manufactured by college students in the industrial shops at the college—as well as a large basket of early spring vegetables grown by the students in the institution's garden. Blackshear likely got the idea for the gift of the shoes from his mentor Booker T. Washington, who months earlier presented philanthropist and railroad magnate Andrew Carnegie with a pair of shoes made in the shoe shops at Tuskegee. Carnegie was so pleased with the quality and fit of the dress shoes that he ordered two additional pairs![18]

The *Houston Daily Post* noted the governor's response was "somewhat a gem of impromptu eloquence" for his appreciation of the gifts prepared by the students of Prairie View. Supportive of higher education, "he assured his visitors of his appreciation for the gifts and his desire to aid their schools and their race in general. He pointed to the fact that the appropriation approved by him for Prairie View was much larger than any previously made and—he took occasion to refer to the liberality of appropriations made for other schools during his administration." Ever mindful of his statewide constituents, the governor declared that "they would find him always willing to lend a helping hand wherever possible to the Negro race, as well as the white race and the Mexican race." At no point was Prohibition mentioned, but Blackshear surely had a brief private conversation with the governor about concerns of a violent murder spree along the Houston and Central railroad tracks, which news media labeled the "assassination by the 'Axeman.'" Blackshear requested a reward be posted and the governor agreed, offering $250 for the arrest and conviction of any such suspect—yet none was ever apprehended.[19]

Substantial state appropriations were forthcoming, and during early 1913 the Prairie View campus expanded facilities. A decade of successful Prairie View graduates took teaching positions in black schools statewide, many of which had principals trained at Prairie View and thus were excellent "feeders" of students to the college. To address the growth, Texas A&M board member Dr. J. Allen Kyle, chairman of the college committee, urged bold improvements to include a "modernly equipped hospital" under the direction of Dr. E. R. Gravelly. Blackshear was very proud of the recognition that Prairie View was considered the "largest [public] institution of its kind" in the nation with only an appropriation of $30,000 per annum from the state and $12,000 from the federal government (see table 5.1). The library in Academic Hall exceeded two thousand volumes, two new dormitories were added, and the campus laundry expanded—with the "irons" heated by gas.[20]

TABLE 5.1. Federal Morrill Act Funding for Black Higher Education

State	Percent black population of the state	Amount	School
Alabama	43%	$20,640	Huntsville Normal
Arkansas	27%	$12,960	Pine Bluff Normal
Delaware	20%	$9,690	Delaware College
Florida	44%	$22,320	State Normal
Georgia	43%	$23,040	Branch of Georgia
Kentucky	15%	$7,200	State Normal
Louisiana	50%	$24,000	Southern University
Maryland	23%	$11,010	Agricultural College
Mississippi	53%	$27,810	Alcorn College
Missouri	6%	$2,880	Lincoln University
N. Carolina	37%	$17,760	Shaw University
S. Carolina	60%	—	No distribution
Tennessee	26%	$12,880	Fisk University
Texas	**14%**	**$12,000**	**Prairie View Normal**
Virginia	33%	$16,000	Hampton Normal
W. Virginia	4%	$1,920	W. Virginia Institute

Source: US Department of Agriculture.

Blackshear's goodwill had a soft underbelly. The extensive new campus construction and surge in enrollment to nearly one thousand students by March 1913 placed a major strain on the financial management of the college. Newly elected Texas A&M board chairman Edward B. Cushing, a distinguished alumnus of A&M and a Houston railroad executive, received an urgent phone call three days after he was confirmed as chair. In the surprise call, Blackshear informed Cushing that the college was practically without groceries, had no available money in the treasury, and the staff had not been paid—indeed, the college was over $40,000 in debt! Cushing contacted Governor Colquitt to determine what could be done in the interim before the legislature could address new appropriations. The options were few, including closing the college at once, which Blackshear strongly opposed, indicating they were only weeks away from commencement. He estimated it would only take $4,000 to carry the college to the end of the session. The principal was candid that the extensive construction of an ice house, two dormitories, and a new laundry plant, as well as the attendance, which had increased threefold, had completely overwhelmed their efforts to budget properly to address the rapid growth. Cushing informed the governor—who had had numerous personal contacts with Blackshear prior to this— that "he seemed to be squarely up against it." After consulting former A&M board chairman Walter Peteet and the A&M board representative to Prairie View, J. Allen Kyle (brother of Texas A&M dean E. J. Kyle), Cushing inquired about the procedure in Austin to obtain deficiency funding until the next legislative meeting. In the meantime, like he had done in a similar situation at the College Station A&M campus, Cushing advanced immediate cash funding and signed his personal guarantee for Prairie View to obtain groceries. He informed the governor, "I did this on what seemed to be a great emergency, but I do not intend to form this habit."[21]

Dr. Kyle played a pivotal role in this financial crisis, and there is no known public statement on the incident by the governor. The 1913 commencement ceremonies went as planned and Kyle and Cushing both spent a tremendous amount of time, personal money, and political capital to place Prairie View back on a solid financial footing and justify the importance and role of the black teachers' college. Concerned with the ramifications at the college, Blackshear wrote the governor, "It was out of deference to these gentlemen and to other members of the Board of Directors who are your political friends and supporters and my official superiors, who have *been kind enough to continue me up to this point in position here*." Rumors of the situation at Prairie View were soon questioned by the *Houston Post*, with Kyle responding directly that "there is some truth in the rumor of a 'shake up' at the Prairie View Normal," but denying that there was a likelihood of Blackshear being replaced. "[He] is a good man for the place and is well qualified and has invaluable experience. It would be an injustice to the school to remove him." Kyle further noted that the changes required by the board were "made for the reasons of economy and the school managed on a cash basis in the future," with the reduction of the student body—from 913 to 600—and six staff members being eliminated to meet the pending appropriations from the state legislature. Kyle informed the *Post*, "We agreed to make Prairie View a more practical school than it has been and to devote more effort to turning out negro teachers. For some time past the school has been run with this idea and we now intend to emphasize it still more." The *Post*, in the face of the disruption, continued to print articles of support, commending the work of the college: "Graduates of the college receive certificates to teach without further examination and there is always a demand for teachers—graduates of the industrial department never 'go a begging' for work."[22]

The *Houston Post*, after a lengthy campus tour, further noted, "Few people that have not visited Prairie View have any conception of the magnitude of the institution, the scope of the work, what it is doing for the colored race, [and] the influence for good on them throughout the State, for it draws students from all over Texas, and they are going out equipped to take their place as citizens whose influence will be for the betterment of the morals of the race, an inspiration to education, to higher ideals, to a clearer understanding of the dignity of labor."[23]

The further recognition of progress at Prairie View was many times related in legislative accolades, and the legislature confirmed its success by maintaining or increasing state appropriations. The excitement and comments of the Texas Senate Finance Committee in the hearings and observations were published in the *Austin American Statesman*:

> A thing that had a great deal to do with the committee's liberal treatment (i.e., appropriations) of Prairie View was the good report brought back by the subcommittee which visited it last spring, composed of Senators Hudspeth, Astin and Taylor.
>
> "If Blackshear had a white skin," Hudspeth said in reply to a question by Willacy, "he could be at the head of the Agricultural and Mechanical College or the State University [of Texas]."

> In reply to another question Hudspeth stated that the greatest economy is practiced in the management of the school, for everything that is capable of being utilized is made use of; by raising and making many of the commodities consumed by the student body, those in charge succeed in making a little money go a long way.
>
> The Senator expressed the conviction that the school was a very considerable factor in the progress of the Negro race in Texas. "The records show," said he, "that no more than 1 per cent of the graduates have ever been convicted of crime. I confess that I went down there prejudiced against the school, but I came away a strong supporter of it."
>
> "Which is the better conducted," Senator Willacy asked, "the white Agricultural and Mechanical College or the colored Prairie View Normal?"
>
> "The colored school, by all odds," answered the senator. He knew of no school anywhere that is conducted so well.[24]

There is no known response from either Texas A&M or the University of Texas.

With his reputation and authority seemingly unscathed, Professor Blackshear's development of the college was augmented by his leadership efforts to bring better conditions and the latest educational advances to African American farmers' connection with "King Cotton" in Texas and across the South.[25]

Cotton Speculation

A well-publicized gathering of representatives from across the Southern states was convened by Governor Colquitt to address the ways to raise the market price of cotton. This was a critical issue for the state, which Colquitt first addressed as a state senator in his "Anti-Cotton Futures" bill introduced in April 1897.[26] For over two decades, 40 percent of the South's cotton had been grown west of the Mississippi River in Texas, Louisiana, and Oklahoma. Blackshear, already writing articles and speaking to a broad cross section of agricultural groups for over a decade, supported the governor, if for no other reason than the price of cotton was key to the profits of Texas farmers and especially to his increasing constituency of black cotton farmers. Few today realize the impact and hold cotton had on all aspects of the economic, political, and social life across the South.

As historian Gilbert Fite noted, "Southern farmers, then, became 'trapped' in a cotton economy."[27] Cotton was celebrated and even revered—the first bale of cotton ginned annually in each community was cause for cheer. For example, the first bale ginned on August 1, 1913, at Blessing, Texas, brought the incredible price of seventeen cents per pound at auction. The *Daily Herald* in Weatherford, Texas, boasted, "Texas has produced a cotton crop greater than the entire crop of the South in 1860." However, gains in cotton production did not always translate to profits for Southern farmers. Efforts to develop a system to increase farmers' profits dated back to the mid-1880s when the Grange and Farmers' Alliance clamored for an improved system to take the middleman out of the yearly process. Ideas floated included improvement of local cooperatives, the establishment of a statewide cotton exchange, and an old marketing strategy by the Grange dating from a failed 1875 petition to the state legislature for a charter to ship cotton in bulk directly to the manufacturers in England, France, and Germany.[28]

In a guest editorial in the *Atlanta Constitution*, a newspaper with one of the highest circulations in the United States, Professor Blackshear outlined a detailed plan to increase the profits of small family farmers by releasing them from the control of speculators and middlemen. Debate among farmers on cotton pricing, marketing, and farm production cost and profits concerned both Southern leaders and the US Congress, who considered means to control speculators and "short sellers" in the cotton futures markets. Texas had a major stake in the cotton market given the fact that its farms yielded over three million bales in 1910, representing over a third of the nation's production. The world market supply of cotton in 1911, according to the *Jefferson* (Texas) *Jimplecute*, was primarily produced in the American South (50 percent), India (18 percent), Egypt (8 percent), Russia (5 percent), China (4 percent), and Brazil (2 percent)—all controlled by middlemen beholden to the futures market in Liverpool, England. As the leading producers of cotton for the past three-quarters of a century, Southerners wanted more say and control. Thus, Blackshear supported the "Subtreasury Plan" to have the federal government broker cotton and control the negative impact of the middleman, along with the failed "Anti-Option Bill" to limit market speculation.[29]

The Subtreasury Plan was an ambitious scheme and one of the key proposals by the Populist movement. Controversial then and in debates since, as Gregg Cantrell confirms in *The People's Revolt*, "Small oceans of ink have been spilled, in the Populist era and among latter-day historians, arguing the relative merits of the plan." Its major aim was to use public policy and government agencies to control monopolies in the fiber and grain markets. Precursors to the Subtreasury Plan can be tied to limited local and state efforts by the Alliance network to establish "cotton yards" that would weigh, store, and gin cotton—yet this limited scheme did not address supply-and-demand price fluctuations or much-needed farm credit and financial assistance. After these earlier proposals ran headlong into powerful banking and business concerns, in 1889 the Farmers' Alliance proposed a network of federally owned warehousing and elevator facilities for storing nonperishable crops like corn, wheat, and cotton. The warehouses would hold and insure crops at a modest fee and not release crops until selling into a favorable market. James Hogg won the governorship with the backing of the Alliance, but opposed the subtreasury movement. If implemented, farmers would then be eligible to obtain loans up to 80 percent of a crop's value, at 1 percent per annum, as well as low-interest land and mortgage loans. As Cantrell notes, "The Subtreasury Plan had multiple benefits. The loan provision addressed the immediate credit shortage faced by farmers, and the greenback feature effectively took the nation off the gold standard, reversing the deflationary contraction of the currency and making the country's money supply more flexible and adapted to a modern economy." And as historian Robert H. Wiebe concluded: "At one stroke they eliminated the national banks, the market in futures, the commission merchants [middlemen], and the private warehousemen, and in their place a simple 'peoples' currency would satisfy every need." Blackshear, constantly looking for means to improve the lives of rural African Americans,

TABLE 5.2. Cotton Production in the United States and Texas, 1860–1910

Year	United States	Texas	Percent of Total
1860	5,387,052 bales	431,463 bales	8.0
1870	3,011,996 bales	350,628 bales	11.6
1880	5,755,399 bales	805,284 bales	14.0
1890	7,472,511 bales	1,471,242 bales	19.7
1900	9,534,707 bales	2,506,212 bales	26.3
1910	11,965,962 bales	3,072,932 bales	25.7

Source: U.S. Bureau of the Census, *Agriculture* (Government Printing Office, 1890, 1900, 1910).

was greatly influenced by the subtreasury plan for the elimination of middlemen and the opportunity for fair market pricing for Texas farmers.[30]

Blackshear concluded that the biggest impact to further black advancement would be "a national system of industrial education for the United States"—to compliment and assist the small farmer in Texas. In a personal letter to Pres. Woodrow Wilson in March 1913, he encouraged that pending legislation in the House and Senate to support the farmers should "ensure that the negro people shall participate in the benefits of funds . . . and [the federal government] should reserve some definite and fixed proportion or ratio however small."[31] The challenge was not only for equality in educational opportunity, but also fair competitive access and protection from unscrupulous market practices. Learning of a bill in the US Congress introduced by Congressman Hatton Sumner of Dallas in 1915 for a "federal sales agency," Blackshear showed insight into the market dynamics in a detailed letter to Summer, singling out the middleman as the focus of the problem in limiting profits for farmers, remarking, "The middleman, when they do distribute these products, charge an excessive price for them—a price that is really prohibitive or at least prevents a wide distribution and consumption of products. It seems to me that this is a penny wise and pound foolish policy limiting distribution and consumption in the interest of high profits which at the same time are accompanied by relatively small sales. A much larger amount of these products could be sold if there was no extortion. But there is so much of the get-rich-quick spirit in the country especially among middlemen who handle these products that the larger good is overlooked and at the same time a larger amount of profit is also lost. That is, the sum total of profit would be greater on a larger amount of products sold, although the profit per unit of sale would be smaller."[32]

While Blackshear carefully did not advocate any movement toward socialism, he did argue that since cotton was a global commodity, the state should have a larger role in setting (monitoring) prices and marketing Southern cotton—to the benefit of the small farmer. Cotton was the number one cash crop in Texas and increased yearly, yet foreign buyers, middlemen, and market timing invariably undercut Texas farmers. Years later, after the turn of the century, Blackshear boasted that the surest path to success was landownership, and this was confirmed in the 1900 census. Substantial gains were made during the late 1890s; the percentage of farms owned by black Texans (20,139) was the highest (at 31 percent) of the seven leading cotton states of the Deep South in 1900. Arkansas was second in black ownership with 25 percent, followed by South Carolina with 22 percent, and Mississippi and Louisiana at 16 percent each. Thus, not surprisingly, debate on landownership and the pricing of cotton had been a major topic for over a decade at the annual Prairie View Colored Farmers' Congress. Blackshear, as early as 1905, indicated that the Southern cotton industry—especially the Texas producers—could and should be assisted by state agents to overcome the monopolies, expand cotton exports, and ensure "equal rights for all and special privilege to none, in the great cotton business of the South."[33]

"Cotton has guided the destinies of the South. It was cotton, really, not negro slavery," Blackshear concluded. The South had a "natural monopoly in producing the staple," and "that brought on the war—negro slaves were merely [a] convenient and long tried and an acceptable means to cotton raising." In a reply to his editorial, the *Atlanta Constitution* questioned the wisdom of more government control, stating that the plan was very commendable for "its boldness and thorough originality—the plan would level more [income] for the individual and less to the government." While Blackshear was at no time directly linked to the Populist sentiment growing in Texas, his conclusions clearly reflected the debate across the state by Populist proponents. Notwithstanding, Prohibition remained the hot topic.[34]

—•»«•—

In 1912 Blackshear was appointed by Governor Colquitt to lead a delegation representing Texas to the National Negro Educational Congress in St. Paul, Minnesota, in July, followed by a presentation at the National Congress of Colored Educators in Washington, DC, in September. Blackshear gained additional nationwide recognition the following year when Texas commissioner of agriculture Edward R. Kone (1908–14) wrote over thirty governors requesting that each state send a "representative negro" delegate to the National Negro Farmers' Congress in July 1913 in Birmingham, Alabama. The letter to the governors in part said, "I desire to say that, in my opinion Blackshear [a key organizer of the Congress] is intellectually one of the strongest negro men in the South, and of moral worth and achievement as an educator, in keeping with the circumstances, a credit to his people and deserving of aid in this effort to broaden and smooth the road of opportunity for negroes to become better citizens and thereby, a desirable constructive force in the body politic."[35]

The timely endorsement and call by Commissioner Kone and the organization by Blackshear resulted in over five hundred delegates gathered in Birmingham to form the National Negro Farmers' Congress, with keynote speakers from Tuskegee and Hampton Institutes and the USDA. The chief organizer, Edward Blackshear, was elected president of the organization. The model used was the one developed at Prairie View over the past seven years. Delegates at the three-day conference agreed to return home to "take steps to enlist the colored people in the movement" and to form county and regional congresses to advance the most profitable farming methods, develop marketing, and address social problems.[36] The objectives of the congress were drafted and delegates encouraged to energize farmers in their home states. African American farmers were motivated to become landowners, encourage farming among the youth, spread agricultural information, and subscribe to publications on marketing and the best methods of production—for example, crop rotation, fertilizers, rural credit, and improved livestock management. There was a direct correlation between household income from cotton yields and black children's school attendance rates. And all this would occur in the backdrop of better homes, schools, and church life in rural communities.[37] However, as Blackshear wrote, equal access under the law was not yet a reality: "The South enforces its mandates of social separation and political exclusion in the same proportion should Southern sentiment afford us reasonable educational and industrial opportunity and the full protection of the law in the courts of justice. For nothing is diviner than justice and in no other attitude is the white man so much the admiration of the black as when he assumes as he often does in Southern courts of law, the divine attitude and function of impartial human justice."[38]

The increased national exposure was not without consequences. Not everyone was supportive of Blackshear. In response to a letter to Pres. Woodrow Wilson in March 1913 (shortly after his inauguration) requesting that six black delegates be appointed from the District of Columbia to attend the National Farmers' Congress, the White House referred the letter to Secretary of Agriculture David Houston, former president of Texas A&M. Commissioner Kone's successful appeal for delegates to nearly a dozen governors, without assistance from the USDA, was soon made known to Houston. Confirmed as secretary for only a few weeks, Houston displayed a form of opposition Blackshear often faced—and this time from the highest level in the federal government. Houston expressed the anti-black tone and support of segregation, supported by a powerful block of Southern bigots in the Senate, that soon penetrated the Wilson administration. Houston wrote an internal memorandum to the president noting, "I know Mr. Blackshear quite well. He is full of schemes and writes well, but very few things he has to do with give satisfactory results," adding furthermore, "the great difficulty, however, would be to discover six negroes in the District who could render any good service."[39]

Houston was quite disingenuous to Blackshear given his earlier pledge back in Texas only a few years earlier to support Blackshear and the advancement of farmers' education and extension work; Houston even expressed reservations "that the negro race can not safely be entrusted with political responsibility." The records also indicate he did not do much to assist Prairie View when he was president of Texas A&M. Notwithstanding Houston's animus, Blackshear was at the height of his career and influence among educators and agriculturists across the South. His success, for example, with pioneering the Colored Farmers' Congress in Texas a decade earlier, the growth and prominence of Prairie View Normal as the largest public institution in the country for African Americans, his efforts to expand the number of black high schools in Texas, and his mentoring of hundreds of teachers and school administrators, as Houston surely knew, resulted in Blackshear routinely being referred to as the "Booker T. Washington of Texas." Furthermore, Wilson and his cabinet during mid-1913 were dealing almost exclusively with foreign affairs crises: entanglements with the Japanese over immigration into California, a dispute with Great Britain over Panama Canal tolls, and—most taxing—an increasingly more violent revolution in Mexico that threatened to call for American military intervention. While there were a number of qualified prospective delegates in the District of Columbia, primarily at Howard University, to fill the six positions, Houston recommended to the president that he take the proper steps to select a few USDA-sponsored "demonstration agents" (who would undoubtedly report back to Houston) near Birmingham to attend the congress. Blackshear most likely was never fully aware of the discrimination displayed by Houston. It is unknown whom Houston appointed, but it is known that the first nationwide National Farmers' Congress was a tremendous success and set the stage for similar events in states across the nation.[40]

—•⊱⊰•—

After much debate, both the subtreasury and federal sales agency ideas failed to gain acceptance in the congress. However, Blackshear's ideas were forwarded to agricultural secretary David Houston and numerous congressmen, who incorporated many of the farmers' concerns in a detailed proposal introduced into the legislature by Rep. Ashbury F. Lever of South Carolina for the enactment of the Cotton Futures Act and Cotton Warehouse Act of 1914. The warehouse portion of the act provided for federal licensing of facilities whose "certificates" could be used as a limited form of collateral. Yet these actions fell short of farmers' ongoing need for ample access to rural credit. Blackshear's observations gained from the National Negro Farmers' Congress were further addressed when the Cotton Futures Act was revised in 1916, 1919, and 1923 with the promulgation of official standard grades of cotton, as well as the USDA publication of an extensive article on cotton warehousing in the Agricultural Yearbook of 1918 and the inauguration of a weekly bulletin on spot market prices and an assessment of overall market conditions.[41]

Thirty-Fifth Annual Session

After a number of years of cooperation with the A&M Board of Directors to annually improve the curriculum and faculty at Prairie View, much progress was made to use state funding to add laboratories, mechanical shops, and farm demonstration sites. With these improvements well in place, working with Dr. William Bennett Bizzell, Blackshear gained board approval for what he termed a "regular course of study" or "Normal-Industrial Course" that solidified a diverse academic program that would be the framework of Prairie View's curriculum for the next four decades. These programs, while addressing the need to produce teachers, also allowed for students to pursue other careers, with a broad, four-year curriculum that included math and science, along with a touch of classical studies. The program was officially introduced for the thirty-fifth college session, beginning on September 9, 1914. Furthermore, since students entered with varying degrees of preparedness, the courses and degree program were designed to reward achievement and allow for a clear path to teacher certification (see table 5.3).

The approval and implementation of the new blended and expanded course of study reflected Blackshear's long-term plan and was on par with white college offerings across the state. This academic change would be the last major official act by Edward Blackshear as principal of the college.

TABLE 5.3. Normal-Industrial Course, 1914

Fall Term	Winter Term	Spring Term
	First Year	
English Composition	Composition	Rhetoric
Arithmetic	Rhetoric	Algebra
Physical Geography	Arithmetic	Agriculture
History—Grecian	Algebra	Civics
Industrial Practice	Physical Geography	Industrial Practices
	Second Year	
American Literature	American Literature	English Literature
Algebra	English Literature	Bookkeeping
Science—Biology	Biology	Physics
History—Medieval	Physics	School Management
Industrial Practice	History—Medieval to Modern	Industrial Practices
	Third Year	
Plane Geometry	Plane Geometry	Plane Geometry
1st Year Latin	1st Year Latin	1st Year Latin
Chemistry	Chemistry	Bacteriology
Economics	History of Industry	Pedagogy
Industrial Practice	Industrial Practice	Industrial Practice
	Fourth Year	
Psychology	Ethics	History of Education
Geology	Advanced Physics	Advanced Physics
Latin—Caesar	Latin—Caesar	Latin—Cicero
Solid Geometry	College Algebra	Plane Trigonometry
Industrial Practice	Industrial Practice	Industrial Practice

Source: "Circular of Information," Thirty-Fifth Annual Session, *Prairie View Standard*, July 25, 1914.

That Blackshear, at the height of his impact on Prairie View, had the vision and goal for the school to be the leading public institution in the training of African American teachers and administrators was captured in the introduction of the 1914–15 college catalogue, which also wove in the industrial and agricultural programs to provide a broad agenda addressing

The 1914 faculty and staff of the Prairie View Normal and Industrial College. This is the last formal picture with Edward Blackshear (pictured in center) and the last image of him as principal of the college. Note the growth depicted by the new buildings. Courtesy of Prairie View A&M University Archives.

the "practical life" of the future. His well-deserved pride was rooted in the success of the college:

> OBJECT OF THE SCHOOL
>
> Prairie View State Normal and Industrial College has for its object the training of persons desiring to fit themselves for the important profession of teaching, by giving them thorough instruction and practical drill in the best recognized methods of organizing, disciplining, and conducting schools.
>
> The particular aims are to fit colored youths for responsible positions in colored public schools of Texas, to impart something of the scholarly spirit indispensable to excellence in teaching, and to awaken an enthusiasm for the education and for the industrial and moral improvement of the colored race in Texas.
>
> Believing in the value of training in connection with the literary and professional studies, as a means to mental, moral, and economic improvement, the Board of Directors have added agricultural and mechanical departments and a department of Female Industries to give a well-rounded education and to prepare the student for practical life.[42]

Texas politics would soon alter the course of Blackshear's life.

Demon Rum

By mid-1914 the political tide in the black community, influenced by new third-party movements, was being strongly encouraged to shift its views on Prohibition. Edward Blackshear, along with key public and denominational college administrators and teachers, as well as black politicians of all political parties, was encouraged to support the anti-saloon crusade of the prohibitionists. This major political reversal for Blackshear would have a dire impact on his life and career. The educators involved felt, with the encouragement of the Prohibition propaganda, that the Prohibition stance benefited black education institutions and awareness of their needs across the state. Due to Prohibition, political lines and allegiances were shifting in Texas. For the first time since Reconstruction, a broad cross section of blacks and whites from diverse and often hostile opposing factions gathered in Waco, where they were joined by Republican "Gooseneck Bill"

McDonald; M. M. Rogers, chairman of the Negro Statewide Prohibition Association; and an aspiring politician of the white Democrat prohibitionist group, Thomas Ball, to plan voter appeal and a turnout strategy. One key aspect of the Prohibition movement was a focus on the black vote, noting: "By an act of the legislature of Texas the qualified voters will be called upon to decide whether or not whiskey shall be manufactured or sold within the state of Texas, and, as a race and citizens who stand for all that tends to elevate our people and promote the best interest of our state, we should and must exercise the right and cast our ballot as becomes a man and a citizen."[43]

Despite the prohibitionists' tremendous effort and their success in gathering many to the Prohibition cause, the amendment failed at the polls. It was not unusual for Blackshear to join with those promoting education as well as figuring prominently among black leadership statewide, yet in this instance it placed him in the prohibitionist camp. As Prairie View historian George Woolfolk concluded, Blackshear "could not refrain from standing with other Negro leaders" and "his tragic blunder was in joining the factional fight in the Texas Democratic party over the issue of prohibition." As the 1914 gubernatorial election approached, he was committed to the prohibitionist candidate, Thomas Ball. Ball hoped to attract black support and allowed a rumor to circulate that he would have the Terrell voting law repealed. Blackshear's lifelong intention was to advance opportunities for black education across the state, yet his highly public profile and generally cautious approach to political issues soon became a problem for the highly regarded educator—politics makes strange bedfellows and often results in unintended consequences.[44]

In the weeks before the election, the race appeared to be a toss-up with no predetermined winner. Times had changed. Colonel House, who had been the behind-the-scenes Democratic campaign power broker and magician for over a decade, was no longer a controlling force. His focus after 1912 was acting as the chief adviser in the White House to Pres. Woodrow Wilson. Previously, House had assisted the Texas Democratic Party with carefully navigating the contentious Prohibition issue, but this time he was gone, and the "wet vs. dry" debate occupied center stage in the fall gubernatorial race. Edward Blackshear, approaching two decades as the principal of Prairie View, was the titular leader of African Americans in Texas. The success of Prairie View, reflected in its growth as the largest public black college in the country as well as in the continued accomplishments of its graduates as teachers, farmers, and businessmen, was known statewide. Blackshear thus was looked upon as a critical leader in the black community to help shape the direction of voters. Having maneuvered five governors' campaigns, some overtly and most covertly behind the scenes, he unwittingly found himself on a collision course as power politics, religion, and strong personal egos clashed in the final weeks of the campaign. Church leaders were engaged in the statewide political campaign like never before, and Blackshear's role was brought into question by a number of political operatives, white and black, attempting to take advantage of the pre-election turmoil.

Editorials and letters to the editor in papers across the state soon became a hotbed of allegations and counterallegations on the looming impact of black voters in the fall election and who had the most influence over them. While there had been general attacks against Prairie View over the years, this time public attacks were launched directly at Blackshear's role and intentions. Many of these politically motivated affronts were the results of long-standing acquaintances, usually in line with his duties as principal. For example, Blackshear had known Thomas Ball since his days as a US congressman (1896–1903) and had hosted him for a visit and presentation to the Prairie View students and staff as early as the fall of 1900.[45] Following the endorsement of Colonel Ball by the Lincoln Baptist Association, which Blackshear attended, at their annual July convention in Houston, questions were raised by black political and denominational leaders in the *Houston Post*: "Attack on Blackshear—Is Behind Certain Movement It Is Now Alleged."

> It appear[s] on the surface that the report was colored by The Post in order to make political capital among the negroes in Colonel Ball's behalf. He raises the question: "Is there a scheme on to vote the 'blacks' in the primaries in Colonel Ball's interest this year?"
>
> Now I am answering him in this wise: There is a scheme on but it is not a white man's scheme to use the negroes in the interest of Colonel Ball or any other white man; it is a black man's scheme to create capital to be used to influence the white man against one negro personally, and against the common interest of all the citizens of Texas both white and black.
>
> That report was written and handed to the city editor of The Post by a negro, who was trained to carve into his report such a statement with

> a view to stack up something to which certain negro politicians could point when in their final attempt to oust Prof. E. L. Blackshear, principal of the Prairie View State normal, and to disrupt our splendid State school. These men know that when it comes to ability and efficiency they have no chance to get professor Blackshear out. They know deep down in their hearts that he is the most logical man for the place but as some of them put it: "We think it's time for a change." They are not in the line of thought which make institutions great, they would prefer the "change."
>
> They recall how Professor Blackshear was led, against his desire to discuss prohibition, pro or con, to make a statement tantamount to indoring [*sic*] the anti-prohibitionists, and now, as it appears they think these little dirty political grand standing plays in their religious gatherings, . . . they may be able to claim the attention of this administration to the extent of dispatching Professor Blackshear for one of their ilk regardless of the negro education in Texas.[46]

Farmer Jim: Politics, War, and Education

The campaign for governor in mid-1914 and the last months of the Colquitt administration was a confusing and tense time in Texas. Blackshear and his staff grappled with addressing facilities for a growing enrollment and funding to add faculty. In addition to state politics, he directed his attention to both foreign and national affairs. The Texas-Mexican border was in turmoil as Mexico's expanding revolutionary hostilities spilled over into Texas border cities. The governor was publicly and vocally at odds with President Wilson on how best to address the growing border violence. The rising death toll of civilian American citizens, both along the border and in Mexico, and the confiscation of American property (especially in the oil industry) in Mexico filled the newspapers with reports of an imminent US intervention to calm the bloody revolution.[47] In advance of turning his attention to the gubernatorial election, Blackshear wrote Governor Colquitt that in the event of a US armed intervention in Mexico and "the President's call upon the Governor to furnish a quota of troops," Blackshear would be honored to take a leave-of-absence from Prairie View to raise a unit of soldiers. The day after he wrote to the governor, on April 21, 1914, US marines landed at Vera Cruz, Mexico. Blackshear's offer was acknowledged by the governor, but there is no evidence after Vera Cruz that his service was requested.[48]

Blackshear next turned his attention to his concerns about the passage of the first national income tax law, sending a detailed letter to former president Theodore Roosevelt at his home in Oyster Bay, New York. His letter, which he urged Roosevelt to forward to Washington legislators with hopes of amending the tax bill, centered on the inequality of taxing large families without having an exception based on the number of children. "It seems unreasonable to make no allowance as between such a family of one or six children." He recommended a sliding scale or allowance of $250 per child, concluding: "I believe this will appeal to you as a father, and as a believer in large families and as one whose family life is a model for the Nation." His second appeal, as he termed it, "in line with the spirit of the Progressive Party," was to establish in the future a network of presidential primaries and also recommendations for the direct election of the president, and thus "the removal of the decision in national elections from the state lines [i.e., participation] entirely and making it depend on a majority of the total vote cast by the whole majority of the people regardless of the states." He closed the personal letter to Roosevelt with the note, "By strengthening the sentiment and evolution of a genuine nationalism is the high destiny of the American republic to be achieved." With this, Blackshear turned his full attention to the Texas governor race.[49]

The two leading contenders in the 1914 gubernatorial election, Thomas Ball and James "Farmer Jim" Ferguson, were at best mediocre candidates who only had to capture their party's primary nomination. Soon Blackshear was to be lured into the growing debate on how best to attract the black vote across Texas. Progressive opponent Ball, a well-known Houston attorney, after some three years of campaigning for Prohibition made the anti-saloon issue the main plank of his campaign. He assumed that a groundswell during a governor's race would solidify the issue with the Texas voters and place him in the governor's mansion. Ferguson, a country boy from Waco with little formal education and a lot of business experience, straddled the issue as the candidate of the "wets" (with extensive support from the liquor industry) by announcing that when he was governor he would veto any bill that had to do with liquor no matter the source or intent of the legislation, boasting, "I will strike it where the chicken got the axe." On the stump, Ferguson, a colorful speaker, appealed to farmers with agrarian props like a gourd of drinking water and a wooden dipper to seal his image as tied to the rural constituents. A vicious statewide whispering campaign labeled Ball a drunk, untrustworthy philanderer and sealed the outcome.[50]

Farmer Jim won a large victory in the July Democratic primary with 235,062 votes over the lackluster Tom Ball with 191,558 and was easily swept into office in November. Without hesitation, Ferguson headed to Austin to assert what he viewed was a "business-minded," conservative approach to the state's challenges, budgets, and needs. After he was inaugurated on January 19, 1915, he addressed the Texas legislature, stating his door was always open. The open door, however, was slammed on any holdover political appointees. He at once began to use one of the limited (yet far-reaching) powers of the Texas governor by dictating replacements and new appointees in agencies and boards across the state. He followed the customary practice of rewarding friends, regardless of qualifications. Many of the leaders whom Blackshear had worked with for over a decade were quickly dismissed and replaced. For example, new political appointments were made to the State Insane Asylum Board, the State Lunatic Asylum, the Confederate Home, and Pilot Commissioners for the ports of Houston and Galveston, and appointees as Public Weighers were nominated and installed. The governor's new appointments were forwarded to the Texas Senate and generally approved with little fanfare.[51]

Following a whirlwind number of agency appointments across the state, Ferguson turned his attention to higher education. The governor targeted both Texas A&M College and its branch at Prairie View, as well as carrying out a punitive, head-on, continuous assault on the funding, staff, and operations at the University of Texas (UT). Ferguson felt that the state's funding should be redirected to education at the local level—rural, underfunded schools should receive the same funding as higher education. Texas lagged behind the national average in most education metrics, and Ferguson felt more could be done for the nearly 15 percent of Texas's children who were illiterate. He called for legislation to provide liberally for "education of the masses." The legislature at his request passed a compulsory school attendance law in 1915, effective for the fall of 1916, and provided new funding of $1 million for the establishment and expansion of rural high schools—pivotal education issues Blackshear had actively championed for over a decade.[52]

In general Ferguson seemed pleased with the operations at Texas A&M, retaining the members of the board, under Chairman John I. Guion of Ballinger, with only one change during the first few years (L. J. Hart replaced by John T. Dickson of Paris). Previous A&M board chairman Edward B. Cushing of Houston had set the college on a solid financial footing—yet increasing appropriations were always needed and requested.

During the final months of the Colquitt administration in mid-1913, A&M president Col. Robert T. Milner found himself in conflict with the governor and resigned at A&M "under pressure."[53] The A&M board and new president William Bennett Bizzell (1914–25) wanted no further conflict with Austin and the new governor. Blackshear, who had already had a brief confrontation with Colquitt, maintained a low profile as the conflict with Milner at A&M evolved. There were, however, pending issues that needed delicate attention. Texas A&M and the University of Texas were in talks on how to mend athletic program conflicts, resulting in the chartering of the Southwest Athletic Conference in December 1914. Furthermore, an ongoing manifestation of the political rivalry resulted in an appeal by many to fairly divide the Permanent University Funds (talks that had lingered on and on since the Ross administration), between the two flagship institutions. The result was a confusing resolution drafted by the Texas Senate that would in effect do away with Texas A&M and consolidate all educational and extension operations, administration, and classes in Austin at one state university! Furthermore, any such actions to disrupt A&M and UT would potentially be disastrous to the future operations of Prairie View. The legislative fight, supported by the governor, cost President Milner his job, and the citizens of Texas overwhelmingly defeated the proposed PUF amendment by a vote of four to one.[54]

Thus, the political tension over higher education in the state carried over from Colquitt to the incoming Ferguson administration. The first higher education challenge in early 1915, purely on political grounds, was launched by Governor Ferguson not at College Station but instead at Prairie View Normal. For Ferguson, the battle had more to do with punitive, vindictive politics than improving the quality of education. Within days of his inauguration, he was to display his hostile approach. During the end of January, as a courtesy and congratulatory visit to the governor's office, Senator Astin dropped in to introduce Texas A&M professor of engineering David W. Spence, the consulting engineer representing construction planning at Prairie View Normal. During the meeting they took the opportunity to "discuss with him informally" an emergency appropriation item of $29,000 for Prairie View Normal. Very matter-of-factly Ferguson indicated he understood the emergency request and stated that at the proper time he would be glad to review it with officials of the college. However, he tied his approval of any such funding to the removal of the principal of the college, Blackshear, as reported in detail in the *Austin Statesman*:

> And having satisfied the callers on that score [of the potential funding] he told them that there was at the head of the Prairie View Normal a negro of whom he thinks very little and whom he wants removed at the earliest possible moment.
>
> In the gubernatorial campaign, Professor Blackshear wrote letters against Governor Ferguson, some of which were published. It is Governor Ferguson's contention that a negro has no business whatever taking a part in the political affairs of the Democratic party, the white man's party, and he says as long as he is governor no negro under him shall attack any white man in any political campaign—that this is beyond the prerogative of a negro in a Democratic election.[55]

Even before Dr. Spence could return to College Station to brief President Bizzell and the A&M board, news of the governor's demand spread statewide. The message was clear: the governor "requested [A&M's] trustees to remove the Principal of Prairie View"—at once. Blackshear quickly found himself on the losing side of a political fight with the governor and reached out to a number of political supporters, such as Congressmen Hutton Sumner in Dallas and Lt. Gov. William P. Hobby in Austin, to intervene with the governor. However, at the A&M board meeting on March 3, 1915, there is no record of the Blackshear situation being discussed, and Dr. Spence, for the record, reported the affairs and management of Prairie View "as being in splendid shape." (It should be noted, however, that the A&M board minutes appear to have been carefully "sanitized" on numerous occasions.) Friends and leaders across the state came to the defense of Blackshear, and the A&M Board of Directors requested he come before the group to clear up the governor's claims. A supporter wrote the *Houston Post*, "Everything is in safe hands, Principal Blackshear could not be duplicated. He is the man for the place." Behind-the-scenes efforts with the governor's office continued for weeks, but to no avail.[56]

Meanwhile, the quisquous Ferguson made no secret of his distaste for what he termed "the snooty elitists" at the University of Texas. As quiet appeals were being made to the governor to forgo the removal of Blackshear, the governor shifted his attention off Prairie View's principal as he became embroiled in a long running controversy with the administrators at UT. Ferguson's first target at the university was the removal of its acting president William J. Battle, a classical professor deemed to have no management experience. This was followed by the demand to remove a list of additional professors and staff—whom Ferguson noted were "butterfly chasers," "day dreamers," and "educated fools"—including Caswell Ellis, Lindley Keasbey, and John Lomax, all of whom he wanted fired at once due to their superfluous positions! Ferguson was supported by many lawmakers and some regents who believed the faculty thought themselves above the law and therefore insulated from criticism regarding the way they allocated and haphazardly spent state funds. Asked why he wanted the removal of the professors, the governor curtly responded: "I don't have to give any reasons. I am the Governor of the State of Texas."[57]

Battle soon wearied of the pressure and resigned, and the Texas Board of Regents replaced him with Robert E. Vinson, president of the Austin Presbyterian Theological Seminary and a clergyman. Vinson did not have the approval of the governor—who was reported to be "red hot" at not being consulted. Campus personnel were important, but the factor that proved critical was the governor's attack on the university budget, which he felt was bloated and misused. Further complicating the discourse was the decade-long tension (which would ultimately last over six decades) with Texas A&M over use of the PUF—where he sided with A&M (possibly influenced by the fact that Ferguson's older brother was an A&M alumnus). Next, his plan was to replace members of the UT Board of Regents and pack the board with his friends, yet this action stalled. This resulted in the involvement of Will Hogg, the former governor's son. Hogg was a former university board regent and powerful in the influential Ex-Students Association. Lewis Gould concluded in 1983 that Governor Ferguson, who "had a large sense of his own importance," in his attacks on the University of Texas "established a pattern of politicization that persists to the present [day]." The conflict with the University of Texas was delayed when the Texas Senate began an investigation to impeach Ferguson, on charges of bribery and mismanagement of public funds. However, as the bitter fight continued with UT, the governor was soon asking about the Prairie View situation.[58]

Blackshear appeared before the A&M board again on April 24, 1915, and stated he had been active in supporting measures that enhanced education statewide, but that at no time had he attacked Ferguson as a gubernatorial candidate. The board agreed Blackshear made a "clear and satisfactory statement" and any confusion was deemed little more than "trivial charges." The A&M trustees hoped the matter was behind them and that time would heal any ill feelings in Austin. Furthermore, the board approved Blackshear's request to once again sponsor Booker T. Washington as the keynote speaker at Prairie View's upcoming June 1915 commencement ceremonies.[59]

In an attempt to protect Blackshear and to prevent more attacks from Austin, the A&M board maintained close oversight of operations at Prairie View, which in fact was running very smoothly. The board further defined the relationship of the college with the administrators at Prairie View by noting all communications and financial matters were to be transmitted through President Bizzell and then to the board—basically restating procedures already in place—and that the A&M president was to visit Prairie View at least four times each year or oftener as necessary, and the annual report should reflect all the activities of the college.[60]

Dr. Woolfolk noted, "Negro leaders believed that strong whites were behind Blackshear and were trying to 'fix things up'; but others were sure that the strength of his backing would not be sufficient to save his job." There was little the Republican Party leadership, supported by many black Texans, could do, since the position of principal was a job controlled by the Democratic Party and Governor Ferguson—regardless of the wishes of the A&M Board of Directors. Possibly the A&M board thought the broiling conflict between Ferguson and the University of Texas would divert attention away from Blackshear. Notwithstanding, the *Bryan Eagle* reported that the A&M board "at the June [6] meeting re-elected Blackshear" as principal, but no record of this action item appears in the A&M Board minutes.[61]

Booker T. Washington was not able to attend the weeklong commencement activities in late June 1915 at Prairie View. This event marked the largest graduating class up till then. Hundreds of families, friends, and representatives from the A&M College attended. Edward Blackshear, in advance of Judge John Guion, chairman of the A&M board, conferring diplomas, made what was to be his last formal campus presentation as principal of Prairie View (and these remarks were found in the *Kansas City Sun*): "Some white people express the belief that education of the negro makes him less honest and less upright. This institution was established as an agricultural college in 1878, and the next year was made a normal institution. In her history she has graduated 1,111 students and has given certificates to teach to more than twice that number. Figures show that not one of our graduates has committed a capital offense against the peace and dignity of the state. In view of these statements, which are indisputable facts, I do not think that any one can consistently say that the proper kind of education does anything except encourage the negro in his attempt to live a better and more useful life."[62]

Support for Blackshear continued during the summer months. Ignoring the pressure of the governor's attacks and confident the A&M board would prevail with Governor Ferguson, Blackshear ensured the important summer teachers' training and certification programs continued. At the annual Texas Colored Farmers' Congress, one of Blackshear's signature accomplishments, held in late July 1915, hundreds of farmers and ranchers from across the state drafted a unanimous resolution to the governor expressing their gratitude for the continued support of the college and especially the leadership of its principal. Resolved: "We recognize Prof. Blackshear as a safe and sound leader, one whose life has been pure and clean and one who has shown his capacity for guarding the proper relation that must exist between the races. Coming from the farms and rural districts where the masses of our people live we, the colored farmers of Texas, are in a position to know the life of Blackshear as is being reflected in our homes through our boys and girls to be a shining example of morality."[63]

The long saga, dating from the governor's first attack in early February 1915, did not end until after the Prairie View commencement. There was strong speculation that enemies of Blackshear, never formally identified, maintained a continuous whisper campaign to discredit and remove the high-profile principal. Notwithstanding, during the summer the *Waco Morning News*, a newspaper in the Texas town where young Blackshear first arrived in 1882, was under the impression all was resolved: "We are glad Blackshear has been re-elected and hope the governor and board will see to it that he shall not be further embarrassed by slander of political self-seekers who want his position. Blackshear has no business meddling in partisan politics in this state, for there is no question but that Blackshear is the best qualified man in Texas for the job." Satisfied with Blackshear's response and performance at the college, his contract as principal was extended by the A&M board on June 6. The remaining question was the continued hostility of the governor. In a final effort to save Blackshear, Judge Guion went to Austin to confer with the governor and "eloquently proclaimed" that his removal as principal would "be a calamity." Ferguson remained recalcitrant. The *Houston Post*, constantly in support of Blackshear, noted, "The decree had gone forth: Blackshear's head was to [be] removed; Blackshear's head was removed. The veto [of the A&M

budget, threatened by the governor] was the club held over the board to compel obedience to the wishes of the governor."[64]

After failing to prevail with Ferguson, Guion wired the principal his request for him to submit his resignation. The efforts of Guion and others who fought the governor to save Blackshear is a significant indication and testament of his prestige and stature among white leaders and board members. Meeting in Dallas on July 6, just prior to the beginning of an A&M board meeting, Blackshear, "feeling he was at the mercy of the board," tendered his resignation. However, when the board formally convened, they requested that the resignation by Blackshear be withdrawn, and according to the *Bryan Eagle*, the "board decided to rescind its action of June 6 in re-electing the incumbent."[65] Members of the A&M board were divided on terminating Blackshear, despite the pressure from the governor, with member J. Sheb Williams of Paris, Texas, protesting: "I have made investigations throughout the state and have never found even one act of indiscretion or one scantillia [*sic*] of evidence against him. The South has been searching for his kind for more than 50 years and have found only two, Blackshear and Booker T. Washington, as educators and high moral examples for the negro race. He has served Prairie View and Texas with great distinction for 19 years, who was dismissed from the state's service without charges being preferred or the opportunity being given him to defend himself. I shall vote to retain him, and I want my reasons given and my vote recorded."[66]

In essence, the board decided that Edward Blackshear's existing contract as principal at Prairie View, which expired on September 1, would not be renewed, and thus there was no need for him to submit a resignation nor any action needed for the board to terminate him. This gracious means of handling a most regrettable political situation by the A&M board was befitting to honor the two decades of leadership and contributions made by Edward Blackshear at Prairie View. From 1896 to 1915, the Blackshear administration had 1,528 graduates, compared to 172 graduates between 1879 and June 1896. Furthermore, by 1915, due to his efforts with summer teacher programs and community outreach, Texas had more than three dozen black public high schools, more than three times as many as any other Southern state (and more than the combined total of high schools in Georgia, Missouri, and South Carolina). Championing education in general across the state, he encouraged the establishment and staffing with Prairie View teachers of African American high schools across Texas and in particular advanced the growth and development of higher education at Prairie View Normal. The *Houston Daily Post* highly commended his service: "It is his intelligent and unremitting work that has made the institution one of the best of its kind in the country."[67]

In the first detailed federal government study and assessment of "Negro Education" across the United States, the Bureau of Education in the Department of the Interior, sponsored by the Phelps-Stokes Fund, conducted a year-long evaluation that coincided with the final months that Blackshear was principal. While Prairie View was the leading black institution in the state, the evaluation expressed concern that the extensive industrial and agricultural programs "suffered from ineffective organization," without giving any specifics. This conclusion was based in part on the fact that over two-thirds of the more than seven hundred students were girls, and it was recommended that the attendance of young men be increased. All students were expected to work three hours a day in either the agricultural or industrial programs. While the livestock and farm equipment were determined to be ample, only 365 of the college's 1,500 acres were under cultivation. The total faculty and staff numbered forty-six, of whom a quarter were trained at Prairie View. The teacher production programs were commended with the suggestion that "practical teaching" be increased, an item Blackshear addressed in his yearly summer teacher programs across the state. The financial accounts, kept on a simple cash basis, were found to be in good order, except for the cumbersome requisition system for purchasing supplies, possibly because of the approval process in College Station that "entailed unnecessary expense and loss of time and labor," which could be improved with an annual audit. The college, given its rapid growth and ongoing pressure to have adequate facilities for students and staff, was considered in good shape.[68]

Governor Ferguson's boisterous arrogance and arbitrary personal actions soon led to his swift demise, an end to his career not as honorable as Professor Blackshear's: an impeachment on ten counts of mismanagement and fraud by the Texas Senate and his resignation on September 17, 1917. Ferguson's political attacks and repeated onslaughts were fully directed at the termination of Blackshear and thus determined a reprisal to eliminate the primary leader of African Americans in Texas. The first count filed against the governor—referring directly to the attack on Blackshear—was the governor's ineptness in the "removal of able, experienced, administrative heads of state institutions of the highest character and efficiency—for purely political purposes." Fully two years after Blackshear was terminated, however, there was little that could be done to reverse the governor's actions. Furthermore, the senate issued a ruling that Ferguson was forever disqualified to hold public office—a censure he ignored, running unsuccessfully for governor in 1918 and the US Senate in 1922.[69]

Transition

The transition to a new principal at Prairie View was not smooth. In haste, the board selected I. M. Terrell (no relation to Senator Terrell), the former superintendent of schools in Fort Worth, even though he had no higher education background or experience in managing a large institution. Terrell's name had surfaced in August 1913 as a possible principal, following a routine audit by J. Allen Kyle of Houston, chairman of the Prairie View subcommittee representing the A&M board to conduct annual oversight. The *Houston Daily Post* reported rumors, after an impromptu interview with Kyle, of faculty changes prior to the beginning of the 1913 fall semester. While there were changes due to budget concerns, the changes had nothing to do with Blackshear. Kyle said bluntly to the media, "Professor Blackshear is a good man for the place, is well qualified and has invaluable experience. It would be an injustice to the school to remove him." These sentiments did not win the day two years later.[70]

Filling the role and educational experience of Blackshear was going to be very difficult—and finding anyone with his reputation, experience, and respect, near impossible. Terrell was hardly in office when faculty and local community protests to the A&M board demanded his removal. The

TABLE 5.4. African American Illiteracy in Texas, 1880–1920

1880	75.4%
1890	52.5%
1900	38.2%
1910	24.6%
1920	17.8%

Source: Eby, *Development of Education in Texas*, 280. See also Jones, *Negro Education*, vol. 1.

dismissal now allowed President Bizzell and the board to take their time in making their next selection. Upon the strong recommendation of the Prairie View faculty, Bizzell at once contacted his lifelong friend Dr. J. Granville Osborne to be the replacement. Osborne as a youth had saved Bizzell from drowning in the local swimming hole and had gone on to great success as an educator, and after completing Leonard Medical School at Shaw University, a physician. He returned to Navasota, Texas, to practice medicine and also accepted the job as the principal of the black public school. He was well suited and respected to pick up where Blackshear departed. Historian Henry Dethloff often noted that where Blackshear had become the Ross of Prairie View to place the institution on a solid footing, "Osborne became the Bizzell of Prairie View, working in close harmony and purpose with President Bizzell."[71]

Back to School

The shock of Blackshear's termination to the black community and educators statewide did not subside for months. His termination was harsh, he lost his regular access to the media and speaking engagements, and he and his wife also lost their campus home, the state-owned residence they had lived in for two decades. The *Houston Daily Post* posed the question, "If the one school in this State maintained for negroes is to be made a political plaything, or if any of the institutions of this State is to be a plaything of politics, the people of Texas have the right to know it. If one school is to be trifled with that way, no State institution of higher learning is safe." On the national level, the death of Booker T. Washington in November 1915 at age fifty-nine left a major leadership vacuum, soon to be filled by W. E. B. Du Bois, now the driving force of the newly organized National Association for the Advancement of Colored People (NAACP). In spite of Blackshear's departure from Prairie View, he remained the titular leader of African Americans in Texas and was selected to deliver the eulogy at the memorial service in Houston titled: "Life and Times Dr. B. T. Washington." Elections have consequences, and others across the state of Texas wondered who would be the governor's next target. The ongoing fight in Austin between the governor and the University of Texas over personnel and budgets kept higher education in the news for months and into the next gubernatorial elections. After a brief vacation, Blackshear moved to Fort Worth in October 1915 to briefly manage the private Industrial and Mechanical

College. To be closer to home, he accepted a position in Houston as principal of the Holman School at Emancipation Park. Blackshear's service to the state did not end there. The move to Houston was disrupted with the tragic news that his eldest son, William, an instructor in the mechanical department at Prairie View, died on January 13, 1917, in the college hospital built by his father in 1902, from complications with pneumonia.[72]

•» 6 «•

War and Agricultural Extension Service

We pledge ourselves to do all in our power, by enlistment at the front, and by engaging at home in those useful and necessary industrial and agricultural pursuits which are essential to the maintenance both of the army in the field and the people at home—in order to do our part to ensure victory.

EDWARD L. BLACKSHEAR, APRIL 6, 1917

I must and do insist as the head of the negro extension work in Texas that we avoid mooted religious, political or racial problems—because these problems involve questions as to which the public entertains various opinions.

EDWARD L. BLACKSHEAR, MARCH 23, 1919

His abrupt separation and departure from the principalship of Prairie View College did not preclude Edward Blackshear from continuing his career and leadership in education. Following a brief period of teaching in Houston, he returned to Prairie View in 1917 after the United States joined World War I to serve in the Agricultural Extension Service to ensure a robust response from Texas farmers to the food, fiber, and forage needs of the nation. He remained one of the most important and vocal advocates of black education and during the last years of his life was engaged in the development and expansion of agricultural programs, first across Texas and then the Southwest. Blackshear had pioneering agricultural experience with Robert L. Smith's Farmers' Improvement Society of Texas in the

1890s, as well as the USDA and Tuskegee Institute programs with the first "Negro demonstration agents" working exclusively with black farmers. Blackshear's development of the Colored Farmers' Congress, first held in 1906, as well as his knowledge of crop rotation, produce markets, pricing, purchasing, and distribution proved valuable to his preparation for his new extension service role. Among these challenges were the ongoing efforts to diversify crop production among the small sharecropper and tenant farmers into new cash crops in the face of the dominant cotton and cattle ethos of the day (with over 85 percent of black Texans growing only King Cotton). While Southern whites limited black authority and political power, census data indicated that in spite of the blatant discrimination African Americans held deep-seated values that linked landownership to economic and personal independence. In this role Blackshear was a pivotal leader in the establishment of a network of black county extension agents and innovative programs in East Texas that had the respect of both black and white farmers and ranchers. The challenges his new team of extension agents faced included assisting farmers with the unrelenting pressures that included the boll weevil, the limited credit system, unpredictable markets, and postwar price deflation of agricultural products. Thus, the Great War in Europe and the struggle for equal rights and opportunities shaped the political, economic, and social dynamics in Texas during the early twentieth century and for decades to come.[1]

World War I: "Fight Them We Must"

As a well-respected leader, Blackshear took a lead role in making sure the black community did not suffer any prejudicial attacks due to propaganda that surfaced during World War I. The war had begun in Europe in August of 1914, but the general feeling was that most Texans had no interest in the faraway conflict. With few exceptions, generations of European immigrants to the state wanted no part of the fight in their former homeland—they had come to Texas to settle and avoid other people's wars. Gradually these sentiments shifted following the announcement of unrestricted Atlantic submarine warfare and the sinking of the *Lusitania*, which killed hundreds of Americans. Further inflaming public opinion was the interception by British intelligence agents of the inflammatory, top-secret Zimmermann telegram from the German high command in Berlin to Mexico City pledging to help Mexico recover "all the stolen territory" of Texas, New Mexico, and Arizona after Germany won the war. Outrage in Texas slowly grew in advance of the congressional declaration of war on April 6, 1917. Especially concerning were the articles and rumors that German secret agents and spies were in Texas and active along the Texas-Mexican border. The aim of the agents was to create disruption, as clearly noted by the Plan of San Diego and the secret efforts in El Paso to assist ousted dictator Gen. Victoriano Huerta to launch a counterattack in Mexico, as well as to incite the black community in Texas to rise up and rebel in support of Germany and against the state. Huerta was arrested near El Paso attempting to cross the border, and the *Southland Farmer* agreed: "Germany has ruthlessly disregarded the rights of our people, as of other neutral nations, and fight them we must."[2]

On the surface these claims to incite African Americans seemed baseless, but in fact they were taken seriously by black leaders, and especially by Edward Blackshear. The rumors of some form of black community response had swirled in Houston among church congregations as well as in the dock workers union in Houston and Galveston. In fact, German agents trained in Mexico City were well organized and looking for any weak spot to create confusion and dissent in Texas.[3] On the eve of the declaration of war, Blackshear called a mass community meeting of black leaders to emphasize the loyalty of black Americans and to pledge to "denounce efforts of German agents in downtown Houston to stir them up."[4] Texans soon were informed in headline stories of the threat of espionage: "ALLIED ARMIES RESIST STUBBORN GERMAN ARMY: All Spies Caught Are Promptly Executed."[5] Once again, Blackshear, as program chairman, crafted a resolution intended to quash the rumors and put the black community on alert that they should be wary of German propaganda, agitators, espionage, and subterfuge and not be baited by them:

> In the view of the honorable military record made by American negroes in the war of the revolution, the war of 1812, the war between the states, the Spanish-American war, and recently at Carrizal [Mexico, under Gen. J. J. Pershing], where negro regulars became the victims of Mexican treachery, we predict that if negroes are called to enlist they will bear arms against the nation's foes in a mannor [*sic*] that will be in line with the negroes' past record and loyalty to this nation and to the Stars and Stripes.
>
> We denounce the efforts alleged in the daily press of enemies of the nation to stir up discontent and disloyalty among American negroes,

> and to turn this discontent to treason and revolt, and urge American negroes everywhere to be on the alert and not become trapped unwarily in these efforts. We pledge ourselves to do all in our power, by enlistment at the front, and by engaging at home in those useful and necessary industrial and agricultural pursuits which are essential to the maintenance both of the army in the field and the people at home—in order to do our part to ensure victory.[6]

There were protests in Texas by a narrow group of pacifists, socialists, and pro-German political radicals, yet there was no overwhelming anti-war movement. The sheriff in Rosser, Texas, arrested an alleged German agent "charged with inciting negroes to revolt against the United States government and he promised free passage to Mexico and freedom from the oppression of the white man in the South." There were also professors at the University of Texas and Rice University in Houston who spoke out to encourage pacifist organizations and protest against conscription and what some viewed as the suppression of civil liberties. Notwithstanding these few protesters, universities and colleges across the state reorganized their campus operations to support the war effort to train and support the troops. Any question as to where the state stood on the war was confirmed by the Texas legislature making it a criminal offense to criticize the United States or its participation in the war. And with the Espionage Act passed by the US Congress on June 15, 1917, shortly after the declaration of war, stringent sentences were enacted for any dissent or interference with recruiting or military training.[7]

In Houston, in contrast to isolated protests, Blackshear led an overwhelming outpouring of loyalty and patriotic support from the African American community. In the backdrop of the "enthusiasm" of a band playing "Dixie," he delivered "The Negro as a Patriot," what the *Houston Post* termed as "an impressive and a stirring address" to "prolonged bursts of applause" to an overflow audience of three thousand in the city auditorium. He noted they were proud to be fighting side-by-side with the soldiers of France on the Western Front: "We cannot afford to be indifferent in this war. And we are not indifferent. I stand here tonight to say to you and for you that our people are ready to give their blood to the common cause of America." The rally was closed with the playing of "The Battle Hymn of the Republic."[8]

The Prohibition advocates maintained an active role during the war, primarily in the larger cities, to position their issues before the voters.

Blackshear remained an active participant, keynoting rallies in Houston in favor of the "drys" ongoing push for statewide Prohibition and not just the local option. One enthusiastic meeting of over three hundred people at the "Big Tree" in the Fifth Ward attracted opposition, as reported by the *Houston Post*: "It was stated that about 25 revelers came out of a nearby saloon and attempted to disturb the meeting, but that the speakers' [Blackshear's] arguments with the crowds soon produced complete quiet and created a strong sentiment in favor of prohibition."[9] However, Blackshear's major focus was on the enhancement of farm production and community improvements in rural areas.

Soon the European war resulted in the federal government's call and encouragement for American farmers to step up efforts both to conserve food at home and to produce more for the troops "over there." President Wilson, on August 10, 1917, named Herbert C. Hoover the administrator of the US Food Administration, with mobilization and oversight of all food, feeds, fibers, and derivative products for the production, saving, and wise use of food. National black leaders such as W. E. B. Du Bois declared Negroes should "close ranks" in support of the American war effort. The primary driver and proponent in Texas was the network of county agricultural agents. There had been some friction prior to the war on the role and authority of black county agents. Not all white Texas Democrats welcomed the increased opportunities for African Americans. White farmers and politicians were concerned with the activities of black agricultural agents, with sentiments ranging from outright hostility to full support and cooperation. Black farmers, already marginalized from many government programs, were suspicious that the black field agents were only spies for the federal government. However, farm demonstration work by the black agents, in spite of low pay, long hours, and a high turnover, slowly gained the confidence of the farmers and gradually improved race relations and production. Blackshear stressed the educational value and results-oriented mandate of the extension service to address the nation's call for increased food production. A slogan to denote a united domestic front and the sacrifice required was coined: "Win the War by Working Six Days per Week," a moniker coined most likely by a Washington bureaucrat, which was generally received humorously by farmers and ranchers, who routinely worked six plus days per week—agriculture was no nine-to-five job.[10]

Shortly after the United States entered the war in the spring of 1917, the War Department began a rapid mobilization of troops, equipment, and training camps. To meet part of the demand in Texas for facilities, two de novo military installations were built in Houston—Ellington Field for Air Service instruction and near downtown, an army training site, Camp Logan. To guard the downtown construction site, the all-black 3rd Battalion of the 24th Infantry Regiment was ordered to Houston. Most of these troops were not from Texas, and the rigidly enforced local Jim Crow laws—which mandated, for example, segregated street cars, water fountains, churches, and cafes—caused immediate friction. Following an incident between white city police officers and a soldier, rumors in camp spread that a black soldier had been shot and killed. The angered troops armed themselves and marched into the San Felipe district of Houston to exact revenge, resulting in an armed confrontation with the police and a riot. By the time the shooting stopped some seventeen people were dead—five policemen, three soldiers, and nine civilians. When army officers and the mayor were unable to stop the confrontation, Edward Blackshear, one of the most prominent community leaders in Houston, was called in to help calm unrest in the black community, like he had done earlier with the German agent threat. He was also recommended—working closely with Dr. J. Allen Kyle (a member of the Texas A&M Board of Directors, 1910–14), chairman of the Houston Public Health Committee—to meet with black troops to advise and "reeducate" them on the social and political norms in Houston to avert further incidents. The deadly incident shattered years of growing goodwill between the races in Houston and much of the earlier fence-mending conducted by Blackshear, his brother John (minister of the Bethel Baptist Church in Houston), and other local black leaders. Blackshear's leadership and reputation were further recognized shortly after the November 1918 Armistice when Texas extension director T. O. Walton advised the secretary of agriculture that steps should be taken to prevent postwar "difficulties" by briefing returning "black soldiers at points of demobilization": "As an illustration of what I mean, I refer to the riots of the negro soldiers at Houston some 16 months ago and to the work of E. L. Blackshear in assisting to control that very delicate and difficult situation. Immediately upon receiving information as to what had occurred, Blackshear got permission to address negro soldiers in the camps, also the negro population near the camps, and I have positive information that his efforts were of material assistance in preventing further difficulties . . . that are likely to occur unless some such step is taken."[11]

Before 1917, with the war in full swing in Europe, there was some growing awareness that the United States would likely become involved. In early 1917, Pres. William Bizzell, representing both the A&M College and Prairie Normal, approached the US Army headquarters in San Antonio with a plan to make the college facilities on both campuses available for military training. Once the United States entered the war in April 1917, the plans were implemented, and within weeks the army and navy began training. In addition to depending on the extension service to assist farmers across Texas, the military used the existing college staff and faculty on each campus to train soldiers. A dozen specialty programs, for example in radio electronics, meteorology, and aircraft mechanics, were established at A&M. Bizzell visited the Prairie View campus often and maintained close contact with Blackshear, who was still connected with the campus through the extension service. The campus was ready and the *Dallas Morning News* reported "No Slackers Found at Prairie View Normal." Campus rallies in support of the combined Red Cross–YMCA drives to raise money for support of "the boys at the front" were a wave of enthusiastic support, as reported by the *San Antonio Express*: "At the psychological moment one of the members [of] the chorus, raised the old familiar song, 'Stay in the field until the war is ended.' The spirit of this song spread like wildfire, having been taken up by the audience with a spontaneity that betokened an indomitable determination to go over the top." Following this patriotic outburst, donations from the crowd quickly exceeded the $1,000 goal.[12]

In advance of the increased military training on campus, Blackshear approved a request for the Prairie View football team to play an exhibition game with the team from the 8th Illinois Regiment during the popular De-Ro-Loc exposition in the fall. US Army captain Robert Butler was dispatched to Prairie View for the purpose of "federalizing" the school and to serve as commandant in charge of the "training institution." Guest speakers from the nearby military training camps made presentations on campus about the role and importance of the armed forces. For the assignment, Butler was accompanied by one junior officer, a surgeon, and a dentist. The first request for Prairie View was to prepare programs to train 150 drafted black men (not yet students of the college) in early 1918: 90 in auto mechanics, 20 as blacksmiths, and 40 in carpentry. One of the most surprising events was the emergency landing by Lt. Gerald Carroll on the college athletic field at midday, with several hundred students and teachers emptying the classrooms to see the first aeroplane doubtless many had ever seen up close—with E. D. Ewell writing the *Houston Post* that "it brought many thrills to the students—resulting [in] a half-day holiday that was not scheduled but educational to all concerned."[13]

By early 1918 over four dozen Prairie View alumni and former students were on active-duty training at army cantonments at Des Moines, Iowa; Camp Funston and Camp Travis, both in Texas; and in the engineering training detachment at Rockford, Illinois—with five men already "stationed somewhere in France." In addition to the special wartime campus training programs, the Reserve Officers' Training Corps (ROTC) was established—under the provisions of an act of Congress of June 3, 1916—primarily at Morrill Land-Grant Act colleges, which mandated the instruction of military tactics to train reserve commissioned officers for the US Army. As with most colleges during this period, a cadet corps was not formally established at Prairie View until after World War I. The first group of voluntary student-cadets was approved in 1917 and activated in late 1918, with acting college principal Osborne notified by the War Department on January 27, 1919, that their application for ROTC had been approved. At the beginning of the program, cadets were under the command of commandant and US Army 1st Lt. Walter A. Giles, a graduate of Prairie View serving as professor of military science and tactics. There was no obligation for students to join either the National Guard or regular army. The Prairie View cadet corps in 1918–19 was under the command of cadet lieutenant Elvin Neal of Yoakum, Texas, and the cadet sergeant major Walter A. Adams of Houston. Future Prairie View president E. B. Evans, first hired as the college veterinarian in 1918, lauded the addition of military training at the college, a mandate and hallmark of land-grant institutions:[14] "In my judgment, one of the most important programs at Prairie View has been the Reserve Officers Training Corps program because it opened a new opportunity for service of young Negroes as commissioned officers in the Army. Secondly, it has done much to teach young negroes the importance of discipline, neatness, self-reliance, punctuality, respect for authority, and has given the institution prestige that could not have been obtained through any other source. It is almost unbelievable to observe the change and effect the military service has brought about on Negroes as a result of exposure to travel and experiences as commissioned officers."[15]

It is ironic that the very expertise and ability to deliver hands-on "industrial training and education" both at Texas A&M and Prairie View after years of curriculum debate proved a major contributor to the critical "technical" training programs in demand for the national war effort. The US Army, for example, was still dependent on the horse for all aspects of operations on the Western Front, resulting in one of the biggest training classes at both A&M and Prairie View centering around farriers' skills and horseshoeing; Prairie View had one of the best wheelwright programs in the nation. Bizzell, a member of the executive committee of the Texas Food Administration and active with the National Security League, stood ready with all the college's resources—and some he didn't (yet) have. Following a meeting with Governor Hobby, Blackshear recommended that W. S. Willis, grand chancellor of the Colored Knights of Pythias, be appointed to the Texas Food and Feed Production campaign to stimulate "interest among the negroes in the cultivation and planting of 'war gardens.'" President Bizzell was also very proactive in meeting with the faculty and staff of Prairie View to ensure a continuity of service. Soon the mechanics courses were expanded, and to address a major demand for medical personnel, in July 1918 a nursing program was added at Prairie View—the first such instruction program at an institution in Texas. Moreover, as A. C. True, a senior USDA official, concluded, as the United States became increasingly entangled in the world war, the relations of the federal government with the states were inevitably changed, and this had a considerable effect in the practical conduct of the extension work. The successful work done in the pilot programs by the Texas A&M Agricultural Extension Service resulted in the placement of over four dozen county agents across Texas.[16]

The work was expanded to agriculturalists across the South. Not all was calm, however. Emmett J. Scott, special assistant to Booker Washington, cast some concern on the out-migration of African Americans from across the South to the North based on letters he had accumulated from 1916–18. Scott concluded, "Here may be seen the effects of the loss resulting from the absence of immigrants from Europe, the conflict of the laboring elements, the evidences of racial troubles and menace of mob rule."[17] However, while there were letters from Texas, the extension network of field agents across the state produced larger crops and profits and allowed them to also assist in raising money for the Red Cross. Blackshear reported his agents had directly or indirectly encouraged cooperation with the Colored War Board (an extension of the Texas Council of Defense). While not an official part of the agent's duties, some one-third of black Texans were encouraged to purchase US Liberty War Bonds. Due to the strong demand and government assistance, farm and ranch incomes among black and white Texans soared during the war as production expanded. The real challenge would begin after the wartime boom ended and domestic markets and demand collapsed some 15 percent.[18]

October 1918: Terror

In the fall of 1918 a deadly influenza epidemic swept across the nation. First reports were that the so-called Spanish influenza started in Boston and spread to Philadelphia. The exact origin of the 1918 flu pandemic remains a mystery, and for weeks its spread remained unchecked. With the massive troop movements by railroad across the country, the flu quickly spread first to army training camps, then to coastal cities and sea ports, and then inland to cities and communities. Epidemics and quarantines had long been routine occurrences in Texas. Both Texas A&M and Prairie View faced deadly outbreaks and quarantines for smallpox in 1890–91, in late 1897, and again in 1905. Then in 1907 came a typhoid outbreak, followed by a polio meningitis scare in 1912–13, but the 1918 influenza wave of infection was far more extensive and deadlier. President Bizzell on September 29, 1918, ordered a mandatory quarantine under armed guard to all college facilities, including Prairie View. When asked by quizzical local reporters why the armed sentinels, the president replied they were posted to protect materials intended for new buildings and to prevent "automobile drivers from driving on the lawns." Orders were issued that all clothes and bedding were to be boiled for reuse or burned. To slow the spread of the deadly "la grippe," as it was called, students, staff, and those visiting the troops training at the campuses could not leave, and no new visitors were allowed.[19]

The flu spread across Texas, infecting and killing thousands of civilians, troops, and students by mid-October. A shortage of doctors and nurses, due to their recruitment to support the war effort in Europe, limited the local response. The first reaction by the military, as well as campuses and cities, was to quickly order forced strict quarantines. Blackshear was concerned with some 340 students and military trainees who were impacted at Prairie View. Orders were issued statewide to prevent all gatherings, all public schools were closed, visitors to army training camps and campuses were prohibited, additional armed guards were stationed as sentinels, and travel was prohibited. In an effort to stem the spread of the pandemic, all local draft board calls for new soldiers were suspended. Federal and state government officials and health officers, who had no idea of the extent of the epidemic, imposed a news blackout and issued no statements, official or unofficial, in spite of the increasing number of infections and deaths, remarking only, "The situation is well in hand." The spike of the influenza attack and the extent of deaths was kept from the public by orders from Washington. Over five thousand people died in Philadelphia in a single week, with thousands of deaths across Texas. President Wilson, preoccupied with ending the war (as well as concerned with the success of a Liberty War Bond drive across the county), made absolutely no formal statements whatsoever to the American public as the pandemic swept the nation and deaths reached into the tens of thousands. The federal government was paralyzed and there were no congressional investigations regarding the pandemic. And as the deaths mounted it was clear there was no known immediate cure for the flu, and for every thousand cases of influenza, there were an average of one hundred cases of pneumonia.[20]

Mortality from the pandemic soared and soon turned very deadly, with thousands infected in the army training camps and large cities around the state. During a three-week period in October, there were fifty-one deaths on the Texas A&M campus. Unlike the concentration of cadets and military trainees in College Station, who remained on campus, most of the students at Prairie View departed the campus and went home, and thus by mid-October only twenty deaths were attributed to the flu on the Hempstead campus. As the deaths mounted, there was a shortage of coffins at A&M, in Hempstead, and in the larger cities. When local undertakers in Brazos and Waller Counties could not locate enough caskets, bodies at A&M (many cadets still in their uniforms) were wrapped in blood-stained sheets and stacked in a corner room of Bizzell Hall across from the drill field. Soon authorities resorted, according to A&M engineering cadet Charles Crawford, "to using long wicker baskets shaped like the old Egyptian mummies," prior to bodies being loaded on a train for shipment to their homes. All campus activities, classes, military training, sports, and extension programs continued to be canceled through late November. Volunteers from around the campus arrived to assist the sick and dying, yet there was no known treatment or medicine. While the exact number of deaths in Texas military training camps is unknown, reports indicate, for example, that over two hundred soldiers died at Camp MacArthur near Waco. By mid-November 1918 there were more than four thousand deaths reported across the state, and the exact count was never determined. The overall reaction by civic leaders and the government was both confusing and disingenuous. As A. A. Hoehling in the *Great Epidemic* (1961) described the influenza response, "There was, apparently, a tacit conspiracy among the nation's news editors to hush-hush the ever-mounting ravages, as though they hoped that if they were not noticed, the infection would go away." The pandemic lingered on into mid-1919, but after an estimated eight hundred thousand deaths nationwide, it ended, seemingly as abruptly as it had started.[21]

Extension Roots

A number of efforts and programs predate the formalized, federally-sponsored extension programs in Texas. A black immigrant from South Carolina, Robert Lloyd Smith, arrived in Texas in the 1880s and settled in Oakland. Smith was a year older than Blackshear, born free in Charleston in 1861. After teaching a number of years at the normal school in Colorado County, he founded the Farmers' Improvement Society (FIS) in 1890, which soon spread statewide for the purpose of supporting black farmers in gaining economic independence and distancing its program from political connections or implied support or endorsements. Smith was inspired by Booker T. Washington and Edward Blackshear and formulated plans for his organization after participation at the Tuskegee Institute's Negro Conference. Earl Crosby notes, "Suspicious whites were less likely to oppose a program viewed as a part of [or styled after] Tuskegee than a federal program for black farmers employing black agents." Thus, this Texas grassroots self-help organization, generally known prior to 1908 as the "farmers' cooperative demonstration work," focused on a few practical solutions and key objectives for farmers: improve methods of farming, cooperate to purchase supplies in volume, avoid the onerous credit system, develop programs to improve both the home environment and community, and give aid to members in sickness and death. At its peak in 1912, FIS had some twelve thousand members. Furthermore, black land ownership, a major first step toward agricultural self-sufficiency, was strongly promoted. There was a considerably increased interest in developing and improving land owned by the farmer—leading to a slogan of the day: "Ten acres clear of debt are better than a hundred with an overdue mortgage."[22]

These objectives, along with Blackshear's introduction of the Colored Farmers' Congress in 1906, educated farmers on the latest advancements in farming and promoted long term goals such as crop diversification.

Blackshear's congress concept, forerunner of the short-course extension programs, attracted hundreds of farmers and agricultural leaders annually to Prairie View for programs at the college farm. Farmers heard firsthand presentations on dairying, home gardening, truck farming, and—important to Blackshear—improving rural schools. Debra Reid notes, "The programs gave farmers a sense of purpose and a forum for self-governance as they organized a board of officers and planned to share the information with neighbors." Furthermore, it was a great opportunity to publicize Prairie View programs and connect with rural African Americans. Aware of the success, the Texas legislature in May 1911 approved a bill that gave each county-agent extension program a firm base in Texas by noting each county could allocate $1,000 for cooperative demonstration work.[23]

As Texas farmers worked with the FIS and educational programs sponsored by Texas A&M and Prairie View, the federal government selected Texas for a number of federally funded projects, most notably in the production of rice and cotton. Texas ranked fifth in the nation in number of black farmers. The leader of the federally funded efforts in Texas was Seaman A. Knapp, who gained agricultural experience in Iowa, where he introduced some of the earliest concepts of the agricultural experiment stations. Concerned with increased production, Knapp as president of the Rice Growers Association of America was contracted by Secretary of Agriculture James Wilson in 1898 to travel to Japan, China, and the Philippines to investigate new rice varieties, production, and milling techniques in order to expand rice production in Louisiana and Texas. The primary intent, other than obtaining the latest information, was to diversify production by adding other crops to the growing of cotton. Following a return trip to Asia, Knapp introduced his results to reluctant farmers. What followed was a meeting in 1903 with farmers and business men in Terrell, Texas. While they were impressed with Knapp's rice research, the aim of the Texas farmers was to better understand the comparative benefits of growing more rice and corn—and less cotton. The key question in the Terrell meetings was how to deal with the infestation and havoc to the cotton growers caused by the boll weevil.[24]

The boll weevil had entered Texas in 1892 from Mexico, and by the early 1900s had spread through Texas and threatened crops across the South. It was of such significant concern that the secretary of agriculture and the chief of the Bureau of Plant Industry made a personal on-site visit to Texas to assess the damage. They returned to Washington and immediately requested an emergency appropriation of $250,000 to combat the boll weevil. From this funding $40,000 was assigned to Seaman Knapp to set up USDA offices in Houston to develop a plan of attack. Knapp met with representatives at Texas A&M and Principal Blackshear at Prairie View and had both colleges' full support. Houston, and the programs at A&M, had received attention when James Wilson noted that A&M was "more nearly fulfilling its mission than any other similar institution in the United States." What followed was a statewide campaign, paid for by matching money from the railroads, farmers, and businesses, to hold town meetings with farmers statewide. Robert Smith advised his FIS members that the weevil was not a black or white issue but a threat of grave concern to all Texas farmers. With the assistance of twenty trained "demonstration agents," over one thousand meetings were held and some seven thousand farmers agreed to implement new methods in growing cotton as well as to diversify into corn, fruit, and forage crops. A. C. True, in his classic 1928 work on the extension service, concluded: "The benefits of pure seed, deep plowing, frequent cultivation, and growing of home supplies," and "in general, getting ahead of the weevil with early planting, early-maturing varieties, and treatment of the soil [i.e., fertilizer] to promote rapid growth was the secret of success."[25]

Role of Extension

The inception of the formal relationship between the A&M College of Texas and the US Department of Agriculture predates most records. In early November 1903, Secretary of Agriculture James Wilson was in Texas on a personal survey of conditions, especially the boll weevil cotton infestation. Departing Houston, the secretary was joined on a private railroad car (the "Austin," courtesy of a railroad executive) at College Station by Dr. David Houston, president of A&M, for a trip to North Texas. En route they held what the *Houston Post* reported was an "informal conference" whereupon the secretary was interested in "securing a closer relationship between the [federal] department and the Texas A&M institution." The secretary told the president, "The government needs men in securing positive results from the experiments; successful and scientific cultivation of the soil can be realized if engineered by men of scientific minds. The Agricultural and Mechanical College must furnish these men—hereafter the college will be awarded larger funds by the government for carrying on its work." Secretary Wilson inquired about the status of Prairie View and acknowledged it should be a partner in these programs. President Houston responded with a "positive declaration regarding these matters." Within a decade, Houston himself would serve as the US secretary of agriculture in the Wilson administration and be tasked to carry on the work he had learned from Texas farmers and expand the agricultural programs nationwide.[26]

A significant event that was often overlooked in 1912, Texas A&M signed a formal memorandum of understanding (MOU) with the USDA signifying that A&M housed, developed, and managed all statewide farm programs in the newly created Texas Agricultural Extension Service. Clarence Ousley was selected the first director of this critical farmers' assistance agency, and Secretary Houston was pleased with the actions, noting: "This meant more than cooperation. It meant that careful joint planning would supplant impulsive and ill-considered action." Some have noted that this MOU, with the endorsement of the Texas Department of Agriculture, undermined the efforts of the University of Texas. The USDA and the Texas Department of Agriculture were fully aware that Texas A&M was the land-grant university under the covenants of the Morrill Act and since 1876 the primary institution for agricultural programs—teaching, research, and extension—along with Prairie View. Regents and administrators at the University of Texas reluctantly confirmed this a dozen times over some three decades. Nonetheless, the University of Texas disregarded the concern for duplicate programs and made plans to establish a parallel extension program, after seeing a similar program at the University of Wisconsin, for rural farmers and ranchers, and if necessary, also urban programs. The Texas Department of Agriculture, with this information, held an annual "Rural School Week" each July to foster support from rural communities and school districts, with Professor Blackshear giving the keynote address at the 1914 gathering on the benefits of agricultural and mechanical training in high school. To that date the university had conducted "soft" courses in baby care, gardening, public school improvements, home welfare, and hygiene. What is often not mentioned was that A&M and UT were in the middle of sometimes heated discussions and negotiations in 1911–12 (and dating back to 1885) over the allocation of the Permanent University Funds. In an attempt to resolve the issue, Clarence Ousley presided over a joint meeting of the regents of the University of Texas and the directors of A&M at the Driskill Hotel in Austin on January 27, 1911. After hours of talking, the group drafted a constitutional amendment and special tax bill for consideration by the legislature, but both failed to pass the Texas House. The so-called special statewide property tax was proposed in return for Texas A&M not pressing the issue of dividing the PUF.[27]

Discussions on funding were resumed and carried into 1913 and 1914. Further complicating the negotiations, the University of Texas had abruptly decided, after being defeated three times in two seasons by Coach Charlie Moran's Texas Aggies, not to play any more football games with A&M. The university unilaterally organized the University Interscholastic League to promote high school sports events as a means of attracting quality athletes to their teams, further fueling the institutional rivalry. Following the Driskill meeting, it is highly probable that John A. Lomax, a former English professor, was lured away from Texas A&M (an "impulsive action") and advised the UT regents of the USDA's plans to fund more projects in Texas. He likely advised UT to make a grab for the federal appropriations by claiming they were going to start an expanded extension program. Lomax advised Ousley they could raid the A&M faculty to secure the proper personnel to staff the Texas extension programs—as well as lobbying the legislature to reduce the appropriation to the University of Texas as well as Texas A&M and Prairie View. However, A&M signed the MOU without consulting either the University of Texas or the Texas Department of Agriculture. Aware of the political maneuvering in Austin, Edward Cushing, chairman of the Texas A&M board, contacted Governor Colquitt with an urgent request that the Smith-Lever bill covenants be immediately accepted because "we are greatly in need of money for this most important work of agricultural extension." Many at the University of Texas had been irritated for years at the steady flow of federal funding A&M received from the Morrill Acts, Hatch Act, and Smith-Lever Act—which were the purview of each land-grant university in each state across the nation. Since no clear agreement could be reached, the university submitted a proposed bill to the legislature that the two institutions, to reduce duplication and reduce expenses, be consolidated, proposing "that the A. and M. College property shall be converted into the state hospital for the insane" and that the faculty and students on the College Station campus be moved to Austin "as soon as practicable." A highly publicized hazing incident at the University of Texas that resulted in a student being shot and killed as well as a hazing investigation at Texas A&M further delayed the final dispensation of the PUF. Notwithstanding, A&M established the Ag Extension Service in

1912, and football between A&M and UT resumed with the creation of the Southwest Intercollegiate Athletic Conference in late 1914. In January 1915, the state legislature formally accepted the provisions of the Smith-Lever Act, "attaching extension work in agriculture exclusively to the A&M College." Negotiations continued over the PUF for many years longer, until an equitable adjustment to the fund was resolved in April 1930.[28]

Black Extension Work

Edward Blackshear soon became a key figure championing the work and expansion of statewide black extension agents and their programs. While not a farmer himself, for over a decade he oversaw the extensive agricultural programs at Prairie View as well as founding and expanding the Texas Colored Farmers' Congress programs. Blackshear was fond of quoting former governor Roberts, whom he termed "the Socrates of Texas," that "civilization begins and ends with the plow. When a nation ceases to plow it ceases to live and grow, and begins to decline and die."[29] In fall 1917, he took a leave of absence from his Houston teaching job and returned to the Prairie View campus as a USDA extension representative. Congress had determined that all USDA extension service activities were to be administered, planned, staffed, and conducted through state land-grant colleges of agriculture. His new extension role was as a special agent to "work among Negros [*sic*] for the emergency food administration" in cooperation with the Texas Agricultural Extension Service (TAEX) and the Texas A&M Department of Agriculture in College Station under the guidelines established by the Smith-Lever Act of 1914. Extension was the third leg of the land-grant model, which also included teaching and research, as well as significant outreach and travel in the field. The hands-on cooperative demonstration idea rapidly spread across Texas. Once again Blackshear—the leading black agrarian educator in the state—now directing a separate TAEX division to serve only black farmers, was traveling and speaking to groups statewide. His first goal was to explain the role and goals of the extension service. Second, he sought to ensure that the black community understood its critical part of the war effort, with "the negro rural schools the social, industrial, and mechanical center" of rural programs. For example, at a mass meeting of over two thousand members at the Ebenezer Tabernacle in Austin, where he spoke on the vital role they could play, Blackshear, still held in very high regard, was addressed and introduced as "President" Blackshear of Prairie View and was joined on the stage by federal district food administrator W. E. Long and the president of the University of Texas, R. E. Vinson. And in Wharton, Texas, a large crowd of farmers turned out for a parade to highlight local ag production and hear addresses by Blackshear and R. L. Smith.[30]

The Negro Division of the Extension Service was created by TAEX in September 1915. To begin the work, Director Clarence Ousley visited Prairie View for a meeting with the faculty in the chapel on the proposed plans for the new service and requested that Blackshear recommend candidates to be extension agents. The first three selected were Robert L. Smith, longtime friend and president of FIS; Texan and teacher Jacob H. "Jake" Ford, who served as an agronomist; and recent Prairie View A&M graduate Mary Evelyn Hunter, who supervised women's programs. These progressive, results-minded rural black agents would be critical in the early days of extension work. Ousley made clear that their performance and acceptance in the rural communities, at times in the face of white opposition to black extension agents, would be pivotal. If they failed, "there would be no other Negro Agents employed in the near future." The challenge was accepted. Traveling together in East Texas to meet with black community leaders and farmers at churches, schools, and county fairs was an effective first step. Smith, a veteran of organizing events, selected eight targeted, black-majority counties. Fully aware of the legacy of King Cotton, they concentrated their early programs on production, crop diversification, and on the basic needs of "raising feed crops for stock and food for man." A study by the Texas A&M Extension Service in 1916 detailed the evils of the crop mortgage credit system, which stipulated banks and merchants would only finance cotton for tenants, as the leading cause for one-crop cotton farming.[31] The annual cost for this credit bondage varied from 10 percent to more than 60 percent. Merchants and bankers based credit exclusively on cotton; planting other food crops, many felt, reduced the amount of cotton grown and thus reduced the dependence on the crop-lien lenders. Breaking the all-cotton tradition of over fifty years and promoting diversification proved difficult. This was slowly accomplished by demonstration plots of corn and cereals, oftentimes adjacent to cotton fields to allow for real-time comparisons. To help fund the extension programs in the countryside, Blackshear and Smith met with county commissioners to secure modest local funding. An example of cooperation, the commissioners in adjoining Brazos and Burleson Counties agreed to split the cost

TABLE 6.1. Texas Cotton Farm Production, 1880–1930

Year	Number of farms	Number of tenant farms	Number of bales produced	Percentage of US total
1880	174,184	65,468	805,284	14.0
1890	228,126	95,510	1,471,242	19.7
1900	352,190	174,991	2,584,810	27.1
1910	417,770	219,575	2,455,174	23.1
1920	436,033	232,309	2,971,757	26.1
1930	495,489	301,660	3,793,392	26.0

Source: U.S. Bureau of the Census, *Reports of Agriculture Production* (Government Printing Office, 1880–1930).

of a county agent to serve the region. Mrs. Hunter, home demonstration agent, organized a multicounty visitation to introduce extension methods into homes and farms of African Americans across East Texas. One of the most successful was the introduction of a canning course and process for a group of women in Stumptoe, Gregg County.[32]

While traditional rural habits and farming methods were slow to change, positive results were gradually achieved. The extension outreach programs grew in large part based on the success of the agents as well as the increased acceptance by farmers. The challenge was convincing farmers there was a better way to manage and improve farm work. A plan to encourage better living conditions was set by agents on these objectives:

1. Improvement of the economic, social, and spiritual well-being of the farm family.
2. Conservation of natural resources.
3. Improvement of farm income through applications of science and mechanization.
4. Improvement of health through better nutrition and more adequate rural health facilities.
5. Improvement of family living through better housing, rural electrification, and labor-saving equipment.
6 Improvement of educational and recreational facilities.
7. Encouraging people to be wiser consumers.[33]

Tenant Farmers

Blackshear's work as special agricultural agent took on new urgency when he was called upon to head a team to combat fraud and corruption by unscrupulous salesmen who flooded the South to defraud black farmers. The war limited access to overseas markets in Europe, dropping cotton below seven cents per pound. Clarence Ousley, director of extension, recalled the market disruption: "Cotton prices dropped suddenly from more than twelve cents a pound to six or less; there was no 'market place' except local town or shipping stations; cotton merchants had no means of 'hedging' their purchase and only the most daring ventured to buy cotton at any price. . . . These were trying times to farmers and their creditors." With the low cotton prices and the rise in the cost of provisions, more and more "croppers"—black and white—were in a perpetual state of indebtedness and thus were at the mercy of their creditors. By 1900 white croppers outnumbered black by about five to four in Texas. Notwithstanding, one-fifth of tenant farmers were African American, and cotton represented 86 percent of black farmers' income in Texas. Because of larger yields due to extension training and programs, many small farmers "had more money for their cotton than they ever expected to possess and those who worked for wages in the fields were paid twice the wages of a few years ago." The 1920 US census indicates that the number of farm wage labors declined, while the number of farmers increased among both owners and tenants—with 70 percent of farm operators being tenant farmers.[34]

The inequities of the cotton market and concerns with a lost opportunity to instill more competition in the cotton manufacturing industry to benefit both Texas and the South was a major concern of Blackshear. These ideas were not without merit, given the fact that one of the main accomplishments of David Houston while president of Texas A&M was to establish a textile engineering department on the College Station campus. A building to teach textile engineering was erected by 1904, and Houston, along with Lt. Gov. George T. Jester and key A&M staff, toured New England to acquire the latest know-how and purchase textile equipment. The Texas Cotton Manufacturers Association, with a special $30,000 Texas legislative appropriation, agreed to install a chemical laboratory, a power-loom weaving department, a cloth room, and a finishing department. Every effort was made to install realistic training in 1904 to ensure "the essential feature of a regular factory."[35] Well aware of the A&M textile engineering program,

Blackshear proposed to Governor Colquitt that the state of Texas take a larger role in its own destiny with the following manufacturing proposal:

> Texas needs cotton factories to round out its economic development and that it appears to me that if in addition to your other activities you could give your attention to the organization of a system or series of cotton factories in Texas to be located on the ship channel in Houston on account of its relation to ocean traffic and to be either under private auspices entirely or under joint State and private auspices. [This] would confer a great boon upon the State of Texas. At the same time Houston as a great interior cotton market would furnish ample cotton for manufacturing purposes; and it is entirely possible, it seems to me, to make Houston a new Manchester district for cotton manufacture—and might become the greatest cotton manufacturing center in the world. Indeed, it seems to be a reflection upon the intelligence of the Southern white people that they content themselves with the mere growing of cotton and do not use their intelligence and capital to engage in its manufacture and thus derive a double profit from the cotton business. Why is the South content to ship their cotton across the ocean and then buy the cloth from European factories when they could manufacture the cotton and sell it to world markets instead of selling simply the raw cotton. So long as Europe manufactures cotton—so long Europe will control the price of raw cotton.[36]

These were lofty plans to advance textile manufacturing in Texas after establishing a viable manufacturing program at Texas A&M, in the heart of the cotton belt, yet by 1910 these schemes were overwhelmed by the rush to capitalize on "black gold"—petroleum exploration and production. And to this day no such efforts have been made to manufacture cotton products in Texas.

In the meantime, few farmers had bank accounts; most held only cash and the few assets they had accumulated. The actions of rogue highwaymen and confidence men aroused the ire of both the state and federal government, who were concerned their duplicity might be part of "enemy propaganda." Blackshear sent a circular statewide outlining the fraud: "Negroes are being offered cheap and often worthless goods with the assurance that their war savings and thrift stamps and liberty bonds are not of par value and will not be for several years. It is then casually suggested by the salesmen that the negro may be dead before his holdings reach par value, and emphasis is laid on the enjoyment he would get by the immediate purchase of their goods, possibly cheap trinkets, a worthless sewing machine, a dazzling bit of jewelry, or musical instrument."[37] Blackshear's warning against "Liberty Bonds" fraud was reprinted in a dozen states, followed by additional rural meetings and circular letters to the black community declaring, "Let the law deal with these swindlers, whether black or white." In fact, African Americans contributed willingly to the war effort. The enlistment of black troops from Texas represented about 25 percent—some thirty-one thousand—of the troops called up from the state, at a time when African Americans represented only 14 percent of the state's population. Blackshear's twenty-year-old second son, Theodore Roosevelt Blackshear, a Prairie View graduate (class of 1915) and at the time employed by Prairie View, registered for the draft on September 12, 1918.[38]

In return for their active-duty service, black Texans hoped to receive added privileges and increased civil rights once back home. Following the war, as part of a federal effort, Prairie View established vocational training programs to assist over one hundred disabled soldiers. Prairie View students also collected funds to assist the recovery of children in postwar Europe. However, as C. Vann Woodward noted, "The war-bred hopes of the Negro for first-class citizenship were quickly smashed" as white fears that black Americans expected greater social and political equality after the war resulted in a new wave of intimidation across the South. This response and denial of equal rights is counter to what historian Oscar Martinez concluded should be the result: "Military service has been one of the most significant avenues for acculturating members of minority groups to American culture." This was not the case after World War I for the over three hundred thousand returning black soldiers. Little research has been done on the record of black Texans' military and civil service during World War I.[39]

The Naked Earth

Blackshear was able to articulate as few could the role and impact of the Texas farmer and the benefits of cooperating with extension agents to adopt and reap "secure results if effectively organized." He clearly saw the connection between farming and education as well economic benefits for African Americans: "Farming is coming to be regarded as one of the greatest of vocations as seen in the fact that the nation and the States are annually expending hundreds of thousands of dollars cooperatively to improve American agriculture, and any man who can take his stand on *the naked earth* and wrest a living from its soil with its physical, chemical and biological forces has done no small thing and deserves the commendation of others. And the American negro farmer, many of them, have proven they can do this, by doing it from year to year."[40]

The growing demands and extent of extension programs resulted in the announcement in December 1918 by Bradford Knapp, chief of the federal extension work in the South, that the Southern region would be divided into three "strategic centers." The three regions were headed by Field Representatives E. L. Blackshear at Prairie View, Thomas M. Campbell of Tuskegee (Alabama), and John P. Pierce of Hampton (Virginia). This was a major compliment and recognition of years of work by both Blackshear and Prairie View, linking the college with the two premier black educational and agricultural programs in the nation—Tuskegee and Hampton. Blackshear oversaw program development and extension agent training in Texas, Oklahoma, Louisiana, and Arkansas. This was, perhaps, a tacit admission that the conditions and scope of demands west of the Mississippi River differed from those in the Old South. Each supervisor reported directly to Washington on the extension work in their area and assessed the general status and needs of black farmers in their territory. In addition to establishing training programs, the extension agents worked to alleviate a growing cotton crisis. Once again, middlemen and market speculators, as Blackshear had chronicled a decade earlier in the subtreasury debacle, derailed any solution. Federal government efforts to establish a "cotton loan fund" languished as borrowing requirements were so strict that tenant farmers and sharecroppers could not qualify.[41]

Regardless of significant contributions made by the black extension agents to improve farm and ranch conditions in Texas, some detractors "criticized the colored government workers [agents] in the South, declaring they were a political machine working in the interest of the North." Racial and political tension, regardless of the positive economic impact of the black county extension agents, threatened certain whites who failed to recognize these advances.[42] Concerned about the attacks, Blackshear, in clear and concise terms, wrote directly to his staff across the region, warning them not to involve "other problems" with extension work. The local-regional letter found its way to the desk of Secretary of Agriculture David Houston and then on to the president (confirmed when the author found a copy in Woodrow Wilson's presidential papers). The rapid mobilization of the extension agents during the war placed a tremendous strain on effectively deploying services, yet in return provided a much-needed boost and new life into the funding and staffing as well as the evolving image of the agents in the field. While as historian Debra Reid notes, "Blackshear's stance represented increasingly old fashioned ideas, even in 1919," Blackshear wanted to caution his agents as well as ensure that they would receive credit for their good works:[43]

> This is not true so far as the Texas Negro Extension workers are concerned, but this charge reveals one or more facts: First, it reveals that there are influential people who do not favor a special negro extension force; second, that we must be careful in all our public utterances not to give ground for the charge that we are mixing other problems with the extension work that have no official connection with it. I must and do insist as the head agent of the negro extension work in Texas that we avoid mooted religious, political or racial problems—because these problems involve questions as to which the public entertains various opinions.
>
> Our opinions are doubtless identical on this problem, but there is a large body of citizens who do not think on this problem as we do, hence when we refer to the race problem it should be done judiciously and in a way to make peace between the races and not discord. And in conclusion I should think we could all see that what we need is the confidence and friendship of the white people to replace the present attitude of suspicion and distrust with which many of them regard us.[44]

The combined impact of the Hatch Act of 1887 and the Smith-Lever Act of 1914, followed by the Smith-Hughes Act of 1917, triggered significant enhancements to Prairie View's extension contributions and demonstrated the value of the land-grant A&M College model. Surprisingly, "experiment" (research) and "extension" had not been fully accounted for or funded in the first two Morrill Acts. Both programs were underfunded and not given the importance due to them. Secretary Houston proved to be a major proponent and champion of these programs, deeming it important that his agency and the agricultural colleges work together with the Association of American Agricultural Colleges and Experiment Stations in the development of the plans and goals to improve and expand extension programs. Houston noted, "In the aggregate [these programs] represent the largest and, in my judgment, in many respects the most significant piece of educational work that any nation has ever undertaken." Experimenters in the lab and field began to successfully test and develop agricultural knowledge and best practices directly relevant to extension agents to assist the farm and ranch. Dr. Sears correctly concludes, "The experiment station act had been so successful at land-grant agricultural campuses that 'academic agriculture' was actually born as a result of the act[s]." Furthermore, the results could be written into textbooks, enhance class lectures, assist extension agents with field training manuals, and generate publications for annual continuing education programs or short courses. For example, the *Prairie View Standard* in 1915 published "School Lessons in Cotton."[45]

Working closely with Clarence Ousley, T. O. Walton, R. L. Smith, and other progressive extension agents and teachers, Edward Blackshear greatly influenced the early development of the Extension Service. The experienced Blackshear, with what Reid termed "old fashioned ideas," applied years of trial and error to work within a system he did not always like and that he felt was unfair to African Americans' opportunities. His experience and leadership were critical in training a younger generation of teachers and extension agents on how to foster support among whites while advancing black Americans. The job of the agents was to promote efficiency, and this was the theme of Blackshear's last major public presentation, as presiding congress president, to the hundreds of delegates at the August 1917 Eighth Annual State Colored Farmers' Congress. The war strengthened and gave credibility to the extension specialist, with Dr. William B. Bizzell concluding, "By the time the War came to an end, the Extension Service organization had become organized thoroughly and the county agent had become a recognized factor in the promotion of agricultural endeavor." Long a goal of African American educators in Texas, the extension program helped promote and expand educational infrastructure in rural black communities. This enhanced both the role and leadership of teachers (as well as school and church elders) in the smaller communities by encouraging more public-private collaboration, with the potential to provide participation in policy development and setting community priorities. By 1920, the number of black farmers had increased by over 20 percent.[46]

The Calvert "Street Exhibit"

One measure of the success of the extension agency can be found in considering the agricultural programs and means to improve production, as well as highlighting the marketing of produce. T. O. Walton, director of extension in Texas, detailed the steady advancements under the programs directed by extension agents. An example of this was seen in the Robertson County "street exhibit" in Calvert, Texas. Reported as a "real eye-opener to the agricultural possibilities," black farmers from across the country, after working with agents for over a year, exhibited the finest corn, garden vegetables, canned goods, and field produce. The event, which was supported by Calvert merchants and attended by over one thousand citizens, was organized by Blackshear with the assistance of high school principal T. H. Brawley. Extension agent specialists included J. H. Ford, agronomist of the Negro division extension service, and Mrs. M. E. V. Hunter, demonstrator of home economics. Furthermore, the event was supported by the Farmers' Improvement Society and Robert L. Smith. This model of community improvement with hands-on extension service agents' assistance gradually spread statewide.[47]

For all its benefits, the extension program under the Smith-Lever Act unwittingly perpetuated segregation by underpinning the "separate but equal" treatment of the black population. States were given a free hand to allocate federal funds, oftentimes reducing support of the "Negro" divisions to a subsistence budget. This unequal practice continued for decades. In spite of the resistance of the white power structure to expanding extension educational programs, Blackshear, with the reluctant encouragement of statewide director Clarence Ousley, remained focused on assisting small farmers regardless of the political circumstances. Blackshear continued to have articles on farming and ranch management published in Texas and across farm communities in the Midwest and was instrumental, due to years of experience, in implementing farmers' demonstration farms, expanding the short courses he pioneered at the Prairie View Farmers' Congress, and developing some of the first agricultural correspondence courses offered in the South. Director of Extension T. O. Walton agreed that black county agents should meet with the Commissioners' Courts in each county to secure additional funding for home and farm demonstration programs, which they did successfully. Furthermore, Walton, a future president of Texas A&M, recognized and honored Blackshear's experience and leadership.[48]

While finding the separate but equal mantra distasteful, Blackshear and other seasoned black leaders used the unjust mandate of segregation to their advantage, building influential and oftentimes relatively autonomous reform programs. Smith and Blackshear both championed the diversification of crop production and land ownership among black farmers and worked to reduce or eliminate the crop liens, as well as to increase access to farm credit. These two dedicated leaders were the key to the remarkably successful extension system in Texas, which was one of the first nationwide programs to employ, as George B. Tindall noted, "a unique collaboration of federal, state, and county governments with private agencies." The direct results of the improvement methods introduced by the extension agents paid great dividends to improve the social and economic conditions of rural farmers. Cotton production in Texas had steadily increased during the war and was only disrupted by market forces after the Armistice that dramatically depressed cotton prices. Agricultural agents of the railroads, striving to increase commercial rail tonnage, helped promote the experimental farms and provided free passes for farmers to attend short courses. The war proved to be a watershed period. In the span of a few years, by 1919 Texas A&M and Prairie View emerged with a proven statewide extension record of service, and, as Dethloff notes, "a high degree of penetration into the everyday affairs of Texas." This was confirmed by a Texas extension agent field report from the Rural Women's Division: "One of the best features of the work is the growth of the co-operative spirit of these women as shown in their working together to make money for their churches and their schools." Thus, informed educational programs and short courses, cooperation with government agencies, increased public support, improved local schools, and a strong work ethic were the hallmarks of Blackshear's crusade to improve the lives and futures of African Americans in Texas and across the South, who remained committed to rural Southern life.[49]

—⋄⋄—

The extensive career of Edward Blackshear ended on December 12, 1919, at the age of fifty-seven. His politically motivated firing as principal of Prairie View in late 1915 by Governor Ferguson had threatened to end his career four years earlier. However, Blackshear's love for education and teaching, coupled with a well-earned reputation, took him back to his roots in primary education teaching and administrating the Holman School in

Houston. He retained his home near the Prairie View campus and for a short period lived in Houston with his daughter Eddie. The call to return to campus to take a major leadership role in the growing statewide extension service would once more place him in the state and national spotlight. Working with Robert L. Smith and officials at Texas A&M, Blackshear spent the last few years of his life training and mentoring the next generation of black educators and leaders. And in working for the US Department of Agriculture, he became a leader in a multistate outreach program that set the model for future extension efforts to advance the fortunes and well-being of black farmers and ranchers and their families.[50]

From the time he arrived in Texas to teach in a one-room country schoolhouse, Blackshear was concerned and committed to the improvement of rural education. Over the span of his career, he was a part of and witness to the tremendous impact of the land-grant colleges and the related extension programs that dramatically changed agricultural and rural life across the South. The *San Antonio Express* noted its appreciation for his work, reporting that "a majority of the colored teachers have been educated at the Prairie View Normal school." Furthermore, during his final years as the assistant state agent, the Negro Division of the Texas Agricultural Extension Service was the vanguard of programs and black-led education and reform—impacting the gradual overall improvement of quality of life in rural Texas. The soil, crops, and family helped shape what Debra Reid in *Reaping a Great Harvest* concluded were the "deep-seated values that linked landownership to economic and personal independence."[51]

In a span of four decades, Blackshear rose to become one of the leading educational advocates in the South. His early work in Texas included promoting the Black Teachers Association, fostering the growth and contribution of the largest black public university in the country, as well as advancing agrarian programs with the inception of the Colored Farmers' Congress in the early 1900s. These associations and programs became the model of training and encouraging farmers in each of their local communities to work to advance their livelihoods and support of education. Public education is always political, and Blackshear learned early in his career the need to work within the system—mentored by Bishop Grant, Sul Ross, Booker Washington, Hightower Kealing, and Col. Edward House—while maintaining his honor in the face of vocal opposition by Jim Crow whites to advances in black education in Texas. Blackshear was well aware of what researcher Gunner Myrdal concluded years later: "The Jim Crow statues were effective means of tightening and freezing—in many cases instigating—segregation and discrimination." Blackshear learned early to manage often-cutthroat relationships with political leaders and elected officials of all parties as well as denominational and civic organizations, in order to support the advancement of African American education. Furthermore, by 1910 Blackshear had become a leading national figure, especially through his cooperation with Booker T. Washington and progressive groups dedicated to advancing education, equal rights, and economic advancement for their race. In Texas, he succeeded in securing legislative appropriations from the state that were unequaled by those received by any other similar public institution in the nation.[52]

Edward Blackshear's eloquent literary writings, correspondence, poems, and books dating from 1882 through 1919 rival those produced by his contemporaries such as Washington, Du Bois, and Kealing. A volume of Blackshear's writings is forthcoming, which will permit future researchers to study the political challenges and dynamics of the fight for black educational opportunities and equal rights in Texas in the works of one who was involved in the fight for some four decades. In the educator's honor, students and faculty at Prairie View named their first campus association after him—the Blackshear Literary Society. Blackshear's fight to advance the status of African American education began, it is obvious, in Texas, far from the East Coast–dominated educational theories on how to approach education in the South. Many stepped forward to participate, most notably African Americans, but also the white missionary societies and Northern-based philanthropists, who looked to both Washington and Du Bois for advice and guidance. For three decades prior to World War I, these two fine scholars and educators were the gatekeepers for those working to advance education in the South, but with little effect in Texas. For example, the well-known and much-touted Peabody Fund, whose money was spread across the South, had little impact on black education in Texas. Blackshear pointedly noted in a December 1905 presentation in New Orleans to the American Association for the Advancement of Science, "Texas alone has contributed for Negro public schools a greater amount probably than Northern philanthropy has given in all the South for the endowment of negro colleges and a greater amount than the national government has ever given for negro education directly." Promoters and scholars of the day, like many of the recent scholars who have written on the post-Reconstruction quest to improve and advance black education opportunities across the South, often did not fully consider Texas in the mix of their efforts and evaluations—and therein lies the significance of Blackshear's contributions. It is fascinating—and frustrating—to note the exhaustive scholarly writings on Tuskegee, Hampton Roads Institute, and Alcorn A&M with barely a mention of not only Prairie View Normal but also of any black colleges in Texas and in other states west of the Mississippi River.[53]

Texas was different. Texas had been an independent republic for a decade. While dominated by King Cotton and cattle before and after the Civil War, in many respects Texas was as Western as it was Southern—with many then and now debating where to fit the Lone Star State in the national pantheon. Texas was also a newer state, the frontier being a recent memory, as opposed to the much older states to the east. Land was cheaper, more readily available, and less "farmed out." And Texas was large. Generalizations that equate conditions in Dallas, Galveston, Austin, Brownsville, and El Paso are obviously problematic. Yet, beyond a doubt, the Southern influence, especially in East Texas, and the politics, culture, and habits that succeeding waves of white settlers from the lower Southern states and from Europe brought with them had a clear impact. However, moving westward of the piney woods, Texas was all Western in scope and culture. As one scholar noted, immigrants "took 'Texas fever' and headed for the trans-Mississippi" with the lure of new opportunities and the offer of fresh land. And black Americans from the Old South also headed west, seeking new opportunities.[54]

Edward Blackshear died much too early, yet the impact he had was lasting and inspirational for those who followed. Over a dozen schools and facilities in Texas have been named for him. His wife, Rachel, continued his work in the extension service as the home demonstration extension agent in Harris County, Texas. The *Houston Post* in a feature editorial, "A Good Man's Memory Worthily Honored," wrote: "He labored for a generation for the moral, mental and economic advancement of his race. He worked along practical lines, holding to the belief that the Negro could improve only as he became a more useful and more responsible citizen. He at all times stood for the best interests of the Negro people, sometimes against strong opposition."[55]

7

Crusader with a Cause

> He labored unceasingly for a generation for the moral, mental and economic advancement of his race. He worked along practical lines, holding to the belief that the negro could improve only as he became a more useful and more responsible citizen. He at all times stood for the best interests of negro people, sometimes against strong opposition.
>
> *HOUSTON POST*, JANUARY 16, 1920

> Some people are very careful as to who handles their fine horse or fine dog, but not specially anxious about who trains the minds of their children.
>
> EDWARD BLACKSHEAR, MARCH 1900

During his professional career between 1882 to 1919, Edward Blackshear had a tremendous impact on education in Texas—lifting thousands out of illiteracy and training an entire generation of teachers, school administrators, farmers, and extension agents. His teaching service started in a one-room elementary school for poor black children in rural Ellis County, and he rose to the highest position in Austin as its superintendent of African American schools. During the summers he traveled across Texas to teach and mentor young teachers on best practices in the classroom. In 1896 he assumed his greatest challenge, the principalship of Prairie View A&M Normal College. A gifted writer and orator, Blackshear became active in civic, political, agrarian, fraternal, and church organizations, in addition to his educational duties, often rising to the top leadership positions. Lifelong relationships and cooperation in each of these groups proved pivotal to his career. Furthermore, these activities had a direct complimentary impact and influence on his political and social education. Blackshear's primary goal was to improve the educational opportunities, economic well-being, and access to equality for black Texans, which resulted in the elevation of their standard of living.

Blackshear's intellect and his breadth of knowledge are self-evident. His commitment to education and to the advancement of his race are beyond question. Blackshear's leadership in education and the civic life of African Americans more generally is demonstrated time and again. And his skill at navigating the politics of race relations in the polarizing environment of Jim Crow Texas is filled with both successes and setbacks. The challenge facing the scholar is that while Blackshear left a rich legacy of public writings and his academic and civic actions are well documented, his private family life, thoughts, and actions remain obscure. His thinking and perspective on the social and political issues of the day in his formative years in the 1880s were considerably impacted by mentors H. T. Kealing, William Holland, Bishop Abraham Grant, Booker T. Washington, Gov. Sul Ross, Edward House, and his brother, Baptist minister John J. Blackshear. However, after scouring over a dozen archives, pouring over census records, and contacting extended family members, little has been found about his private life or his private writings. Notwithstanding, a reasonable conclusion is that, to accomplish his long-term goals, Blackshear played a pivotal public role in turn-of-the-century Texas.

Born into slavery and raised during his youth in Montgomery, Alabama, as a young teenager he traveled to Iowa to attend Tabor College. His extensive collegiate preparation shaped his career and focus on higher education. Upon graduation Blackshear was lured to Texas by classmate and lifelong friend Hightower T. Kealing. The benefits of their extensive classical college education became evident in their professional careers and their authorship of detailed articles and presentations on a broad cross section of topics. Blackshear's primary focus and writings were on educational issues in Texas and, by extension to Southern and national audiences, on the plight and condition of African Americans. Unlike Booker T. Washington, Blackshear employed no ghostwriters and had no large philanthropic funding source to expand college programs. To garner support for his collegiate work, Blackshear had to deftly curry the favor of white politicians. In addition to his passion for education, Blackshear crafted articles, editorials, and books on topics ranging from the challenge of African Americans seeking to escape their conditions in the South, to mine safety, to the cotton futures markets, to Prohibition, to childcare, and to professional boxing. Addressing the political and social issues of the day, his views were routinely published in over three dozen newspapers in Texas and in a dozen leading national papers and journals, as well as in at least six foreign publications.

Blackshear learned from his experiences in the mid-1880s and early 1890s with the AME Church and congregation in Austin that there was power in the ability to organize and influence groups of people. African American churches, one of the few gatherings free from direct white control, were a pivotal place to learn the dynamics of leadership and how to shape a message. Without downplaying the spiritual role of the church, it is worth noting that few could escape the social and political ramifications of organized denominational groups. The closed-door debates, admonitions, and opinions of both evangelistic preachers and lay speakers were a timely gauge on the issues and trends of the day. Rev. John J. Blackshear was a significant influence on his brother Edward's life until his tragic death in April 1907. Furthermore, the church was a critical link to the development and financial support of black rural community schools and educational programs like those sponsored and provided by the agricultural extension service. Blackshear's experience with the Colored Teachers State Association exposed him to the value and intricacies of the statewide education network, an asset he increasingly utilized and developed as time passed.

Prairie View

Edward Blackshear assumed the job as principal at Prairie View in 1896 under a scattering of media reports questioning the unjustified dismissal of sitting principal L. C. Anderson. An honorable and accomplished educator, Anderson became involved with firebrands like Norris Cuney as a Republican in the turbulent elections of the mid-1890s—fought over by the Lily-Whites and upstart Populist partisans—whose outcome sealed the dominant position of the Texas Democrats for decades to come. Activist Calvert teacher John Rayner lamented the involvement of the African American community in the Populist movement as black Americans lost what little political influence they had. Though a quiet, introverted man, Anderson as principal of the primary black public college in the South had made tremendous strides in advancing the mission of the institution and was considered a leading spokesman on educational issues—which were often political in nature—for black Texans. Thus, he was a prime target of the victorious Democrats as they silenced opponents and exercised their demand for a change. The confrontation at the A&M College board meeting that triggered Anderson's dismissal—an attack on his strongly held position on equal rights—was irresponsible and unjustified, yet it reflected the contentious Jim Crow political environment of the period facing black leaders. Within weeks, Anderson assumed the administrative position Blackshear had held as head of black schools in Austin, and for the next three decades he was an active educational advocate in both local and state educational issues. The two men thereafter remained friends and served jointly on a number of boards and education committees. The *Dallas Express* noted that Blackshear, who in 1915 confronted his own dismal at Prairie View due to injurious, vindictive politics, "was generous, for he guarded carefully his predecessor's interest and gave him all the prominence possible."

Some speculated that Professor Blackshear aspired to the job at Prairie View. That cannot be confirmed, but what is known is that he rose to the challenge and was for two decades able to navigate the white, Democratic, Jim Crow–controlled social and political dynamics of Texas and the South. Blackshear's goal and mission was to advance—within the limits of the white power structure—the educational, social, and equal rights opportunities for black Americans. He was well spoken and by the mid-1890s politically astute enough to constantly manage his image as well as the image and expectations of the college. While some have questioned the wisdom of Booker T. Washington's "accommodationist" philosophy at Tuskegee—after which Blackshear modeled much of the educational and industrial training programs at Prairie View—few can criticize the results of Blackshear's strategic approach and incremental enhancements of educational programs for black Texans. These educational advances at Prairie View, coupled with Blackshear's work to enhance the lifestyle and success of black farmers and ranchers, helped build the foundation for a black middle class in Texas.

Dating from the administration of Gov. Sul Ross, Blackshear had maintained close working relationships and contacts at the highest level of Texas elected officials. And in terms of support and funding for the college, he was astute and careful with the success he managed to garner. As principal and chief operating officer at Prairie View, he reported directly to the Texas A&M president and maintained for two decades a professional and productive working relationship with a variety of administrations. Notwithstanding, being head of the largest public institution of higher learning for African Americans in Texas vaulted him to a position of leadership among his people. As Woolfolk noted, "The basic danger that lay ahead for men of his stripe, especially in Texas, was the desire to play a larger role in the political life of a region in spite of the fact that a special compromise had come out of Atlanta which the white South had accepted in principle as a *modus vivendi*."

Rivalries, strains, and prejudices threatened to derail his long-term goals. However, Blackshear had the ability to work with a broad cross section of organizations—both black and white—while effectively championing his concerns. He advanced Prairie View to the largest enrollment of any black public university in the nation. He quadrupled the faculty from ten in 1897 to over forty by 1915 and attracted distinguished graduates and professionals from the leading African American institutions. He maintained excellent relations with the A&M Board of Directors and especially the designated board representatives, who over time proved critical partners, often as important as the sitting A&M president. The most important representatives during Blackshear's tenure at Prairie View were William Cavitt of Bryan, Dr. J. Allen Kyle of Houston, and T. M. Scott of College Station. Texas A&M presidents Ross, Foster, and Bizzell were engaged on a personal level with Blackshear to ensure the success of the college. Their attention to detail and their counseling Blackshear on what was possible in terms of funding, growth, and political landmines helped him navigate the often-hostile political dynamics of Austin. Blackshear's eagerness to have members of the public, former students, and Austin politicians visit the campus proved a successful strategy and was instrumental in advancing the image and accomplishments of the college. Blackshear was particularly adept at fostering positive press coverage by the *Houston Post*—a paper owned and edited by a former Confederate soldier.

While questions remain about Blackshear's involvement in national affairs, he took the initiative to build relationships and exchange ideas across the country. What motivated the A&M Board of Directors and the A&M college president to permit Blackshear's extensive travels? Many trips took place during the summer, when Prairie View was in recess, but others occurred during the school year. How did the college administrators, and state legislators and governors, feel about his often highly opinionated national writings and speeches—especially his high-profile advocacy in the late 1890s for the creation of a black university in Austin? Surely they received some negative feedback from whites and blacks, perhaps considerable criticism in some cases. Readers should note that Blackshear and Booker T. Washington were both state employees. As Blackshear eventually discovered, they had to exercise care in what they did and said, lest they jeopardize their jobs—and their public platforms. However, in Washington's case he had powerful political ties, a growing national image, and extensive private financial backing from Northern philanthropists, thus allowing him more flexibility and perceived credibility.

South or West

At the midpoint of Edward Blackshear's career in education and extension in 1900, both he and Texas were at a crossroads. Since he arrived in Texas in 1881 the population had more than doubled. And the 1900 census demonstrated the changing landscape of the demographic, political, social, and economic dynamics of the state in transition. In-migration by thousands of whites from Southern states looking for a new start, the arrival of Europeans via the Port of Galveston, and a growing number of Mexicans moving north across the border had a dramatic effect on the social-demographic order and shifted the Texas electorate. In the process, black Texans increasingly became a smaller percentage of the overall state population—and thus faced a diminished opportunity to gain and exercise suffrage, achieve effective judicial fairness, and enjoy equal rights. In addition, the passage of Jim Crow laws limited African Americans' access to the political process.

The crusade to realize the dream of the black university was stalled by the turn of the century. The dominant Democratic Party at both the state and local level gave scant lip service to funding black education. With the departure from the state legislature in 1898 of Blackshear's friend and collaborator in education Rep. Robert Smith (president of the FIS), the last elected black Texas legislator for the next seven decades, black Texans had little or no political voice in Austin. Nonetheless, in 1900 Blackshear was probably at the happiest point in his life both professionally and privately. The focus at last fell on Prairie View Normal and its improvements to advance the scale and expanse of public higher educational opportunities for black Texans. Enrollment increased and new facilities were added yearly.

One interesting challenge faced by the author in writing this book has been the debate, confusion, and general uneasiness over the last few decades on where to place Texas in that transition period straddling the late nineteenth and early twentieth century—was Texas to be identified with the frontier West or part of the Old South? For that matter, should different regions in the state, given its size, be viewed differently? Scholar and historian George Woolfolk of Prairie View unequivocally declared that "Texas is not the deep South." In matters of education the Texas Constitution of 1876 upheld the sentiments of the Old South that dictated that races could not be educated together, "but the rough democracy of the new West said that they should have an equal chance—a monument to the public conscience of Texas." In contrast, Gregg Cantrell notes that Texas straddled the divide between the South and West: "Texas partook of the political culture of both sections, although its southern heritage remained the dominant strain." The indelible economic, political, and social link for decades was with "King Cotton." Furthermore, the debate on the role, impact, and meaning of "the West" and "frontier" has been ongoing since the famed Frederick Jackson Turner thesis on the closing of the American frontier in the mid-1890s. While the state grew dramatically via immigration from 1880 through World War I, with many new arrivals coming from the deep South, Texas, with its opening of the lands west of Austin, looked to develop westward and not to the south.

Texas and the trans-Mississippi West were dominated by cotton and cattle, along with sugar and rice—while the economy of the Old South was first based on the manufacture of tobacco, the deep South's oldest staple crop, followed by cotton. These two traditional crops through decades of overplanting stripped the soil of productivity, which caused the westward migration of thousands of farmers looking for a new future. Texas, in spite of the Southern hype of Henry Grady and the rise of the "New South" (more cosmopolitan and industrial), was overwhelmingly a country of rural people, by far one of the most rural sections of the nation. Agricultural growth in Texas was made possible by improved methods of farming—actively espoused by the agricultural extension service—hallmarked by dry land farming, water wells and windmills, new fertilizers, crop rotation, mechanized farm equipment, and barbwire. Blackshear capably worked with African Americans across Texas, not just those in the traditional cotton belt, and worked to expand efforts to demonstrate the benefits of land ownership and education. However, as historian Leigh A. Soares noted, "Like many others before him, Edward Blackshear came to learn the cruel lesson that no amount of goodwill accrued over decades of devoted work could protect him from political retaliation." Notwithstanding, Blackshear astutely navigated the political and social pressures of his era like few others—both in Texas, the West, and in the South. In time and at the height of his career in 1914, he was increasingly referred to in the news media as the "Booker T. Washington of the Southwest."

Crusader

From the first time Blackshear stepped into the primitive, one-room school house with a dozen barefoot black children eager to learn, and during his entire adult life, he championed education, self-sufficiency, and equality. His long crusade ended on December 19, 1919, at the age of fifty-seven, after a short illness. Reports of his death appeared in newspapers across the state. The *Dallas Express* noted his passing, "Professor Blackshear was looked upon by both white and black as one of the leading Negro educators in the country." The *Houston Post* instead of an obituary ran an editorial commenting that his contributions on education made him the most influential African American in Texas prior to World War I. "He labored unceasingly for a generation for the moral, mental and economic advancement of his race—a life every negro youth might well emulate. He at all times stood for the best interests of the Negro people, sometimes against strong opposition." He was buried alongside his son William, after a small family ceremony near the Prairie View campus. He left behind an extensive legacy of work on behalf of his race not just in Texas, but across the South. His wife, Rachel, remained at Prairie View and split her time between the campus and Houston, staying with her daughter Eddie, and working as a home demonstration extension agent for Harris County.

Arriving in Texas in 1882 fresh out of an extensive college education at Tabor College—something that was virtually unknown and unavailable for the great mass of African Americans during the post–Civil War years—Edward Blackshear faced the grim realities confronting freedmen across the South. The extent of his contribution and the leadership role he played in Texas has been both largely ignored and vastly overlooked. For far too long, Washington and Du Bois, while clearly worthy and accomplished leaders, have dominated the narrow narrative of African Americans' efforts to find their place in the postwar South. And only in recent years has there been scholarship to chronicle the efforts of such black Texas leaders as Lawrence Minor, George T. Ruby, Norris W. Cuney, John N. Johnson,

William Holland, Ida Wells, Abram Grant, and John B. Rayner. Thus, this work should encourage and further expand knowledge in this dynamic area of study.

Blackshear's early Texas years teaching in country schools galvanized his quest to promote the education, equality, and decades of stolen justice due his race. It soon became very apparent that in addition to educational needs, the social fabric and economic attainment of African Americans had to be improved in order to prosper and succeed. Unlike some in the Deep South who felt they could solve the "Negro problem" by promoting the exodus of black Americans to Africa, Haiti, Mexico, or Cuba, Blackshear was adamant that the best place for African Americans to prosper was America. An ethos of self-improvement, a strong nuclear family, and hard work to take control of their own lives were the foundation of the hundreds of speeches and articles he penned over four decades. He drilled this philosophy of education and family as the foundation for success into over two decades of students and young teachers while principal of Prairie View.

By the early 1900s, Blackshear's breadth of experience focused his drive to employ whatever tactics necessary to advance these views. Advancing his crusade required measured and well-placed political alliances to obtain the support and resources needed from the white Democratic-controlled power structure that dominated Texas throughout his lifetime. The struggle against a never-ending social structure of white supremacy and its refusal to fully recognize black Texans as equal under the law was a daily challenge. To not have acted as he did would have hampered his goals of advancing opportunities for his people to attempt to gain social equality.

Blackshear embraced the industrial education philosophy and programs crafted by his mentor Booker T. Washington, which he employed well into the classes at Prairie View. Yet all the while, aware of the needs of rural schools—and ever mindful of W. E. B. Du Bois's championing of higher education—Blackshear's passion was equally as strong to educate and certify African American teachers and place them in classrooms. The measure of his success is demonstrated by the fact that fully 80 percent of the "right kind of teachers" in black primary schools across the state had been educated at Prairie View by the time of his departure in 1915. It was here that Prairie View gained its early laudable reputation as the only black public college of higher education in Texas. Furthermore, in the decade following his death, over twenty schools and educational facilities in Texas were named in his honor. In his first—prophetic—report to the A&M

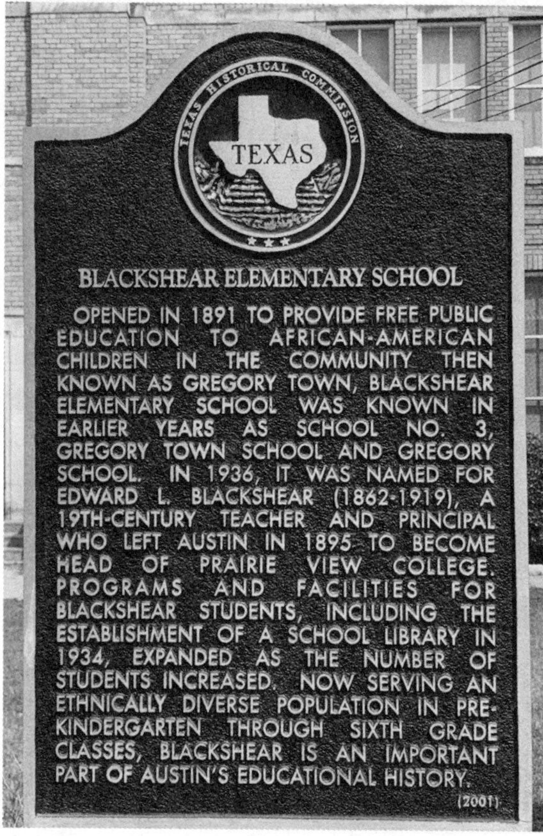

The Texas Historical Commission marker for Edward L. Blackshear at Blackshear Elementary School in Austin is only one of many recognitions of his contributions to education across the state. Approximately twenty schools and other facilities carry Blackshear's name. From the collection of John A. Adams Jr.

Board of Directors in the fall of 1896, only months after arriving at Prairie View, Blackshear noted: "There is a great demand everywhere among our people for teachers of character, culture, ability and professional skill. It is the personality of the teachers, the direct, immediate influence of his mind and character upon the pupils, that educate. As is the teacher, so is the school, so are the scholars. Excellent systems of public instruction and liberal appropriations therefore are valueless and ineffective without true teachers. There is no economy in poor teachers at any price. The state is expending annually large sums of money for the impartial education of all the children in her borders, and this money is worse than wasted unless skilled and devoted teachers are employed to carry out the spirit and letter of her schools . . . with a sufficient number of *the right kind of teachers*."

The lofty goal of equality of achieving opportunity for African Americans through education, economic opportunities, and equal justice was not fully realized at the time of Blackshear's death, nor has it been fully accomplished in today's America. While the Du Bois mantra of the "talented tenth' was expected to lead the way to prosperity for black Americans, it fell short. Many were left behind. There is a dynamic "talented tenth" of black doctors, lawyers, college professors, and entrepreneurs, yet in their wake there is a vast void of generations of economically challenged blacks and whites who have not found prosperity or social equality.

In Blackshear's honor the following was penned by a student:

BLACKSHEAR
Napoleon B. Edward

Your name shall live in Texas' heart and home,
Your deeds shall meet the coming years in peace,
Your love shall soothe and bid the sorrows gone,
And free the soul and give the poor release.

You touched the virgin youth with wisdom's hand,
And made the great and lowly hear thy voice,
Ignorance was driven from the land,
And hope arose mid a loud rejoice.

As Master, Teacher, kind and just and wise,
The truths you planted in the souls of earth,
Are beaming bright beyond the cloudy skies,
And ages about the glory of your birth.

You came to teach and bind the broken heart,
And nations loved and honored thee,
And cried and moaned and wept when you'd depart,
You lit a torch and made the meek and humble see.

—•⟫⟪•—

At the head of the Texas Institution is E. L. Blackshear who is the peer of Booker T. Washington in practical things and in common sense.

DAILY HERALD (WEATHERFORD, TX), DECEMBER 5, 1912

APPENDIX

"The Education of the Colored Race"
AN OPEN LETTER FROM SUL ROSS

An Exhibit of what Texas, under Democratic Rule, Has Done in the past and is Doing for the education and betterment of the Colored Race

by Governor L. S. Ross

For the Information of the People of the United States

The Democrats have been in power in Texas about fourteen years, but the present school system has been in operation only about ten years. During the last ten years the Democrats of Texas have paid to support public schools for the colored children as follows:

School Year	Colored Children	Pro Rata	Amount Distributed
1879–80	57,701	$3.00	$173,103.00
1880–81	66,777	$3.00	$200,331.00
1881–82	68,015	$3.25	$221,048.75
1882–83	75,341	$3.61	$271,981.01
1883–84	80,065	$4.50	$360,292.50
1884–85	103,536	$5.00	$517,680.00
1885–86	115,941	$5.20	$602,893.20
1886–87	124,842	$4.75	$592,999.50
1887–88	125,515	$4.50	$564,817.50
1888–89	135,184	$4.00	$540,736.00
		Total	$4,045,882.46

In ten years the colored scholastic population increased 134 percent and white 113 percent.

Owing to overestimates of the available school fund in 1885 and 1886, there were deficiencies which had to be met out of the school revenues of the years 1888 and 1889, reducing the pro rata by which reduction the white and colored suffered equally.

Speculative colored and white republican politicians have hatched schemes to carry off to Kansas, Missouri, California, and South America the colored population of Texas. Thousands have gone to Kansas and California. If Cuney, Allen, Radcliff Platt and other bloody shirt shriekers in Texas are correct, many of their race have been murdered by the white Democrats. But the race has more than doubled in Texas in ten years. There is mystery in this growth of the colored population. The only explanation of it is the Democrats of Texas are not able to kill off the colored population as rapidly as they are brought into the State for that purpose. The ability to destroy lags behind the will. The Texas Democrats have not got on to the dynamite process.

The increase of colored children in Texas, notwithstanding the bloody reign of the democracy, is a remarkable circumstance. It is far greater than the natural increase and greater than the rate of increase of the white children. Where have the colored children come from?

The foregoing figures are to be found in the reports of the educational department. In the ten years up to this date the Democrats of Texas have established 2,981 colored schools, employing as many colored teachers. These teachers are officers of the State, and 99 out of 100 of them are Republicans. Their politics are not inquired into. Then for some ten years the State has been educating colored teachers at the State Normal School near Hempstead. Not less than 100 teachers have been rendered proficient as pedagogues by that institute. Large and commodious additions to it are now under construction, paid for in the main by Democratic tax payer[s].

The State is now building a large and handsome brick addition to the deaf and Dumb and Blind Asylum for Colored Inmates. About $50,000 has been expended on that institution. A colored Republican has charge of it, appointed by Democrats, although there were white Democratic applicants for the place, and among them a surgeon in the State Lunatic Asylum. The Democrats have also supported colored summer normal schools when such schools for the white race were supported.

The State receives colored lunatics into its insane asylums without inquiry as to color, race, or previous condition. They cost the State $40,000 per annum.

1. The scholastic population of the State of Texas for the fiscal year ending August 31, 1889, is 523,116.
2. The scholastic population is divided with reference to color in the proportion of one negro child to three white children.
3. The amount of public money expended during the fiscal year ending August 31, 1889, for educational purposes from school funds was $2,998,347.39. To this amount should be added expenditures from funds derived from sales of bonds in cities and towns for building and equipping school houses, $300,000, making a total expenditure for educational purposes, $3,298,347.39. This amount does not include the expenditures for the State University, the Agricultural and Mechanical College, and the Deaf and Dumb and Blind Institutes, which aggregate $200,000, giving a total of $3,498,347,39.
4. No distinction is made on the basis of color in the distribution of the school fund, such distinction being forbidden both by the organic and statutory law, and as a matter of fact none has been made.
5. The proportion of taxes levied for school purposes, paid by the colored tax payer of the State is about one-third of the entire amount of taxes levied and paid for this purpose.
6. One State Normal School—the Sam Houston Institute—is supported by the State for the education of white teachers, and one State Normal School—the Prairie View Institute—is supported by the State for the education of colored teachers. The annual State appropriations to these schools pay the salaries of the faculties of the schools and furnish scholarships to about two hundred students in addition. The building and grounds of the normal school for the negroes are superior to those of the normal school for white teachers.
7. During the past ten years the public school system of this State has been built up, practically *ab initio*, so that the average school term of the State is about 5 8/10 months and the average salaries

of the teachers of about $45 per month, which is about $4 more than the average in the United States. The steady growth of the public school sentiment is conclusively shown by the extension of local taxation by which the State and county funds are being supplemented.

8. The permanent school fund of the State is increasing at the rate of about $1,000,000 per annum. The annual receipts of school funds are increasing by interest of this increase of the permanent school fund of the State, the increase of the permanent county school fund, and by the extension of local taxation in school districts. The annual expenditures for school purposes for the fiscal year ending August 31, 1889, exceeded the expenditures for the year ending August 31, 1888, about $400,000.

The policy of the Democrats in paying 2,981 colored teachers $590,000 per annum, in caring for colored lunatics at a cost of $40,000 per annum, in supporting the colored normal at about $20,000 per annum, in supporting their Deaf and Dumb and Blind Asylum, say $15,000—altogether about $665,000 yearly—is not easily understood away up north.

The Democrat loves his money as well as other people. How is it he pays as liberally to elevate and care for the negroes always found voting against him? Certainly there is only one explanation, and it is that the Democrats of Texas have agreed that the negro shall enjoy equal rights before the law, and cost what it may, they will, whether the party's majority is 165,000 or 5,000, accord the negro whatever the contract calls for. The race has thus been afforded a good chance to improve, and it is known by the white people of Texas that the negro has advanced marvelously. They were for years led as so many chained slaves by their white political leaders; now they rule supremely these old chieftains. They have in Texas thousands of accomplished teachers and preachers and many political orators able to cope with the gifted speakers of the white race. Democrats have contributed largely to this triumph. It is [a] singular notion that the Democrats could be hostile to the negro. It would be idiotic to yearly hand out $665,000 for the Negro's advancement if the Democrats designed to suppress them.

Education will strengthen them for any contest. If kept in blind ignorance they might be governed to extinction by the white race, stronger in numbers, wealth and intelligence.

Notes

List of Abbreviations

AHC: Austin History Center, Austin, TX

CLA: Coleman Library and Archives, Prairie View A&M University, Prairie View, TX

DBC: Dolph Briscoe Center for American History, University of Texas, Austin, TX

ELCA: Evans Library and Cushing Archives, Texas A&M University, College Station, TX

NARA: National Archives, Washington, DC

THS: Tabor Historical Society, Tabor, IA

TSLA: Texas State Library and Archives Commission, Austin, TX

Chapter 1

1. E. L. Blackshear, "What Is the Negro Teacher Doing in the Matter of Uplifting His Race?," in *Twentieth Century Literature, or A Cyclopedia of Thought on the Vital Topics Relating to the American Negro by One Hundred of America's Greatest Negroes*, ed. D. W. Culp (J. L. Nichols, 1902), 334.
2. Thomas M. Owen, *History of Alabama and Dictionary of Alabama Biography* (Reprint Company, 1978), 1373; Elizabeth W. Sheehan, "The Pollard House," *Alabama Historical Quarterly* 1, no. 4 (1930): 8–12; Edward B. Reuter, *The Mulatto in the United States: A Study of the Role of Mixed-Blood Races Throughout the World* (Richard G. Badger, 1918; repr., University Press of the Pacific, 2004), 225–27, 267–69; Ira Berlin, *Slaves Without Masters: The Free Negro in the Antebellum South* (New Press, 1974), 152; Joe M. Richardson, *Christian Reconstruction: The American Missionary Association and Southern Blacks, 1861–1890* (University of Georgia Press, 1986), 71–84, 245–47; "Work of Prairie View College," *Afro-American Ledger* (Baltimore), October 4, 1913. See also Society of Pioneers, *Pioneers: Past & Present, 1855–2001* (Society of Pioneers of Montgomery, 2001), 91; Henry A. Bullock, *A History of Negro Education in the South from 1619 to the Present* (Harvard University Press, 1967), 21–36.
3. US Census, Montgomery, 5th Ward, Alabama, July 27, 1870, p. 40; "Biography of Prof. Edward L. Blackshear," n.d., Edward L. Blackshear File, AHC.

4. U.S. Department of the Interior, Bureau of Education, *Report of the Commissioner of Education for the Year 1902*, vol. 1 (Government Printing Office, 1903), 285–92; Richardson, *Christian Reconstruction*, 109–19.
5. Edward L. Blackshear, "Present Needs of the Colored Race," *Christian Recorder* (Philadelphia), July 20, 1882; Blackshear, "What Is the Negro Teacher Doing," 334.
6. Blackshear, "What Is the Negro Teacher Doing," 334. For an early general history of "Negro education," see also Loretta Funke, "The Negro in Education," *Journal of Negro History* 5, no. 1 (1920): 1–21.
7. Charles W. Ramsdell, "Presidential Reconstruction in Texas," *Quarterly of the Texas State Historical Association* 11, no. 4 (1908): 288–94; William L. Richter, *Overreached on All Sides: The Freedmen's Bureau Administration in Texas, 1865–1868* (Texas A&M University Press, 1991); Virginia L. Denton, *Booker T. Washington and the Adult Education Movement* (University Press of Florida, 1993), 19–24, 58–60; Claude F. Oubre, *Forty Acres and a Mule: The Freedmen's Bureau and Black Ownership* (Louisiana State University Press, 1978).
8. Alwyn Barr, *Black Texans: A History of African Americans in Texas, 1528–1995*, 2nd ed. (University of Oklahoma Press, 1996), 60–64; Claude Elliott, "The Freedmen's Bureau in Texas," *Southwestern Historical Quarterly* 56, no. 1 (1952): 1–24; Barry A. Crouch, *The Freedmen's Bureau and Black Texans* (University of Texas Press, 1992), 59–64, 83–90; Randolph B. Campbell, *A Southern Community in Crisis: Harrison County, Texas, 1850–1880* (Texas State Historical Association, 2016), 261, 297, 304; Bullock, *History of Negro Education*, 31–43; Richardson, *Christian Reconstruction*, 82; U.S. Department of the Interior, *Report of the Commissioner of Education for the Year 1902*, vol. 1, 293–302; R. Grant Seals, "The Formation of Agricultural and Rural Development Policy with Emphasis on African-Americans: II. The Hatch-George and Smith-Lever Acts," *Agricultural History* 65, no. 2 (1991): 13. See also Richard White, *The Republic for Which It Stands: The United States During Reconstruction and the Gilded Age, 1965–1896* (Oxford University Press, 2017), 42–50.
9. John Habberton, *Our Country's Future* (International Publishing, 1889), 582; Richardson, *Christian Reconstruction*, 127–40; Alton Hornsby, "The Freedmen's Bureau Schools in Texas," *Southwestern Historical Quarterly* 76, no. 4 (1973): 397–417; Hilary Green, *Educational Reconstruction* (Fordham University Press, 2016), 6, 16. See also Dwight O. W. Holmes, *The Evolution of the Negro College* (Arno Press, 1949), 76–101.
10. Tabor College Registration Book, entry "Edward L. Blackshear, age 14, P. O., Montgomery, Ala., parent, Abram," p. 6, THS; US Census, Tabor, Ross Township, Iowa, June 29, 1880, p. 9; E. L. Blackshear, "Training of African Youths," *African Mail*, May 14, 1909, 317. See also Wesley A. Hotchkiss,

"Congregationalists and Negro Education," *Journal of Negro Education* 29, no. 3 (1960): 289–93. *Lux in tenebris* means "light in darkness."

11. Edward L. Blackshear academic grade reports, 1877–81, Tabor College Records, THS.
12. E. L. Blackshear, "Memories of Tabor," Blackshear Papers, THS.
13. Fifteenth Annual Commencement program of Tabor College, June 15, 1881, THS; H. T. Kealing, '81, Alumni Address, *Tabor Talisman*, April 1904, THS; "Useful Career of H. T. Kealing Comes to Close," *Afro-American* (Baltimore), March 1, 1918.
14. Perry L. Blackshear Jr., *Blacksheariana* (Atlanta: Perry L. Blackshear, n.d.), 106–9; *Catalog of Tabor College, 1877–78*, "Freshman Class" (Tabor, IA, 1878), 8; J. J. Pipkin, *The Story of a Rising Race: The Negro in Revelation, in History and in Citizenship* (St. Louis: N. D. Thompson, [1902?]), 432–36; "Work of Prairie View College," *Afro-American* (Baltimore), October 4, 1913; Richardson, *Christian Reconstruction*, 123–24; Thomas T. Smith, *The U.S. Army & the Texas Frontier Economy, 1845–1900* (Texas A&M University Press, 2007), 159.
15. Edward Blackshear, "Evolution of Society," *Christian Recorder* (Philadelphia), March 29, 1883; Blackshear, "Present Needs of the Colored Race."
16. Barr, *Black Texans*, 94.
17. W. E. B. Du Bois, ed., *The Negro Church: Report of a Social Study Made upon the Direction of Atlanta University* (Atlanta University Press, 1903), 57, quoted in Richardson, *Christian Reconstruction*, 157; Lawrence Rice, *The Negro in Texas, 1877–1900* (Louisiana University Press, 1971), 271–75. Gunnar Myrdal concludes, "The Negro church was, from the beginning, the logical center for community life—much more than a place of worship." *An American Dilemma: The Negro Problem and Modern Democracy* (Harper Torchbooks, 1944), vol. 2, 867.
18. N. W. Hartlee, "Four Veteran Teachers," *Dallas Express*, December 13, 1919. Edward Blackshear died on December 12, 1919. A "hod" is a wooden trough or harness to carry heavy loads on the shoulders.
19. "A Fine School Building for Eastern Austin," *Austin American Statesman*, August 23, 1883; Larry Willoughby, *Austin: A Historical Portrait* (Donning, 1985), 41.
20. E. L. Blackshear, "A Few Suggestions to the Officials of the Church," July 12, 1883; Edward Blackshear, "Word from Texas," *Christian Recorder* (Philadelphia), April 3, 1884; "Bishop Grant and Wife Dead," *Chicago Defender*, January 28, 1911; C. Vann Woodward, *Origins of the New South* (Louisiana State University, 1951; repr., 1971) 169. "Veni, vidi, vici" (I came, I saw, I conquered) was first reported to be used by Julius Caesar in a 47 BC letter to the Roman Senate and seen in Plutarch's *Life of Caesar*. Bishop Abraham Grant, who was often referred to as Abram, was born on an oxcart

to an enslaved mother on a trip between Jacksonville and Lake City, Florida, on August 25, 1848, and was originally named for his master, Rollins. Following the Emancipation Proclamation, he changed his name to the first name of the president and the last name of his favorite Union general, Grant. See "Colored Bishop Dead," *Daily Republican* (Cherryvale, KS), January 23, 1911.

21. "Emancipation," *Austin Daily Statesman*, June 19, 1884; Douglas Hales, *A Southern Family in White and Black: The Cuneys of Texas* (Texas A&M University Press, 2003), 19.
22. State Convention of Colored Men of Texas, *Proceedings of the State Convention of Colored Men of Texas, July 10–12, 1883* (Houston, 1883), TSLA; "Mortuary [William H. Holland]," *Austin Statesman*, June 21, 1907; "Colored Men Meet," *Galveston Daily News*, March 24, 1895; Alwyn Barr, "Black State Conventions," in *Handbook of Texas*, vol. 1, ed. Ron Tyler (Texas State Historical Association, 1996), 575.
23. "State Papers," *Galveston Daily News* [reprinted from the *Argus*], September 1, 1891.
24. E. L. Blackshear, "The Negro Problem," *Fort Worth Daily Gazette*, December 20, 1888; "A Gubernatorial Tilt," *Dallas Morning News*, October 14, 1888; "Mortuary [William H. Holland]"; James Markham, "Texas Blind, Deaf, and Orphan School," in *Handbook of Texas*, vol. 6, ed. Ron Tyler (Texas State Historical Association, 1996), 295.
25. *Tri-Weekly Herald* (Marshall, TX), August 18 and 28, 1883, and September 4 and 6, 1883; *Spectator* (Galveston), September 15, 1883, as quoted in the *New York Times*, September 23, 1883; *Houston Post*, October 18, 1883; Alwyn Barr, "The Texas 'Black Uprising' Scare of 1883," *Phylon (1960–)* 41, no. 2. (1980): 179–86.
26. E. L. Blackshear, "Negro Outbreaks," *Austin Statesman*, June 4, 1884.
27. Blackshear, "Present Needs of the Colored Race"; Blackshear, "Evolution of Society"; E. L. Blackshear, "Equal Rights in Texas," *Evening World* (New York), December 7, 1888.
28. Governor Oran Roberts General Message to Special Session, April 6, 1882, in *Governors' Messages: Coke to Ross, 1874–1891* (Texas State Library, 1916), 389–90. See also L. L. Foster, *Forgotten Texas Census: First Annual Report of the Agricultural Bureau of the Department of Agriculture, Insurance, Statistics, and History, 1887–88* (Austin, 1889; repr., Texas State Historical Association, 2001), 216, 312.
29. Oscar H. Cooper, *Special Report of the Superintendent of Public Instruction for the Years Ending Aug. 31, 1987* (Austin, 1888), 26–32, TSLA; Texas State Constitution of 1876, ratified February 15, 1876, art. 7, sec. 7, TSLA; State Convention of Colored Men of Texas, *Proceedings*, 17–19; Carlos K. Blanton, *The Strange Career of Bilingual Education in Texas, 1836–1981* (Texas A&M

University Press, 2004), 44–45. For a detailed overview of the evolution of education in Texas, see George R. Woolfolk, *Prairie View: A Study in Public Conscience, 1878–1946* (Pageant Press, 1962), 1–17.

30. William B. Bizzell, *The Green Rising* (MacMillan, 1926), 121–26; Alwyn Barr, *Reconstruction to Reform: Texas Politics, 1876–1906* (Southern Methodist University Press, 2001), 9; Barr, *Black Texans*, 100; Bullock, *History of Negro Education*, 172–82; William R. Davis, *The Development and Present Status of Negro Education in East Texas* (Columbia University Bureau of Publication, 1934), 478; Frederick Eby, *The Development of Education in Texas* (Macmillan, 1925), 195–96, 212, 223–25.
31. Rev. E. L. Blackshear, "Interesting Notes from Austin, Tex.," *Christian Recorder* (Philadelphia), August 14, 1890; "The Church," *Freeman* (Philadelphia), June 18, 1892; Edward W. Gilliam, "The African in the United States," *Popular Science Monthly*, February 1883; John Henry Brown, *A History of Texas from 1865–1892* (St. Louis, 1893), 509–10. See also G. F. Richings, *Evidences of Progress Among Colored People* (Geo. S. Ferguson, 1904), 136–38, 373–74.
32. E. L. Blackshear, "Colored Man's Letter," *Austin Daily Statesman*, October 15, 1885. See also "Biography of Prof. Edward L. Blackshear," and Austin Independent School District File, n.d., both at the AHC; Eby, *The Development of Education in Texas*, 230–31; Barr, *Black Texans*, 98–99. The compulsory attendance law was passed following a recommendation by Governor Ferguson in early 1915, over the objections that the new "mild compulsory law . . . would interfere with the sanctity of the [Texas] family."

    Student absenteeism ranged daily from 26–33 percent in Texas in 1887:

    Student enrollment and average attendance in selected Texas counties in 1887.

County	Students	Attendance	County	Students	Attendance
Dallas	4,577	3,004	Galveston	4,577	3,000
Bexar	1,595	1,108	Atascosa	1,887	967
Bandera	830	625	Bastrop	3,533	3,333
Austin	2,492	1,730	Erath	2,211	1,822

Source: Texas State Library and Archives Commission.

33. Blackshear, "Colored Man's Letter."
34. Blackshear, "Colored Man's Letter."
35. "Texas News by Telegraph," *Galveston Daily News*, October 23, 1877; "Act to Establish an Agricultural and Mechanical College of Texas, for the Benefit of the Colored Youths," Session of the Fifteenth Legislature, ch. 92, pp. 136–37, April 18, 1876, General Laws of the State of Texas, TSLA; "Act for the Organization and Support of a Normal School at Prairie View

(formerly called Alta Vista)," Regular Session of the Sixteenth Legislature, ch. 159, pp. 181–82, April 24, 1879, General Laws of the State of Texas, TSLA; Minutes of the Board of Directors of the A&M College of Texas, November 18–24, 1879, ELCA; John W. Davis, "The Negro Land-Grant College," *Journal of Negro Education* 2, no. 3 (1933): 317–18. See also Merline Pitre, *Through Many Dangers, Toils, and Snares: The Black Leadership of Texas, 1868–1900* (Texas A&M University Press, 2016), 72–76; Marie G. Tomlinson, "The State Agricultural and Mechanical College of Texas, 1871–1879: The Personalities, Politics, and Uncertainties" (master's thesis, Texas A&M University, 1976); Woolfolk, *Prairie View*, 28–33. There was only one A&M board of directors. A number of authors cite the "Prairie View Board of Directors," but there was none and this is incorrect; Prairie View, as a branch of the A&M College, reported through its principal to the president of Texas A&M and then to the A&M board. Part of the confusion could be that Prairie View did submit a separate biannual report to the A&M board.

36. John A. Adams Jr., "How Alta Vista Became Prairie View: Lawrence Washburne Minor and the Beginnings of Public Higher Education for African Americans in Texas," *Southwestern Historical Quarterly* 127, no. 3 (2024): 268–86; Joel Schor, *Agriculture in the Black Land-Grant System to 1930* (Florida A&M University Press, 1982), 71–72.
37. "The News from Austin: President Gathright Given Charge of the Colored College," *Galveston Daily News*, January 23, 1878; E. L. Blackshear, "Relation of Industrial Education to Prairie View Curriculum," in Proceedings of the Annual Session of the Colored Teachers State Association, January 1, 1901, p. 19, TSLA; David Brooks Cofer, *First Five Administrations of Texas A. & M. College* (Association of Former Students, 1952), 7–8; *Houston Post*, May 21, 1908; Henry C. Dethloff, *A Centennial History of Texas A&M University, 1876–1976*, vol. 1 (Texas A&M University Press, 1975), 54; Eby, *The Development of Education in Texas*, 271–74; Alton Hornsby Jr., "The 'Colored Branch University' Issue in Texas—Prelude to *Sweatt vs. Painter*," *Journal of Negro History* 61, no. 1 (1976): 51–53. In the mid-1870s Texas was one of eight Southern states approving a new constitution.
38. "The News from Austin," *Galveston Daily News*, January 23, 1878, and March 15, 1878; *Weekly Democratic Statesman* (Austin), February 7, 1878; *Dallas Weekly Herald*, February 9, 1878; "Agricultural and Mechanical College for Colored Youths at Alta Vista," *Austin American Statesman*, February 6, 1879; Office of Government Reports, "Information Digest," no. 454, April 30, 1942, Government Printing Office; "Negro College in Texas to Get ROTC Unit," *Dallas Morning News*, May 2, 1942; Woolfolk, *Prairie View*, 33.
39. Eby, *The Development of Education in Texas*, 187–89; "Secession Convention," in *Texas Almanac, 1857–1874*, ed. James M. Day (Texian Press, 1967), 475–93.

40. "The Colored College: Can We Afford to Let It Drop?," *Galveston Daily News*, February 8, 1879; "Agricultural and Mechanical College for Colored Youths at Alta Vista," *Galveston Daily News*, February 6, 1879; O. M. Roberts, "Governor's Message," *Journal of the Senate of the Sixteenth Legislature, Extra Session*, June 10, 1879, pp. 8, 11, 46–50, 57–58, ELCA. See also Adams, "How Alta Vista Became Prairie View," 268–86.
41. Thomas S. Gathright, *Reports of the Agricultural and Mechanical College of Texas, Alta Vista College for Colored Youths* (Galveston, 1878); William R. David, *The Development and Present Status of Negro Education in East Texas* (Columbia University Press, 1934), 122; Dethloff, *Centennial History of Texas A&M*, vol. 1, 54–56; Woolfolk, *Prairie View*, 44–47. Between 1891 to 1906, Prairie View funding from Peabody totaled $5,924. See also "A History of the A. and M. College," *Houston Daily Post*, June 6, 1909; Joan Malczewski, "Weak State, Stronger Schools: Northern Philanthropy and Organizational Change in the Jim Crow South," *Journal of Southern History* 75, no. 4 (2009): 963–1000. George Peabody established the Peabody Fund of $2.4 million in 1866–69 (in 2025 that would be an estimated value of over $48.3 million) for stipends for the improvement of education in the South. The Peabody Fund was liquidated in 1914 and its assets transferred to the Slater Fund.
42. Thomas S. Gathright, "Prairie View School Report," *Journal of the Senate of the Sixteenth Legislature*, June 2, 1879, pp. 57–58, ELCA; Jared R. Stallones, "Education and Politics in Texas: The Legacies of Laurine C. Anderson and Edward L Blackshear," in *Pedagogies of Black Educators*, special issue, *Vitae Scholasticae* 28, no. 2 (2011): 9; Cofer, *First Five Administrations*, 8–21.
43. Gathright to L. L. McInnis, March 9, 1880, Gathright Papers, ELCA; "President's Report: Plan of Reorganization," *Biennial Report*, Texas A&M, July 1, 1880, 9–11, ELCA; Cofer, *First Five Administrations*, 14–20; Seals, "Formation of Agricultural and Rural Development Policy," 15. See also Dethloff, *Centennial History of Texas A&M*, vol. 1, 50–69.
44. "Act for the Organization and Support of a Normal School," 181–82; "State Normal School of Texas," *Galveston Daily News*, October 1, 1880; "Agricultural and Mechanical College," *Galveston Daily News*, June 26, 1881; O. M. Roberts, "General Message on the Judiciary, Education, Insurance, Statistics and History, Railroads, Etc.," Seventeenth Legislature, Austin, January 26, 1881, pp. 753–64, quoted in Frederick Eby, *Education in Texas: Source Materials*, University of Texas bulletin no. 1824, April 25, 1918, TSLA; E. H. Anderson, "Prairie View Normal School," *Biennial Report*, Texas A&M, January 20, 1881, 46–48, ELCA.
45. O. M. Roberts to Col. J. M. Burroughs, March 16, 1882, and June 12, 1882, J. M. Burroughs Papers MSS 04-0049, Rosenberg Library Special Collections, Galveston, TX; "Texas Exchanges," *Forth Worth Daily*

Democrat-Advance, February 10, 1882; Woolfolk, *Prairie View*, 71. See also "Governor's Message, April 6, 1882," *Weekly Democratic Statesman*, April 13, 1882. Six hundred dollars in 1882 would be worth $18,700 in 2025 value.

46. "The Colored People of Austin," *Austin Daily Statesman*, August 29, 1882; Texas Secretary of State, *Report* (Austin, 1882), 5, TSLA; "Chapter 29 (Prairie View deficiency funding)," in *General Laws of the State of Texas* (A. H. Belo, 1882), 37–38, TSLA; *Houston Daily Post*, September 21, 1882; John Mason Brewer, *Negro Legislators of Texas and Their Descendants* (Mathis, 1935), 83–84; Woolfolk, *Prairie View*, 68–72, 86–91; "Biography of Prof. L. C. Anderson," n.d., L. C. Anderson File, AHC; Hornsby, " 'Colored Branch University' Issue," 52; Dudley G. Wooten, ed., *A Comprehensive History of Texas, 1685–1897*, vol. 2 (Dallas, 1898), 462–63.

47. Junior N. Nelum, "A Study of the First Seventy Years of the Colored Teachers State Association of Texas" (PhD diss., University of Texas, 1955); Woolfolk, *Prairie View*, 77–80; Rice, *Negro in Texas*, 224–25. See also Edward A. Hollins, "The Colored Teachers State Association of Texas as Revealed in the Texas Press" (master's thesis, Prairie View A&M College, 1948); John A. Adams Jr., "A Promise Unfulfilled—Edward L. Blackshear: Crusader for the 'Colored University' in Texas 1882–1901," forthcoming with *East Texas Historical Journal.*

48. E. L. Blackshear, "Colored People Moving," *Austin American Statesman*, September 3, 1885; Lauren N. Henley, "'Devilish Deeds': Serial Murder and Racial Violence in Austin, Texas, 1884–1885," *Journal of African American History* 105, no. 1 (2020): 1–25.

49. "Outlook for the State University," *Galveston Daily News*, September 12, 1882; "Another Word with You, Judge Terrell," *Austin Statesman*, August 10, 1891, and March 20, 1892; *Dallas Morning News*, March 22 and 24, 1892; Lewis L. Gould, *Alexander Watkins Terrell: Civil War Soldier, Texas Lawmaker, American Diplomat* (University of Texas Press, 2004), 57, 79–81, 120–23; Oran M. Roberts, "Fifty Years of Politics, Legislation and Judicial History of Texas," in Wooten, *Comprehensive History of Texas*, vol. 2, 246–50; Frank E. Vandiver, "John William Mallet and the University of Texas," *Southwestern Historical Quarterly* 53, no. 4 (1950): 422–42; H. Y. Benedict, *A Source Book Relating to the History of the University of Texas* (University of Texas, 1917), 264–69. See also John W. Mallet, "Reminiscences of the First Year of the University of Texas," *Alcalde*, April 1913, 14–17; W. H. Wilson, "Recollections of Dr. R. L. Dabney," *Alcalde*, March 1914, 415–32; Frank W. Johnson, *A History of Texas and Texans*, vol. 3 (American Historical Society, 1914), 1063–64; and Wooten, *Comprehensive History of Texas*, vol. 2, 445–49.

50. "Judge Ireland and the Education of the Masses," *Galveston Daily News*, September 12, 1882, and September 29, 1884; John J. Lane, *History of the University of Texas* (Austin, 1891), 56, 70–72; W. J. Battle, "A Concise History

of the University of Texas, 1883–1950," *Southwestern Historical Quarterly* 54, no. 4 (1951): 391–411. See also Roscoe C. Martin, "The Grange as a Political Factor in Texas," *Southwestern Political and Social Science Quarterly* 6, no. 4 (1926): 363–83.

51. J. N. Johnson to Governor John St. John, June 21, 1879, transcription of Governor St. John's Exoduster Correspondence, https://www.kansashistory.gov/research/pdfs/st.john_exoduster_transcription.pdf; "Colored Colonization Society," *Colorado Citizen*, April 10, 1879; "Colored State Conference," *Galveston Daily News*, July 2 and 4, 1879; "Colored Conference: Negroes Urged to Emigrate," *Galveston Daily News*, July 5, 1879; *Brenham (TX) Weekly Banner*, August 29, 1879; Gregg Cantrell, *Feeding the Wolf: John B. Rayner & the Politics of Race, 1850–1918* (Harlan Davidson, 2001), 19–20. See also Nell I. Painter, *Exodusters: Black Migration to Kansas After Reconstruction* (W. W. Norton, 1986).
52. C. Vann Woodward, *The Strange Career of Jim Crow*, 3rd ed. (Oxford University Press, 2002), 21.
53. C. Vann Woodward, *The Burden of Southern History* (Louisiana State University Press, 1968), 65; Abraham Lincoln, "Address on Colonization to a Deputation of Negros," August 12, 1862, in *The Collected Works of Abraham Lincoln*, vol. 5, ed. Roy P. Basler (Lincoln Sesquicentennial Commission, 1959), 371–72. See also E. L. Blackshear, "Negro Colonization Schemes," *Houston Post*, July 13, 1914.
54. E. L. Blackshear, "Colored Man's Letter," October 15, 1885; Gilliam, "The African in the United States"; Henry Gannell, "Are We to Become Africanized?," *Popular Science Monthly*, June 1885; James B. Craighead, "The Future of the Negro in the South," *Popular Science Monthly*, November 1884, 39–46; Carl T. Moneyhon, *George T. Ruby: Champion of Equal Rights in Reconstruction Texas* (Texas Christian University Press, 2020), 351–57; Barr, *Black Texans*, 96–98; Blackshear, "A Refuge for Negroes," *Washington Post*, December 5, 1898; Debra A. Reid, "Reaping a Greater Harvest" (PhD diss., Texas A&M University, 2000), 23; Myrdal, *American Dilemma*, vol. 2, 185–86; August Meier, *Negro Thought in America, 1880–1915* (University of Michigan Press, 1963), 66. Cuba and Mexico were also considered as locations for resettlement. Blackshear repeated his views many times, such as, "I don't believe in the deportation proposition. I believe your logical home is here in the south where the race has good friends." *Waxahachie Daily Light*, September 15, 1904.
55. "One by One," *Texan-Telephone* (Canton, TX), February 21, 1885.
56. E. L. Blackshear, "Advice from His Colored Brethren," *Austin Daily Statesman*, March 9, 1894. See also Christine Lutz, "'The People! The People!': African American Leaders on Africans and Asians at the Turn of the Nineteenth Century," *Journal of GAH* 28 (2009): 33–54. Blackshear

was in complete agreement with Washington, who did not favor migration as a solution, on the best place for the African American to succeed and prosper. Washington declared, "Cast down your buckets where you are. It is in the South that the Negro is given a man's chance in the commercial world." Booker T. Washington, *Up from Slavery: An Autobiography* (New York, 1900), 220.

57. W. E. B. Du Bois to Paul Hagemans, Council-General of Belgium, c. 1897, quoted in in Du Bois, *Against Racism: Unpublished Essays, Papers, Addresses, 1887–1961*, ed. Herbert Aptheker (University of Massachusetts Press, 1985), 43–49; N. S. Shaler, "The Future of the Negro in the Southern States," *Popular Science Monthly*, June 1900; "Pan African Association," *Colored American* (Washington, DC), February 1901; E. L. Blackshear, "Congo Horrors," *New York Age*, January 17, 1907; Jacqueline M. Moore, *Booker T. Washington, W. E. B. Du Bois, and the Struggle for Racial Uplift* (SR Books, 2003), 8. In 1919, Du Bois attended the first conference of the Pan-African movement, in Paris. See also Ryan E. Tickle, "For Their Brethren Across the Sea: The African-American Protest to Abuses in the Congo Free State, 1885–1908" (master's thesis, California State University, 2009).

58. "A Gubernatorial Tilt," *Dallas Morning News*, October 14, 1888; "Hearne," *Galveston Daily News*, September 14, 1879; *Dallas Herald*, October 2, 1889; Painter, *Exodusters*, 200–201; J. Fred Rippy, "A Negro Colonization Project in Mexico, 1895," *Journal of Negro History* 6, no. 1 (1921): 66–73; Woolfolk, *Prairie* View, 78–80; Rice, *Negro in Texas*, 200–208; Barr, *Black Texans*, 96–98; U.S. Department of Commerce, Bureau of the Census, *Negro Population in the United States, 1790–1915* (Government Printing Office, 1918), 43–44, 51, 91–92. The overall state population grew from 1,591,749 in 1880 to 2,235,521 in 1890 and to 3,048,000 in 1900. Debra Reid, in *Reaping a Greater Harvest: African Americans, the Extension Service, and Rural Reform in Jim Crow Texas* (Texas A&M University Press, 2007), notes, "Even if four thousand left Texas for Kansas, the number represents only 1.02 percent of the state's total black population" (181). See also Bruce A. Glasrud, "Black Texans, 1900–1930: A History" (PhD diss., Texas Tech University, 1969), 318–27. Furthermore, little has been researched about the movement of Mexican immigrants northward from South Texas during 1890 to 1920. See Arnoldo De Léon and Kenneth L Stewart, "Lost Dreams and Found Fortunes: Mexican and Anglo Immigrants in South Texas, 1850–1900," *Western Historical Quarterly* 14, no. 3 (1983): 291–310; Robert Oppenheimer, "Acculturation or Assimilation: Mexican Immigrants in Kansas, 1900 to World War II," *Western Historical Quarterly* 16, no. 4 (1985): 429–48. The phrase to "wave the bloody shirt" was a post–Civil War term referring to the strategy of recalling the passions and hardships of the recent

war that was actively employed by the Radical Republicans on controversial issues facing the country.

59. E. L. Blackshear, "Industrial Training and the Race Question," *Southern Workman*, July 1906, 399; Faculty Minutes of Prairie View, May 9, 1909, May 20, 1910, May 9, 1911, CLA; James H. Quarles, "Student of Prairie View Grandson of African King," *Houston Daily Post*, July 11, 1909; "Colored Youth, Come South!" *Freedman* (Indianapolis), September 5, 1908; "Training of African Youths," *African Mail* (Liverpool), May 14, 1909; John A. Lomax, "Stories of an African Prince: Yoruba Tales," *Journal of American Folk-Lore* 26, no. 4 (1913): 1–12.
60. "Prairie View Normal School," *Texas School Journal*, February 1885, 37; David A. William, *Bricks Without Straw: A Comprehensive History of African Americans in Texas* (Eakin Press, 1977), 258–60, 387–88.
61. Edward L. Blackshear, *The Education of Childhood* (New York, 1911), 54; "Mr. Ed Blackshear," *Austin American Statesman*, April 25, 1886; "Mrs. Blackshear Funeral," *Austin Daily Statesman*, June 30, 1889; *Freie Presse für Texas* (San Antonio), July 1, 1889.
62. Blackshear to Walter Graham, Secretary City School Board, July 10, 1895, Blackshear File, AHC; Blackshear to Mamie North, July 31, 1895, Blackshear File, AHC.
63. "Work of Prairie View College," *Afro-American*, October 4, 1913; Michael Fultz, "African American Teachers in the South, 1890–1940: Powerless and the Ironies of Expectations and Protest," *History of Education Quarterly* 35, no. 4 (1995): 403–4. See also Bullock, *History of Negro Education*.

Chapter 2

1. U.S. House, *Report of the Commissioner of Education*, 1880–81, p. 308, TSLA; Paul Casdorph, *A History of the Republican Party in Texas, 1865–1965* (Pemberton Press, 1965), 30–45; Claude Elliott, "The Freedmen's Bureau in Texas," 7–13; Henry L. Swint, *The Northern Teacher in the South* (Octagon Books, 1967), 128–33; Edward King, *Texas: 1874* (Houston: Cordovan Press, 1874; repr., 1974), 68. See also Charles W. Ramsdell, "Presidential Reconstruction in Texas," *Quarterly of the Texas State Historical Association* 11, no. 4 (1908): 277–313; Charles W. Ramsdell, "Presidential Reconstruction in Texas: III. The Restoration of State Government," *Quarterly of the Texas State Historical Association* 12, no. 3 (1909): 204–30; Moneyhon, *George T. Ruby*.
2. Gould, *Alexander Watkins Terrell*, 74–75; Barr, *Reconstruction to Reform*, 203–5; Stephen J. DeCanio, *Agriculture in the Postbellum South: The Economics of Production and Supply* (Massachusetts Institute of Technology Press, 1974), 17–23; Woodward, *The Strange Career of Jim Crow*, 23.
3. "Church and State and Education," *Galveston Daily News*, August 18, 1882; Patrick G. William, *Beyond Redemption: Texas Democrats After*

Reconstruction (Texas A&M University Press, 2007), 19–24; Lewis L. Gould, *Progressives and Prohibitionists: Texas Democrats in the Wilson Era* (University of Texas Press, 1973), 48–49; William L. Richter, *Overreached on All Sides* (Texas A&M University Press, 1991), 94–100; Reid, *Reaping a Greater Harvest*, 30–32; Myrdal, *American Dilemma*, vol. 1, 481–85.

4. *Report of the Commissioner of Education for 1877*, 245, TSLA. See also Willie A. Tarrow, "A University for Negroes of Texas—A Promise Unfulfilled" (master's thesis, Prairie View University, 1946).
5. Gould, *Alexander Watkins Terrell*, 74, 78, 117, 149; Woodward, *The Strange Career of Jim Crow*, 84; Dick Smith, "Texas and the Poll Tax," *Southwestern Social Science Quarterly* 45, no. 2 (1964): 167–73; David Montejano, *Anglos and Mexicans in the Making of Texas, 1836–1986* (University of Texas Press, 1987), 143.
6. "Contest in Sixth District: A Record of Election Corruption," *Southern Mercury*, November 29, 1894; "Why a People's Party," *Southern Mercury*, January 31, 1895; J. C. Kearby v. Jo Abbott, *Report on Electoral Fraud*, H.R. Rep. No. 1596, 54th Cong., 1st Sess. (1897), pp. 1895–96; Williams, *Beyond Redemption*, 169–72; Barr, *Black Texans*, 79–81; Woodward, *The Strange Career of Jim Crow*, 84. See also Myrdal, *American Dilemma*, vol. 1, 39–40, 65–67, 191, 446–48.
7. "Afternoon Session," *Galveston Daily News*, July 5, 1879; "Agricultural and Mechanical College," *Galveston Daily News*, June 26, 1881; Eby, *The Development of Education in Texas*, 175–80, 190–91, 207–13; Fultz, "African American Teachers in the South," 403–4; Barr, *Black Texans*, 99; Barr, *Reconstruction to Reform*, 42–43, 63, 77–80.
8. "Biography of Prof. L. C. Anderson," AHC; "State Education," *Hempstead Ledger*, December 4, 1885; "Hempstead," *Galveston Daily News*, October 3, 1886; Woolfolk, *Prairie View*, 78–82, 94–100. See also Eby, *The Development of Education in Texas*, 243.
9. Seals, "Formation of Agricultural and Rural Development Policy," 16–18; Alfred C. True, *A History of Agricultural Education in the United States, 1785–1925*, pub. no. 36 (Government Printing Office, 1929), 155. See also Ralph Smith, "The Grange Movement in Texas, 1873–1900," *Southwestern Historical Quarterly* 42, no. 4 (1939): 397–415; Woodward, *Origins of the New South*, 192–93.
10. "Colored Grangers," *Galveston Daily News*, September 22, 1876; Walton C. John, ed., *Land-Grant College Education 1910–1920*, U.S. Department of Interior, Bureau of Education bulletin no. 24 (Government Printing Office, 1925), 9–26; Dethloff, *Centennial History of Texas A&M*, vol. 1, 96–97; Donna A. Barnes, *Farmers in Rebellion: The Rise and Fall of the Southern Farmers Alliance and People's Party of Texas* (University of Texas Press, 1984), 67.

11. Scrapbook, A. J. Rose Papers, DBC. See also Robert A. Calvert, "A. J. Rose and the Agrarian Concept of Reform," *Agricultural History* 51, no. 1 (1977): 181–96; C. N. Ousley, ed., *Texas Farm and Ranch* [pamphlet], July 10, 1888, seen in David Brooks Cofer, *Early History of Texas A. and M. College Through Letters and Papers* (Association of Former Students, 1952), 188.
12. James B. Craighead, "The Future of the Negro in the South," *Popular Science Monthly*, November 1884, 41; Stallones, "Education and Politics in Texas," 11; Eby, *The Development of Education in Texas*, 270–27; Seals, "Formation of Agricultural and Rural Development Policy," 6. During the early 1870s there were a number of thriving denominational schools scattered across east-central Texas. King, in *Texas: 1874*, noted that the Baptists had schools in Independence and Waco; the Presbyterians in Huntsville; the Lutherans in Columbus; the Methodists in Chappell Hill; and the Odd Fellows in Bryan.
13. "Requirements for State Students," quoted in Tarrow, "University for Negroes," 50.
14. "Colored Baptists Meet," *Dallas Morning News*, August 26, 1992; Cecil E. Evans, *The Story of Texas Schools* (Steck, 1955), 211–12.
15. W. D. Robertson, "Education," *Southern Mercury*, May 6, 1889.
16. Irvin M. May, "The Origins and Development of the Texas Agricultural Experiment Station," *Political and Social Science Quarterly*, March 1976, 363–83; Debra A. Reid, "People's College for Other Citizens," in *Science as Service: Establishing and Reformulating American Land-Grant Universities, 1865–1930*, ed. Alan I. Marcus (University of Alabama Press, 2015), 157–58.
17. Article by A. D. Jackson, *Farm and Ranch*, March 5, 1921, quoted in Clarence Ousley, *History of the Agricultural and Mechanical College of Texas*, bulletin no. 8 (A&M College, December 1, 1935), 107–10, ELCA; Schor, *Agriculture in the Black Land-Grant System*, 72–73. See also Robert L. Haney, *Milestones Marking Ten Decades of Research: Texas Agricultural Experiment Station* (Texas Agricultural Experiment Station, 1989), vii–viii, 2–5, 11–14.
18. Foster, *Forgotten Texas Census*, xxvii–xxix; "Agricultural Experiment Station," *Biennial Report*, Texas A&M, 1889, p. xviii, 11, ELCA; Dethloff, *Centennial History of Texas A&M*, vol. 1, 143, 317–18; "The Cotton Market," *Galveston Daily News*, May 12, 1896; "Cotton Statistics," *Galveston Daily News*, July 16, 1896; "Cotton," *Galveston Daily News*, September 12, 1882; Woodward, *Origins of the New South*, 410–12; "The Outlook," *Southern Mercury*, October 21, 1897; Irvin M. May Jr., "Reform, 1874–1900," in *The Texas Heritage*, ed. Ben Procter and Archie P. McDonald (Harlan Davidson, 1998), 82; Haney, *Milestones*, 4. Programs sponsored by the Experiment Station began almost at once to investigate the cause of the cotton blight or "root rot," test new types of fertilizers, conduct feeding tests for beef and dairy cattle, and test new varieties of grasses. See "About Experiments," *Galveston Daily News*, July 4, 1896; "Use of Fertilizers," *Galveston Daily*

News, July 18, 1896; Ousley, *History of the Agricultural and Mechanical College*, 107–11, 126–28. A. H. Belo had by the mid-1880s established an extensive network of branch offices for distribution, not only across Texas but also in New York; Washington, DC; St. Louis; and New Orleans. Belo founded the *Dallas Morning News* as a satellite daily publication in October 1885.

19. *Rockdale (TX) Reporter*, January 17, 1889, seen in Stallones, "Education and Politics in Texas," 12; Foster, *Forgotten Texas Census*, xxiv–xxvi; Evans, *The Story of Texas Schools*, 289–91; Woolfolk, *Prairie View*, 100. See also Martin, "The Grange as a Political Factor in Texas," 363–83.
20. "Want Cuney's Scalp," *Galveston Daily News*, May 17, 1896; "Lily White Faction," *Galveston Daily News*, July 16, 1896; "Bishop Grant," *Freedman* (Indianapolis), May 10, 1890; Paul D. Casdorph, "Norris Wright Cuney and Texas Republican Politics, 1883–1896," *Southwestern Historical Quarterly* 68, no. 4 (1965): 455–64; Virginia N. Hinze, "Norris Wright Cuney" (master's thesis, Rice University, 1965), 1–150; Maud Cuney Hare, *Norris Wright Cuney: A Tribune of the Black People* (G. K. Hall, 1995), 1–6, 167–71; Hales, *Southern Family*, 6.
21. "The Colored Alliance," *Southern Mercury*, October 23, 1888; Richard M. Humphrey, "History of the Colored Farmers' Alliance and Co-Operative Union," in *The Farmers' Alliance History and Agricultural Digest*, ed. Nelson A. Dunning (Washington, DC, 1891); Woodward, *Origins of the New South*, 192, 217. See also White, *Republic for Which It Stands*, 612–15.
22. "The State Press," *Galveston Daily News*, January 24, 1889; Hare, *Norris Wright Cuney*, 64–68, 167–71; May, "Reform, 1874–1900," 89; Wooten, *Comprehensive History of Texas*, vol. 2, 275; Barnes, *Farmers in Rebellion*, 18–20; Judith Ann Benner, *Sul Ross: Soldier, Statesman, Educator* (Texas A&M University Press, 1983), 160–65. It was estimated that there were from seventy-five thousand to one hundred thousand members of the Alliance in Texas in 1886.
23. "Song of the Texas Farmer," *Southern Mercury*, October 29, 1896. Blackshear published some sixteen poems in publications across Texas and the nation.
24. Foster, *Forgotten Texas Census*, 2; Woodward, *Origins of the New South*, 287; Dewey W. Grantham, "Texas Congressional Leaders and the New Freedom, 1913–1917," *Southwestern Historical Quarterly* 53, no. 1 (1949): 35–48; Gould, *Progressives and Prohibitionists*, 7; Arthur Smith, *The Real Colonel House* (George H. Doran, 1918), 46–63.
25. Woodward, *The Strange Career of Jim Crow*, 62; Joe L. Coker, *Liquor in the Land of the Lost Cause: Southern White Evangelicals and the Prohibition Movement* (University of Kentucky Press, 2007), 200–233. By the 1890s the Greenback and Gold Democrat political parties or movements had faded away as the Populists rose to dominate the alternate discourse.

26. John A. Adams Jr., *Sul Ross at Texas A&M* (Texas A&M University Press, 2022), 13–50; "Texas," *Southern Mercury*, October 23, 1888; Benner, *Sul Ross*, 160–76; Bill Minutaglio, *A Single Star and Bloody Knuckles* (University of Texas Press, 2021), 39–40.
27. Curl L. Webb, "Religious and Educational Efforts Among Texas Indians in the 1850's," *Southwestern Historical Quarterly* 69, no. 1 (1965): 32–34; Benner, *Sul Ross*, 13–66; C. Allan Jones, *Texas Roots: Agriculture and Rural Life Before the Civil War* (Texas A&M University Press, 2005), 195–201.
28. May, "Reform, 1874–1900," 90; Barr, *Black Texans*, 96; Williams, *Beyond Redemption*, 164–66; Foster, *Forgotten Texas Census*, xl–xlvii. L. L. Foster was president of the A&M College of Texas from 1898 to 1901 following the death of Sul Ross.
29. "Joint Resolution to Amend Section 20 of Article 16 of the State Constitution," approved March 4, 1887, TSLA; Wooten, *Comprehensive History of Texas*, vol. 2, 268; "Hon. Samuel J. Jenkins," *Austin American Statesman*, March 23, 1902; Benner, *Sul Ross*, 165. Two early graduates of Prairie View who were directors of the Deaf, Dumb, and Blind Asylum were Samuel J. Jenkins and his wife, the former Irene B. Washington of Marlin, Texas.
30. Randolph B. Campbell, *Gone to Texas: A History of the Lone Star State* (Oxford University Press, 2003), 320; Gould, *Progressives and Prohibitionists*, 50–51; Barr, *Reconstruction to Reform*, 85–92; Woodward, *Origins of the New South*, 187. See also "Senator Coke's Speech," *Austin Daily Statesman*, August 16, 1885; "Jeff Davis vs. Prohibition," *Dallas Morning News*, July 27, 1887; Brendan J. Payne, "Defending Black Suffrage: Poll Taxes, Preachers, and Anti-Prohibition in Texas, 1887–1916," *Journal of Southern History* 83, no. 4 (2017): 815–52. During the first votes for the local option, only three of forty county elections adopted Prohibition.
31. *Austin Daily Democratic Statesman*, August 26, 1874; *Journal of the Constitutional Convention Begun and Held in Austin, September 6, 1875* (Galveston, 1875), 15, 35, 228, 339, 395, 404, 802–7; E. L. Blackshear, "Colored Man's Letter," *Austin American Statesman*, October 13, 1885; Foster, *Forgotten Texas Census*, xxxi; "Texas Letter," *Christian Recorder*, October 11, 1888. To curb violence in and around McLennan County, in August 1874 Ross convened representatives from sixty-five counties at the courthouse in Corsicana to form the Sheriff's Association of Texas; while expressing a key objective to protect citizens, their first major action was to condemn "the spirit of mob law."
32. "The State Press," *Galveston Daily News*, September 22, 1886; William R. Childs, *The Texas Railroad Commission* (Texas A&M University Press, 2005), 55–66; Barr, *Reconstruction to Reform*, 94; Kenneth E. Hendrickson, *The Chief Executives of Texas* (Texas A&M University Press, 1995), 111–13; Benner, *Sul Ross*, 163–73; Myrdal, *American Dilemma*, vol. 1, 9–12, 457–58;

Wooten, *Comprehensive History of Texas*, vol. 2, 268; Jerry D. Thompson, *Tejano Tiger: José de los Santos Benavides and the History of the Texas-Mexico Borderlands, 1823–1891* (Texas Christian University Press, 2017), 315–16.

33. Gould, *Alexander Watkins Terrell*, 57; *Journal of the House of Representatives of the Twentieth Legislature, Extra Session* (hereafter House Journal, April 1888), April 6, 1888 (Austin, 1888), 34.
34. *Report of the Board of Regents of the University of Texas* (Austin, 1886), 19.
35. House Journal, April 1888, 18–19, 26–36, 45–46; Lewis B. Cooper, *The Permanent School Fund of Texas* (Texas State Teachers Association, 1934), 26–51, 238–41; Wooten, *Comprehensive History of Texas*, vol. 2, 441.
36. "An Industrial School: Galveston Colored Citizens Pass Resolutions," *Galveston Daily News*, January 21, 1887; "Industrial School for Colored Youths," *Austin American Statesman*, February 2, 1887; "An Industrial College," *Austin American Statesman*, February 3, 1887; "Unveiling a Monument," *Galveston Daily News*, June 3, 1891; "Colored Masons," *Houston Post*, July 23, 1904.
37. "A Gubernatorial Tilt," *Dallas Morning News*, October 14, 1888, 4; "The Prairie View Normal," *Galveston Daily News*, July 24, 1888; "Democrats at Sunset," *Galveston Daily News*, October 14, 1888.
38. E. L. Blackshear, "Equal Rights in Texas," *Evening World*, December 7, 1888.
39. David L. Chapman, "Lynching in Texas" (master's thesis, Texas Tech University, 1973), 94; John A. Adams Jr., *Conflict and Commerce on the Rio Grande: Laredo,1775–1955* (Texas A&M University Press, 2008), 124–25. See also Jerry D. Thompson, *Warm Weather & Bad Whiskey: The 1886 Laredo Election Riot* (Texas Western Press, 1991).
40. C. L. Sonnichsen, *I'll Die Before I'll Run: The Story of the Great Feuds of Texas* (Devin-Adair, 1962), 188. See also "Unchanged: Affairs at Richmond—Woodpeckers Obstinate," *Austin Statesman*, August 20, 1889; "The Richmond Trouble," *Austin Daily Statesman*, August 23, 1889.
41. Sonnichsen, *I'll Die Before I Run*, 233–77; Rice, *Negro in Texas*, 120–22; "Condemning Mob Law," *Gainesville Daily News*, March 8, 1888; "The Lynching in Forsyth," *Dallas Morning News*, March 7, 1888; "Letter of Governor Ross," *Austin Statesman*, January 5, 1890.
42. Hare, *Norris Wright Cuney*, 127; Eby, *The Development of Education in Texas*, 268. Maud noted that he was being flattered with public schools given his name, for example in Whitesboro, Texas (which has since been changed).
43. U.S. Statutes at Large, Second Morrill Act, Pub. 51-841, 26 Stat. 417 (1890); Dethloff, *Centennial History of Texas A&M*, vol. 1, 159–60; Davis, "The Negro Land-Grant College," 312–17; Reid, "People's College for Other Citizens," 144–45; Stallones, "Education and Politics in Texas," 14; Thomas L. Miller, *The Public Lands of Texas, 1519–1970* (University of Oklahoma

Press, 1972), 185–211. See also John R. Wennersten, "The Travail of Black Land-Grant Schools in the South, 1890–1917," *Agricultural History* 65, no. 2 (1991): 54–62; Robert L. Jenkins, "The Black Land-Grant Colleges in Their Formative Years, 1890–1920," *Agricultural History* 65, no. 2 (1991): 63–72; Carolyn B. Brooks and Alan I. Marcus, "The Morill Mandate and a New Moral Mandate," *Agricultural History* 89, no. 2 (2015): 247–62. The state of Texas accepted the covenants of the Second Morrill Act on March 14, 1891.

44. Lawrence S. Ross, "The Education of the Colored Race" (Austin, 1890), CLA; Holmes, *The Evolution of the Negro College*, 151–52. Governor Ross noted, "I have appointed a colored Republican superintendent of the state colored asylum. And my private secretary was a Union soldier. Is there any governor of a northern state who will appoint a colored man to such a responsible position and place an ex-Confederate soldier on his staff?" "Governor Ross," *Fort Worth Daily Gazette*, May 22, 1890.

45. *Governor's Messages, Coke to Ross, 1874–1891*, 670–72; H. P. Gammel, ed., *The Laws of Texas, 1822–1897*, vol. 9 (Austin, 1898), 45–46; *Reports of the Agricultural and Mechanical College of Texas* (Austin, 1891), 3, ELCA; Minutes of the Board of Directors, February 10, 1891, ELCA; Davis, "The Negro Land-Grant College," 317; Wennersten, "Travail of Black Land-Grant Schools," 54–62. By 1930, the percent of funding from the Act of 1890 ranged from 6.2 percent in Missouri to a high of 53.4 percent in Mississippi.

46. Stanley P. Hirshson, *Farewell to the Bloody Shirt: Northern Republicans and the Southern Negro* (Quadrangle Books, 1962), 192–200; Leslie H. Fishel and Benjamin Quarles, *The Negro American: A Documentary History* (Scott, Foresman, 1967), 316–19.

47. E. L. Blackshear, "The Negro Problem: The Race Can Be Educated and Is Rapidly Improving," *Fort Worth Star Gazette*, December 20, 1888. See also Carrie B. White, "The Development of Higher Education for the Negro in the South from 1890–1914, with Special Reference to the Land-Grant Colleges" (master's thesis, Prairie View Agricultural and Mechanical College, 1947); Fishel and Quarles, *Negro American*, 364–69.

48. "Grimes County Colored Fair," *Dallas Morning News*, October 17, 1891; "The Colored University," *Dallas Morning News*, January 30, 1892; W. T. Harris, "The Education of the Negro," *Atlantic Monthly*, June 1892, 722–24; Oswald Villard, "Higher Education of Negroes," *Nation*, May 1902, 381; U.S. Department of the Interior, Bureau of Education, *Report of the Commissioner of Education for the Year Ending June 30, 1907* (Government Printing Office, 1908), 3–4, 31–32; Schor, *Agriculture in the Black Land-Grant System*; Raymond Wolters, *Du Bois and His Rivals* (University of Missouri Press, 2002), 40–54; Hornsby, "'Colored Branch University' Issue," 51–96; Michael R. Heintze, *Private Black Colleges in Texas, 1865–1954* (Texas A&M University Press, 1985), 51–58, 84–86, 180.

49. Wooten, *Comprehensive History of Texas*, vol. 2, 279–84, 767–72; Hare, *Norris Wright Cuney*, 159; Heintze, *Private Black Colleges*, 53–58. Art. 16, sec. 11, of the Texas Constitution of 1876 set a maximum rate of 12 percent per annum.
50. Wooten, *Comprehensive History of Texas*, vol. 2, 268–75; "Called to the College," *Galveston Daily News*, July 6, 1890; "In a New Field of Service," *Galveston Daily News*, July 12, 1890; Benner, *Sul Ross*, 184–97, 233–36. See also Adams, *Sul Ross at Texas A&M*.
51. E. L. Blackshear, "Gives His Views of the Negro's Condition in Texas and the South," *Austin Statesman*, April 30, 1890; J. M. Carlisle, *Eighth Biennial Report of the State Superintendent of Public Instruction* (Austin, 1893), 22, TSLA.
52. U.S. Statutes at Large, Second Morrill Act, Pub. 51-841, 26 Stat. 417 (1890).
53. The primary African American papers varied in the time span they were published, with many lasting only a few years and other quickly replacing those that ended publication. Some were daily and others weekly editions. The primary black papers in the late 1880s included the *Blade* (Austin), the *Citizen* (Austin), *Southern Guide* (Austin), the *Echo* (Dallas), the *Echo* (Navasota), and the *Monitor* (Wharton). In 1890 a new generation of papers were found in the following cities: Austin (the *Colored Alliance* and the *Metropolitan Sun*), Denison (*Texas Reformer*), Dallas (the *Tribune* and the *Alliance Record*), Beaumont (the *Record*), Fort Worth (the *Torchlight Appeal*), Waco (the *Baptist*), San Antonio (*Tonquelet*), and Galveston (the *Freeman's Journal*). See also Charles W. Grose, "Black Newspapers in Texas, 1888–1970" (PhD diss., University of Texas, 1972).
54. "The Second Day [of the CTSA Conference]," *Galveston Daily News*, June 27, 1891.
55. "To Call on Gov. Hogg," *Galveston Daily News*, December 17, 1891; "Want a Colored Branch," *Galveston Daily News*, December 30, 1891; "The Colored University," *Galveston Daily News*, January 2, 1892; "To Wait on Governor Hogg," *Austin Weekly Statesman*, December 31, 1891; "Prairie Lea," *Galveston Daily News*, October 10, 1892; Woodward, *Origins of the New South*, 238–39. Any question of Blackshear's political involvement was confirmed in early 1893, when he was "unanimously endorsed by members of the legislature for commissioner of deeds for the District of Columbia." While deemed a great honor, no action was taken. "Colored Supporter of Cleveland," *Galveston Daily News*, March 31, 1893, and *Christian Recorder*, April 13, 1893, noted that he was "a popular and promising representative of the 'Lone Star.'"
56. "The Colored University," *Galveston Daily News*, January 2, 1892.

57. "Austin, Tex. Special," *Freedman* (Indianapolis), May 13, 1892; "For a Colored University," *Galveston Daily News*, February 12, 1893; E. L. Blackshear, "Dear Editor," *Southwestern Christian Advocate* (New Orleans), February 9, 1893.
58. "Petition," *Christian Recorder*, February 16, 1883. A sample of the more than one hundred petitions submitted: Kaufman County, February 13, 1893; Victoria County, February 1893; Lamar County, February 9, 1893; Colored Citizens of the City of Houston and Harris County, January 30, 1893; Bastrop County, February 20, 1893; San Marcos and Hays County, February 4, 1893; Lavaca County, January 20, 1893; Nueces County, January 30, 1893. Texas, memorials and petitions, 1834–1929, TSLA.
59. "Modern Political Methods," *Southern Mercury*, June 25, 1896.
60. "The Alcalde's Speech," *Galveston Daily News*, February 19, 1913; Texas Legislature, House of Representatives, *House Journal*, 23rd Leg., reg. sess. (1893), 526–31; Cantrell, *Feeding the Wolf*, 66; "The Education Committee," *Austin American Statesman*, February 12, 1893; Wooten, *Comprehensive History of Texas*, vol. 2, 288–94. See also Roscoe Martin, *The People's Party in Texas: A Study in Third Party Politics*, University of Texas bulletin no. 3308 (1933), 26–40; Rice, *Negro in Texas*, 78–82; Robert C. Cotner, *James Stephen Hogg: A Biography* (University of Texas Press, 1959), 255–58.
61. "Colored Supporter of Cleveland"; "A Candidate for Recorder of Deeds," *Freeman* (Philadelphia), April 29, 1893; quote from the *Illuminator* in "Endorses Sayers," *Brenham Daily Banner*, October 4, 1894. At this time Blackshear was the superintendent of all black public schools in Austin, with one thousand pupils and twenty-one teachers.
62. E. L. Blackshear, "Semi-Centennial: Texas Should Celebrate and Austin Is the Place," *Austin Weekly Statesman*, February 14, 1895.
63. E. L. Blackshear, "Salutatory," *Texas School Journal*, November 1895, 466; George Clark, *A Glance Backward* (Rein and Sons, 1914), 91.
64. E. L. Blackshear, "An Address: To the People of Texas by the Colored State Teachers," *Galveston Daily News*, June 29, 1894; *Dallas Morning News*, June 30, 1894.
65. Blackshear to House, March 27, 1897, March 29, 1898, May 25, 1898, December 15 and 18, 1898, and November 21, 1903, House Papers, Yale University Archives, New Haven, CT. See also Rupert N. Richardson, *Colonel Edward M. House: The Texas Years, 1858–1912* (Abilene Printing & Stationary, 1964), 219–22.
66. E. L. Blackshear to House, March 27, 1897, March 29, 1898, May 25, 1898, December 15 and 18, 1898, and November 21, 1903; Smith, *The Real Colonel House*, 25–26, 41–44, 55–63; Rupert N. Richardson, "Edward M. House and the Governors," *Southwestern Historical Quarterly* 61, no. 1 (1957): 51–65; Woodward, *Origins of the New South*, 289; Ernest W. Winkler, ed.,

Platforms of Political Parties in Texas (University of Texas Press, 1916), 388; Brewer, *Negro Legislators of Texas*, 108; Minutaglio, *A Single Star and Bloody Knuckles*, 67–68.

67. *Texas School Journal*, May 1896, 191, and February 1897, 336.
68. E. L. Blackshear, "Colored University," *Galveston Daily News*, March 28, 1895. See also Miller, *Public Lands of Texas*, 185–200.
69. N. Q. Henderson to A. J. Rose, March 31, 1896, in "Negro Education," *Austin American Statesman*, April 12, 1896; "Prairie View Normal," *Galveston Daily News*, June 15, 1896; "From a Colored Teacher," *Houston Daily Post*, October 23, 1896. See also Merline Pitre, "The Evolution of a Black University in Texas," *Western Journal of Black Studies* 3, no. 3 (1979): 216–23.
70. "Not Done Yet!," *Southern Mercury*, June 3, 1897; "The African Plank of the Platform," *Galveston Daily News*, May 17, 1897.
71. "Editorial," *Texas School Journal* (1896), 191, 266, 398, TSLA; John J. Lane, *History of Education in Texas*, U. S. Bureau of Education (Government Printing Office, 1903), 55–56; Woodward, *Origins of the New South*, 117–18; Reuben McKitrick, *The Public Land System in Texas, 1823–1910*, University of Wisconsin bulletin no. 905, vol. 9 (1918), 70; Woolfolk, *Prairie View*, 82–84; Charles Seymour, *The Intimate Papers of Colonel House* (Houghton Mifflin, 1926), vol. 1, 28–38. See also Adams, "Promise Unfulfilled."
72. Quoted in *Abilene Reporter*, April 5, 1895.
73. Pitre, *Through Many Dangers, Toils, and Snares*, 182; E. L. Blackshear, "A Circular Letter," *Dallas Morning News*, October 28, 1896.
74. E. L. Blackshear, "Industrial Education," *Texas School Journal*, October 1899, 682–83; Hales, *Southern Family*, 61; "The Passing of Wright Cuney," *El Paso Daily Herald*, March 5, 1898; Hare, *Norris Wright Cuney*, 214–15. In 1945, Prairie View was renamed a "university" until such time as a permanent "colored university" was "legally established." In advance of a lawsuit filed by Herman M. Sweatt for admission to the University of Texas, Texas Southern at Houston was established as a university. See also Hornsby, "'Colored Branch University' Issue," 51–60.

Chapter 3

1. Minutaglio, *A Single Star and Bloody Knuckles*, 54–79.
2. E. D. Ball, "The Land-Grant Colleges in Relation to National Development," in *Land-Grant College Education, 1910–1920*, U.S. Department of the Interior, Bureau of Education bulletin no. 30 (Government Printing Office, 1925), 19; Gilbert C. Fite, *Cotton Fields No More: Southern Agriculture, 1865–1980* (University Press of Kentucky, 1984), 4–7, 12. See also Bizzell, *Green Rising*, 173–75; Roger Ransom and Richard Sutch, "The 'Lock-in' Mechanism and Overproduction of Cotton in the Postbellum South," *Agricultural History* 49, no. 2 (1975): 405–25.

3. Oran M. Roberts, "The Political, Legislative, and Judicial History of Texas," in Wooten, *Comprehensive History of Texas*, vol. 2, 220, 308–14; Eby, *The Development of Education in Texas*, 224–25; Woodward, *Origins of the New South*, 269; J. Evetts Haley, *Charles Goodnight: Cowman & Plainsman* (University of Oklahoma Press, 1949), 381–401; Myrdal, *American Dilemma*, vol. 1, 32, 441. See also Lewis Nordyke, *Cattle Empire* (William Morrow, 1949).
4. *Texas Stock and Farm Journal*, January 11, 1895; John S. Spratt, *The Road to Spindletop: Economic Change in Texas, 1875–1901* (Southern Methodist University Press, 1955), 72; John D. Hicks, *The Populist Revolt: A History of the Farmers' Alliance and the People's Party* (University of Minnesota Press, 1931), 45; Wooten, *Comprehensive History of Texas*, vol. 2, 764–65; Louis J. Wortham, *A History of Texas*, vol. 5 (Wortham-Molyneaux, 1924), 127–34; Roger Ransom and Richard Sutch, "Debt Peonage in the Cotton South After the Civil War," *Journal of Economic History* 32, no. 3 (1972): 641–69.
5. Reagan v. Farmers' Loan & Trust Co., 154 U.S. 362 (1894); "Gold Democrats Electoral Ticket," *Houston Daily Post*, October 23, 1896; "Texas Delegations," *Galveston Daily News*, June 13, 1896; E. L. Blackshear, "The Negro of the South," *Fort Worth Morning Register*, July 22, 1900; Woolfolk, *Prairie View*, 60, 117; Woodward, *Origins of the New South*, 146–47, 264–73; Myrdal, *American Dilemma*, vol. 1, 230–32, 292; Martin, "The Grange as a Political Factor in Texas," 381–82; Fite, *Cotton Fields No More*, 47; Edward L. Ayers, *The Promise of the New South: Life After Reconstruction* (Oxford University Press, 1992), 87. Henry Grady visited Texas in October 1888 and met with then-governor Ross. *Austin Weekly Statesman*, November 1, 1888; *Atlanta Constitution*, October 30, 1888; Louis R. Harlan, *Booker T. Washington* (Oxford University Press, 1972), 165.
6. "A 'Peter Jackson' Club," *Freedman* (Indianapolis), October 8, 1892; "The Colored Y. M. C. A.," *Austin American Statesman*, March 22, 1896; Hendrickson, *The Chief Executives of Texas*, 125–30; Ayers, *Promise of the New South*, 143–46, 326–27; Cotner, *James Stephen Hogg*; Robert L. Peterson, "State Regulation of Railroads in Texas, 1836–1920" (PhD diss., University of Texas, 1960), 314–16. For example, nine Southern states enacted railroad segregation laws between 1887–91. Segregation was further entrenched into law with the US Supreme Court ruling on "separate but equal" in *Plessy v. Ferguson* in 1896, followed by *Williams v. Mississippi* in 1898, in which the court refused to condemn recent disenfranchisement maneuvers written into new Southern state constitutions.
7. "Board of Directors Meeting," *Bryan Eagle*, June 13, 1896; *Galveston Daily News*, July 11, 1896; Woolfolk, *Prairie View*, 1–19, 122–23. Investment and improvements in the Port of Galveston and adjacent channels from 1870 to 1900 exceeded $8 million, more than the total invested (about $7.1 million)

in all other Texas coast facilities, bays, and rivers combined. See Smith, *U.S. Army*, 147.

8. Barr, *From Reconstruction to Reform*, 176.
9. Winkler, *Platforms of Political Parties in Texas*, 427; Blackshear and Maxwell, "The Branch University," *Texas School Journal*, October 1896, 398; "S. W. Texas Association," *Texas School Journal*, December 1896, 477–78; Woolfolk, *Prairie View*, 121–24; Hornsby, "'Colored Branch University' Issue," 54–56. See also Horace A. Young, "A History and Appraisal of the Colored Teachers' State Association of Texas" (master's thesis, University of New Mexico, 1949); Hales, *Southern Family*, 61–93.
10. Plessy v. Ferguson, 163 U.S. 537 (1896); A. Robinson Henry, "Perpetuating Inequality: *Plessy v. Ferguson* and the Dilemma of Black Access to Public and Higher Education," *Journal of Law and Education* 27, no. 1 (1998): 1–5; Thomas J. Davis, *Plessy v. Ferguson* (Greenwood, 2012); Michael J. Klarman, *From Jim Crow to Civil Rights: The Supreme Court and the Struggle for Racial Equality* (Oxford University Press, 2004); Harlan, *Booker T. Washington*, 230. See also "Plessy v. Ferguson (1896)," National Archives, last updated February 8, 2022, http://www.ourdocuments.gov/doc.php?doc=52; Steve Luxenbury, *Separate: The Story of Plessy v. Ferguson* (W. W. Norton, 2019); Kermit Roosevelt, *The Nation That Never Was: Reconstructing America's Story* (University of Chicago Press, 2022). In a strange turn of events, three years after the *Plessy* decision, Justice Louis Harlan instead held that *Plessy* protected the right of states to set their own "fairness" doctrine: *Cumming v. Richmond Board of Education* upheld a local school board's decision to close a black high school while continuing to operate two white schools.
11. Arntie Edward Hollins, "The Colored Teachers State Association of Texas as Revealed in the Texas Press" (master's thesis, Prairie View A&M College, 1948), 28–32. See also Casdorph, "Norris Wright Cuney," 455–64.
12. "Board of Director's Meeting," *Bryan Eagle*, June 13, 1896; "Teachers Elected," *Galveston Daily News*, July 2, 1896, and July 11, 1896; "State Capital," *Dallas Morning News*, July 6, 1896; E. L. Blackshear to J. W. Smith, president of the Austin School Board, July 6, 1896, Blackshear File, AHC. Blackshear had the strong support of both Sul Ross and W. R. Cavitt. See "Committee on Education," *Austin American Statesman*, February 12, 1893.
13. Woolfolk, *Prairie View*, 123, 154.
14. L. S. Ross to John D. McCall, comptroller, September 22, 1892, *Report of the Texas Comptroller of Public Accounts* (1893), 130, TSLA; meetings with the building committee and contractors at Prairie View noted in *Bryan Daily Eagle*, February 27, 1896, June 13, 1896, August 2, 1896, August 21, 1896, November 26, 1896, and December 23, 1896; "Bids Needed," *Austin Daily Statesman*, June 2, 1893; "To Colored Voters," *Houston Post*, November 1, 1896.

15. "This Is Negro Day," *Atlanta Constitution*, December 26, 1895; "Educational Event: The Coming Lecture of Booker T. Washington," *Houston Daily Post*, May 23, 1897; Booker T. Washington to E. L. Blackshear, June 7, 1897, and Blackshear to Washington, June 10, 1897, in "The Negro Debt," *Houston Daily Post*, June 10, 1897; David W. Blight, *Frederick Douglass: Prophet of Freedom* (Simon & Schuster, 2018), 757–59.
16. "Educational Event," *Houston Daily Post*, May 23, 1897; "Mr. Booker T. Washington," *Galveston Daily News*, June 6, 1897; Washington, *Up from Slavery*, 220. See also Ayers, *Promise of the New South*, 322–27; "Colored Delegates," *Houston Daily Post*, December 8, 1895.
17. "Lecture at Prairie View," *Houston Daily Post*, December 7, 1897; Douglas C. Brennan, "The Address in Atlanta," in "Booker T. Washington and the Myth of Accommodation" (master's thesis, University of North Texas, 1994), 36–47; Woolfolk, *Prairie View*, 126–27; Woodward, *Origins of the New South*, 350–67; "State Schools of Methods," *Dallas Morning News*, June 27, 1897.
18. "The University," *Austin Weekly Statesman*, March 26, 1885; "State Teachers' Association," *Freedman* (Indianapolis), July 25, 1896; "Prairie View Normal: The University Plan Recommended," *Houston Daily Post*, January 5, 1897; "Prairie View School," *Houston Daily Post*, September 4, 1898; E. L. Blackshear, "A Circular Letter," *Houston Daily Post*, October 27, 1896; E. L. Blackshear, "A Circular Letter," *Dallas Morning News*, October 28, 1896; *Texas School Journal*, October 1896, 398; David A. Williams, "The History of Higher Education for Black Texans, 1872–1977" (PhD diss., Baylor University, 1978), 21–31.
19. "D. A. Paulus, Esq.," *Hallettsville Herald*, July 9, 1896.
20. L. S. Ross to Cavitt, May 18, 1896, Ross Papers, ELCA; "Henderson to Rose," *Dallas Morning News*, April 12, 1896; Dethloff, *Centennial History of Texas A&M*, vol. 1, 318.
21. "State Schools of Methods," *Dallas Morning News*, June 27, 1897. See also E. L. Blackshear, "Lines of Negro Education," *AME Church Review*, January 1897, 309–11.
22. Minutes of the Board of Directors, January 17, 1898, vol. 1, 199–201, ELCA; Dethloff, *Centennial History of Texas A&M*, vol. 1, 175–78; *Bryan Eagle*, January 4, 1898; Edward L. Blackshear, "Sul Ross," *Houston Daily Post*, January 9, 1898.
23. Report of the principal, Edward L. Blackshear, *Report of the Prairie View State Normal School*, January 3, 1899 (Austin, 1899), ELCA; Ida Belle Luckie, "President Winston at Prairie View," *Southwestern Christian Advocate* (New Orleans), March 24, 1898.
24. "Lecture at Prairie View," *Houston Daily Post*, October 23, 1898; "Address to Graduates," *Houston Daily Post*, June 7, 1899; H. M. Tarver, "The Colored

University," *Texas School Journal*, February 1899, 490, TSLA; Young, "History and Appraisal," 22–24.

25. W. E. B. Du Bois, "The Two Sorts of Schooling," *Texas School Journal*, May 1900, 150–51, TSLA. Verse from "Barclay of Ury Poem," by John Greenleaf Whittier, 1890.
26. Blackshear, "What Is the Negro Teacher Doing," 334–37; "The Work of R. L. Smith: It Is a Labor of Love for the Up-Building of the Negroes of Texas," *Houston Daily Post*, October 14, 1901; "Prairie View Normal," *Houston Daily Post*, June 4, 1899. See also Richings, *Evidences of Progress*.
27. "Endorses Sayers," *Brenham Daily Banner*, October 4, 1894; J. N. Johnson, "Negroes in the Flood District," *Washington Post*, July 20, 1899; "Aid for Flood Suffers," *Washington Times*, July 23, 1899; "Distress in Texas," *Colored American* (Washington, DC), August 5, 1899. See also John A. Adams Jr. and Bill Page, "John Nathaniel Johnson: The Great Political Agitator Educator, Journalist, Attorney, and Doctor," *East Texas Historical Journal* 61, no. 1 (2023): 7–47.
28. Adams and Page, "John Nathaniel Johnson," 7–41.
29. E. L. Blackshear, "A Remarkable Speech," *Williamson County Sun*, June 14, 1900; Hendrickson, *The Chief Executives of Texas*, 137–40; Rice, *Negro in Texas*, 259. The statue of Lincoln was added to the Capitol rotunda in 1871, followed by Lee in 1909, Davis in 1931, and Douglass in 2013.
30. Minutes of the Board of Directors, April 17, 1901, ELCA; Richardson, *Colonel Edward M. House*, 220–21.
31. "Prairie View Normal," *Houston Daily Post*, March 27, 1900 and September 1, 1900; "New from Prairie View," *Austin American Statesman*, May 25, 1900; "Prairie View Normal," *San Antonio Express*, December 31, 1898; "Henry Rollins, '97," *Battalion*, January 1, 1900; "Prairie View Normal: Contract for Dormitory," *Houston Post*, November 11, 1899, and August 11, 1901; "Expenses," *Annual Catalogue* (1900–1901), 43, CLA. See also Blackshear, "Industrial Education," 682–83. In early November 1899, Blackshear took extreme caution to quarantine the campus from a major smallpox outbreak; the epidemic passed without major hardship to students or staff.
32. "Prairie View State Normal," *Austin Daily Statesman*, November 18, 1900; "Prairie View School," *Austin Daily Statesman*, November 23, 1900; "Professor E. H. Holmes," *Texas School Journal*, March 1900, 76; "Estimated," *Brenham Daily Banner*, December 2, 1900; Du Bois, "The Two Sorts of Schooling," 150–55; Bruce A. Glasrud, "Jim Crow's Emergence in Texas," *American Studies* 15, no. 1 (1974): 47–60; Clarence L. Mohr, "Minds of the New South: Higher Education in Black and White, 1880–1915," *Southern Quarterly* 46, no. 4 (2009): 13, 15, 26–27. For a contemporary view of the South and education, see N. S. Shaler, "The Future of the Negro in

the Southern States," *Popular Science Monthly*, June 1900. Equivalent purchasing power of $3,500 in 1900 would be about $133,200 in 2025.

33. "Mr. Foster's Work Appreciated," *Houston Daily Post*, January 6, 1901; N. Q. Henderson, "Negro Industrial Training," *Houston Daily Post*, February 11, 1901; Woolfolk, *Prairie View*, 128. A sample of citizen petitions include those submitted by Robertson County, March 2, 1901; Lampasas County, February 20, 1901; Caldwell Country, March 2, 1901; Brazoria County, February 22, 1901; DeWitt County, February 22, 1901; and Falls County, February 23, 1901. The legislature approved the classical studies request with the first year of the biennium at $2,500 and the second year at $1,800, out of the general revenue.
34. H. T. Kealing, "The Prairie View School," *Houston Post*, February 19, 1901.
35. E. L. Blackshear, "The Negro Question," *Houston Post*, January 7, 1901; E. L. Blackshear to George Cortelyou, White House, March 7, 1901, and April 9, 1901, McKinley Presidential Papers, series 3, reel 76, ELCA; "Prof. Blackshear," *Houston Post*, January 16, 1901; "The Negro Question," *Houston Post*, January 7, 1901; "President Stops at Houston," *Post Signal* (Pilot Point, TX), April 5, 1901; "To Visit Normal," *Galveston Tribune*, April 6, 1901; Catalogue of Officers and Students (1903), 6, Howard University Archives, Washington, DC; Harlan, *Booker T. Washington*, 286. Blackshear also received information from Emmett J. Scott, a former reporter in Houston and graduate of Wiley College, who became Washington's private secretary in 1897 and who helped arrange President McKinley's visit to Tuskegee in the fall of 1898. Blackshear first mentioned the possible visit in the *Houston Post* in early January 1901. Burleson served seven terms in Congress (1899–1913), and in March 1913 he was appointed postmaster general in the Woodrow Wilson cabinet (1913–21), due largely to his close friendship with Colonel House.
36. "President's Visit," *Houston Daily Post*, April 30, 1901; "The President's Train," *Houston Daily Post*, May 3, 1901; "Presidential Excursion: Round trip—$2.00," *Galveston Daily News*, May 2, 1901; Edward O. Frantz, *The Door of Hope* (University of Florida Press, 2011), 129.
37. Speech of Governor Sayers, May 3, 1901, McKinley Presidential Papers, series 4, reel 84, ELCA; "The President at Prairie View," *Houston Daily Post*, May 4, 1901; "Prairie View College," *Houston Daily Post*, April 13, 1901; "The President's Remarks," *Galveston Daily News*, May 4, 1901; "Will Escort McKinley," *Galveston Tribune*, May 1, 1901; Oscar K. Davis, *The Life of William McKinley* (Princeton University Press, 2009), 90. A formal railway depot resolution by the Texas Senate was passed in September 1901 to request the Houston and Texas Central to build a site where "the public road [HW 290] crosses the railroad at a point in front of the college." See "Afternoon Session," *Houston Daily Post*, September 26, 1901. Presidents

Warren Harding and Franklin Roosevelt were also members of the Knights of Pythias, as well as Blackshear himself.

38. Roger D. Cunningham, "'A Lot of Fine, Sturdy Black Warriors': Texas's African American 'Immunes' in the Spanish American War," *Southwestern Historical Quarterly* 108, no. 3 (2005): 345–67. See also Charles J. Crane, *The Experiences of a Colonel of Infantry* (Knickerbocker Press, 1923). Prairie View former student Charlie Taylor served in the US Army in the Philippines, 1899–1900. "Colored State Normal," *Houston Daily Post*, June 1, 1902; Elmer A. Carter, "Prairie View Teacher Praises Negro Regiment," *Houston Daily Post*, February 23, 1919.
39. "McKinley's Last Speech to the Negroes of America at the Prairie View State College," *Freeman* (Philadelphia), November 30, 1901. See also Willard B. Gatewood, *Black Americans and the White Man's Burden, 1898–1903* (University of Illinois Press, 1975).
40. Woodward, *The Strange Career of Jim Crow*, 72–75, 87.
41. Edward O. Frantz, "Goin' South: Republican Presidential Tours of the South, 1877–1933" (PhD diss., University of Wisconsin–Madison, 2002), 232–38; Cunningham, "A Lot of Fine, Sturdy Black Warriors," 362, 366–67. Col. C. J. Crane was commandant of cadets at Texas A&M from 1917–18.
42. Ousley, *History of the Agricultural and Mechanical College*, 59–65; "Petition: To Honorable R. H. Welles, Red River County," March 1901, TSLA. The petition to Representative Wells urged the approval of $12,500 for industrial programs; $2,500 for "female industries"; and $2,500 to "inaugurate" a college course of classical and scientific studies.
43. "About Co-Education: Strong Endorsement from the Secretary of Agriculture," *Houston Daily Post*, February 22, 1901.
44. "Sorrow at Prairie View," *Dallas Morning News*, December 7, 1901; Minutes of the Board of Directors, December 10, 1901, vol. 1, 251–53, and April 7, 1902, vol. 1, 260, ELCA; David F. Houston, *Eight Years with Wilson's Cabinet, 1913–1920*, vol. 1 (Doubleday, 1926), 1–14; Richardson, *Colonel Edward M. House*, 221; Walter P. Webb and H. Bailey Carroll, eds., *The Handbook of Texas*, vol. 1 (Texas State Historical Association, 1952), 844–45. In 1938 President Foster's grave was moved to a cemetery on the south side of campus. Houston departed Texas A&M to be president of the University of Texas in 1905, and then resigned to accept the presidency of Washington University, St. Louis, in 1908. Mezes replaced him as president of the University of Texas in 1908.
45. Dethloff, *Centennial History of Texas A&M*, vol. 1, 188–92; Reid, *Reaping a Greater Harvest*, 31; Ousley, *History of the Agricultural and Mechanical College*, 63–65, 89.
46. "Bids and Proposals," *Houston Post*, July 24, 1901; Rice, *Negro in Texas*, 110, 228; W. E. Curtis, "Hope of the Negro," *Evening Star* (Washington, DC),

May 14, 1905; Reid, *Reaping a Greater Harvest*, 10, 17; Houston, *Eight Years with Wilson's Cabinet*, vol. 1, 203–4; Andrea R. Roberts, "The Farmers' Improvement Society and the Women's Barnyard Auxiliary of Texas: African American Community Building in the Progressive Era," *Journal of Planning History*16, no. 3 (2017): 222–45.

47. E. L. Blackshear, "The Burden of the South," *Galveston Daily News*, August 4, 1904; "Prairie View Special," *Galveston Daily News*, May 29, 1905; Holmes, *The Evolution of the Negro College*, 112–14; Dethloff, *Centennial History of Texas A&M*, vol. 1, 191; *Bryan Eagle*, November 25, 1904; Thomas J. Jones, *Negro Education: A Study of the Private and Higher Schools for Colored People in the United States*, U.S. Department of Interior, Bureau of Education bulletin no. 39, 2 vols. (Government Printing Office, 1918), 567–606. See also Davis, "The Negro Land-Grant College," 312–28; William H. Baldwin, "Negro Education in the South," *National Municipal Review*, January 1918, 53–57.
48. Woolfolk, *Prairie View*, 142; "Industrial School: For Negro Girls Is Now Asked of the Legislature," *Houston Post*, March 4, 1905.
49. "Will Lecture in Colored Churches," *Houston Daily Post*, July 29, 1900; "Education in Texas: The Prairie View State Normal, the Pride of the State," *Colored American* (Washington, DC), April 23, 1904; "Old Landmark Association," *Galveston Daily News*, July 9, 1904; "Negro Baptists," *Waxahachie (TX) Daily Light*, September 4, 1904; "Colored Farmers' Congress," *Dallas Morning News*, June 24, 1906; *Houston Daily Post*, November 7, 21, and 30, 1909, December 9, 1910, and November 11, 1914. See also Howard Beeth and Cary D. Wintz, eds., *Black Dixie: Afro-Texan History and Culture in Houston* (Texas A&M University Press, 1992).
50. "Doing Great Work," *Houston Daily Post*, January 18, 1904.
51. "An Organization for Oratorical Contests," *Austin American Statesman*, March 20, 1904; "Education in Texas," *Colored American* (Washington, DC), April 23, 1904; Heintze, *Private Black Colleges*, 20–31, 44–46; Eby, *The Development of Education in Texas*, 267–68.
52. "Colored Schools," *Houston Daily Post*, May 12, 1898; "Professional Summer School for Negroes," *Austin Statesman*, April 18, 1904.
53. "The Southern Education Board and the Negro," *Houston Post*, July 15, 1902.
54. "Education in Texas: The Prairie View State Normal the Pride of the State," *Colored American* (Washington, DC), April 23, 1904; "Blackshear Will Not Resign," *Houston Post*, June 30, 1904; E. L. Blackshear, "Boll Weevil," *Galveston Daily News*, February 21, 1905. See also F. A. Gulley, *First Lessons in Agriculture* (New York, 1892).
55. "Hope of the Negro," *Evening Star* (Washington, DC), May 15, 1905; Bullock, *History of Negro Education*, 82–88, 165, 174, 191–93. A contrary view was expressed by Donald Spivey in *Schooling for the New Slavery: Black*

Industrial Education, 1868–1915 (Greenwood Press, 1978). Spivey argued that such industrial education kept black Americans in a subservient position and as nothing more than a pool of cheap, uneducated labor.

56. Interview with W. M. McDonald, April 16, 1945, in Douglass G. Perry, "Black Populism: The Negro in the People's Party of Texas" (master's thesis, Prairie View University, 1945), 34, 41; Bizzell, *Green Rising*, 170–81; Dale Baum, *Counterfeit Justice* (Louisiana State University Press, 2009), 9–10. See also *AME Church Review*, April 1895, 525–26; Gould, *Alexander Watkins Terrell*, 154–55.
57. Cantrell, *Feeding the Wolf*, 36–38, 92; *Daily Examiner* (Navasota, TX), April 4, 1900, quoted in Lawrence C. Goodwyn, "Populist Dreams and Negro Rights: East Texas as a Case Study," *American Historical Review* 76, no. 5 (1971): 1439; Walter L. Buenger, *The Path to a Modern South: Northwest Texas Between Reconstruction and the Great Depression* (University of Texas Press, 2001), 85–88; Jack Abramowitz, "John B. Rayner—A Grass Roots Leader," *Journal of Negro History* 36, no. 2 (1951): 160–93. See also Matthew Hild, "The Knights of Labor and the Third-Party Movement in Texas, 1886–1896," *Southwestern Historical Quarterly* 119, no. 1 (2015): 25–43; Worth R. Miller and Stacy G. Ulbig, "Building a Populist Coalition in Texas, 1892–1896," *Journal of Southern History* 74, no. 2 (2008): 255–96.
58. Fred A. Shannon, *The Farmer's Last Frontier* (M. E. Sharpe, 1973), 276–77, 326–28; Barr, *Black Texans*, 78–80; Smith, *The Real Colonel House*, 54–56; Myrdal, *American Dilemma*, vol. 1, 452–55. See also Woodward, *The Burden of Southern History*, 104–20, 255, 277, 325, 461; Perry, "Black Populism," 48–49; "Colored Delegates' Resolutions Adopted at State Convention," August 7, 1896, CLA.
59. J. B. Rayner, "A Negro on the Negro," *Houston Daily Post*, December 14, 1902.
60. "Blackshear's Address," and "Was Highly Pleasing to Convention in Richmond," *Houston Post*, August 13, 1905; "Negro Farmers Adjourn," *Austin American Statesman*, August 1, 1911; U.S. Department of Commerce, Bureau of the Census, *Negro Population in the United States, 1790–1915* (Government Printing Office, 1918); Reid, *Reaping a Greater Harvest*, xxii. Italian immigration into Texas began in the mid-1880s. In many counties they were not considered white and were categorized as minorities and thus blocked from voting in the white primaries.
61. Frederick L. Hoffman, *Race Traits and Tendencies of the American Negro* (New York, 1896), 261; "Colored Farmers' Congress," *Dallas Morning News*, June 24, 1906; "Negro Farmers' Congress Meets at Prairie View," *Houston Post-Dispatch*, August 6, 1924; "2000 Colored Farmers Attend Short Course: Twentieth Annual Negro Farmers' Congress," *Tyler Journal*, August 19, 1927. See also *Prairie View Standard*, August 5, 1916, CLA.

62. Moore, *Booker T. Washington, W. E. B. Du Bois*, 61–113; Pero G. Dagbovie, "Exploring a Century of Historical Scholarship on Booker T. Washington," *Journal of African American History* 92, no. 2 (2007): 239–64; Frederick Dunn, "The Educational Philosophies of Washington, Du Bois, and Houston: Laying the Foundations for Afrocentrism and Multiculturalism," *Journal of Negro Education* 62, no. 1 (1993): 24–34; Mohr, "Minds of the New South," 8–34; Meier, *Negro Thought in America*. This in no way is a complete list, only a sample; see also Monroe N. Work, *A Bibliography of the Negro in Africa and America* (H. W. Wilson, 1928), which has over one hundred entries of items authored by Washington and Du Bois.
63. "A Notable Address to Negroes," *Houston Daily Post*, September 21, 1902. See also Whitney Battle-Baptiste and Britt Rusert, eds., *W. E. B. Du Bois's Data Portraits: Visualizing Black America; The Color Line at the Turn of the Twentieth Century* (Princeton Architectural Press, 2018).
64. W. E. B. Du Bois, *The Souls of Black Folk* (Atlanta, 1903; repr., Millennium Publications, 2014), 28, 48; Myrdal, *American Dilemma*, vol. 2, 889–907; Harlan, *Booker T. Washington*, 265–69; H. W. Brands, *American Colossus* (Doubleday, 2010), 548. Dr. George Woolfolk provided an interesting assessment of Washington: "There will probably never be a satisfactory end to the argument of whether Booker T. Washington was the most unprincipled opportunist his race has ever known or a real statesman who had taken the measure of the whirlwind and sought to bring peace to the troubled water." *Prairie View*, 120. See also James A. Levy, "Narratives of Progress: Black Elites, the 'Folks,' and the Politics of Knowledge, 1890–1915" (PhD diss., Rutgers University, 2006), 101–14.
65. E. L. Blackshear, "Economy in Teaching School," *School Journal*, December 27, 1902, 682; W. E. B. Du Bois, "Of the Training of Black Men," *Atlantic*, September 1902, 17–23; August Meier, "Booker T. Washington and the Negro Press: With Special Reference to the Colored America Magazine," *Journal of Negro History* 38, no. 1 (1953): 67–90; James Levy, "Forging African American Minds: Black Pragmatism, 'Intelligent Labor,' and a New Look at Industrial Education, 1879–1900," *American Nineteenth Century History* 17, no. 1 (2016): 44–45; Wooten, *Comprehensive History of Texas*, vol. 2, 462–63. Meier concludes, "Washington's tone was accommodating, but there was a peculiar militancy about his emphasis on self-help, economic advancement and moral improvement, his concern with developing manhood and race pride." "Booker T. Washington," 78–79. See also Adams, "How Alta Vista Became Prairie View," 268–86; and Fishel and Quarles, *Negro American*, 364–72.
66. "Negro's Day," *Houston Post*, September 7, 1909; "Negro's Needs," *Houston Daily Post*, December 9, 1910. See also "The Educators Meet," *Colored American* (Washington, DC), March 21, 1903.

67. "From Booker Washington," *Houston Daily Post*, January 27, 1903; Booker T. Washington to E. L. Blackshear, n.d., quoted in *Washington (DC) Bee*, August 21, 1909; "Wants Exposition for Louisville," *Negro Business League Herald*, September 15, 1909; "E. L. Blackshear Appointed," *Dallas Morning News*, October 25, 1909; "The National Negro Exposition," *Advocate* (Charleston, WV), October 28, 1909; "Give All a Chance," *Advocate* (Charleston, WV), October 28, 1909; John H. Burrows, *The Necessity of Myth: A History of the National Negro Business League, 1900–1945* (Hickory Hill Press, 1988); Meier, *Negro Thought in America*, 124–28. At the same time as Blackshear's appointment, Dr. C. T. Walker of the Walker Baptist College in Augusta, GA, and Major R. R. Moton of the Hampton Institute were added to the executive committee. See also Bruce A. Glasrud, "Early NAACP Struggles in Texas, 1914–1932," *Journal of South Texas* 29, no. 2 (2016): 24–33.
68. "Dr. Washington's Trip Through Texas," *Richmond (VA) Planet*, October 14, 1911.
69. E. L. Blackshear to B. T. Washington, October 16, 1911, and Horace D. Slatter, Resume of Trip, October 14, 1911, 331–38, 345–46, in Louis R. Harlan and Raymond W. Smock, eds., *The Booker T. Washington Papers*, vol. 11 (University of Illinois Press, 1990).
70. "Letter of Appreciation," Booker T. Washington to E. L. Blackshear, October 10, 1911, quoted in *Houston Post*, October 21, 1911; Rice, *Negro in Texas*, 193.

Chapter 4

1. Woolfolk, *Prairie View*, 116, 148.
2. Woolfolk, *Prairie View*, 27–28; "College for the Negroes," *Dallas Morning News*, May 18, 1900.
3. W. R. Cavitt, "Negro Vote for Sayers," *Houston Post*, November 1, 1898; "The Prairie View Normal," *Houston Daily Post*, March 27, 1900; Woolfolk, *Prairie View*, 96–97, 150. Rose remained an active advocate for Prairie View after departing the A&M board and when he served as the Texas state commissioner of agriculture.
4. "Prairie View Normal," *Houston Post*, November 15, 1896, and January 5, 1897; "Great Work for Negroes," *Houston Post*, June 8, 1902; Minutaglio, *A Single Star and Bloody Knuckles*, 37.
5. "Prairie View School," *Houston Daily Post*, September 4, 1898; "Prairie View Normal," *Houston Daily Post*, January 30, 1899; Woolfolk, *Prairie View*, 77.
6. Woolfolk, *Prairie View*, 83–84, 123–27; "Prairie View Normal," *Houston Daily Post*, January 30, 1899.
7. Dethloff, *Centennial History of Texas A&M*, vol. 1, 317.
8. General Laws of the State of Texas, 1897–1902, 325, TSLA.

9. E. L. Blackshear, "Industrial Training and the Race Question," *Southern Workman*, June 1906, 396–401; Myrdal, *American Dilemma*, vol. 2, 883–99; Dethloff, *Centennial History of Texas A&M*, vol. 1, 316. Myrdal indicated that his research in the early 1940s showed that "no effective industrial training was ever given the Negroes in the Southern public schools."
10. E. L. Blackshear, "Economy in Teaching School," *School Journal*, December 27, 1902, 682; "Prairie View," *Houston Daily Post*, February 14, 1901, and June 13, 1901; Woolfolk, *Prairie View*, 127–30. For contemporary negative assessment of African American higher education programs in 1902, see "The Southern Education Board and the Negro," *Houston Daily Post*, July 15, 1902.
11. A. J. Rose, President, "For Negro Youths," *Galveston Daily News*, January 5, 1897 (emphasis added).
12. Texas State Department of Education, *Biennial Report of the State Superintendent of Public Instruction* (State Board of Education, 1902), 44–134, 225–344, and *Biennial Report of the State Superintendent of Public Instruction* (State Board of Education, 1906), 78–210, DBC; "Will Lecture in Colored Church," *Houston Daily Post*, July 29, 1900; "Colored Educator: Addressed Negroes at Court House," *Hallettsville (TX) Herald*, November 8, 1900; Woolfolk, *Prairie View*, 128–29, 135. See also Deborah L. Morowski and O. L. Davis, "Through a Heavy Fog: Public High Schools in Texas for African Americans, 1900–1930," *American Educational History Journal* 32, no. 2 (2005): 183–91; Fite, *Cotton Fields No More*, 39–43.
13. E. L. Blackshear, "Tuskegee as I Saw It," *Texas School Journal*, January 1900, 790–91.
14. Woolfolk, *Prairie View*, 134.
15. Woolfolk, *Prairie View*, 131. See also Daniel T. Rodgers, *The Work Ethic in Industrial America, 1850–1920* (University of Chicago Press, 1974), 83–90.
16. Biennial Report of the Board of Directors of the Prairie View Normal and Industrial College, October 1902, quoted in the *Galveston Daily News*, December 30, 1902; "Bids and proposals," *Houston Post*, November 1, 1907; "Improvements at the A. and M.," *Houston Post*, October 19, 1907; "Directors Green and McInnis Visit Prairie View School," *Houston Post*, March 31, 1908; "Professional Summer Schools for Negroes," *Austin Statesman*, April 18, 1904.
17. E. L. Blackshear, "Boll Weevil," *Galveston Daily News*, February 21, 1905; "Colored Farmers' Congress," *Dallas Morning News*, June 24, 1906; "The Work of R. L. Smith: It Is a Labor of Love for the Up-Building of the Negroes of Texas," *Houston Daily Post*, October 14, 1901; "Negro Farmers: Many Land Owners," *Houston Post*, July 6, 1906; "Negro Farmers Meet," *Houston Post*, July 5, 1907; Pitre, *Through Many Dangers, Toils, and Snares*, 180–83.

18. Blackshear, *Education of Childhood*, 50–52; "Doing Great Work: What Was Seen on Visit to Prairie View," *Houston Daily Post*, January 18, 1904; Woolfolk, *Prairie View*, 135.
19. Faculty Committee Minutes, January 14, 1908, CLA.
20. Faculty Minutes, January 10, 1905, October 10, 1905, December 12, 1905, April 23, 1907, October 8, 1907, September 28, 1909, November 2, 1909; "Prairie View Normal Band," *Houston Post*, April 13, 1905; E. B. Evans, "Down Memory Lane: The Story of Edward B. Evans, and the Early History of Prairie View A&M University" (1970), 34, 45–49, CLA.
21. Lomax, "Stories of an African Prince," 3; "Some General Rules," *Annual Catalogue* (1905–6), 42, CLA.
22. Faculty Minutes, May 11 and 25, 1905, October 25, 1905, December 6, 1905, June 30, 1906, March 5, 1907, February 11, 1908; "At Prairie View," *Houston Post*, July 11, 1909; "Call for Troops from a School," *Houston Post*, October 1, 1904; Woolfolk, *Prairie View*, 139; Dethloff, *Centennial History of Texas A&M*, vol. 1, 204–9. See also Paul D. Casey, *The History of the A. and M. College Trouble* (J. S. Hill, 1908); Blackshear, "Annual Address of President E. L. Blackshear," in Proceedings of the Annual Session of the Colored Teachers' Association, Marshall, Texas, December 28, 1904, 40, TSLA.
23. General Laws of the State of Texas, 1879, ch. 159, sec. 2, pp. 181–82, TSLA.
24. "Prairie View Normal," *Houston Daily Post*, January 30, 1899; "At Prairie View," *Houston Post*, May 11, 21, and 26, 1911. The Peabody Fund contributed twenty-five dollars to ten students at Prairie View in the spring semester of 1894. "Revenue Pouring in," *Galveston Daily News*, February 8, 1894.
25. Faculty Minutes, February 27, 1906; "The Daily Routine," *Annual Catalogue* (1907–8), 14, CLA.
26. Faculty Minutes, May 29, 1906; "Prairie View Plan," *Houston Post*, May 26, 1911; "Adopt a Uniform," *Houston Post*, July 16, 1911.
27. Faculty Minutes, April 5, 1905, February 20, 1906, January 21, 1908, February 1, 1910, March 9, 1911; 1908 Alumni Association Program, ELCA; "Negro Industrial Training," *Houston Daily Post*, February 11, 1901.
28. "Supt. Blackshear to Governor," *Bastrop Advertiser*, September 15, 1900.
29. Minutes of the Texas A&M Board of Directors, April 17, 1901, ELCA; "Board Adopts Designs," *San Antonio Daily Express*, August 6, 1907; "Making Brick at Prairie View," *Houston Post*, January 21, 1908; "Industrial Training of Negroes Is Urged," *Houston Post*, May 21, 1908; "Take Care of All," *Houston Post*, October 10, 1910; Woolfolk, *Prairie View*, 151–53; Moore, *Booker T. Washington, W. E. B. Du Bois*, 29. When Booker T. Washington decided to build permanent brick buildings at Tuskegee in the late 1880s, he opened a brickyard on campus for building projects, with the surplus sold to the surrounding community. A second campus service for local farmers was established to grind sugar cane and make syrup in September 1911.

30. "Directors at Prairie View," *Bryan Daily Eagle*, May 27, 1909; "A. and M. Directors Met: Prairie View Improvements Approved," *Houston Post*, May 25, 1909; "Negro's Pride," *Houston Post*, May 26, 1909; "At Prairie View," *Houston Post*, September 11, 1911.
31. "Prairie View," *Crisis* (New York), May 1913, 4. *The Crisis* has been in continuous print since 1910 and is the oldest black-oriented magazine in the world. The Prairie View advertisement ran beside those of Fisk University, Atlanta University, Knoxville College, and the agricultural and mechanical colleges in Greensboro, NC, and Normal, AL.
32. Janet Schmelzer, *Our Fighting Governor: The Life of Thomas M. Campbell and the Politics of Progressive Reform in Texas* (Texas A&M University Press, 2014), 8–21, 43, 56.
33. Schmelzer, *Our Fighting Governor*, 39–40, 86–89, 144.
34. Sidney T. Matthews, "The Negro Problem in the South" (honors thesis, University of Richmond, 1934), http://scholarship.richmond.edu/honors-theses. Lord Banquo, the Thane of Lochaber, is a character in William Shakespeare's 1606 play *Macbeth*. There were a number of euphemisms for the "Negro Problem," for example: race problem, Negro question, race issue, and race consciousness.
35. The bibliography on the "negro problem" is exceedingly extensive, and a full assessment of these documents is not a part of this book. However, the following sources were some of the items consulted and are included to give the reader a very brief selection of sources for further study: W. E. B. Du Bois, *A Select Bibliography of the Negro American* (Atlanta University Press, 1905); Du Bois, "The Study of the Negro Problems," *Annals of the American Academy of Political and Social Science*, January 1898, 1–23; Booker T. Washington, *The Negro Problem* (J. Pott, 1903); N. S. Shaler, "The Negro Problem," *Atlantic*, November 1884; Edward Eggleston, *The Ultimate Solution of the American Negro* (R. G. Badger, 1913); "The Negro Question," *New York Times*, April 25, 1903; Moore, *Booker T. Washington, W. E. B. Du Bois*; Marcus Garvey, "Aims and Objects of Movement for Solution of Negro Problem," 1924, available on "The Making of African American Identity," vol. 3, National Humanities Center, rev. February 2011, www.nationalhumanitiescenter.org/pds; John Pepper, *American Negro Problems* (Workers Library, 1928); Myrdal, *American Dilemma*; Meier, *Negro Thought in America*; E. L. Blackshear, L. S. Ross, and Andrew N. Cleven, *Future of the Negro: The Race Problem Discussed* (Cameron, TX: Colored Teachers Institute, 1898), TSLA; Pitre, *Through Many Dangers, Toils, and Snares*, 180.
36. "Religious Problem," *Houston Daily Post*, November 17, 1890; "Race Problems," *Houston Daily Post*, August 2, 1890.

37. E. L. Blackshear, "Evolution of Society"; E. L. Blackshear, "The Negro Problem," *Fort Worth Daily Gazette*, December 20, 1888.
38. James N. Leiker, "Racial Borders: Black Soldiers and Race Relations Along the Rio Grande, 1866–1916" (PhD diss., University of Kansas, 1999), 314–40; "Congo Horrors, *New York Age*, January 17, 1907. See also John D. Weaver, *The Brownsville Raid* (Texas A&M University Press, 1992).
39. "Prof. Blackshear Addressed Colored Teachers," *Houston Post*, February 3, 1907; "Secretary Taft on the Brownsville Affair," *Outlook*, December 15, 1906, 897–98; "Secretary Taft and the Negro Soldiers," *Independent*, July 23, 1908, 189–90; "Desired Prairie View Appropriation Stricken Out," *Bryan Morning Eagle*, April 7, 1907; Denton, *Booker T. Washington*, 156–58. See also Emma L. Thornbrough, "The Brownsville Episode and the Negro Vote," *Mississippi Valley Historical Review* 44, no. 3 (1957): 469–83; J. A. Tinsley, "Roosevelt, Foraker and the Brownsville Affray," *Journal of Negro History* 41, no. 1 (1956): 43–65.
40. Myrdal, *American Dilemma*, vol. 1, 123–25.
41. E. L. Blackshear, "Gives His Views of the Negro's Condition in Texas and the South," *Austin American Statesman*, April 30, 1890; Woodward, *The Strange Career of Jim Crow*, 68–69.
42. E. L. Blackshear, "An Address: To the People of Texas by the Colored State Teachers," *Galveston Daily News*, June 29, 1894; E. L. Blackshear, "A Circular Letter," *Houston Daily Post*, October 27, 1896; E. L. Blackshear, "Lines of Negro Education," *AME Church Review*, January 1897; Franklin W. William, "How Foreign Immigration Will Ultimately Solve Negro Problem," *Denver Colorado Statesman*, April 13, 1912.
43. E. L. Blackshear, "The Negro Problem Settling Itself," *Austin Weekly Statesman*, December 9, 1897.
44. John Higham, *Stranger in the Land: Patterns of American Nativism, 1860–1925* (Atheneum, 1972), 168–69, 174–76; Booker T. Washington, "Races and Politics," *Outlook* 97 (1911): 264; Arnold Shankman, "The Menacing Influx: Afro-Americans on Italian Immigration to the South, 1880–1915," *Mississippi Quarterly* 31, no. 1 (1977–78): 78, 86; Anne Boykin, ed., *The Italians of Steele's Store, Texas & Brazos Valley Italians*: (Left-Write Ink Books, 2019), 13–31. See also Barbara Rozek, *Come to Texas: Attracting Immigrants, 1865–1915* (Texas A&M University Press, 2003); David J. Hellwig, "Strangers in Their Own Land: Patterns of Black Nativism, 1830–1930," *American Studies* 23, no. 1 (1982): 85–98; Cassandre Durso, "Two States with One Goal: Texas and Louisiana Recruit Italians," *Texas Gulf History & Biographical Record* 48 (November 2012): 25–42; Susan R. Breitzer, "Race, Immigration, and Contested Americanness: Black

Nativism and the American Labor Movement, 1880–1930," *Race/Ethnicity: Multidisciplinary Global Context* 4, no. 2 (2011): 269–83.

45. "Solution of Negro Problem," *Houston Daily Post*, August 16, 1899. Washington made his conclusion against sending black Americans to Africa after a visit to London in the summer of 1899, noting, "There is no part of Africa to which the colored man could immigrate in which he would not be under some European power except Liberia, and that is an unhealthy country." AME Church bishop Henry M. Turner objected, stating, "The government should establish a line of steamships between this country and Africa to carry negroes at a nominal price. The Anglo-Saxon never does and never will live with any other race without trampling it under foot. I believe emigration the only practicable solution of the problem." See also Charles S. Smith, *Race Question Reviewed* (Nashville, 1899).
46. E. L. Blackshear, "A Refuge for Negroes," *Washington Post*, December 5, 1898; E. L. Blackshear, "The Numerous Possibilities: The Pathway of the Colored Race," *Houston Daily Post*, March 20, 1899; E. L. Blackshear, "Negro Colonization Schemes," *Houston Post*, July 13, 1914.
47. E. L. Blackshear, "Industrial Training and the Race Question," *Southern Workman*, June 1906; E. L. Blackshear, "News of the State Capital," *Galveston Daily News*, July 28, 1900; E. L. Blackshear, "The South's Difficulties," *Houston Post*, August 1, 1904; Langston quote seen in Meier, *Negro Thought in America*, 78; Blackshear to colleague, March 23, 1919, Woodrow Wilson Presidential Papers, ELCA; O. B. Martin, *A Decade of Negro Extension Work, 1914–1924*, U.S. Department of Agriculture circular no. 72 (Government Printing Office, 1924), 1.
48. E. L. Blackshear, "Pugilism and Race Question," *New York Times*, May 11, 1910; "Jack Johnson Knocks Out Jeffries," *San Diego Union*, July 5, 1910; Schmelzer, *Our Fighting Governor*, 123–24.
49. Jacob Bogage, "Boxer Jack Johnson Is Posthumously Pardoned," *Washington Post*, May 24, 2018; James W. Byrd, "Jack Johnson, 1878–1946," in *Handbook of Texas*, vol. 3, ed. Ron Tyler (Texas State Historical Association, 1996; rev. ed., 2020), 395–96.
50. E. L. Blackshear, "The South's Difficulties," *Houston Post*, August 1, 1904.
51. E. L. Blackshear, "Negro Education in Texas," *Houston Post*, May 26, 1908. See also "More Room Is Needed," *Austin Statesman*, December 8, 1908; "At the Capital: Principal Blackshear Reports on Prairie View," *Houston Post*, December 10, 1908; "The Work at Prairie View Normal," *Houston Daily Post*, May 23, 1909.
52. Woolfolk, *Prairie View*, 154; "Negro's Needs," *Houston Post*, December 9, 1910; "At Prairie View," *Houston Post*, May 21, 1911; "Usefulness of Prairie View Normal for Colored," *Galveston Daily News*, December 18, 1910.

Chapter 5

1. "Last Day for Donations," *Houston Post*, October 31, 1908; Gould, *Progressives and Prohibitionists*, 7, 28. See also Myrdal, *American Dilemma*, vol. 1, lxxv, 29, 41, 65, 455.
2. "Asked for Location," *Washington Herald*, October 24, 1909. The paper further noted: "Mr. Taft is turning the animals loose as fast as he gets them [apparently he was gifted with at least four possums], and there ought to be a fat find for anybody who will follow along the Taft trail from New Orleans to the Atlantic seaboard."
3. "Taft in Texas," *Houston Post*, October 25, 1908.
4. "A Great Stir," *Temple Daily Telegram*, July 23, 1912; E. L. Blackshear, "The Progress of the Negro in Texas," *Houston Daily Post*, September 27, 1914; U.S. Bureau of the Census, *Thirteenth Census: Supplement for Texas*, 1910, 595, 659. See also Shannon, *The Farmer's Last Frontier*, 372–78; Woodward, *Origins of the New South*, 169–72. Blackshear concluded the relative percentage decline in the Negro population in the electorate was threefold: an increased death rate, the exodus of African Americans out of Texas, and the increase in white Southerners and Europeans immigrating into Texas.
5. "A Big Demonstration," *New York Times*, July 27, 1887; Williams, *Beyond Redemption*, 172; Gould, *Progressives and Prohibitionists*, 29–33, 47–57; Myrdal, *American Dilemma*, vol. 1, 457–58; Benner, *Sul Ross*, 164–65; Billy M. Jones, *The Search for Maturity* (Steck-Vaughn, 1965), 139. Ross's up-and-coming Progressive-minded attorney general James Hogg agreed with the governor, noting that the "measure was impractical. . . . Men cannot be made moral, forced into temperance, or whipped into religion."
6. "Must Investigate," *Rockdale Reporter and Messenger*, August 3, 1911; Terry G. Jordan, "A Century and a Half of Ethnic Change in Texas, 1836–1986," *Southwestern Historical Quarterly* 89, no. 4 (1986): 394, 402; Larry D. Hill, "Texas Progressivism: A Search for Definition," in *Texas Through Time: Evolving Interpretations*, ed. Walter L. Buenger and Robert A. Calvert (Texas A&M University Press, 1991), 231, 247; Gregg Cantrell, *The People's Revolt: Texas Populists and the Roots of American Liberalism* (Yale University Press, 2020), 335–40. See also De Léon and Stewart, "Lost Dreams and Found Fortunes," 291–310.
7. "Mr. Ousley Statement," *Austin American Statesman*, June 5, 1911; "After Blackshear's Scrap," *Houston Daily Post*, August 21, 1911; "The Negro and Prohibition," *Jefferson (TX) Jimplecute*, August 25, 1911.
8. James H. Quarles to Governor Colquitt, January 31, 1911, and O. B. Colquitt to Walton Peteet, July 30, 1912, Oscar B. Colquitt Papers, TSLA; Colquitt to Robert H. Hopkins, January 2, 1913, Oscar B. Colquitt Papers, DBC; Hendrickson, *The Chief Executives of Texas*, 153–56; George B. Tindall, *The Emergence of the New South, 1913–1945* (Louisiana State University Press,

1967), 19; Cantrell, *People's Revolt*, 154; Walter L. Buenger and Walter D. Kamphoefner, eds., *Preserving German Texan Identity: Reminiscences of William A. Trenckmann, 1859–1935* (Texas A&M University Press, 2019), 29–30, 109, 154–56, 159–60.

9. Payne, "Defending Black Suffrage," 824.
10. Gould, *Progressives and Prohibitionists*, 44–55, 88–90; Barr, *Black Texans*, 113; James M. McPherson, "White Liberals and Black Power in Negro Education, 1865–1915," *American Historical Review* 75, no. 5 (1970): 1371–72; Woodward, *Origins of the New South*, 61–66; Kyle G. Wilkison, "The End of Independence: Social and Political Consequences of Economic Change in Texas, 1870–1914" (PhD diss., Vanderbilt University, 1995), 227–31; Robert H. Wiebe, *The Search for Order, 1877–1920* (Hill and Wang, 1967), 104–5, 110; Myrdal, *American Dilemma*, vol. 1, 9–12; *Galveston Daily News*, December 30, 1910. For an insightful essay on the early underpinnings of the black church in the South, see Chandra Manning, "Faith and Works: A Historiographical Review of Religion in the Civil War Era," *Journal of the Civil War Era* 10, no. 3 (2020): 373–96.
11. "Ball's Statement Blackshear Case," *Galveston Daily News*, May 30, 1911; "How Does This Strike the American Voter of El Paso?," *El Paso Herald*, July 21, 1911.
12. Barr, *Reconstruction to Reform*, xv, 18; Myrdal, *American Dilemma*, vol. 2, 858–78; Daina R. Berry and Kali N. Gross, *A Black Women's History of the United States* (Beacon Press, 2020), 113; Rebecca Sharpless, *Fertile Ground, Narrow Choices: Women on Texas Cotton Farms, 1900–1940* (University of North Carolina Press, 1999), 204–8.
13. Gould, *Alexander Watkins Terrell*, 88, 117, 149; Woolfolk, *Prairie View*, 155–57; Casdorph, *History of the Republican Party*, 107; *Texas Christian Advocate*, January 9, 1890; Rice, *Negro in Texas*, 133–39; Sharpless, *Fertile Ground, Narrow Choices*, 202–10; Myrdal, *American Dilemma*, vol. 2, 870–72; Cantrell, *People's Revolt*, 163, 400.
14. "Prof. Blackshear," *Jefferson (TX) Jimplecute*, August 4, 1911.
15. Adams and Page, "John Nathaniel Johnson," 7–47.
16. "Compliments to Blackshear by Washington on Prairie View," *Houston Post*, September 29, 1911.
17. E. L. Blackshear, "Right of Suffrage," *Houston Post*, January 3, 1911; Cantrell, *Feeding the Wolf*, 88–90. See also J. Morgan Kousser, *The Shaping of Southern Politics: Suffrage Restriction and the Establishment of the One-Party South, 1880–1910* (Yale University Press, 1974); Bullock, *History of Negro Education*, 219–21.
18. *New York Times*, November 26, 1906.
19. "Industrial Pupils Proved Efficiency: Principal of Prairie View Normal Presented Colquitt with Campaign Outfit," *Houston Daily Post*, April 14,

1912; "Colquitt Offers Reward for Axeman," *Amarillo Daily News*, April 20, 1912. The hat and shoes presented to the governor were exact counterparts of those worn by him during the previous (1910) campaign. Professor Blackshear brought the originals along with the new articles of head and foot adornment, but he did not say just how he had contrived to get hold of them. He said only he used the originals as patterns.

20. "Principal of Prairie View on Speaking Tour," *Houston Post*, May 1, 1914.
21. E. B. Cushing to Gov. O. B. Colquitt, April 4, 1913, Oscar B. Colquitt Papers, TSLA; "E. B. Cushing President," *Houston Post*, April 1, 1913; "Houstonians at Prairie View," *Houston Post*, April 9, 1913.
22. Blackshear to Governor Colquitt, July 16, 1913, Oscar B. Colquitt Papers, TSLA; "'Shake Up' at Prairie View: Lack of Money Liable to Reduce Enrollment," *Houston Post*, August 23, 1913; "Prairie View State Normal: Industrial School for Negros," *Houston Post*, June 8, 1913.
23. "Prairie View Normal Largest of Its Kind," *Houston Post*, February 1, 1913; "Work at Prairie View a Revelation," *Houston Daily Post*, February 9, 1913.
24. "Normal Gets Appropriations," *Austin American Statesman*, August 7, 1913.
25. "Program for Colored Farmers' Congress at Prairie View," *Houston Chronicle*, March 22, 1913; O. B. Colquitt, "Educational Amendment Elucidated: Proposition Helps A. and M," June 27, 1913, Oscar B. Colquitt Papers, TSLA; Barbara Donalson, *Kyle Tough* (Oaks Press, 2003), 137.
26. "Anti-Cotton Futures," *Houston Daily Post*, April 4, 1897.
27. Fite, *Cotton Fields No More*, 21, 27.
28. "First Bales in Texas," *Houston Post*, August 2, 1913; "Texas Cotton Crop," *Daily Herald* (Weatherford, TX), December 5, 1912; Foster, *Forgotten Texas Census*, xxxv–xxxvi, xl; Barnes, *Farmers in Rebellion*, 54–67, 80–83; Myrdal, *American Dilemma*, vol. 1, 234. See also Wortham, *A History of Texas*, vol. 5, 123–32.
29. "Reasons for the Anti-Option Bill," *Southern Mercury*, October 27, 1892; "Cotton Acreage 1910," *Jefferson (TX) Jimplecute*, August 4, 1911; "Sketch of King Cotton," *Jefferson (TX) Jimplecute*, August 25, 1911; Woodward, *Origins of the New South*, 198–200. See also James C. Malin, "The Farmers' Alliance Subtreasury Plan and European Precedents," *Mississippi Valley Historical Review* 31, no. 2 (1944): 255–60.
30. Cantrell, *People's Revolt*, 118, 129–34; E. L. Blackshear, "He Would Make the State the Cotton Middleman," *Atlanta Constitution*, April 21, 1912; Wiebe, *Search for Order*, 72. See also Malin, "The Farmers' Alliance Subtreasury Plan"; Fite, *Cotton Fields No More*, 56–59; Buenger, *Path to a Modern South*, 60–66; Myrdal, *American Dilemma*, vol. 1, 234.
31. E. L Blackshear to Pres. Woodrow Wilson, March 10, 1913, Woodrow Wilson Presidential Papers, microfilm, series 4, reel 229, ELCA. See also A. S. Steitous to Wilson, representative of Philadelphia-based "The Joint

Organization of the Association for Equalizing Industrial Opportunities and the League of Civic and Political Reform," March 10, 1913, Woodrow Wilson Presidential Papers, ELCA; William P. Morton, "The Future of the Negro in Politics," February 13, 1913, Woodrow Wilson Presidential Papers, reel 229, ELCA.

32. Blackshear to Congressman Hatton Sumners, January 26, 1915, Sumner Papers, Dallas Historical Society, Dallas, TX. See also DeCanio, *Agriculture in the Postbellum South*, 94–119.
33. E. L. Blackshear, "Cotton Manufacture," *Houston Daily Post*, July 3, 1905; Data from the 1900 US Census in Oubre, *Forty Acres and a Mule*, 179–80, tables 1 and 2. See also "The Sims Reunion," *Dallas Morning News*, July 28, 1896; "State Schools of Methods," *Dallas Morning News*, June 27, 1897; Shennette Garrett-Scott, "'The Hope of the South': The New Century Cotton Mill of Dallas, Texas, and the Business of Race in the New South, 1902–1907," *Southwestern Historical Quarterly* 116, no. 2 (2012): 138–66.
34. "Cotton Statistics," *Galveston Daily News*, July 16, 1896; Blackshear, "He Would Make the State the Cotton Middleman"; "A Unique Slant on Cotton," *Atlanta Constitution*, April 21, 1912; "Public Schools in the South," *Pittsburgh Courier*, June 6, 1912; "A Practical Aid," *Fort Worth Star-Telegram*, August 9, 1912. See also Woodward, *Origins of the New South*, 147. David Blight in *Frederick Douglass* (371) noted, "Lincoln shockingly blamed the war on the presence of blacks, 'But for your race among us there could not be war, although many men engaged on either side do not care for you one way or another. We should be separated.'"
35. Blackshear to Governor Colquitt, May 4, 1912, June 13, 1912, and April 1, 1913, Oscar B. Colquitt Papers, TSLA; "Negro Farmers' Congress," *Houston Post*, April 27, 1913; "Negro Farmers' Congress," *Galveston Daily News*, June 6, 1913.
36. "Negro Farmers to Meet Tomorrow," *Birmingham Age-Herald*, July 3, 1913; "Large Attendance at First Meeting of Negro Farmers," *Birmingham Age-Herald*, July 5, 1913; "Negro Farmers Organize for Economic Progress," *Austin Statesman*, July 10, 1913.
37. "Colored Farmers' Congress," *Dallas Morning News*, June 24, 1906. See also E. L. Blackshear, "Industrial Training and the Race Question," *Southern Workman*, July 1906, 396–401; Paul Lombardi, "Examining the Effect of Economic Shocks on the Schooling Choices of Southern Farmers," *European Review of Economic History* 23, no. 2 (2018): 99, 214–40. Lombardi notes that black men earned 50 percent less than white men and that there was a three-and-a-half-year schooling gap between blacks and whites; fewer years of parental education had a positive correlation with lower wages and household assets, and contributed directly to the next generation of blacks receiving less formal schooling.

38. E. L. Blackshear, "Three Phases of Rural Education for Negroes in Texas County Schools," *Houston Post*, December 21, 1914.
39. David F. Houston to the president, May 1, 1913, Woodrow Wilson Papers, ELCA; A. Scott Berg, *Wilson* (G. P. Putnam's Sons, 2013), 309–11.
40. "Professor Houston on Women's Work," *Austin Statesman*, November 26, 1905; "Negro Farmers Elect Officers," *Houston Post*, August 2, 1913; Houston, *Eight Years with Wilson's Cabinet*, vol. 1, 51–84; Berg, *Wilson*, 280–319; Friedrich Katz, *The Secret War in Mexico: Europe, the United States and the Mexican Revolution* (University of Chicago Press, 1981), 161–82; John A. Adams Jr., *Murder and Intrigue on the Mexican Border: Governor Colquitt, President Wilson, and the Vergara Affair* (Texas A&M University Press, 2018), 5–50.
41. Roy L. Newton and James M. Workman, "Cotton Warehousing—Benefits of an Adequate System," in *USDA Yearbook 1918* (Government Printing Office, 1919), 399–432; Tindall, *Emergence of the New South*, 13, 36–37; James E. Boyle, *Cotton and the New Orleans Cotton Exchange* (Garden City, NY, 1934), 88–90; George O. Gatlin, *Cooperative Marketing of Cotton*, USDA bulletin no. 1392 (Government Printing Office, 1926). See also Ransom and Sutch, "The 'Lock-in' Mechanism," 405–15.
42. E. L. Blackshear, "Object of the School," *Annual Catalogue* (1914–15), 11, CLA.
43. Quoted in Woolfolk, *Prairie View*, 157.
44. Woolfolk, *Prairie View*, 155, 158; "Principal of Prairie View on Speaking Tour," *Houston Daily Post*, May 1, 1914; "Delegates," *Brenham Daily Banner-Press*, July 15, 1914; Barr, *Black Texans*, 161. See also "Regrading the Negro Voters," *Houston Post*, July 23, 1912.
45. "Ball at Hempstead," *Houston Daily Post*, October 29, 1900.
46. "Attack on Blackshear," *Houston Post*, July 11, 1914.
47. Adams, *Murder and Intrigue*, 11–34.
48. Governor Colquitt's private secretary to E. L. Blackshear, April 22, 1914, Oscar B. Colquitt Papers, Box 301–370, TSLA. See also John A. Adams Jr., *William F. Buckley: Witness to the Mexican Revolution, 1908–1921* (University of Oklahoma Press, 2023).
49. E. L. Blackshear to Hon. Theodore Roosevelt, May 27, 1914, Theodore Roosevelt Presidential Papers, ELCA. Blackshear's three-page letter (typed single space) was not on Prairie View Normal letterhead and carries a notation that it was "Ack 6/2/14."
50. "James Furgeson [*sic*] Spoke in Bonham," *Bonham (TX) News*, May 1, 1914; "Col. Ball Completes East Texas Campaign," *Austin Statesman*, July 23, 1914; Hendrickson, *The Chief Executives of Texas*, 157–62; Gould, *Progressives and Prohibitionists*, 126; Gould, "Progressives and Prohibitionists," *Southwestern Historical Quarterly* 75, no.1 (1971): 13.

51. *Austin Statesman*, February 1, 1915; Gould, *Progressives and Prohibitionists*, 142, 155–57.
52. "Text of Resolutions Adopted at Waco," *Houston Post*, June 15, 1915; Campbell, *Gone to Texas*, 348–50; Eby, *The Development of Education in Texas*, 230–31; Gould, *Progressives and Prohibitionists*, 185–86.
53. "Politics Puts Out Col. Milner," *Waco Morning News*, June 12, 1913; "Milner Gives His Side of Dispute," *Dallas Morning News*, July 27, 1913.
54. Minutes of the A&M Board of Directors, March 3 and 15, 1914, June 10 and 14, 1914, and August 25, 1914, ELCA; Governor Colquitt to Robert H. Hopkins, January 2, 1913, Oscar B. Colquitt Papers, DBC; Dethloff, *Centennial History of Texas A&M*, vol. 1, 162–63, 258–59, 318–19, and vol. 2, 508–10; Gould, *Progressives and Prohibitionists*, 187–91. See also Benner, *Sul Ross*, 188, 221; Miller, *Public Lands of Texas*, 120–25, 183–84; "S. J. R. 18 defeated 4 to 1," *Dallas Morning News*, July 20, 1913. The PUF had about 2,100,000 acres in twenty West Texas counties. The item that caused the controversy was Senate Joint Resolution No. 18, introduced in early 1913. The unstated reason for the interest in the PUF was the result of an assessment of university lands and the status of mineral rights. The state owned no mineral rights in lands it sold previous to September 1, 1895. In 1901, Land Commissioner Charles Rogan (a graduate in 1879 of the first class at Texas A&M College) was the first commissioner to appraise and amend all Texas land records to establish a mineral classification, beyond the myopic view that the only possible revenue was from grazing and lumber leases. These actions, unknown to most at the time, established the generation of substantial revenue from oil and gas discoveries to fund higher education in the state for generations. See Octavia F. Rogan, *Land Commissioner Charles Rogan and the Mineral Classification of Texas Public School Lands* (San Felipe Press, 1968); "Protecting School Fund: Land Commissioner Rogan Has Taken Steps to That End," *Houston Daily Post*, October 11, 1901.
55. "Negro Educator Arouses Ire of Gov. Ferguson," *Austin Statesman*, February 2, 1915. No such anti-Ferguson letters by Blackshear have been found.
56. Woolfolk, *Prairie View*, 156–59; Charles F. Smith, "The State's Opportunity: Train Her Colored Citizens to Become Modern Farmers," *Houston Post*, February 2, 1914; Blackshear to Hatton Sumners, February 9, 1915, and Hatton Sumners to Governor Ferguson, February 15, 1915, Hatton Sumner Papers, Dallas Historical Society; Blackshear to William P. Hobby, February 3, 1915, William P. Hobby Papers, TSLA; Minutes of the A&M Board of Directors, March 3, 1915, ELCA; Barr, *Black Texans*, 161.
57. Lewis L. Gould, "The University Becomes Politicized: The War with Jim Ferguson, 1915–1918," *Southwestern Historical Quarterly* 86, no. 2 (1983): 255–66; Gould, *Progressives and Prohibitionists*, 185–87; Carl J. Erkhardt,

Presidents of the University of Texas at Austin (Austin, [1973?]); Susan R. Richardson, "Oil, Power, and Universities: Political Struggle and Academic Advancement at the University of Texas and Texas A&M, 1876–1965" (PhD diss., Pennsylvania State University, 2005), 70–71.

58. Gould, "The University Becomes Politicized," 256, 259–60. See also Gould, *Progressives and Prohibitionists*, 187–99; John A. Lomax, "Governor Ferguson and the University of Texas," *Southwest Review* 28, no. 1 (1942): 11–29; Battle, "Concise History of the University of Texas," 391–411; Charles R. Matthews, "The Early Years of the Permanent University Fund from 1836 to 1937" (PhD diss., University of Texas, 2006), 73–98.
59. Minutes of the A&M Board of Directors, April 24, 1915, ELCA. See also "Blackshear Vindicated," *Waco Morning News*, June 12, 1915; "Let the Public Have the Truth," *Houston Daily Post*, August 5, 1915.
60. Minutes of the Texas A&M Board of Directors, July 6, 1915, ELCA.
61. "Blackshear Lost Prairie View Head," *Bryan Eagle*, August 12, 1915; Woolfolk, *Prairie View*, 159.
62. "E. L. Blackshear," *Kansas City Sun*, June 26, 1915.
63. "Negroes Thankful for Aid to School," *Houston Post*, July 31, 1915. See also "No Principal Yet for Prairie View," *Bryan Daily Eagle*, July 8, 1915.
64. W. D. Hornaday, "The Real Issue Which Has Been Raised by Ferguson," *Houston Post*, June 18, 1917; Barr, *Black Texans*, 161.
65. "The Removal," *Bryan Daily Eagle*, August 24, 1915; "The Public Entitled to Know," *Wichita Daily Times*, August 12, 1915; "Waco, Texas," *Washington Bee*, February 27, 1915.
66. Quoted in Evans, "Down Memory Lane," 64–65. Evans—who stated the principal was "unceremoniously and ruthlessly summarily dismissed"—reflected on the events: "Blackshear's name and accomplishments will be remembered when the names of great men have been recorded in the annals of higher education in Texas and the South."
67. "Blackshear Vindicated"; "Let the Public Have the Truth"; "Blackshear Lost Prairie View Head"; "History of School," *Prairie '17* (Prairie View annual, 1917), 15, CLA; Dethloff, *Centennial History of Texas A&M*, vol. 1, 319; Du Bois, *Atlanta University Publication*, no. 16, quoted in Funke, "The Negro in Education," 12; James D. Anderson, *The Education of Blacks in the South, 1860–1935* (University of North Carolina Press, 1988), 191, 199–200. In 1915, 25 percent of all black high schools in the South were in Texas.
68. Jones, *Negro Education*, vol. 2, 598–600.
69. Hornaday, "The Real Issue Which Has Been Raised by Ferguson."
70. "'Shakeup' at Prairie View," *Houston Daily Post*, August 23, 1913.
71. Dethloff, *Centennial History of Texas A&M*, vol. 1, 319–20; Woolfolk, *Prairie View*, 163–77.

72. "Let the Public Have the Truth"; "Ft. Worth Industrial & Mechanical College," *Tulsa Star*, October 8, 1915; "Negro Students to Work Way in School," *Fort Worth Star-Telegram*, October 31, 1915; "W. A. Blackshear Dead," *Houston Daily Post*, January 14, 1917; "Prof. E. L. Blackshear," *Prairie View Standard*, March 25, 1916, 2, CLA; "Freeman Headquarters," *Freeman* (Philadelphia), November 27, 1915. See also Mark Bauerlein, "Washington, Du Bois, and the Black Future," *Wilson Quarterly* 28, no. 4 (2004): 74–86.

Chapter 6

1. "The Boll Worm," *Galveston Daily News*, September 20, 1894; E. L. Blackshear, "The Work of R. L. Smith," *Houston Daily Post*, October 14, 1901; W. B. Mercier, *Extension Work Among Negros—1920*, USDA Cooperative Extension Work in Agriculture circular 190 (Government Printing Office, 1921), 3; Myrdal, *American Dilemma*, vol. 1, lxxv, 234–35; Reid, *Reaping a Greater Harvest*, xx–xxii.
2. Ambassador James Gerard to Colonel House, June 16, 1915, in Seymour, *The Intimate Papers of Colonel House*, vol. 2, 13–14, 451–55; Ralph A. Wooster, *Texas and Texans in the Great War* (State House Press, 2009), 11–24, 32, 107; Earl W. Crosby, "The Struggle for Existence: The Institutionalization of the Black County Agent System," *Agricultural History* 60, no. 2 (1966): 133; Katz, *Secret War in Mexico*, 210–49, 339–78; Enrigue Krauze, *Mexico: Biography of Power* (HarperCollins, 1977), 368; Campbell, *Gone to Texas*, 352–54; Gould, *Progressives and Prohibitionists*, 159–63, 222.
3. Mark Benbow, "All the Brains I Can Borrow: Woodrow Wilson and Intelligence Gathering in Mexico, 1913–15," *Studies in Intelligence* 51, no. 4 (2007): 1–15. See also Thomas Boghardt, *The Zimmermann Telegram: Intelligence, Diplomacy, and America's Entry into World War I* (Naval Institute Press, 2012).
4. "Appeal for Negro Race for Loyalty," *Dallas Morning News*, September 14, 1917.
5. "Allied Armies Resist Stubborn German Army," *Bryan Daily Eagle*, August 19, 1914.
6. "Reports of German Agents Denounced," *Houston Daily Post*, April 6, 1917. See also Crosby, "Struggle for Existence," 133.
7. "Charged with Inciting Negroes Against U.S.," *Houston Daily Post*, April 8, 1917; William E. Nicholas, "World War I and Academic Dissent in Texas," *Arizona and the West* 14, no. 3 (1972): 215–30; Neil Foley, *The White Scourge: Mexicans, Blacks, and Poor Whites in Texas Cotton Culture* (University of California Press, 1997), 114–16; Tindall, *Emergence of the New South*, 50–51, 66.
8. "Colored Mass Meeting at City Auditorium," *Houston Post*, April 10, 1017; "Patriotic Appeal Made to Negroes," *Houston Post*, April 11, 1917.

9. "Colored Pros Held Meeting at Big Tree," *Houston Post*, August 18, 1917.
10. Crosby, "Struggle for Existence," 123–36; W. E. B. Du Bois, "Close Ranks," *Crisis* (New York), July 1918, 111; A. C. True, *A History of Agricultural Extension Work in the United States, 1785–1923*, pub. no. 15 (Government Printing Office, 1928), 134–43; Wooster, *Texas and Texans in the Great War*, 56–57. For a response of German American Texans during the war to anti-German attacks and spies, see Buenger and Kamphoefner, *Preserving German Texas Identity*, 169–74; True, *History of Agricultural Education*, 296–300. True has extensive bibliography on each state except Texas.
11. "Wharton Is Chairman of War Commission," *Houston Daily Post*, August 19, 1917; "War Service Board," *Houston Daily Post*, September 9, 1917; Robert V. Haynes, *A Night of Violence: The Houston Riot of 1917* (Louisiana State University Press, 1976), 202–3; R. Douglas Hurt, ed., *African American Life in the Rural South, 1900–1950* (University of Missouri Press, 2003), 166–69; T. O. Walton to Bradford Knapp, December 31, 1918, record group 16, ID 5772459, Office of the Secretary, Department of Agriculture, NARA. In the military court-martial for mutiny held during November 1917 in San Antonio at Fort Sam Houston, nineteen were executed and forty-one were sentenced to life in prison.
12. Minutes of the Texas A&M Board of Directors, March 23, 1917, vol. 3, 212–13, ELCA; William B. Bizzell, "The Service of the College to the Nation," *A&M College Alumni Quarterly*, November 1917, 3–6; "Capt. Allen Addressed Prairie View Students," *Houston Post*, October 14, 1917; "Bizzell Tendered Government for Training at Prairie View," *Fort Worth Star-Telegram*, April 5, 1918; "Prairie View School Offered to U.S. Army," *Austin American Statesman*, April 6, 1918; "Prairie View Normal Raises War Funds Quota," *San Antonio Express*, February 4, 1918.
13. "Preparing Plans for De-Ro-Loc Exposition," *Houston Post*, September 30, 1917; "Prairie View Normal School Federalized Tuesday," *Houston Post*, October 4, 1918; "Weather Prophets in the Army," *San Antonio Express*, September 1, 1918; J. C. Nagle, "War Training Activities: Prairie View Training Department," Society for the Promotion of Agricultural Education, *Proceedings of the Twenty-Sixth Annual Meeting* (1918), 63–77, CLA; "Regret at Death of Lt. Carroll," *Houston Post*, January 21, 1918. See also Myrdal, *American Dilemma*, vol. 1, 193–95; C. W. Crawford, *One Hundred Years of Engineering at Texas A&M, 1876–1976* (pub. by the author, 1976), 38–46; Emmett J. Scott, *Scott's Official History of the American Negro in the World War* (pub. by the author, 1919), 330. A week after Lieutenant Carroll's landing at Prairie View, he was killed in training.
14. "In Negro Camps at Des Moines, Iowa," *Houston Post*, July 17, 1917; "Capt. Allen Addressed Prairie View Students," *Houston Post*, October 14, 1917; Frank E. Burkhalter, "Spirit of Patriotism High in Prairie View

Normal," *Austin American Statesman*, January 20, 1918, repr. in "Prairie View Students Are Doing a Part of the War Work," *Houston Post*, January 28, 1918; "R. O. T. C. Application Approved," *San Antonio Express*, January 28, 1919; "Military Training," *Annual Catalogue* (1918–19), 63–65, 81, CLA; Monro MacCloskey, *Reserve Officers Training Corps: Campus Pathways to Service Commissions* (Richards Rosen Press, 1965), 36–37.

15. Evans, "Down Memory Lane," 3; Myrdal, *American Dilemma*, vol. 1, 419–22. Evans was the first African American licensed veterinarian in Texas, license number 237.
16. Bizzell, *Green Rising*, 198–204; "Prairie View State Normal Director Here," *Courier-Gazette* (McKinney, TX), May 4, 1918; "Blackshear Doing Extension Service Work with Negroes," *Bryan Weekly Eagle*, November 8, 1917; David B. Danbom, "The Agricultural Extension System and the First World War," *Historian* 41, no. 2 (1979), 315–31.
17. Emmett J. Scott, "Letters of Negro Migrants of 1916–1918," *Journal of Negro History* 4, no. 3 (1919): 290–340.
18. "Prairie View Normal Prospects Are Bright," *Houston Post*, August 26, 1917; "Colored Farmers' Congress a Success," *Houston Post*, August 5, 1917; "Will Meet at State Capital," *La Grange (TX) Journal*, February 28, 1918; "Bizzell National War Council," *Houston Post*, April 3, 1918; "Nursing at Prairie View," *Bryan Daily Eagle*, June 4, 1918; "Auto Mechanics," *Corsicana Daily Sun*, October 12, 1918; "Men Go to A. & M. and Prairie View," *Fort Worth Star-Telegram*, June 15, 1918; Edward E. Dale, *The Range Cattle Industry: Ranching on the Great Plains from 1865 to 1925* (University of Oklahoma Press, 1960), 167. See also Reid, *Reaping a Greater Harvest*, 39–42. See growth of county agents below:

Extension Agent Growth in the 254 Texas Counties

	1914	1915	1916	1917		1918
Men	98	99	90	92		178
Women	26	27	38	31		67
					Total (1918)	245

Source: True, *History of Agricultural Extension Work*, 200–201.

19. "Vaccinations for La Grippe," *Houston Daily Post*, December 26, 1898; "Typhoid at College: Total Twenty-Five Cases," *Dallas Morning News*, May 25, 1907; "A. and M. Closing," *Houston Post*, May 26, 1907; "Meningitis in Bryan," *Bryan Daily Eagle*, January 27, 1912; "A. & M. Cadet Dies: Meningitis at College Station," *Dallas Morning News*, January 16, 1913; John H. Barry, *The Great Influenza: The Story of the Deadliest Pandemic in History* (Penguin Books, 2004), 176–93; "Spanish Influenza," *Bryan Daily*

Eagle, October 2, 1918; "Uncle Sam's Advice on Flu," *Bryan Daily Eagle*, October 18, 1918. See also John A. Adams Jr., *Over There in the Air: The Fightin' Texas Aggies in World War I, 1917–1918* (Texas A&M University Press, 2020), 49–56; Jeremy Brown, *Influenza* (Touchstone, 2018), 51–53.

20. "Pneumonia Kills Four at Travis: Influenza Grows," *San Antonio Express*, October 10, 1918; "Pneumonia Cases Are Decreasing in Army Camps," *San Antonio Express*, October 15, 1918; "All Draft Calls for October Are Suspended," *Shiner Gazette*, October 17, 1918; Berg, *Wilson*, 474–75, 505–6; Brown, *Influenza*, 50–60; Catherine Arnold, *Pandemic 1918* (St. Martin's Griffin, 2018), 145–52.
21. "Seven More Dead in 48 Hour College Death Toll," *Bryan Daily Eagle*, October 14, 1918; "Deplorable College Conditions Condemned by Defense Council," *Bryan Daily Eagle*, October 10, 1918; "La Epidemia de la Influenza esta Decreciendo Notablemente en el Campo Travis," *San Antonio La Presa*, October 12, 1918; interview with Charles Crawford, March 30, 1971, quoted in Dethloff, *Centennial History of Texas A&M*, vol. 1, 280; "Football for 1918," *A&M College Alumni Quarterly*, November 1918, 5. See also Arnold, *Pandemic 1918*.
22. Purvis Carter, "Robert L. Smith and the Farmers' Improvement Society, a Self-Help Movement in Texas," *Negro History Bulletin* 29 (1966): 175–91; Merline Pitre, "Robert Lloyd Smith: A Black Lawmaker in the Shadow of Booker T. Washington," *Phylon (1960–)* 46, no. 3 (1985): 262–68; Barr, *Black Texans*, 105–7; Earl W. Crosby, "The Roots of Black Agricultural Extension Work," *Historian* 39, no. 2 (1977): 228–47; General Laws of Texas (1911), 105–6, TSLA; Ousley, *History of the Agricultural and Mechanical College*, 138–40; Martin, *Decade of Negro Extension Work*, 3, 11–12, 21–22. Quote on "ten acres" from Earl W. Crosby, "Limited Success Against Long Odds," *Agricultural History* 57, no. 3 (1983): 277–88. For the early roots and evolution of the extension service, see Allen W. Jones, "The Role of Tuskegee Institute in the Education of Black Farmers," *Journal of Negro History* 60, no. 2 (1975): 254–56; True, *History of Agricultural Extension Work*, 3–41.
23. Reid, *Reaping a Greater Harvest*, 14.
24. True, *History of Agricultural Extension Work*, 58–61; Reid, *Reaping a Greater Harvest*, 17; "Silver Anniversary," Texas A&M Extension Service, Historical File, box 2, ELCA; Pete Daniel, *Breaking the Land: The Transformation of Cotton, Tobacco, and Rice Culture since 1880* (University of Illinois Press, 1986), 41–45. See also Wiebe, *Search for Order*, 119–27; Henry C. Dethloff, *A History of the American Rice Industry, 1685–1985* (Texas A&M University Press, 2000), 78–80.
25. Houston, *Eight Years with Wilson's Cabinet*, vol. 1, 203–4; Ousley, *History of the Agricultural and Mechanical College*, 137–40; Woodward, *Origins of the*

New South, 410–11. Houston in his memoir refers to the A&M College of Texas as "Texas State College of Agriculture."

26. "Wilson's Views," *Houston Post*, November 4, 1903. It was not unusual for a newspaper reporter to accompany visiting parties and thus be present on the train trip to record a firsthand report.
27. E. L. Blackshear to Governor Colquitt, July 14 and 16, 1914, Oscar B. Colquitt Papers, TSLA; "Declares City Teacher in Rural School Outrage," *Austin Statesman*, July 14, 1914; Minutes of the A&M Board of Directors, June 30, 1896, ELCA; Larry D. Hill and Robert A. Calvert, "The University of Texas Extension Services and Progressivism," *Southwestern Historical Quarterly* 86, no. 2 (1983): 231–35; Matthews, "The Early Years of the Permanent University Fund," 81–85; Houston, *Eight Years With Wilson's Cabinet*, vol. 1, 204; Reid, *Reaping a Greater Harvest*, 16.
28. E. B. Cushing to O. B. Colquitt, June 3, 1914, Oscar B. Colquitt Papers, TSLA; O. B. Colquitt, *Educational Amendment Elucidated* [pamphlet], June 27, 1913, Oscar B. Colquitt Papers, TSLA; Minutes of the A&M Board of Directors, June 10, 1914, ELCA; Ousley, *History of the Agricultural and Mechanical College*, 81; Dethloff, *Centennial History of Texas A&M*, vol. 1, 231–35; Hill and Calvert, "The University of Texas Extension Service," 235–39; True, *History of Agricultural Extension Work*, 60–61; Gould, "The University Becomes Politicized," 259. The Smith-Lever Act was passed by Congress in May 1914 and the Texas legislature accepted provisions of the act on January 29, 1915. For an excellent overview of the Hatch Act and Smith-Lever Act, see Seals, "Formation of Agricultural and Rural Development Policy," 12–34. See also Miller, *Public Lands of Texas*, 185–211.
29. "Negro's Needs," *Houston Daily Post*, December 9, 1910; E. L. Blackshear, "To the Colored Farmers of Texas," *Hallettsville Herald*, July 2, 1915.
30. E. B. Cushing to O. B. Colquitt, June 3, 1914; "Blackshear Speaks on Negro Rural Schools," *Dallas Morning News*, July 17, 1914; "Blackshear Doing Extension Service Work with Negroes," *Bryan Weekly Eagle*, November 8, 1917; "Will Do Extension Work," *Houston Daily Post*, November 20 and 28, 1917; "Food Conservation," *Houston Daily Post*, January 13, 1918; "Blackshear to Teach Negroes to Save Food," *Bellville Times*, November 29, 1917; "2,000 Negros at Patriotic Mass Meeting," *Austin Statesman*, March 11, 1918; "Wharton Grand Parade," *San Antonio Express*, May 17, 1918; Reid, *Reaping a Greater Harvest*, 35. See also Davis, "The Negro Land-Grant College," 319–21; Schor, *Agriculture in the Black Land-Grant System*, 35–36. Some expressed concerns that a black cooperative extension program would be difficult to start, but this was not the case in Texas. See Carmen V. Harris, "'The Extension Service Is Not an Integration Agency': The Idea of Race in the Cooperative Extension Service," *Agricultural History* 82, no. 2 (2008): 193–219.

31. "Brief History of Extension Work Among Negroes in Texas, 1915–1948," Texas Agricultural Extension Service Papers, file 4, box 4, ELCA; Walton Peteet, *Farming Credit in Texas*, 5, 10–11, 22, 79, A&M College Extension, bulletin no. B-34 (February 1917), ELCA; "Extension Department," *Annual Catalogue* (1918–19), 70. See also Gatlin, *Cooperative Marketing of Cotton*, 3–4.
32. "Extension Service: Boll Weevil Dispersion," *Prairie View Standard*, September 18, 1915, CLA; "Extension Work," *Prairie View Standard*, September 25, 1915, CLA; "Facts About Negro Home Demonstration Work in Texas," ELCA; Mary Hunter, "History of Extension Service Among Negroes in Texas, Brief History Summary," TAEX Historical File, ELCA; Woolfolk, *Prairie View*, 340–42; Reid, *Reaping a Greater Harvest*, 22–38; Barr, *Reconstruction to Reform*, 95.
33. "Brief History of Extension Work Among Negroes in Texas"; E. L. Blackshear, "The Capacity of the Negro Race," *Houston Post*, April 25, 1915. In 1915 Blackshear published a revised list from information gained from Seaman Knapp, his "Ten Agricultural Commandments":

    1. Remove all surplus water from soil
    2. Deep fall plowing and winter cover
    3. Proper spacing of plants
    4. Intensive cultivation & rotation of crops
    5. Use best seeds available for quality
    6. Judicious use of manure and fertilizers
    7. Home production of food for family
    8. Use more horsepower and machinery
    9. Raise more stock and forage
    10. Keep accurate records on farm operations

34. "To Colored Farmers," *Bryan Eagle*, March 18, 1918; U.S. Bureau of the Census, *Agriculture: Texas*, 14th census, 1920 (Government Printing Office, 1922), 4; U.S. Bureau of the Census, *Farm Tenancy in the United States*, Census Monographs, IV (Government Printing Office, 1924), 214; Ousley, *History of the Agricultural and Mechanical College*, 138; Dethloff, *Centennial History of Texas A&M*, vol. 2, 382–404; Shannon, *The Farmer's Last Frontier*, 88–100; Myrdal, *American Dilemma*, vol. 1, 246; Rice, *Negro in Texas*, 165.
35. General Laws of the State of Texas (1903), 74, TSLA; General Laws of the State of Texas (1909), 220, TSLA; *Biennial Report*, Texas A&M, 1903 and 1904, 4–5, 20–21, ELCA; *Dallas Morning News*, July 7, 1902; *Bryan Eagle*, May 5, 1904; Dethloff, *Centennial History of Texas A&M*, vol. 1, 249.
36. E. L. Blackshear to Governor O. B. Colquitt, December 1, 1914, Oscar B. Colquitt Papers, TSLA. See also Shannon, *The Farmer's Last Frontier*, 90–95, 110–17, 338–41.

37. "Southern Negro Is Being Robbed," *Austin Statesman*, August 5, 1918; "Blackshear's Letter on Swindlers," *Dallas Morning News*, July 7, 1918; Gould, *Progressives and Prohibitionists*, 151–52.
38. "Attempts to Cheat Negroes out of Liberty Bonds Reported," *Dallas Morning News*, May 1, 1918, and July 7, 1918; "Prairie View's Record," *Houston Post*, December 26, 1920; Wooster, *Texas and Texans in the Great War*, 104–6, 166–67; Theodore Roosevelt Blackshear registration card, September 12, 1918, order number 620, Local Board Waller County, Hempstead, Texas, CLA; "A. & M. to Assist in After-War Work," *Daily Bulletin* (Brownwood, TX), February 12, 1818; Barr, *Black Texans*, 114–15; Prairie View, *Alumni Directory, 2004* (Prairie View Alumni Association, 2005), 524. See also Margaret B. Baker, "The Texas Negro and the World War" (master's thesis, University of Texas, 1938).
39. Woodward, *The Strange Career of Jim Crow*, 114; Oscar J. Martinez, *Border People: Life and Society in the U. S.–Mexico Borderlands* (University of Arizona Press, 1994), 262–63.
40. E. L. Blackshear, "To Better Farming Skills of Negros," *Houston Daily Post*, January 13, 1918 (emphasis in original). See also "Negro Framers Praised for Patriotic Work," *Galveston Daily News*, February 1, 1919.
41. "Conservation Was Theme of Meeting," *Houston Post*, January 7, 1918; "E. L. Blackshear Interested in Government Insurance for the Negro," *Dallas Express*, March 15, 1919; "Tuskegee, Alabama," *Kansas City Sun*, March 22, 1919; Crosby, "Struggle for Existence," 135–37; Gould, *Progressives and Prohibitionists*, 135, 153–54; "Strategic Centers," *Star of Zion*, June 24, 1920.
42. Earl W. Crosby, "Struggle for Existence," 123–36.
43. Reid, *Reaping a Greater Harvest*, 35–41.
44. E. L. Blackshear to Dear Colleague, March 23, 1919, MS 100011, Race and Segregation Collection, Woodrow Wilson Presidential Papers, ELCA.
45. Seals, "Formation of Agriculture and Rural Development Policy," 31; True, *History of Agricultural Extension Work*, 110–12, 116, 123; Bullock, *History of Negro Education*, 138; Wooster, *Texas and Texans in the Great War*, 70–71. President Wilson agreed with Secretary Houston that the Smith-Lever Act was "one of the most significant and far reaching measures for education of adults ever adopted by the government." See also *Prairie View Standard*, September 18, 1915, CLA.
46. E. L. Blackshear, "Industrial Training and the Race Question," *Southern Workman*, July 1906, 398–400; "State Colored Farmers' Congress," *Prairie View Standard*, July 7, 1917, CLA; Bizzell, *Green Rising*, 200; Fultz, "African American Teachers in the South," 401–22; Joan Malczewski, "Philanthropy and Progressive Era State Building Through Agricultural Extension Work in the Jim Crow South," *History of Education Quarterly* 53, no. 4 (2013): 370, 398–99.

47. T. O. Walton, *Annual Report of the Extension Service of the A&M College of Texas* (A. and M. Extension Service, 1920), 110–11, ELCA; "Negroes to Give Exhibit of Farm Products," *Houston Post*, July 17, 1918; "Colored Farmers' Congress a Success," *Houston Post*, August 5, 1917; "Negroes to Give Exhibit," *Calvert Courier*, July 19, 1918. See also Mercier, *Extension Work Among Negroes—1920*, 3–11.
48. E. L. Blackshear, "To Better Farming Skill of Negroes," *Monitor* (Omaha), February 9, 1918; "Prairie View Estimates Filed," *Dallas Morning News*, January 9, 1915; T. O. Walton to Bradford Knapp, December 31, 1918, record group 16, NARA; Woolfolk, *Prairie View*, 340–42. See also Jones, *Negro Education*, vol. 2, 567–606.
49. Memo, Mrs. Nat P. Jackson to Clarence Ousley, January 4, 1917, Annual Report, Texas Extension Service, box 2, ELCA; Mercier, *Extension Work Among Negroes—1920*, 1–24; "Vote to Reduce Cotton Crop of South One-Third," *Houston Post*, February 23, 1919; Tindall, *Emergence of the New South*, 15; Buenger, *Path to a Modern South*, 46–47. For the national extension service impact, see Danbom, "Agricultural Extension," 315–31; Schor, *Agriculture in the Black Land-Grant System*, 78–79; Dethloff, *Centennial History of Texas A&M*, vol. 1, 265–66, 285.
50. Edward L. Blackshear, Standard Certificate of Death, Bureau of Vital Statistics, Hempstead, Texas, filed February 5, 1920; *Houston City Directory* (1918), 277, TSLA.
51. Reid, *Reaping a Greater Harvest*, xxi. See also "Educating the Negroes," *San Antonio Express*, December 3, 1913.
52. "Veteran Teachers," *Dallas Express*, December 13, 1919; Blackshear to President Wilson, March 23, 1919, MS 100011, Woodrow Wilson Presidential Papers, ELCA; "To the Colored Farmers of Texas," *Hallettsville Herald*, July 2, 1915; Woodward, *The Strange Career of Jim Crow*, 105.
53. E. L. Blackshear, "Industrial Training and the Race Question," *Southern Workman*, December 1905, 400; "E. L. Blackshear, Noted Man of His Race Dies at His Home, Prairie View," *Dallas Express*, December 20, 1919; Woolfolk, *Prairie View*, 40–43; "Blackshear Literary Society," *Prairie View Standard*, July 7, 1917, CLA; C. Fred Williams, "Frustrations Amidst Hope: The Land Grant Mission of Arkansas AM&N College, 1873–1972," *Agricultural History* 65, no. 2 (1991): 115–30. See also *Galveston Daily News*, March 7, 1879.
54. George R. Woolfolk, *The Cotton Regency* (Octagon Books, 1979), 95–97. See also Frank E. Vandiver, *The Southwest: South or West?* (Texas A&M University Press, 1975).
55. "A Good Man's Memory Worthily Honored," *Houston Post*, January 16, 1920; Mercier, *Extension Work Among Negroes—1920*, 24; "Bryan Negro Girl Wins First Prize," *Bryan Daily Eagle*, November 30, 1925; Woolfolk, *Prairie View*, 248.

Selected Bibliography

Archives

Austin History Center, Austin, TX

Wheatville Papers

E. L. Blackshear File

L. C. Anderson File

Auburn University Archives, Auburn, AL

Clarence Ousley Papers

Baylor University Archives, Waco, TX

The Texas Collection

Farmers' Improvement Society of Texas

Smith-Cobb Family Papers

Bennett Library, Rice University, Houston, TX

Norris W. Cuney Collection

Coleman Library and Archives, Prairie View A&M University, Prairie View, TX

Alumni Directory, 2004. Prairie View Alumni Association, 2005.

Annual Catalogue, 1901, 1905, 1914, 1918

Annual Reports

Biennial Report of the Board of Directors of the Prairie View Normal School, December 1890. Austin, 1891.

Biennial Report of the Board of Directors of the Prairie View Normal School, 1894.

Biennial Report of the Prairie View Normal and Industrial College, for the Two Years Beginning September 1, 1904, and Ending August 31, 1906. Austin: Von Boeckmann and Schutze State Printers, 1906.

Blackshear, Edward. "Future of the Negro." *Education of the Colored Race*. Unpublished manuscript, Cameron, Texas, 1898.

Blackshear, Edward L., to the Secretary of State, May 13, 1912. U.S. Department of State, Records of the Department of State Relating to the Internal Affairs of Haiti, 1910–1929.

Blackshear, E. L., clippings file

Calvin Hoffman Waller Papers, 1880–1919

Evans, E. B. "Down Memory Lane: The Story of Edward B. Evans, and the Early History of Prairie View A&M University." 1970.

Negro Extension Photo Inventory

Prairie View Standard, 1913–41
The Prairie '17 (Prairie View annual), 1917
Report of the A&M College for Colored Youths, Alta Vista College. Texas State Press, December 1878; Texas State Government Press, 1878.
Report of the Board of Directors of the State Agricultural and Mechanical College of the State of Texas, Located in Brazos County, March 28, 1882. Austin, 1882.
Report of Prairie View Normal School, December 9, 1882. Austin, 1883.
Report of the Prairie View Normal School for 1885–86. Austin, 1887.
Report of the Prairie View State Normal School. Austin, 1896.
Report of the Prairie View State Normal School. Austin, 1899.
Report of the Prairie View State Normal School, Waller County, Texas. Austin, 1899.
Ross, Lawrence S. "The Education of the Colored Race." Austin, 1890.
Tuskegee Institute. *Negro Year Book, 1912*.

Dallas Historical Society, Dallas, TX
Hatton Sumners Papers

Dolph Briscoe Center for American History, University of Texas, Austin, TX
Archibald J. Rose Papers
James E. Ferguson Collection
James Pearson Newcomb Collection
James S. Hogg Papers
Oscar B. Colquitt Papers
Potts, Charles S. *Railroad Transportation in Texas*. Bulletin of the University of Texas no. 119. Austin, 1909.
Report of the Board of Regents of the University of Texas. Austin, 1886.
Texas Almanac and State Industrial Guide, 1910. A. H. Belo, 1910.
Texas State Department of Education. *Biennial Report of the State Superintendent of Public Instruction of Texas*. State Board of Education, 1916–18 and 1920–22.
Texas State Department of Education. *Historical and Statistical Data as to Education in Texas, 1919–1921*. Bulletin no. 133. Department of Education, 1921.
William P. Hobby Papers
White, E. V., and William E. Leonard. *Studies in Farm Tenancy in Texas*. Bulletin of the University of Texas no. 21. Austin, 1915.

Evans Library and Cushing Archives, Texas A&M University, College Station, TX
Bizzell, William B. "Farm Tenantry in the United States: A Study of the Historical Development of Farm Tenancy and Its Economic and Social Consequences on Rural Welfare, with Special References to Conditions in the South and Southwest." *Texas Agricultural Experiment Station Bulletin*, no. 278. April 1921.

David F. Houston file

Gathright, Thomas S. *Reports of the Agricultural and Mechanical College of Texas, Alta Vista College for Colored Youths*. Galveston, 1878.

Kyle, E. J., et al. *Money Crops in Place of Cotton*. A&M College of Texas bulletin no. 2. College Station, 1914.

McKinley Presidential Papers

Ousley, Clarence. *History of the Agricultural and Mechanical College of Texas*. Bulletin no. 8. A&M College, December 1, 1935.

Page, Bill, ed. "African Americans on College Station and at Texas A&M." April 2, 2014.

———, ed. "The Gathright Papers." March 2016.

———, ed. "John N. Johnson: Bryan's First African American Attorney." March 1, 2019.

———, ed. "Lawrence Sullivan Ross and E. L. Blackshear and Prairie View." August 2022.

———, ed. "Lawrence Sullivan Ross: Working Notes," August 1, 2020

———, ed. "Matthew Gaines." June 6, 2019.

———, ed. "Meetings of the Texas A&M Board of Directors, 1875–1886—with notes on Prairie View." January 25, 2016.

———, ed. "Prairie View in World War I." 2019.

———, ed. "Sources Concerning the Brazos Bottoms and Bravos Valley." March 17, 2017.

Patrons of Husbandry. "Minutes of the Sixth Annual Meeting of the Texas Co-Operation Association, Patrons of Husbandry." Dallas, 1884.

Peteet, Walton. *Farming Credit in Texas*. Bulletin no. B-34. A&M College, February 1917.

Prairie View University Papers, 1915–71

Reports of the Agricultural and Mechanical College of Texas. Austin, 1891–94, 1896, 1899.

Reports on the Agricultural & Mechanical College of Texas and Alta Vista College for Colored Youths. 1878–81.

Ross, Lawrence S. "Education of the Colored Race." Austin, 1890.

Texas Agricultural Extension Service & Historical Files, 1900–20

William H. Taft Presidential Papers, microfilm, 1910

Woodrow Wilson Presidential Papers, microfilm, 1913

Fort Worth Public Library, Fort Worth, TX

Farmers' Alliance Papers, 1874–1893

Franklin Library Special Collections and Archives, Fisk University, Nashville, TN

George Edmund Haynes Collection

Howard University Archives, Washington, DC

Catalogue of Officers and Students, 1901–3

National Archives, Washington, DC

U.S. Bureau of Refugees, Freedmen, and Abandoned Lands. Records of the Superintendent of Education for the State of Texas [part of Record Group 105, on microfilm].

Records of the Office of the Secretary, Record Group 16

Oberlin College Archives, Oberlin, OH

Henry Churchill King Papers

Rosenberg Library Special Collections, Galveston, TX

J. M. Burroughs Papers MSS 04-0049

Rubenstein Library Special Collections, Duke University, Durham, NC

Industrial Training of African Natives, March 1909

Special Collections at the Morris Library, Southern Illinois University, Carbondale, IL

Open Court Publishing Company Records

Texas State Library and Archives Commission, Austin, TX

Blackshear, E. L., L. S. Ross, and Andrew N. Cleven. *Future of the Negro: The Race Problem Discussed*. Cameron, TX: Colored Teachers Institute, 1898.

Colored Teachers State Association. Proceedings, 1895–1904

Constitution of the State of Texas, ratified February 15, 1876

Cooper, Oscar H. *Special Report of the Superintendent of Public Instruction for the Years Ending Aug. 31, 1887*. Austin, 1888.

Eby, Frederick. *Education in Texas: Source Materials*. University of Texas bulletin no. 1824. April 25, 1918.

Eleventh Biennial Report of the State Superintendent of Public Instruction: Years Ending August 31, 1897, and August 31, 1898. Austin, 1898.

Foster, L. L. *Forgotten Texas Census: First Annual Report of the Agricultural Bureau of the Department of Agriculture, Insurance, Statistics, and History, 1887–88*. Austin, 1889.

General Laws of the State of Texas

"Act for the Organization and Support of a Normal School at Prairie View (formerly called Alta Vista)." Regular Session of the Sixteenth Legislature, ch. 159, pp. 181–82, April 24, 1879.

"Act to Establish an Agricultural and Mechanical College of Texas, for the Benefit of the Colored Youths." Session of the Fifteenth Legislature, ch. 92, pp. 136–37, April 18, 1876.

Journal of the House of Representatives of the Twentieth Legislature, Extra Session. Austin, 1888.

Journal of the House of Representatives of the Twenty-Third Legislature, Regular Session. Austin, 1893.

Members of the Texas Legislature, 1846–1962. Texas State Legislature, 1962.

Oscar B. Colquitt Papers

Report of the State Superintendent of Public Schools. Austin, 1893.

State Convention of Colored Men of Texas. *Proceedings of the State Convention of Colored Men of Texas, July 10–12, 1883*. Houston, 1883.
Tenth Biennial Report of the State Superintendent of Public Instruction: Years Ending August 31, 1895, and August 31, 1896. Austin, 1897.
Texas Almanac and Emigrants Guide. Galveston, 1869–74.
Texas School Journal, 1884–1920
Texas State Board of Education Reports
Texas State Journal, 1887–1915
University of Texas. *Investigation by the Board of Regents of the University of Texas Concerning the Conduct of Certain Members of the Faculty*. University of Texas bulletin no. 59. 1916.
William P. Hobby Papers

Tabor Historical Society, Tabor, IA
E. L. Blackshear college records, 1878–81
Hightower M. Kealing college records, 1878–81

Texas Women's University, Denton, TX
Clarence Ousley Papers
Minutes of the CIA/TWU Board of Directors

Woodrow Wilson Presidential Library, Princeton, NJ
Race and Segregation Collection

Yale University Archives, New Haven, CT
Edward M. House Papers

United States Government Documents

Andrews, Benjamin F. *The Land Grant of 1862 and the Land-Grant Colleges*. U.S. Department of Interior, Bureau of Education bulletin no. 18. Government Printing Office, 1918.

Brunner, Henry S. *Land-Grant Colleges and Universities, 1862–1962*. U.S. Department of Health, Education, and Welfare, Office of Education bulletin no. 13. Government Printing Office, 1962.

Caliver, Ambrose, ed. *Bibliography of Education of the Negro*. U.S. Department of Interior, Bureau of Education bulletin no. 17. Government Printing Office, 1931.

Campbell, Thomas M. *The First Historical Report of Agricultural Extension Work Among Negroes in the States of Alabama, Georgia, Florida, Mississippi, Louisiana, Oklahoma, and Texas*. U.S. Department of Agriculture circular no. 1. Government Printing Office, 1920.

Du Bois, W. E. B. "The Negro Farmer." *Negros in the United States*. Bureau of the Census bulletin no. 8. Government Printing Office, 1904.

———. *What the Negro Has Done for the United States and Texas*. Government Printing Office, 1936.

Evans, James A. *Extension Work Among Negroes: Conducted by Negro Agents, 1923*. USDA circular no. 355. Government Printing Office, 1925.

Hall, Charles E. *Progress of the Negro in Texas*. U.S. Department of Commerce, Bureau of the Census, 1936.

Hare, Butler B. "Statistics of Land-Grant Colleges and Agricultural Experiment Stations, 1912." In *Annual Report of the Office of Experiment Stations*, 233–77. Government Printing Office, 1912.

Houston, David F. "Report of the Secretary." *Yearbook of the United States Department of Agriculture*. Government Printing Office, 1914.

John, Walton C., ed. *Land-Grant College Education 1910–1920*. U.S. Department of Interior, Bureau of Education bulletin no. 24. Government Printing Office, 1925.

Jones, Thomas J. *Negro Education: A Study of the Private and Higher Schools for Colored People in the United States*. U.S. Department of Interior, Bureau of Education bulletin no. 39. 2 vols. Government Printing Office, 1916.

Knapp, Seaman A. "The Farmers' Cooperative Demonstration Work." In *USDA Yearbook of Agriculture 1909*, 153–70. Government Printing Office, 1909.

Lane, John J. *History of Education in Texas*. U.S. Bureau of Education. Government Printing Office, 1903.

Martin, O. B. *A Decade of Negro Extension Work, 1914–1924*. U.S. Department of Agriculture circular no. 72. Government Printing Office, 1924.

Mercer, W. B. *Extension Work Among Negroes, 1920*. USDA circular no. 190. Government Printing Office, 1921.

Newton, Roy L., and James M Workman. "Cotton Warehousing—Benefits of an Adequate System." In *USDA Yearbook 1918*. Government Printing Office, 1919.

Plessy v. Ferguson, 163 U.S. 537 (1896).

Select Committee to Investigate the Causes of the Removal of the Negroes from the Southern States to the Northern States. S. Rep. 693-46 (1880).

True, Alfred C. *A History of Agricultural Education in the United States, 1785–1925*. Pub. no. 36. Government Printing Office, 1929.

———. *A History of Agricultural Extension Work in the United States, 1785–1923*. Pub. no. 15. Government Printing Office, 1928.

U.S. Bureau of the Census. *Agriculture: Texas*. 14th census, 1920. Government Printing Office, 1922.

———. *Farm Tenancy in the United States*. Census Monographs, IV. Government Printing Office, 1924.

———. *Population: Occupations, 1920*. Government Printing Office, 1923.

———. *Reports of Agriculture Production*. Government Printing Office, 1880–1930.

U.S. Department of Agriculture. *USDA Yearbook of Agriculture, 1901*. Government Printing Office, 1901.

U.S. Department of Commerce, Bureau of the Census. *Negroes in the United States, 1920–1932*. Government Printing Office, 1935.

———. *The Negro Farmer in the United States*. Government Printing Office, 1933.

———. *Negro Population in the United States, 1790–1915*. Government Printing Office, 1918.

U.S. Department of the Interior, Bureau of Education. National Parks Service. National Register of Historical Places. "Historic and Architectural Resources of Prairie View A&M University, Waller County, Texas." Submitted April 21, 1999.

———. *Report of the Commissioner of Education for the Year Ending June 30, 1907*. Government Printing Office, 1908.

———. *Report of the Commissioner of Education for the Year 1902*. Government Printing Office, 1903.

———. *Report of the United States Commissioner of Education for 1900–1901*. Government Printing Office, 1902.

U.S. Statutes at Large. First Morrill Act. Pub. L. 37-108, 12 Stat. 503 (1862).

U.S. Statutes at Large. Second Morrill Act. Pub. 51-841, 26 Stat. 417 (1890).

Wilkerson, Doxey A. *Agricultural Extension Services Among Negroes in the South*. Conference of Presidents of Negro Land Grant Colleges, 1942.

Interviews

Wayne Sadberry, interview by Todd Moye, July 8, 2015. Civil Rights in Black and Brown Oral History Project, Portal to Texas History, https://texashistory.unt.edu/ark:/67531/metapth836702/m1/.

Captain Frank Johnson, interview with the author, July 1, 2020. Prairie View University.

Books

Adams, John A., Jr. *Murder and Intrigue on the Mexican Border: Governor Colquitt, President Wilson, and the Vergara Affair*. Texas A&M University Press, 2018.

———. *Sul Ross at Texas A&M*. Texas A&M University Press, 2022.

———. *William F. Buckley: Witness to the Mexican Revolution, 1908–1921*. University of Oklahoma Press, 2023.

Anderson, James D. *The Education of Blacks in the South, 1860–1935*. University of North Carolina Press, 1988.

———, ed. *New Perspectives on Black Educational History*. G. K. Hall, 1978.

Avary, Myrta L. *Dixie After the War: An Exposition of Social Conditions Existing in the South*. Doubleday, 1906.

Ayers, Edward L. *The Promise of the New South: Life After Reconstruction*. Oxford University Press, 1992.

Barnes, Donna A. *Farmers in Rebellion: The Rise and Fall of the Southern Farmers Alliance and People's Party in Texas*. University of Texas Press, 1984.

Barr, Alwyn. *The African Texans*. Texas A&M University Press, 2004.

———. *Black Texans: A History of African Americans in Texas, 1528–1995*. 2nd ed. University of Oklahoma Press, 1996.

———. *Reconstruction and Reform: Texas Politics, 1876–1906*. University of Texas Press, 1971.

Barr, Alwyn, and Robert A. Calvert, eds. *Black Leaders: Texans for Their Times*. Texas State Historical Association, 1981.

Basler, Roy P., ed. *The Collected Works of Abraham Lincoln*. Vol. 5. Sesquicentennial Commission, 1959.

Bateman, David A., Ira Katznelson, and John S. Lapinski. *Southern Nation: Congress and White Supremacy After Reconstruction*. Russell Sage Foundation, 2018.

Battle-Baptiste, Whitney, and Britt Rusert, eds. *W. E. B. Du Bois's Data Portraits: Visualizing Black America; The Color Line at the Turn of the Twentieth Century*. Princeton Architectural Press, 2018.

Beard, Augustus F. *A Crusade of Brotherhood: A History of the American Missionary Association*. Pilgrim Press, 1909.

Beeth, Howard, and Cary D. Wintz, eds. *Black Dixie: Afro-Texan History and Culture in Houston*. Texas A&M University Press, 1992.

Benedict, H. Y. *A Source Book Relating to the History of the University of Texas*. University of Texas, 1917.

Benner, Judith Ann. *Sul Ross: Soldier, Statesman, Educator*. Texas A&M University Press, 1983.

Berlin, Ira. *Slaves Without Masters: The Free Negro in the Antebellum South*. New Press, 1974.

Berry, Daina R., and Kali N. Gross. *A Black Women's History of the United States*. Beacon Press, 2020.

Bizzell, William B. *The Green Rising*. Macmillan, 1926.

Blackshear, Edward L. *The Education of Childhood*. New York, 1911.

———. *Future of the Negro: The Race Problem Discussed*. Prairie View, 1898.

Blackshear, Edward L., and J. Weslay Hoffman. *Industrial Training of African Natives*. State Normal & Industrial College, March 1909.

Blanton, Carlos K. *The Strange Career of Bilingual Education in Texas, 1836–1981*. Texas A&M University Press, 2004.

Blight, David W. *Frederick Douglass: Prophet of Freedom*. Simon & Schuster, 2018.

Boykin, Anne, ed. *The Italians of Steele's Store, Texas & Brazos Valley Italians*. Left-Write Ink Boos, 2019.

Brands, H. W. *American Colossus: The Triumph of Capitalism, 1865–1900*. Doubleday, 2010.

Brannon-Wranosky, Jessica, and Bruce A. Glasrud, eds. *Impeached: The Removal of Texas Governor James E. Ferguson*. Texas A&M University Press, 2017.

Brewer, John Mason. *Negro Legislators of Texas and Their Descendants*. Mathis, 1935.

Britton, Karen G. *Bale o' Cotton: The Mechanical Art of Cotton Ginning*. Texas A&M University Press, 1992.

Brown, John Henry. *History of Texas, from 1685 to 1892*. Vol. 2. St. Louis, 1893.

Bryson, Conrey. *Dr. Lawrence A. Nixon and the White Primary*. Texas Western Press, 1972.

Buenger, Walter L. *The Path to a Modern South: Northwest Texas Between Reconstruction and the Great Depression*. University of Texas Press, 2001.

Buenger, Walter L., and Robert A. Calvert, eds. *Texas Through Time: Evolving Interpretations*. Texas A&M University Press, 1991.

Buenger, Walter L., and Walter D. Kamphoefner, eds. *Preserving German Texan Identity: Reminiscences of William A. Trenckmann, 1859–1935*. Texas A&M University Press, 2019.

Bullock, Henry Allen. *A History of Negro Education in the South from 1619 to the Present*. Harvard University Press, 1967.

Burrows, John H. *The Necessity of Myth: A History of the Negro Business League, 1900–1945*. Hickory Hill Press, 1988.

Campbell, Randolph B. *Gone to Texas: A History of the Lone Star State*. Oxford University Press, 2003.

———. *Grass-Roots Reconstruction in Texas, 1865–1880*. Louisiana State University Press, 1997.

———. *A Southern Community in Crisis: Harrison County, Texas, 1850–1880*. Texas State Historical Association, 2016.

Cantrell, Gregg. *Feeding the Wolf: John B. Rayner & the Politics of Race, 1850–1918*. Harlan Davidson, 2001.

———. *The People's Revolt: Texas Populists and the Roots of American Liberalism*. Yale University Press, 2020.

Casdorph, Paul D. *A History of the Republican Party of Texas, 1865–1965*. Pemberton Press, 1965.

Catalog of Tabor College, 1877–78. Tabor, IA, 1878.

Clark, George. *A Glance Backwards, or Some Events in the Past History of My Life*. Rein & Sons, 1914.

Cofer, David Brooks, ed. *Early History of Texas A. and M. College Through Letters and Papers*. Association of Former Students, 1952.

———. *First Five Administrations of Texas A. & M. College*. Association of Former Students, 1952.

Compayre, Gabriel. *The History of Pedagogy*. London, 1900.

Cooper, Lewis B. *The Permanent School Fund of Texas*. Texas State Teachers Association, 1934.

Cotner, Robert C., ed. *Addresses and State Papers of James S. Hogg*. University of Texas Press, 1951.

———. *James Stephen Hogg: A Biography*. University of Texas Press, 1959.

Crawford, C. W. *One Hundred Years of Engineering at Texas A&M, 1876–1976*. Privately published, 1976.

Crouch, Barry A. *The Freedmen's Bureau and Black Texans*. University of Texas Press, 1992.

Culp, D. W., ed. *Twentieth Century Negro Literature, or A Cyclopedia of Thought on the Vital Topics Relating to the American Negro by One Hundred of America's Greatest Negroes*. J. L. Nichols, 1902.

Curry, J. L. M. *A Brief Sketch of George Peabody and a History of the Peabody Education Fund Through Thirty Years*. Cambridge, MA, 1898.

Dailey, Maceo C., Will Guzmán, and David H. Jackson, eds. *Emmett J. Scott*. Texas Tech University Press, 2023.

Dale, Edward E. *The Range Cattle Industry: Ranching on the Great Plains from 1865 to 1925*. University of Oklahoma Press, 1960.

Daniel, Pete. *Breaking the Land: The Transformation of Cotton, Tobacco, and Rice Cultures Since 1880*. University of Illinois Press, 1986.

Davis, William R. *The Development and Present Status of Negro Education in East Texas*. Columbia University Bureau of Publication, 1934.

DeCanio, Stephen. *Agriculture in the Postbellum South: The Economics of Production and Supply*. Massachusetts Institute of Technology Press, 1974.

Denton, Virginia L. *Booker T. Washington and the Adult Education Movement*. University Press of Florida, 1993.

Dethloff, Henry C. *A Centennial History of Texas A&M University, 1876–1976*. 2 vols. Texas A&M University Press, 1975.

———. *A History of the American Rice Industry, 1685–1985*. Texas A&M University Press, 1988.

———. *A List of References for the History of the Farmers' Alliance and the Populist Party*. Agricultural History Center, University of California, 1973.

Dethloff, Henry C., and Irvin M. May, eds. *Southwestern Agriculture: Pre-Columbian to Modern*. Texas A&M University Press, 1982.

Donalson, Barbara. *Kyle Tough*. Oaks Press, 2003.

Drimmer, Melvin, ed. *Black History: A Reappraisal*. Doubleday, 1968.

Du Bois, W. E. B. *Against Racism: Unpublished Essays, Papers, Addresses, 1887–1961*. Edited by Herbert Aptheker. University of Massachusetts Press, 1985.

———. *The Autobiography of W. E. B. Du Bois: A Soliloquy of Viewing My Life from the Last Decade of the First Century*. International Publishers, 1968.

———. *Black Reconstruction*. Russell and Russell, 1935.

———, ed. *The College-Bred Negro: Report of a Social Study Made Under the Direction of Atlanta University, Together with Proceedings of the Fifth*

Conference for the Study of the Negro Problem, Atlanta, May 29–30, 1900. Atlanta University Press, 1900.
———. *John Brown: A Biography.* George W. Jacobs, 1909.
———, ed. *The Negro Church: Report of a Social Study Made upon the Direction of Atlanta University.* Atlanta University Press, 1903.
———. *A Select Bibliography of the Negro American.* Atlanta University Press, 1905.
———. *The Souls of Black Folk.* Atlanta, 1903. Reprint, Millennium Publications, 2014.
Duster, Alfreda M., ed. *Crusade for Justice: The Autobiography of Ida B. Wells.* University of Chicago Press, 2020.
Eby, Frederick. *The Development of Education in Texas.* Macmillan, 1925.
Eddy, Edward D. *Colleges for Our Land and Time: The Land-Grant Idea in American Education.* Harper & Row, 1957.
Erkhardt, Carl J. *Presidents of the University of Texas.* Austin, [1973?].
Evans, Cecil E. *The Story of Texas Schools.* Steck, 1955.
Fishel, Leslie H., and Benjamin Quarles. *The Negro American: A Documentary History.* Scott, Foresman, 1967.
Fite, Gilbert C. *Cotton Fields No More: Southern Agriculture, 1865–1980.* University Press of Kentucky, 1984.
Foley, Neil. *The White Scourge: Mexicans, Blacks, and Poor Whites in Texas Cotton Culture.* University of California Press, 1997.
Foreman, P. Gabrielle, Jim Casey, and S. L. Patterson. *The Colored Conventions Movement: Black Organizing in the Nineteenth Century.* University of North Carolina Press, 2021.
Frantz, Edward O. *The Door of Hope.* University of Florida Press, 2011.
Gammel, H. P., ed. *The Laws of Texas, 1822–1897.* Vol. 8. Austin, 1898.
———, ed. *The Laws of Texas, 1822–1897.* Vol. 9. Austin, 1898.
Gantt, Fred. *The Chief Executive in Texas: A Study in Gubernatorial Leadership.* University of Texas Press, 1964.
Gardner, Eric. *Black Print Unbound: The Christian Recorder, African American Literature, and Periodical Culture.* Oxford University Press, 2015.
Gatewood, Willard B. *Black Americans and the White Man's Burden, 1898–1903.* University of Illinois Press, 1975.
Glasrud, Bruce A., ed. *African Americans in South Texas History.* Texas A&M University Press, 2011.
Glasrud, Bruce A., and Deborah M. Liles, eds. *African Americans in Central Texas History.* Texas A&M University Press, 2018.
Glasrud, Bruce A., and Merline Pitre, eds. *Black Women in Texas History.* Texas A&M University Press, 2008.
Goodwin, Ronald E. *Remembering the Days of Sorrow.* State House Press, 2013.

Gould, Lewis L. *Alexander Watkins Terrell: Civil War Soldier, Texas Lawmaker, American Diplomat*. University of Texas Press, 2004.
———. *Progressives and Prohibitionists: Texas Democrats in the Wilson Era*. University of Texas Press, 1973.
Gems of Poesy. Delhaye, 1905.
Governors' Messages: Coke to Ross, 1874–1891. Texas State Library, 1916.
Grady, Henry W. *The New South*. New York, 1890.
Green, Hilary. *Educational Reconstruction*. Fordham University Press, 2016.
Gulley, F. A. *First Lessons in Agriculture*. New York, 1892.
Gutman, Herbert G. *The Black Family in Slavery and Freedom, 1750–1925*. Pantheon Books, 1976.
Hales, Douglas. *A Southern Family in White and Black: The Cuneys of Texas*. Texas A&M University Press, 2003.
Haney, Robert L. *Milestones Marking Ten Decades of Research: Texas Agricultural Experiment Station*. Texas Agricultural Experiment Station, 1989.
Hare, Maud Cuney. *Norris Wright Cuney: A Tribune of the Black People*. G. K. Hall, 1995.
Harlan, Louis R. *Booker T. Washington: The Making of a Black Leader, 1856–1901*. Oxford University Press, 1972.
———. *Booker T. Washington: The Wizard of Tuskegee, 1901–1915*. Oxford University Press, 1983.
Harlan, Louis R., and Raymond W. Smock, eds. *The Booker T. Washington Papers*. 12 vols. University of Illinois Press, 1990.
Haynes, Robert V. *A Night of Violence: The Houston Riot of 1917*. Louisiana State University Press, 1976.
Heintze, Michael R. *Private Black Colleges in Texas, 1865–1954*. Texas A&M University Press, 1985.
Hendrickson, Kenneth E. *The Chief Executives of Texas*. Texas A&M University Press, 1995.
Hesseltine, William B., and David L. Smiley, eds. *The South in American History*. Prentice Hall, 1960.
Hicks, John D. *The Populist Revolt: A History of the Farmers' Alliance and the People's Party*. University of Minnesota Press, 1931.
Hirshson, Stanley P. *Farewell to the Bloody Shirt*. Quadrangle Books, 1962.
Hoffman, Frederick L. *Race Traits and Tendencies of the American Negro*. New York, 1896.
Holmes, Dwight O. W. *The Evolution of the Negro College*. Arno Press, 1949.
Houston, David F. *Eight Years with Wilson's Cabinet, 1913–1920*. 2 vols. Doubleday, 1926.
Hullinger, Edwin W. *Plowing Through: The Story of the Negro in Agriculture*. William Morrow, 1940.

Hunt, Robert L. *A History of Farmer Movements in the Southwest, 1873–1925*. Texas A. & M. Press, 1935.

Hurt, R. Douglas, ed. *African American Life in the Rural South, 1900–1950*. University of Missouri Press, 2003.

Industrial Advantages of Houston, Texas and Environs. Akehurst, 1984.

Johnson, Frank W., et al. *A History of Texas and Texans*. American Historical Society, 1914.

Jones, Billy M. *The Search for Maturity: The Saga of Texas, 1875–1900*. Steck-Vaughn, 1965.

Jones, C. Allan. *Texas Roots: Agriculture and Rural Life Before the Civil War*. Texas A&M University Press, 2005.

Jones, Howard. *The Red Dairy: A Chronological History of Black Americans in Houston and Some Neighboring Harris County Communities—122 Years Later*. Nortex Press, 1991.

Jones, Lance G. E. *Negro Schools in the Southern States*. Clarendon Press, 1928.

Katz, Fredrick. *The Secret War in Mexico: Europe, the United States and the Mexican Revolution*. University of Chicago Press, 1981.

Kealing, H. T. *History of African Methodism in Texas*. Waco, 1885.

Kendi, Ibram X. *Stamped from the Beginning*. Bold Type Books, 2016.

Kennedy, David M. *Over Here: The First World War and American Society*. Oxford University Press, 1980.

Kousser, J. Morgan. *The Shaping of Southern Politics: Suffrage Restriction and the Establishment of the One-Party South, 1880–1920*. Yale University Press, 1974.

Lamb, Daniel S., ed. *Howard University Medical Department: A Historical, Biographical and Statistical Souvenir*. Washington, DC, 1900.

Lane, John J. *History of the University of Texas Based on Facts and Records*. Austin, 1891.

Luxenberg, Steve. *Separate: The Story of Plessy v. Ferguson, and America's Journey from Slavery to Segregation*. W. W. Norton, 2019.

Marcus, Alan I., ed. *Science as Service: Establishing and Reformulating American Land-Grant Universities, 1865–1930*. University of Alabama Press, 2015.

Martin, O. B. *The Demonstration Work: Dr. Seaman A. Knapp's Contribution to Civilization*. Naylor, 1941.

Martin, Roscoe. *The People's Party in Texas: A Study in Third-Party Politics*. University of Texas bulletin no. 3308. 1933.

Martinez, Oscar J. *Border People: Life and Society in the U.S.–Mexico Borderlands*. University of Arizona Press, 1994.

Mather, Frank L. ed. *Who's Who of the Colored Race*. Vol. 1. Chicago, 1915.

Matthews, Charles R. *Higher Education in Texas: Its Beginnings to 1970*. University of North Texas Press, 2018.

McDaniel, Curtis E. *Educational and Social Interests of the Grange in Texas, 1873–1905*. Austin, 1938.

McDaniel, Vernon. *History of the Teachers State Association of Texas*. National Education Association, 1977.

McKay, Seth S., ed. *Debates of the Texas Constitution of 1875*. Texas Technological College Press, 1942.

———. *Making the Texas Constitution of 1876*. University of Pennsylvania Press, 1924.

———. *Seven Decades of the Texas Constitution of 1876*. S. S. McKay, 1942.

Mears, Michelle M. *And Grace Will Lead Me Home*. Texas Tech University Press, 2009.

Meier, August. *Negro Thought in America, 1880–1915*. University of Michigan Press, 1963.

Miller, Thomas L. *The Public Lands of Texas, 1519–1970*. University of Oklahoma Press, 1972.

Minutaglio, Bill. *A Single Star and Bloody Knuckles: A History of Politics and Race in Texas*. University of Texas Press, 2021.

Moneyhon, Carl L. *George T. Ruby: Champion of Equal Rights in Reconstruction Texas*. Texas A&M University Press, 2020.

Montejano, David. *Anglos and Mexicans in the Making of Texas, 1836–1986*. University of Texas Press, 1987.

Moore, Jacqueline M. *Booker T. Washington, W. E. B. Du Bois, and the Struggle for Racial Uplift*. SR Books, 2003.

Moore, James T. *Through Fire and Flood: The Catholic Church in Frontier Texas, 1836–1900*. Texas A&M University Press, 1992.

Morris, Robert C. *Reading, 'Riting, and Reconstruction: The Education of Freedmen in the South, 1861–1870*. University of Chicago Press, 1981.

Myrdal, Gunnar. *An American Dilemma: The Negro Problem and Modern Democracy*. 2 vols. Harper Torchbooks, 1944.

The New Texas Reader: Designed for the Use in Schools of Texas. Houston, 1864.

Neyland, Leedell W. *Historically Black Land-Grant Institutions and the Development of Agricultural and Home Economics, 1890–1990*. Florida A&M University Foundation, 1990.

Nordin, D. Sven. *Rich Harvest: A History of the Grange, 1867–1900*. University Press of Mississippi, 1974.

Olmsted, Frederick Law. *The Cotton Kingdom: A Traveller's Observations on Cotton and Slavery in the American Slave States, 1853–1861*. New York, 1861.

Oubre, Claude F. *Forty Acres and a Mule: The Freedmen's Bureau and Black Land Ownership*. Louisiana State University Press, 1978.

Owen, Thomas M. *History of Alabama and Dictionary of Alabama Biography*. Reprint Company, 1978.

Painter, Nell I. *Exodusters: Black Migration to Kansas After Reconstruction*. W. W. Norton, 1976.

Pipkin, J. J. *The Story of a Rising Race: The Negro in Revelation, in History and in Citizenship*. St. Louis: N. D. Thompson, [1902?].

Pitre, Merline. *Through Many Dangers, Toils, and Snares: The Black Leadership of Texas, 1868–1900*. Eakin Press, 1985. Reprint by Texas A&M University Press, 2016.

Platt, Harold L. *City Building in the New South: The Growth of Public Services in Houston, Texas, 1830–1910*. Temple University Press, 1983.

Procter, Ben, and Archie P. McDonald, eds. *The Texas Heritage*. Harlan Davidson, 1998.

Ramsdell, Charles W. *Reconstruction in Texas*. Columbia University Press, 1910.

Red Book of Houston: A Compendium of Social, Professional, Religious, Educational and Industrial Interests of Houston's Colored Population. Houston: Sotex, [1915?].

Reed, St. Clair G. *A History of the Texas Railroad*. St. Clair, 1941.

Reid, Debra A. *Reaping a Greater Harvest: African Americans, the Extension Service, and Rural Reform in Jim Crow Texas*. Texas A&M University Press, 2007.

Reuter, Edward B. *The Mulatto in the United States: A Study of the Role of Mixed-Blood Races Throughout the World*. Richard G. Badger, 1918. Reprint, University Press of the Pacific, 2004.

Rice, Lawrence. *The Negro in Texas, 1877–1900*. Louisiana University Press, 1971.

Richardson, Joe M. *Christian Reconstruction: The American Missionary Association and Southern Blacks, 1861–1890*. University of Alabama Press, 2009.

Richardson, Rupert N. *Colonel Edward M. House—The Texas Years, 1858–1912*. Abilene Printing, 1964.

Richings, G. F. *Evidences of Progress Among Colored People*. Geo. S. Ferguson, 1904.

Richter, William L. *Overreached on All Sides: The Freedmen's Bureau Administration in Texas, 1865–1868*. Texas A&M University Press, 1991.

Rodgers, Daniel T. *The Work Ethic in Industrial America, 1850–1920*. University of Chicago Press, 1974.

Roosevelt, Kermit. *The Nation That Never Was: Reconstructing America's Story*. University of Chicago Press, 2022.

Rozek, Barbara. *Come to Texas: Attracting Immigrants, 1865–1915*. Texas A&M University Press, 2003.

Rudwick, Elliott M. *Propagandist of the Negro Protest*. Atheneum, 1968.

Saloutos, Theodore. *Farmer Movements in the South, 1865–1933*. University of California Press, 1960.

Schor, Joel. *Agriculture in the Black Land-Grant System to 1930*. Florida A&M University Press, 1982.

Schor, Joel, and Cecil Harvey. *A List of References for the History of Black Americans in Agriculture, 1619–1974*. Agricultural History Center, 1975.

Schmelzer, Janet. *The Fighting Governor: The Life of Thomas M. Campbell and the Politics of Progressive Reform in Texas*. Texas A&M University Press, 2014.

Scott, Roy V. *The Reluctant Farmer: The Rise of Agricultural Extension to 1914*. University of Illinois Press, 1970.

Shabazz, Amilcar. *Advancing Democracy: African Americans and the Struggle for Access and Equity in Higher Education*. University of North Carolina Press, 2004.

Shannon, Fred A. *The Farmer's Last Frontier*. M. E. Sharpe, 1973.

Sharpless, Rebecca. *Fertile Ground, Narrow Choices: Women on Texas Cotton Farms, 1900–1940*. University of North Carolina Press, 1999.

Shepardson, Whitney H. *Agricultural Education in the United States*. Macmillan, 1929.

Sitton, Thad, and James H. Conrad. *Freedom Colonies: Independent Black Texans in the Time of Jim Crow*. University of Texas Press, 2005.

Smith, Charles S. *Race Question Reviewed*. Nashville, 1899.

Smith, Thomas T. *The U.S. Army & the Texas Frontier Economy, 1845–1900*. Texas A&M University Press, 1999.

Sonnichsen, C. L. *I'll Die Before I'll Run: The Story of the Great Feuds of Texas*. Devin-Adair, 1962.

Sorber, Nathan M. *Land-Grant Colleges and Popular Revolt*. Cornell University Press, 2018.

Spratt, John S. *The Road to Spindletop: Economic Change in Texas, 1875–1901*. Southern Methodist University Press, 1955.

Stampp, Kenneth M. *The Era of Reconstruction, 1865–1877*. Vintage Books, 1965.

Sweet, Leonard I. *Black Images of America, 1784–1870*. W. W. Norton, 1976.

Swint, Henry L. *The Northern Teacher in the South, 1862–1870*. Vanderbilt University Press, 1941.

Tindall, George B. *The Emergence of the New South, 1913–1945*. Louisiana State University Press, 1967.

Thompson, Jerry D. *Tejano Tiger: José de los Santos Benavides and the History of the Texas-Mexico Borderlands, 1823–1891*. Texas Christian University Press, 2017.

———. *Warm Weather & Bad Whiskey: The 1886 Laredo Election Riot*. Texas Western Press, 1991.

Tyler, Ron, ed. *New Handbook of Texas*. 6 vols. Texas State Historical Association, 1996.

Vandiver, Frank E. *The Southwest: South or West?* Texas A&M University Press, 1975.

Washington, Booker T. *The Negro Problem*. New York, 1899.

———. *Up from Slavery: An Autobiography*. New York, 1900.

Waugh, Frank A. *The Agricultural College*. Orange Judd, 1916.
Weaver, John D. *The Brownsville Raid*. Texas A&M University Press, 1993.
Webb, Walter P., and H. Bailey Carroll, eds. *The Handbook of Texas*. 2 vols. Texas State Historical Association, 1952.
Welch, June R. *The College of Texas*. GLA Press, 1981.
White, Richard. *The Republic for Which It Stands: The United States During Reconstruction and the Gilded Age, 1865–1896*. Oxford University Press, 2017.
Wiebe, Robert H. *The Search for Order, 1877–1920*. Hill and Wang, 1967.
Williams, David A. *Bricks Without Straw: A Comprehensive History of African Americans in Texas*. Eakin Press, 1997.
Williams, Patrick G. *Beyond Redemption: Texas Democrats After Reconstruction*. Texas A&M University Press, 2007.
Willoughby, Larry. *Austin: A Historical Portrait*. Norfolk, VA, 1885.
Winegarten, Ruthe. *Black Texas Women: 150 Years of Trial and Triumph*. University of Texas Press, 1995.
Winkler, Ernest W., ed. *Platforms of Political Parties in Texas*. University of Texas Press, 1916.
Wolters, Raymond. *Du Bois and His Rivals*. University of Missouri Press, 2002.
Woodward, C. Vann. *The Burden of Southern History*. Louisiana State University Press, 1968.
———. *Origins of the New South*. Louisiana State University Press, 1967.
———. *The Strange Career of Jim Crow*. Oxford University Press, 1974.
Woolfolk, George R. *The Cotton Regency: The Northern Merchants and Reconstruction, 1865–1880*. Bookman Associates, 1958.
———. *The First Seventy-Five Years, 1876–1951*. Texas A&M Press, n.d.
———. *Prairie View: A Study in Public Conscience, 1878–1946*. Pageant Press, 1962.
Wooster, Ralph A. *Texas and Texans in the Great War*. State House Press, 2009.
Wooten, Dudley G., ed. *A Comprehensive History of Texas, 1685–1897*. 2 vols. Dallas, 1898.
Work, Monroe N., ed. *A Bibliography of the Negro in Africa and America*. H. W. Wilson, 1928.
———, ed. *Negro Year Book: An Annual Encyclopedia of the Negro, 1921–1922*. Negro Book Publishing, 1922.
Wortham, Louis J. *A History of Texas: From Wilderness to Commonwealth*. 5 vols. Wortham-Molyneaux, 1924.
Wright, Galvin. *The Political Economy of the Cotton South: Households, Markets, and Wealth in the Nineteenth Century*. W. W. Norton, 1978.
Yafa, Stephen. *Cotton: The Biography of a Revolutionary Fiber*. Penguin Books, 2005.
Yelderman, Pauline. *The Jay Bird Democratic Association of Fort Bend County*. Texian Press, 1979.

Articles and Book Chapters

Abramowitz, Jack. "John B. Rayner—A Grass Roots leader." *Journal of Negro History* 36, no. 2 (1951): 160–93.

Adams, John A., Jr. "How Alta Vista Became Prairie View: Lawrence Washburne Minor and the Beginnings of Public Higher Education for African Americans in Texas." *Southwestern Historical Quarterly* 127, no. 3 (2024): 268–86.

———. "A Promise Unfulfilled—Edward L. Blackshear: Crusader for the 'Colored University' in Texas 1882–1901." Forthcoming with *East Texas Historical Journal.*

Adams, John A., Jr., and Bill Page. "John Nathaniel Johnson: The Great Political Agitator Educator, Journalist, Attorney, and Doctor." *East Texas Historical Journal* 61, no. 1 (2023): 7–47.

Atwood, Rufus. "Origins and Development of the Negro Public College with Special Reference to the Land-Grant College." *Journal of Negro Education* 31, no. 3 (1962): 240–50.

Baldwin, William H. "Negro Education in the South." *National Municipal Review*, January 1918, 53–57.

Barr, Alwyn. "Advancing from History's Hollow to History's Mountain: Sources on African American History in Texas." *East Texas Historical Journal* 38, no. 1 (2000): 28–34.

———. "The Impact of Race in Shaping Judicial Districts, 1876–1907." *Southwestern Historical Quarterly* 108, no. 4 (2005): 423–39.

———. "The Texas 'Black Uprising' Scare of 1883." *Phylon (1960–)* 41, no. 2 (1980): 179–86.

Battle, W. J. "A Concise History of the University of Texas, 1883–1950." *Southwestern Historical Quarterly* 54, no. 4 (1951): 391–411.

Bauerlein, Mark. "Washington, Du Bois, and the Black Future." *Wilson Quarterly* 28, no. 4 (2004): 74–86.

Baum, Dale, and Robert Calvert. "Texas Patrons of Husbandry: Geography, Social Contexts and Voting Behavior." *Agricultural History* 63, no. 4 (1989): 36–55.

Blackshear, Edward L. "Appeals to Negro Voters." *Dallas Morning News*, November 1, 1912.

———. "Colored Man's Letter." *Austin Daily Statesman*, October 13, 1885.

———. "Colored University." *Galveston Daily News*, March 28, 1895.

———. "Congo Horrors." *New York Age*, January 17, 1907.

———. "The Evolution of Society." *Christian Recorder*, March 29, 1883.

———. "He Would Make the State the Cotton Middleman." *Atlanta Constitution*, April 21, 1912.

———. "Industrial Education." *Texas School Journal*, October 1899, 682–83.

———. "Industrial Training and the Negro Problem in the United States." *Science Journal*, April 20, 1906, 606–8.

———. "Industrial Training and the Race Question." *Southern Workman*, June 1906, 396–401.

———. "Lines of Negro Education." *AME Church Review* 13 (January 1897): 309–11.

———. "Man's Moral Nature, the Key to Human Education and Evolution." *Journal of Education* 81, no. 9 (1915): 231–33.

———. "The Negro as Passive Factor in American History." *AME Church Review* 20 (1901): 352–63.

———. "Negro Influence on Southern Character." *Literary Digest*, May 21, 1904, 732.

———. "The Progress of the Negro in Texas." *Houston Daily Post*, September 27, 1914.

———. "A Refuge for Negros." *Washington Post*, December 5, 1898.

———. "Safety in Mines." *Scientific American*, February 5, 1910, 123.

———. "Texas: National Water Power." *Outing Magazine*, May 1909, 227.

———. "To Better Farming Skills of Negroes." *Houston Daily Post*, January 13, 1918.

———. "What Is the Negro Teacher Doing in the Matter of Uplifting His Race?" In *Twentieth Century Literature, or A Cyclopedia of Thought on the Vital Topics Relating to the American Negro by One Hundred of America's Greatest Negroes*, edited by D. W. Culp. J. L. Nichols, 1902.

———. "Word from Texas." *Christian Recorder*, April 3, 1884.

Breitzer, Susan Roth. "Race, Immigration, and Contested Americanness: Black Nativism and the American Labor Movement, 1880–1930." *Race/Ethnicity: Multidisciplinary Global Contexts* 4, no. 2 (2011): 269–83.

Brooks, Carolyn, and Alan I. Marcus. "The Morrill Mandate and a New Moral Mandate." *Agricultural History* 89, no. 2 (2015): 247–62.

Burton, Orville V. "African American Status and Identity in a Postbellum Community." *Agricultural History* 72, no. 2 (1998): 213–40.

Calista, Donald J. "Booker T. Washington: Another Look." *Journal of Negro History* 49, no. 4 (1964): 240–55.

Calvert, Robert A. "A. J. Rose and the Granger Concept of Reform." *Agricultural History* 51, no. 1 (1977): 181–96.

———, ed. "The Freedman and Agriculture Prosperity." *Southwestern Historical Quarterly* 76, no. 4 (1973): 461–72.

Campbell, Jack. "The Politics of Pedagogy in Reconstruction Texas." *Journal of Thought* 18, no. 3 (1983): 37–47.

Cantrell, Gregg, and D. Scott Barton. "Texas Populists and the Failure of Biracial Politics." *Journal of Southern History* 55, no. 4 (1989): 659–92.

Carter, Purvis. "Robert Lloyd Smith and the Farmers' Improvement Society, a Self-Help Movement in Texas." *Negro History Bulletin* 29 (1966): 175–91.

Casdorph, Paul D. "Norris Wright Cuney and Texas Republican Politics, 1883–1896." *Southwestern Historical Quarterly* 68, no. 4 (1965): 455–64.

Cotton, Barbara R., ed. "The 1890 Land-Grant Colleges: A Centennial View." Special issue, *Agricultural History* 65, no. 2 (1991).

Craighead, James B. "The Future of the Negro in the South." *Popular Science Monthly*, November 1884, 39–46.

Crosby, Earl W. "Limited Success Against Long Odds: The Black County Agent." *Agricultural History* 57, no. 3 (1983): 277–88.

———. "The Roots of Black Agricultural Extension Work." *Historian* 39, no. 2 (1977): 228–47.

———. "The Struggle for Existence: The Institutionalization of the Black County Agent System." *Agricultural History* 60, no. 2 (1986): 123–36.

Crough, Barry A. "Hesitant Recognition: Texas Black Politicians, 1865–1900." *East Texas Historical Association*, no. 1 (1993): 41–58.

Cunningham, Roger D. "'A Lot of Fine, Sturdy Black Warriors': Texas's African American 'Immunes' in the Spanish American War." *Southwestern Historical Quarterly* 108, no. 3 (2005): 345–67.

Cuthbertson, Gilbert. "The Jaybird-Woodpecker War." *Texana* 10, no. 4 (1972): 297–309.

Dagbovie, Pero G. "Exploring a Century of Historical Scholarship on Booker T. Washington." *Journal of African American History* 92, no. 2 (2007): 239–64.

Dailey, Maceo C., Jr. "The Business Life of Emmett Jay Scott." *Business History Review* 77, no. 4 (2003): 667–86.

Danbom, David B. "The Agricultural Extension System and the First World War." *Historian* 41, no. 2 (1979): 315–31.

Daniel, Walter C. "W. E. B. Du Bois' First Efforts as a Playwright." *CLA Journal* 33, no. 4 (1990): 415–27.

Davis, John W. "Land-Grant College for Negroes." *West Virginia State College Bulletin* 21, no. 5 (1934).

———. "The Negro Land-Grant College." *Journal of Negro Education* 2, no. 3 (1933): 312–28.

Davis, O. L., and Thomas Wacker. "From Freedman's Dream to Desegregation Consolidation: A Black School Survival Saga from Texas." *American Educational History Journal* 33 (2006): 107–16.

Du Bois, W. E. B. "Of the Training of Black Men." *Atlantic*, September 1902, 17–24.

———. "The Study of the Negro Problems." *Annals of the American Academy of Political and Social Science*, January 1898, 1–23.

Dunn, Frederick. "The Educational Philosophies of Washington, Du Bois, and Houston: Laying the Foundations for Afrocentrism and Multiculturalism." *Journal of Negro Education* 62, no. 1 (1993): 24–34.

Durso, Cassandre. "Two States with One Goal: Texas and Louisiana Recruit Italians." *Texas Gulf Historical & Biographical Record* 48 (November 2012): 25–42.
Elliott, Claude. "The Freedmen's Bureau in Texas." *Southwestern Historical Quarterly* 56, no. 1 (1952): 1–24.
Fairclough, Adam. "'Being in the Field of Education and Also Being Negro . . . Seems . . . Tragic': Black Teachers in the Jim Crow South." *Journal of American History* 87, no. 1 (2000): 65–91.
———. "Tuskegee's Robert R. Moton and the Travails of the Early Black College President." *Journal of Blacks in Higher Education*, no. 31 (Spring 2001): 94–105.
Fultz, Michael. "African American Teachers in the South, 1890–1940: Powerlessness and the Ironies of Expectations and Protest." *History of Education Quarterly* 35, no. 4 (1995): 401–22.
Funke, Loretta. "The Negro in Education." *Journal of Negro History* 5, no. 1 (1920): 1–21.
Gannett, Henry. "Are We to Become Africanized?" *Popular Science Monthly*, June 1885.
Garrett-Scott, Shennette. "'The Hope of the South': The New Century Cotton Mill of Dallas, Texas, and the Business of Race in the New South, 1902–1907." *Southwestern Historical Quarterly* 116, no. 2 (2012): 138–66.
Generals, Donald. "Booker T. Washington and Progressive Education: An Experimentalist Approach to Curriculum Development and Reform." *Journal of Negro Education* 69, no. 3 (2000) 215–34.
Gilliam, Edward W. "The African in the United States." *Popular Science Monthly*, February 1883.
Glasrud, Bruce A. "Asians in Texas: An Overview, 1870–1900." *East Texas Historical Journal* 39, no. 2 (2001): 10–22.
———. "Early NAACP Struggles in Texas, 1914–1932." *Journal of South Texas* 29, no. 2 (2016): 24–33.
———. "Jim Crow's Emergence in Texas." *American Studies* 15, no. 1 (1974): 47–60.
Goodwyn, Lawrence C. "Populist Dreams and Negro Rights: East Texas as a Case Study." *American Historical Review* 76, no. 5 (1971): 1435–56.
Gould, Lewis L. "Progressives and Prohibitionists: Texas Democratic Politics, 1911–1921." *Southwestern Historical Quarterly* 75, no.1 (1971) 5–18.
———. "The University Becomes Politicized: The War with Jim Ferguson, 1915–1918." *Southwestern Historical Quarterly* 86, no. 2 (1982): 255–76.
Griffin, Roger A. "To Establish a University of the First Class." *Southwestern Historical Quarterly* 86, no. 2 (1982): 135–60.
Harris, Angela P. "[Re]Integrating Spaces: The Color of Farming." *Savannah Law Review* 2, no. 1 (2015): 157–99.

Harris, Carmen V. "'The Extension Service Is Not an Integration Agency': The Idea of Race in the Cooperative Extension Service." *Agricultural History* 82, no. 2 (2008): 193–219.

Harris, W. T. "The Education of the Negro." *Atlantic Monthly*, June 1892, 722–24.

Hellwig, David J. "Afro-American Reactions to the Japanese and Anti-Japanese Movement, 1906–1924." *Phylon (1960–)* 38, no. 1 (1977): 93–104.

———. "Strangers in Their Own Land: Patterns of Black Nativism, 1830–1930." *American Studies* 23, no. 1 (1982): 85–98.

Henley, Lauren N. "'Devilish Deeds': Serial Murder and Racial Violence in Austin, Texas, 1884–1995." *Journal of African American History* 105, no. 1 (2020): 1–27.

Hild, Matthew. "The Knights of Labor and the Third-Party Movement in Texas, 1886–1896." *Southwestern Historical Quarterly* 119, no. 1 (2015): 25–43.

Hill, Caroline M. "Prairie View Farm School." *Elementary School Teacher* 8, no. 1 (1907): 24–28.

Hill, Larry D., and Robert A. Calvert. "The University of Texas Extension Service and Progressivism." *Southwestern Historical Quarterly* 86, no. 2 (1983): 230–54.

Holmes, William F. "The Demise of the Colored Farmers' Alliance." *Journal of Southern History* 41, no. 2 (1975): 187–200.

Hornsby, Alton. "The 'Colored Branch University' Issue in Texas—Prelude to *Sweatt vs Painter*." *Journal of Negro History* 61, no. 1 (1976): 51–60.

———. "The Freemen's Bureau Schools in Texas, 1865–1870." *Southwestern Historical Quarterly* 76, no. 4 (1973): 397–417.

Hotchkiss, Wesley A. "Congregationalists and Negro Education." *Journal of Negro Education* 29, no. 3 (1960): 289–98.

Houston, David F. "Soldiers of the Soil." *National Geographic*, March 1917, 273–77.

Huchison, John E. "The Texas Agricultural Extension Service: A Historical Overview." In *Southwestern Agriculture: Pre-Columbian to Modern*, edited by Henry C. Dethloff and Irvin M. May. Texas A&M University Press, 1982.

Humphries, Frederick S. "1890 Land-Grant Institutions: Their Struggle for Survival and Equality." *Agricultural History* 65, no. 1 (1991): 3–11.

Jenkins, Robert L. "The Black Land-Grant Colleges in Their Formative Years, 1890–1920." *Agricultural History* 65, no. 2 (1991): 63–72.

Jones, Allen W. "Thomas M. Campbell: Black Agricultural Leader of the New South." *Agricultural History* 53, no. 1 (1979): 42–59.

Kealing, M. T. "Are All the Great Men Dying?" *Christian Recorder*, August 11, 1881.

———. "Titular Twaddle." *Christian Recorder*, October 26, 1882.

Levy, James. "Forging African American Minds: Black Pragmatism, 'Intelligent Labor,' and a Look at Industrial Education, 1879–1900." *American Nineteenth Century History* 17, no. 1 (2016): 43–73.

Little, Monroe H. "The Extra-Curricular Activities of Black College Students, 1868–1940." *Journal of Negro History* 65, no. 2 (1980): 135–48.

Lomax, John A. "Governor Ferguson and the University of Texas." *Southwest Review* 28, no. 1 (1942): 11–29.

———. "Stories of an African Prince: Yoruba Tales." *Journal of American Folklore* 26 (1913): 1–12.

Lombardi, Paul. "Examining the Effect of Economic Shocks on the Schooling Choices of Southern Farmers." *European Review of Economic History* 23, no. 2 (2019): 214–40.

Lutz, Christine. "'The People! The People!': African Leaders on Africans and Asians at the Turn of the Nineteenth Century." *Journal of GAH* 28 (2009): 33–54.

Malczewski, Joan. "Philanthropy and Progressive Era State Building Through Agricultural Extension Work in the Jim Crow South." *History of Education Quarterly* 53, no. 4 (2013): 369–400.

———. "Weak State, Stronger Schools: Northern Philanthropy and Organizational Change in the Jim Crow South." *Journal of Southern History* 75, no. 4 (2009): 963–1000.

Malin, James C. "The Farmers' Alliance Subtreasury Plan and European Precedents." *Mississippi Valley Historical Review* 31, no. 2 (1944): 255–60.

Martin, Roscoe. "The Grange as a Political Factor in Texas." *Political and Social Science Quarterly* 6, no. 4 (1926): 363–83.

May, Irvin M. "The Origins and Development of the Texas Agricultural Experiment Station." *Panhandle Plains Historical Review* 49 (1976): 55–79.

Mays, Benjamin E. "The Significance of the Negro Church-Related College." *Journal of Negro Education* 29, no. 3 (1960): 245–51.

McKay, Seth A. "Social Conditions in Texas in the Eighteen Seventies." *West Texas Historical Association* 14 (1938): 32–51.

McPherson, James M. "White Liberals and Black Power in Negro Education, 1865–1915." *American Historical Review* 75, no. 5 (1970): 1357–86.

Meier, August. "Booker T. Washington: With Special Reference to the Colored American Magazine." *Journal of Negro History* 38, no. 1 (1953): 67–90.

Miller, Joseph D. "John W. Hoffman." *Alexander's Magazine*, September 15, 1906, 32–35.

Miller, Worth R., and Stacy G. Ulbig. "Building a Populist Coalition in Texas, 1892–1896." *Journal of Southern History* 74, no. 2 (2008): 255–96.

Mohr, Clarence L. "Minds of the New South: Higher Education in Black and White, 1880–1915." *Southern Quarterly* 46, no. 4 (2009): 8–34.

Morowski, Deborah L., and O. L. Davis. "Through a Heavy Fog: Public High Schools in Texas for African Americans, 1900–1930." *American Educational History Journal* 32, no. 2 (2005): 183–91.

Myers, Lois E. "'Like Water to the Body': Women and the African American Rural Church." *Sound Historian* 10 (2007): 26–38.

The Nation. "Higher Education for the Negro." May 15, 1902, 381.

Nicholas, William E. "World War I and Academic Dissent in Texas." *Arizona and the West* 14, no. 3 (1972): 220.

Nieman, Donald G. "Black Political Power and Criminal Justice: Washington County, Texas, 1868–1884." *Journal of Southern History* 55, no. 3 (1989): 391–420.

Nier, Charles L. "The Shadow of Credit: The Historical Origins of Racial Predatory Lending and Its Impact upon African American Wealth Accumulation." *University of Pennsylvania Journal of Law and Social Change* 11, no. 2 (2007): 131–94.

Osborn, William S. "Curtains for Jim Crow: Law, Race, and the Texas Railroads." *Southwestern Historical Quarterly* 105, no. 3 (2002): 393–427.

Page, William R. "'I'se Gwine to Ride in Dat Car': African Americans' Fight to Integrate Texas Railroads, 1866–1891." Forthcoming with *Southwestern Historical Quarterly*.

Payne, Brendan J. "Defending Black Suffrage: Poll Taxes, Preachers, and Anti-Prohibition in Texas, 1887–1916." *Journal of Southern History* 83, no. 4 (2017): 816–52.

Pickens, William. "Jim Crow in Texas." *Nation*, August 15, 1923, 155.

Pitre, Merline. "The Evolution of a Black University in Texas." *Western Journal of Black Studies* 3, no. 3 (1979): 216–23.

———. "Robert Lloyd Smith: A Black Lawmaker in the Shadow of Booker T. Washington." *Phylon (1960–)* 46, no. 3 (1985): 262–68.

Plummer, Brenda G. "The Afro-American Response to the Occupation of Haiti, 1915–1934." *Phylon (1960–)* 43, no. 2 (1982): 125–143.

Ramsdell, Charles W. "Presidential Reconstruction in Texas." *Quarterly of the Texas State Historical Association* 11, no. 4 (1908): 277–313.

———. "Presidential Reconstruction in Texas: III. The Restoration of State Government." *Quarterly of the Texas State Historical Association* 12, no. 3 (1909): 204–30.

Ransom, Robert, and Richard Sutch. "Debt Peonage in the Cotton South After the Civil War." *Journal of Economic History* 32, no. 3 (1972): 641–69.

———. "The 'Lock-in' Mechanism and Overproduction of Cotton in the Postbellum South." *Agricultural History* 49, no. 2 (1975): 405–25.

Reese, James V. "The Evolution of an Early Texas Union: The Screwmen's Benevolent Association of Galveston, 1866–1891." *Southwestern Historical Quarterly* 75, no. 2 (1971): 158–85.

Reid, Debra. "Rural African American and Progressive Reform." *Agricultural History* 74, no. 2 (2000): 322–39.

Richardson, Rupert N. "Edward M. House and the Governors." *Southwestern Historical Quarterly* 61, no. 1 (1957): 51–65.

Rippy, J. Fred. "A Negro Colonization Project in Mexico, 1895." *Journal of Negro History* 6, no. 1 (1921): 66–73.

Roberts, Andrea R. "The Farmers' Improvement Society and Women's Barnyard Auxiliary of Texas: African American Community Building in the Progressive Era." *Journal of Planning History* 16, no. 3 (2016): 222–45.

Roberts, Oran M. "A History of the Establishment of the University of the State of Texas." *Quarterly of the Texas State Historical Association* 1, no. 4 (1898): 233–65.

Russ, William A. "Radical Disfranchisement in Texas, 1867–1870." *Southwestern Historical Quarterly* 38, no. 1 (1934): 40–52.

Saloutos, Theodore. "The Grange in the South, 1870–1877." *Journal of Southern History* 19, no. 4 (1953): 473–87.

Saunders, Robert. "Southern Populists and the Negro, 1893–1895." *Journal of Negro History* 54, no. 3 (1969): 240–61.

Scott, Emmett J. "Letters of Negro Migrants of 1916–1918." *Journal of Negro History* 4, no. 3 (1919): 290–340.

Scott, Roy V. "American Railroads and Agricultural Extension, 1900–1914: A Study in Railway Development Techniques." *Business History Review* 39, no. 1 (1965): 74–98.

Seals, R. Grant. "The Disparity in Land Grant Funding from State Sources Between Traditionally White Institutions and Traditionally Black Institutions in Louisiana and Mississippi: The Role of Agricultural Development Legislation." *Journal of Rural Studies* 2, no. 3 (1986): 221–32.

———. "The Formation of Agricultural and Rural Development Policy with Emphasis on African-Americans: II. The Hatch-George and Smith-Lever Acts." *Agricultural History* 65, no. 2 (1991): 12–34.

Shaler, N. S. "The Future of the Negro in the Southern States." *Popular Science Monthly*, June 1900.

Shelton, William E. "A Reappraisal of Public Education in Texas During the Reconstruction Period." *Journal of Educational Research* 48, no. 5 (1955): 345–53.

Shook, Robert W. "The Texas 'Election Outrage' of 1886." *East Texas Historical Journal* 10, no. 1 (1972): 20–30.

Sinitiere, Phillip L. "'Outline of Report on Economic Conditions of Negros in the State of Texas': W. E. B. Du Bois's 1935 Speech at Prairie View State College." *Phylon (1960–)* 54, no. 1 (2017): 3–24.

Skocpol, Theda, and Jennifer Lynn Oser. "Organization Despite Adversity: The Origins and Development of African American Fraternal Associations." *Social Science History* 28, no. 3 (2004): 367–437.

Smallwood, James. "Black Texans During Reconstruction: First Freedom." *East Texas Historical Society* 14, no. 1 (1976): 9–19.

Smith, Dick. "Texas and the Poll Tax." *Southwestern Social Science Quarterly* 45, no. 2 (1964): 167–73.

Smith, Ralph. "The Grange Movement in Texas, 1873–1900." *Southwestern Historical Quarterly* 42, no. 4 (1939): 297–315.

Smith, Robert L. "Elevation of Negro Farm Life." *Independent*, August 30, 1900, 2103–6.

———. "The Farmers' Improvement Society of Texas." *AME Review*, January 1909, 289–96.

———. "Village Improvement Among Negroes." *Outlook*, March 31, 1900, 733–36.

Spearman, Mindy. "'Everything to Help, Nothing to Hinder': The Story of the Texas School Journal." *Southwestern Historical Quarterly* 111, no. 3 (2008): 282–302.

Spinler, Frank MacD. "The History of Hempstead and Formation of Waller County, Texas." *Southwestern Historical Quarterly* 63, no. 3 (1960): 404–27.

Stallones, Jared. "Education and Politics in Texas: The Legacies of Laurine C. Anderson and Edward L. Blackshear." In *Pedagogies of Black Educators*, special issue, *Vitae Scholasticae* 28, no. 2 (2011): 7–22.

———. "Struggle for the Soul of a Normal School." *Journal of the Midwest History Society* 23 (1996).

Strong, Donald S. "The Poll Tax: The Case of Texas." *American Political Science Review* 38, no. 4 (1944): 640–53.

Sturdevant, Paul. "The FIS School: A Tuskegee for Texas?" *East Texas Historical Association* 47, no. 1 (2009): 52–59.

Taylor, Quintard. "Texas: The South Meets the West, the View Through African American History." *Journal of the West* 44, no. 2 (2005): 44–52.

True, A. C. "Address of the President of the Association of American Agricultural Colleges and Experiment Stations." *Science*, November 27, 1914, 757–66.

Villard, Oswald G. "Higher Education of Negroes." *Nation*, May 1902, 381.

Washington, Booker T. "Education for the Man Behind the Plow: Tuskegee Institution." *Independent*, April 23, 1908, 918–20.

Webb, Murl L. "Religious and Educational Efforts Among Texas Indians in the 1850's." *Southwestern Historical Quarterly* 69, no. 1 (1965): 22–37.

Wennersten, John R. "The Travail of Black Land-Grant Schools in the South, 1890–1917." *Agricultural History* 65, no. 2 (1991): 54–62.

Williams, C. Fred. "Frustration Amidst Hope: The Land Grant Mission of Arkansas AM&N College, 1873–1972." *Agricultural History* 65, no. 2 (1991): 115–30.

Wood, W. D. "The Ku Klux Klan." *Quarterly of the Texas State Historical Association* 9, no. 4 (1906): 262–68.

Wooten, Mattie L. "Racial, National, and Nativity Trends in Texas, 1870–1930." *Southwestern Social Science Quarterly* 14, no. 1 (1933): 62–69.

Newspapers and Periodicals

Advocate (Charleston, WV), 1909–11
African Mail (London), 1909
Afro-American Ledger (Baltimore), 1904
Alto (TX) Herald, 1911
Atlanta Constitution, 1894–98, 1912
Austin Daily Statesman, 1880–1920
Austin Texas School Journal, 1885–1920
Austin: The Review, 1894
Austin Weekly Statesman, 1889
Bellville (TX) Times, 1917
Birmingham Age-Herald, 1913
Bonham (TX) News, 1914
Brenham (TX) Daily Banner, 1894, 1900
Brenham (TX) Evening Press, 1909
Bryan (TX) Eagle, 1912
Bystander (Des Moines), 1911
Caldwell (TX) News Chronicle, 1899
Calvert (TX) Courier, 1918
Chicago Defender, 1917
Christian Recorder (Philadelphia), 1882–1920
Citizen (Berea, KY), 1909
Colored American (Washington, DC), 1901–4
Crisis (New York), 1913
Dallas Express, 1899
Dallas Morning News, 1888–1919
Dallas Southern Mercury, 1888–1907
Dallas Weekly Herald, 1884
DeBow's Review (New Orleans), 1890–1900
El Paso (TX) Herald, 1911
El Paso (TX) Morning Times, 1906
Evening World (New York), 1888
Fort Worth Daily Gazette, 1888
Fort Worth Star-Telegram, 1907–15
Freedman (Indianapolis), 1892
Freeman (Philadelphia), 1908
Freie Presse für Texas (San Antonio), 1889
Galveston Daily News, 1875–1920

Note: There are few preserved archival runs of African American newspapers published in Texas between 1880–1920. However, many articles, notices, and editorials were subsequently printed in the *Galveston Daily News* during this period, including those from the following papers:

Argus (Galveston)
Austin Herald
Beaumont (TX) Echo
Blade (Austin)
Chronicle (Fort Worth)
Citizen (Austin)
Colored Alliance (Austin)
Echo (Dallas)
Echo (Navasota)
Freeman's Journal (Galveston)
Guide (Dallas)
Hearne Independent
Hearne Southern Guide
Houston Citizen
Houston Texas Freeman
Jasper Burning Light

Paul Quinn Weekly (Waco)
San Antonio Globe
San Antonio Illuminator
Seguin New Test
Tonquelet (San Antonio)
Torchlight Appeal (Fort Worth)
Tyler Leadership
Wharton Southern Journal
Galveston News Idea, 1905
Galveston Tribune, 1901
Hallettsville (TX) Herald, 1900, 1915
Hallettsville, Texas Semi-Weekly New Era, 1918
Hearne (TX) Democrat, 1952
Houston Daily Post, 1882–1920
Houston Informer, 1920
Jefferson (TX) Jimplecute, 1911
Kansas City Sun, 1915
La Grange Journal, 1897, 1904, 1918
La Nacion (Buenos Aires), 1915
Lee County Journal (Leesburg, GA), 1912
Lexington (SC) Dispatch, 1902
Manchester Guardian, 1907
Mexico Herald (Mexico City), 1913
Navasota (TX) Daily Examiner, 1900
Negro Business League Herald (Washington, DC), 1909
News Weekly (Sierra Leone), 1909
New York Popular Science Monthly, 1883–90
New York Times, 1910
Nocona (TX) News, 1913
Nueva Era (El Paso), 1902, 1913
Oakland (CA) Sunshine, 1915
Omaha Daily Bee, 1890–98
Patton (PA) Courier, 1905
Pittsburgh Courier, 1912
Post Signal (Pilot Point, TX), 1901
Rockdale (TX) Reporter and Messenger, 1911
San Antonio Express-News, 1898
San Antonio La Presa, 1910
Schulenberg (TX) Sticker, 1901
Scientific American, 1910
Silver Springs Signal (New York), 1905
Southwestern Christian Advocate (New Orleans), 1893–97
Standard (Clarksville, TX), 1887
St. Landry Clarion (Opelousas, LA), 1901
Tabor (IA) Beacon, 1904
Tabor (IA) Talisman, 1904
Taylor (TX) Daily Press, 1922
Temple (TX) Daily Telegram, 1912
Texan-Telephone (Canton, TX), 1885
Twin City Star (Minneapolis), 1913
Waco (TX) Morning News, 1912
Washington Bee, 1909, 1915
Washington Post, 1898, 2018
Waxahachie (TX) Daily Light, 1902–4
Weatherford (TX): The Daily Herald, 1912
Weekly Democrat Statesman (Austin, TX), 1879
Wichita Daily Times, 1915
Williamson County Sun (Georgetown, TX), 1900

Dissertations and Theses

Baggett, James A. "The Rise and Fall of the Texas Radicals, 1867–1883." PhD diss., North Texas State University, 1972.
Baker, Margaret B. "The Texas Negro and the World War." Master's thesis, University of Texas, 1938.
Barr, Alwyn. "Texas Politics, 1876–1906." PhD diss., University of Texas, 1966.

Blair, John P. "African American Citizen Soldiers in Galveston and San Antonio, Texas, 1880–1906." Master's thesis, Texas A&M University, 2007.

Boyer, Jacob L. "A Survey of Certain Personnel Aspects of the Cooperative Extension Service for Negroes in Texas." Master's thesis, Prairie View University, 1947.

Brennan, Douglas C. "Booker T. Washington and the Myth of Accommodation." Master's thesis, University of North Texas, 1994.

Brophy, William J. "The Black Texan, 1900–1950: A Quantitative History." PhD diss., Vanderbilt University, 1974.

Budd, Harrell. "The Negro in Politics in Texas, 1867–1898." Master's thesis, University of Texas, 1925.

Carrigan, William D. "Between South and West: Race, Violence, and Power in Central Texas, 1836–1916." PhD diss., Emory University, 1999.

Chamberlain, Charles K. "Alexander Watkins Terrell: Citizen, Statesman." PhD diss., University of Texas, 1957.

Chambers, Bill. "The History of the Texas Negro and His Development in Texas." Master's thesis, North Texas State Teachers College, 1940.

Chapman, David L. "Lynching in Texas." Master's thesis, Texas Tech University, 1975.

Chapman, Oscar J. "A Historical Study of Negro Land-Grant Colleges in Relationship with Their Social, Economic, Political, and Educational Backgrounds and a Program for Their Improvement." PhD diss., Ohio State University, 1940.

Chunn, Prentis W. "Education and Politics: A Study of the Negro in Reconstruction Texas." Master's thesis, Southwest Texas State College, 1957.

Clater, Marie. "An Analysis and Appraisal of the Aims of the Negro: Teacher Colleges in Texas in Relation to Their Curriculum Offerings." Master's thesis, Prairie View State Normal School, 1941.

Colby, Ira C. "The Freedmen's Bureau in Texas and Its Impact on the Emerging Social Welfare System and Black-White Social Relations, 1865–1885." PhD diss., University of Pennsylvania, 1984.

Cooper, Arnold. "Five Black Educators: Founders of Schools in the South, 1881–1915." PhD diss., Iowa State University, 1983.

Cripps, Thomas R. "The Lily-White Republicans: The Negro, the Party, and the South in the Progressive Era." PhD diss., University of Maryland, 1967.

Dorsett, Jesse. "Blacks in Reconstruction Texas, 1865–1877." PhD diss., North Carolina Central University, 1881.

Enck, Henry S. "The Burden Borne: Northern White Philanthropy and Southern Black Industrial Education, 1900–1915." PhD diss., University of Cincinnati, 1970.

Evans, Samuel Lee. "Texas Agriculture, 1865–1880." Master's thesis, University of Texas, 1955.

Fine, Bernice R. "Agrarian Reform and the Negro Farmer in Texas, 1886–1896." Master's thesis, North Texas State University, 1971.

Fink, Robert C. "Black College Football in Texas." PhD diss., Texas Tech University, 2003.

Frantz, Edward O. "Goin' Dixie: Republican Presidential Tours of the South, 1877–1933." PhD diss., University of Wisconsin–Madison, 2002.

Gee, Ruth Ella. "The History and Development of the Prairie View Training School, 1916–1946." Master's thesis, Prairie View University, 1946.

Glasrud, Bruce A. "Black Texans, 1900–1930: A History." PhD diss., Texas Tech University, 1969.

Gooden, John E. "Negro Participation in Civil Government with Emphasis on Public Education in Texas." PhD diss., University of Southern California, 1949.

Grose, Charles W. "Black Newspapers in Texas, 1868–1970." PhD diss., University of Texas, 1972.

Hinze, Virginia N. "Norris Wright Cuney." Master's thesis, Rice University, 1965.

Hollins, Arntie Edward. "The Colored Teachers State Association of Texas as Revealed in the Texas Press." Master's thesis, Prairie View A&M College, 1948.

Hornsby, Alton. "Negro Education in Texas, 1865–1917." PhD diss., University of Texas, 1962.

Irvin, Bobbye H. "Black-White Relations in Texas, 1874–1896." Master's thesis, North Texas State University, 1970.

Lanier, Roy H. "Church-Related Colleges for Negroes in Texas." Master's thesis, Hardin-Simmons University, 1950.

Leiker, James N. "Racial Borders: Black Soldiers and Race Relations Along the Rio Grande." PhD diss., University of Kansas, 1999.

Levy, James A. "Narratives of Progress: Black Elites, the 'Folks,' and the Politics of Knowledge, 1890–1915." PhD diss., Rutgers, 2006.

Mason, Kenneth. "Paternal Continuity: African Americans and Race Relations in San Antonio, Texas, 1867–1937." PhD diss., University of Texas, 1994.

Matthews, Charles R. "The Early Years of the Permanent University Fund from 1836–1937." PhD diss., University of Texas, 2006.

Murray, Sean C. "Texas Prohibition Politics, 1887–1914." Master's thesis, University of Houston, 1968.

Nelum, Junior N. "A Study of the First Seventy Years of the Colored Teachers State Association of Texas." PhD diss., University of Texas, 1955.

Parker, Edith H. "History of Land Grants for Education in Texas." PhD diss., University of Texas, 1952.

Pastrano, Jose G. "Industrial Agriculture in the Peripheral South: State, Race, and the Politics of Migrant Labor in Texas, 1890–1930." PhD diss., University of California, 2006.

Payne, John W. "David F. Houston: A Biography." PhD diss., University of Texas, 1953.

Peavler, David J. "Creating the Color Line and Confronting Jim Crow: Civil Rights in Middle America: 1850–1900." PhD diss., University of Kansas, 2008.

Perry, Douglass G. "Black Populism: The Negro in the People's Party on Texas." Master's thesis, Prairie View University, 1945.

Peterson, Robert L. "State Regulation of Railroads in Texas, 1836–1920." PhD diss., University of Texas, 1960.

Platt, Hazel. "Negro Education in Texas." Master's thesis, University of Texas, 1917.

Reid, Debra Ann. "Reaping a Greater Harvest: African Americans, Agrarian Reform, and the Texas Agricultural Extension Service." PhD diss., Texas A&M University, 2000.

Richardson, Susan R. "Oil, Power, and Universities: Political Struggle and Academic Advancement at the University of Texas and Texas A&M, 1876–1965." PhD diss., Pennsylvania State University, 2005.

Smith, Stewart D. "Schools and Schoolmen: Chapters in Texas Education, 1870–1900." PhD diss., North Texas State University, 1974.

Soares, Leigh A. "Higher Ambitions for Freedom: The Politics of Public Black Colleges in the South, 1865–1915." PhD diss., Northwestern University, 2019.

Sullivan, John A. "A Historical Investigation of the Negro Land-Grant College from 1890 to 1964." PhD diss, Loyola University, 1969.

Tarrow, Willie A. "A University for Negroes of Texas—A Promise Unfilled." Master's thesis, Prairie View University, 1946.

Taylor, Douglas B. "Negro Education in Texas." Master's thesis, University of Texas, 1927.

Tickle, Ryan E. "For Their Brethren Across the Sea: The African-American Protest to the Abuses in the Congo Free State, 1885–1908." Master's thesis, California State University, 2009.

Tomlinson, Marie G. "The State Agricultural and Mechanical College of Texas, 1871–1879: The Personalities, Politics, and Uncertainties." Master's thesis, Texas A&M University, 1976.

Watson, Larry J. "Evangelical Protestants and the Prohibition Movement in Texas, 1887–1919." PhD diss., Texas A&M University, 1993.

Webb, Juanita. "The Administration of Governor L. S. Ross, 1887–1891." Master's thesis, University of Texas, 1935.

White, Annie Mae Vaught. "The Development of the Program of Studies of the Prairie View State Normal and Industrial College." Master's thesis, University of Texas, 1938.

White, Carrie B. W. "The Development of Higher Education for the Negro in the South from 1890 to 1914, with Special Reference to the Land-Grant Colleges." Master's thesis, Prairie View Agricultural and Mechanical College, August 1947.

Whiteside, Myrtle. "The Life of Lawrence Sullivan Ross." Master's thesis, University of Texas, 1938.

Wilkison, Kyle G. "The End of Independence: Social and Political Consequences of Economic Change in Texas, 1870–1914." PhD diss., Vanderbilt University, 1995.

Williams, David A. "History of Higher Education for Black Texans, 1872–1977." PhD diss., Baylor University, 1977.

Willingham, William O. "Progress of Negro Education in Texas." Master's thesis, Texas Technological College, 1932.

Wright, Chester W. "A History of Black Land-Grant Colleges, 1890–1916." PhD diss., American University, 1981.

Yancey, William C. "The Old Alcalde: Oran Milo Roberts, Texas's Forgotten Fire-Eater." PhD diss., University of North Texas, 2016.

Young, Horace A., Jr. "A History and Appraisal of the Colored Teachers State Association of Texas." Master's thesis, New Mexico University, 1949.

Index

Page numbers in italics indicate illustrative material.